T0323630

Nashville Cats

Nashville Cats

Record Production in Music City

TRAVIS D. STIMELING

OXFORD
UNIVERSITY PRESS

Oxford University Press is a department of the University of Oxford. It furthers the University's objective of excellence in research, scholarship, and education by publishing worldwide. Oxford is a registered trade mark of Oxford University Press in the UK and certain other countries.

Published in the United States of America by Oxford University Press
198 Madison Avenue, New York, NY 10016, United States of America.

Library of Congress Cataloging-in-Publication Data
Names: Stimeling, Travis D., author.
Title: Nashville cats : record production in Music City / Travis D. Stimeling.
Description: New York : Oxford University Press, 2020. |
Includes bibliographical references and index.
Identifiers: LCCN 2019051796 (print) | LCCN 2019051797 (ebook) |
ISBN 9780197502815 (hardback) | ISBN 9780197502839 (epub) | ISBN 9780197502846 (online)
Subjects: LCSH: Country music—Tennessee—Nashville—History and criticism. |
Country music—Production and direction—Tennessee—Nashville—History—20th century. |
Sound recording industry—Tennessee—Nashville—History—20th century.
Classification: LCC ML3524 .S756 2020 (print) | LCC ML3524 (ebook) |
DDC 338.4/7781642—dc23
LC record available at https://lccn.loc.gov/2019051796
LC ebook record available at https://lccn.loc.gov/2019051797

9 8 7 6 5 4 3 2 1

Printed by Integrated Books International, United States of America

CONTENTS

FIGURES AND TABLE

FIGURES

TABLE

ACKNOWLEDGMENTS

This book has been a dream come true. Having grown up with country music in my background, I have spent untold hours listening to the work of the musicians that form the basis of this study, and this book represents my modest effort to make sense of their world. Many of the musicians profiled here were very generous with their time and energy, offering insightful interviews and connecting me to others who might be helpful in my research. Charlie McCoy, who graciously allowed me to co-author his 2017 memoir, was key to this research, and I'm deeply grateful for his willingness to tell me stories and to confirm or challenge my understandings. Additionally, I would like to thank Carole Ann Bach, Ted Bach, Kent Blanton, Harold Bradley, Justin Croft, Ronnie Dean, Rose Drake, Ray and Polly Edenton, Solie Fott, Cathy Bach Guenther, Pat McCoy, Bill McElhiney, Jr., Leonard Morton, Sr., Wayne Moss, Buddy Spicher, Ray Stevens, and Bergen White for sharing their time, their stories, and their personal archives with me, as they formed the most important archives for this research.

Additionally, I had the great pleasure of working in a number of excellent libraries and archives throughout this project. I would like to thank the staffs at the Country Music Foundation Library, the Rock and Roll Hall of Fame Library and Archives, the Center for Popular Music and Middle Tennessee State University, the Southern Folklife Collection at the University of North Carolina at Chapel Hill, the Nashville Public Library,

Vanderbilt University Special Collections, and Tennessee State University Special Collections. I would also like to thank Mary Smythe, Barbara Hoffman, and Jonathan Marx at the Nashville Symphony for sending along useful information about the symphony's work during the 1950s and 1960s.

This work was generously supported by a number of grants and fellowships, without which this work would not have been possible. A fellowship from the West Virginia Humanities Council and a WVU Faculty Senate Research Grant provided vital early support and facilitated travel to archives and interviews in Nashville and North Carolina, and a fellowship from Case Western Reserve University's Center for Popular Music Studies allowed me to visit the Rock and Roll Hall of Fame Library and Archives. A Big XII Fellowship from WVU's Office of the Provost allowed me to present this work to colleagues within our academic and athletic conference. Finally, a fellowship from National Endowment for the Humanities permitted me to spend a year drafting and revising this manuscript. Any views, findings, conclusions, or recommendations expressed in this book do not necessarily represent those of the National Endowment for the Humanities.

I would also like to thank a remarkable community of people who have supported me throughout this process. Stacey DaBaldo, Sophia Enriquez, and Anne Stickley transcribed interviews and handwritten primary sources. Innumerable students have listened to my ramblings on record production and the Nashville Sound, including especially those in my "Music in an Age of Recording" seminar. Special thanks in that regard go to Phoebe Hughes, Jacob Kopcienski, and Paige Zalman, each of whom provided valuable insights and thoughtful questions along the way. My colleague Evan MacCarthy has been a frequent interlocutor during the research for and writing of this book, and I am especially grateful for his willingness to take on additional work while I was on research leave. WVU College of Creative Arts deans Paul Kreider and Keith Jackson, as well as WVU School of Music director Michael Ibrahim, have also been very supportive throughout this process, and I am grateful for their personal and institutional support. And I would like to thank Melanie Page in the WVU Research Office for encouraging me to seek external funding for this research. Finally, the two peer reviewers at Oxford University Press went above and beyond the call of duty by offering line-by-line suggestions for editing and revising the text.

Much of the work in this manuscript was presented previously in both academic and public settings. I would like to thank my colleagues in the Society for American Music and at the International Country Music Conference for their insightful questions. As well, colleagues at TCU, the University of North Carolina at Chapel Hill, Belmont University, and East Tennessee State University provided opportunities to share work in progress. And the West Virginia Humanities Council's Little Lecture Series offered a venue for me to link this research to my home state, an opportunity that I especially relished.

Finally, I would like to thank my incredible friends and family, who have been steadfast in their support of me. They picked me up when I was down and encouraged me to see the big picture when I was mired in the details. For that, and much more, I am profoundly grateful.

Introduction

When I met Harold Bradley in August 2014, he presented me with a five-page photocopied résumé and biographical statement. An original member of the Nashville "A Team," founding partner (with his brother Owen) of one of the most important recording studios in the city's history, and longtime president of the Nashville Federation of Musicians, Bradley was a significant figure in Nashville since the 1940s, where he played a key role in shaping the sounds, business practices, and physical landscape of the city. Before I started my audio recorder and began my formal interview with him, I skimmed the résumé and found those accomplishments listed alongside such interesting autobiographical tidbits as "lifetime non smoker, non drinker, non use of recreational drugs [*sic*]," "expert rating as a Water Ski Jumper and Slalom Skier [*sic*]," and "offered baseball contract by Chicago Cubs." But perhaps the most shocking nugget of all was tucked away on the second page: "Harold Bradley played on three all time [*sic*] Christmas hits produced by his brother, Owen Bradley": Brenda Lee's "Rockin' Around the

Nashville Cats. Travis D. Stimeling, © Oxford University Press (2020). Oxford University Press.
DOI: 10.1093/oso/9780197502815.001.0001

Christmas Tree" (1958), Bobby Helms's "Jingle Bell Rock" (1957), and Burl Ives's "A Holly Jolly Christmas" (1964).[1]

I probably shouldn't have been surprised to see that Bradley played guitar on three of the most significant Christmas records of the 1950s and 1960s, recordings that were made in the very Nashville studios where he had built a career. But as I processed that information, the sheer import of his work—and the work of his fellow members of the Nashville A Team—began to set in. Anyone who has visited a grocery store, switched on a television, or passively listened to the radio in the last sixty years—regardless of their religious faith, socioeconomic background, or musical tastes—has heard Harold Bradley play the guitar.[2] Like so many of session musicians, though, Bradley's work is central to our individual and collective experiences with popular music, but, outside of Nashville and some music industry circles, his name is not.

Such is the case with nearly all of the people who contributed to recordings made in Nashville during the 1950s, 1960s, and 1970s. The elite musicians who formed the so-called Nashville A Team were some of the most active session musicians in the entire US music industry, contributing to as many as twenty or more sessions each week for, in some cases, twenty years or more. (In fact, some of the musicians discussed in this book still play sessions with some frequency.) Considering that musicians were expected to record four songs in each three-hour session, many members of the A Team participated in the creation of as many as 80,000 individual recordings over the course of their careers. In a city best known for its contributions to country music, the Nashville A Team joined recording artists hailing from not only the *Grand Ole Opry* stage, but also rock, pop, and even jazz. Therefore, it is highly likely that, as is the case with Harold Bradley, even the most passive consumers of popular music have heard the Nashville A Team at some point in their lives and maybe even formed deep emotional attachments to their work, without even knowing their names.

Our collective ignorance of the Nashville A Team's work might be surprising given the sheer volume of their contributions to popular music. But it is perhaps even more surprising when we consider the amount of journalistic coverage that the A Team received during its heyday. When reporters visited Nashville during the 1960s, there was a high probability that they would eventually end up in one of the city's bustling recording studios, where they would watch and listen as a team of recording artists, producers, recording engineers, and session musicians hurriedly worked out arrangements, chased down technical gremlins, nuanced the emotional impact of a vocal performance, and, ultimately, sent another completed recording into the marketplace. In previous decades, journalists who wanted to take in the city's musical culture often found themselves in the audience—or, with the right connections, backstage—at the *Grand Ole Opry*, the august country music barn dance program that could be heard every week over a clear-channel radio signal that blanketed much of North America and that was syndicated over the NBC radio network.[3] But, by the early 1960s, Nashville was becoming known not only for its remarkable pool of talented radio performers, but also for its exceptional group of recording specialists whose work could be heard on jukeboxes, record players, and transistor radios around the United States and even around the world.

The Nashville A Team was not the only pool of session musicians to make significant contributions to popular music during the postwar years. In fact, a significant portion of the popular music—as well as the commercial jingles heard on radio and television broadcasts—that reached the US market in the mid-twentieth century was created by cadres of professional studio musicians working in New York, Los Angeles, Detroit, and, later, Memphis.[4] In a marketplace that constantly demanded new and innovative products and that often profited by only the slimmest of margins, production costs needed to remain low and production outputs high.[5] Professional studio musicians filled that need, bringing their unique musical talents to a variety of projects and, for the most part, putting their own professional identities aside in the service of a bigger project.[6]

In this crowded and very talented marketplace, each city's cohort of session musicians came to be associated with geography, aesthetics, professional behavior, musicianship, race, gender, and class. These identities ultimately led label executives to make production decisions that were informed on essentialized understandings of who these musicians were. Nashville was no different. According to music journalists, trade reporters, and even the musicians themselves, the Nashville A Team stood out among their recording industry peers for a number of reasons. New York and Los Angeles session musicians, for instance, were known throughout the industry not only for their insularity, but for their profound dependence on written arrangements—printed notation that told them exactly what to play and when to play it. The musicians of the Nashville A Team, on the other hand, were commonly viewed through a lens of rusticity, downhome amiability, and natural talent that downplayed the important professional training that all of them had undertaken on their paths to Music Row and that positioned Nashville's recording community as a hospitable (if somewhat backward) alternative to big-city studios. The Nashville A Team seemed more laidback, collaborative, and creative. In a 1966 report for *The Saturday Evening Post*, for instance, writer Charles Portis—later of *True Grit* fame—remarked: "A Nashville recording session is a very casual affair. There are no arrangers, no producers and no written music, except once in a while a lead sheet, and the singer has probably brought that along for the words, not the music."[7] Similarly, a 1964 *Time* reporter noted that "the sidemen on twangy electric guitars . . . are a small, seasoned corps whose musical prowess is more heart than art. Few, lest it cramp their style, have had formal training. In fact, they tend to pride themselves on their inability to read music. . . ."[8] This coverage became so common that, by 1970, journalists John Grissim and Paul Hemphill, in their respective books on the country music commercial juggernaut, highlighted the A Team in extended passages, as did documentary and feature films focusing on country music artists, culminating in Robert Altman's Academy Award–winning 1975 film *Nashville*.[9]

Given their decades-long involvement in recording and their connections to sessions for dozens of labels, exactly who composed the Nashville A Team is a matter of some debate, even among members of the A Team themselves. For the most part, the A Team's membership can best be understood in generational terms (Table I.1). The first generation—what some Nashville musicians refer to as "the original Nashville A Team"—was

TABLE I.1   THE GENERATIONS OF THE NASHVILLE A TEAM

First Generation	Chet Atkins (guitar)
(ca. 1945–ca. 1955)	Harold Bradley (guitar)
	Owen Bradley (piano)
	Billy Byrd (guitar)
	Farris Coursey (drums)
	Joe Zinkan (bass)
Second Generation	Floyd Cramer (piano)
(ca. 1955–ca. 1963)	Hank Garland (guitar)
	Buddy Harman (drums)
	The Jordanaires (background vocals)
	The Anita Kerr Singers (background vocals)
	Grady Martin (guitar)
	Bob Moore (bass)
	Velma Smith (guitar)
Third Generation	Fred Carter, Jr. (guitar)
(ca. 1963–ca. 1975)	Ray Edenton (guitar)
	Charlie McCoy (harmonica, others)
	Wayne Moss (guitar)
	Jerry Reed (guitar)
	Hargus "Pig" Robbins (piano)
	Henry Strzelecki (bass)
Fourth Generation	David Briggs (piano)
(ca. 1967–ca. 1980)	Jerry Carrigan (drums)
	Norbert Putnam (bass)
	Reggie Young (guitar)

involved in the Nashville recording scene from its very beginnings in the late 1950s and, in some cases, remained active until the mid-1970s. These musicians—including guitarists Billy Byrd, Chet Atkins, and Harold Bradley, drummer Farris Coursey, bassist Joe Zinkan, and pianist Owen Bradley—were responsible for drawing country recording sessions from Chicago and Cincinnati to Nashville, and they were at the forefront of many business ventures that helped to establish Nashville as a major music industry center. By the mid-1950s, a second generation of musicians established themselves in Nashville's growing studio scene, joining some members of the first generation on iconic country, pop, and rock and roll recordings. Among these musicians were guitarists Grady Martin and Hank Garland, pianist Floyd Cramer, bassist Bob Moore, and drummer Buddy Harman. A third generation—including multi-instrumentalist Charlie McCoy, pianist Hargus "Pig" Robbins, guitarist Wayne Moss, bassist Henry Strzelecki, and drummer Willie Ackerman—emerged by the mid-1960s to help meet the needs of a still growing studio scene and to bring new musical ideas to town. And by the end of the 1960s, a fourth generation hailing from the soul and rhythm and blues recording scenes in Memphis and Muscle Shoals, Alabama, came to town, offering their own soul-inspired take on country music and working closely with country-rock musicians throughout the early 1970s. Among them were guitarist Reggie Young, bassist Norbert Putnam, and drummer Jerry Carrigan. The musicians in these generational configurations frequently worked with one another, and a new studio musician's arrival in the scene was more often the consequence of increased demand for work than the need to replace the labor of someone who was already established.

Session musicians have played a key role in record production, almost from its inception, and continue to be central to the production of many popular music recordings decades into the digital era.[10] During the recording industry's first few decades, recorded performances were cut directly to a wax or acetate disc, and even after the development of magnetic tape in the 1940s, musicians needed to perform a piece from start to finish without stopping because of the recording media's limitations.[11] Musicians who thrive in a live environment are often daunted by the recording studio.[12] Concerts are ephemeral, and mistakes of timing, intonation, and inflection are easily forgotten. But recordings are more permanent documents of a particular performance that can, through repeated playbacks, amplify mistakes and idiosyncracies.[13] Recording studios can also feel odd for musicians who are accustomed to receiving the feedback of a live concert audience, forcing the musicians to seek out additional sources of inspiration and energy to create memorable recorded performances.[14] And, from an economic perspective, recording studio time is expensive, so musicians seldom have the luxury of making too many mistakes and doing take after take in search of perfection.[15]

The 1950s and 1960s were a particularly important time for the deployment of session musicians in the US popular music marketplace. Following World War II, radio stations increasingly turned away from live, in-studio musical performances and toward "disc jockey shows" that featured charismatic disc jockeys who shaped local, regional, and national taste by curating recordings for increasingly segmented listening audiences.[16] As a consequence, record labels—which had previously been accustomed to providing content for phonograph owners and jukebox jobbers—needed to turn their attention to radio stations, which demanded new content at an almost blistering pace.[17] As musicologist Albin Zak has discussed, the recording industry of the 1950s and 1960s was engaged in a constant search for "novel" sounds that could engage radio listeners and encourage the purchase of new recordings for their expanding collections. At the same time, this push for novelty led to increasing obsolescence of musical styles, as what once sounded "new" and "fresh" quickly became "old" and "worn out."[18]

In New York and Los Angeles, the two major poles of US record production during the 1950s and 1960s, the push for novelty was largely led by staff arrangers, whose job was to take the raw material of a song— provided to them either in a lead sheet that outlined the melody and the chord changes or a demonstration recording ("demo") provided by the song's publisher—and transform it into a hit using an interesting, engaging, and "hooky" arrangement.[19] Working primarily from written notation, these arrangers called upon session musicians to play their scores faithfully. As a consequence, New York and Los Angeles session musicians were widely renowned for their ability to sight-read written notation and to play even the most complicated arrangements cleanly and confidently without prior rehearsal.

The Nashville A Team, on the other hand, largely eschewed standard arranging practices in favor of so-called "head" arrangements that were developed during the recording session itself. That is, the A Team musicians arrived at a session with little to no prior knowledge of the songs that were going to be recorded that day, and they often heard the songs for the first time as the session began. In some cases, the singer or the producer played a demo, while in others, the singer played and sang the song on the spot. As the musicians listened to the first song for the four-song session, they wrote down the song's chord changes using a shorthand known as the "Nashville Number System" and began to think of interesting ways to ornament the singer's melody. In some cases, the accompaniment might draw from cues heard in the demo, but it was just as common for the A Team musicians to think of something on the spot. After trying out a couple of ideas, the musicians sat down for a "take," with the goal of creating a publishable recording in as few takes as possible.[20]

In these "cold turkey" sessions, as Harold Bradley described them, the A Team played the role of both session musician and arranger.[21] As such, A Team musicians were valued not only for their ability to play with precision, but also for their ability to create novel sounds that could attract the attention of radio listeners and record buyers. For record labels, such skills led to significant cost savings, not only by reducing the amount of studio time that was necessary to create a recording, but also by eliminating the expense of hiring an arranger and a copyist to provide written notation for the session. The Nashville A Team might, therefore, be rightfully viewed as co-authors and co-composers of nearly every hit recording to come out of Nashville's Music Row for a span of twenty years or more.[22] Yet, like most session musicians of their generation, their work was seldom credited at the time, and their contributions are little known outside of friends, family, colleagues, and dedicated fans and historians.

The demand for original product in the country genre grew exponentially during the 1950s and 1960s, putting especially strong pressure on the Nashville A Team to work long hours and to be as efficient and creative as possible. These two decades witnessed the emergence of an identifiable country music industry and the centralization of that industry in Nashville, a city that, while internationally known as the home of the *Grand Ole Opry* radio broadcasts, was as well-known for its contributions to education, religious life, and literary culture as it was for music.[23] Emerging from the annual Disc Jockey Convention that was first hosted in 1952, the Country Music Association (CMA)—spearheaded by Jo Walker-Meador and Connie B. Gay—worked to establish Nashville as the industrial home of country music and lobbied radio station owners across the United States, Canada, and even Europe to devote more and more of their broadcast time to playing recordings of country music.[24] As Diane Pecknold notes, one of the most powerful tools that the CMA had at its disposal was the changing demographics of the core country music audience and its growing consumer power.[25] By the end of the 1960s, radio stations were switching over to a full-time, all-country format that demanded new product constantly.[26] Nashville's studio musicians were at the ready, cutting hundreds of tunes a week.

The purpose of this book is to work toward recovering the histories of the session musicians who shaped the sounds of popular music in the United States during the 1950s, 1960s, and 1970s through oral historical, archival, and musical research on the Nashville session scene. This broader project has been the subject of quite a bit of research in recent years, with numerous trade and academic books, as well as documentary films and museum exhibits, contributing to our understanding of how recordings were made during this important time in US popular music history. Motown's Funk Brothers, the Wrecking Crew in Los Angeles, and the Swampers in Muscle Shoals have all been the subject of significant books and documentary films, and the hit documentary *20 Feet from Stardom* highlighted the contributions of predominantly African American and predominantly female backing vocalists to the broad spectrum of US popular music from the 1960s to the present.[27] And the Nashville A Team has been the subject of a major museum exhibition—titled *Dylan, Cash, and the Nashville Cats*—at the Country Music Hall of Fame and Museum in Nashville and has been given a voice in other temporary and permanent exhibits.[28]

This book expands upon these contributions by using new archival documents and oral histories to add depth and nuance to some of the prevailing narratives surrounding not only country music production, but the work of session musicians, more generally. I have conducted original oral histories with many of the remaining members of the Nashville A Team, as well as other musicians who participated in Nashville recording sessions with less frequency. Additional oral histories are drawn from the Country Music Foundation Library's expansive oral history project, which includes the oral testimonies of many deceased session musicians, producers, and Music Row executives. This research also expands upon previous Music Row oral history projects by talking with people who can shed light on the work of some people who have seldom been considered in any detail: orchestral musicians and arrangers. As a consequence, the perspectives of these musicians also figure prominently into this book's narrative.

Nashville's music industry is a surprisingly insular one, and much of what fans of country music see is a carefully polished veneer that often obscures important facts and counternarratives. The history of Nashville's recording industry—and the place of the Nashville A Team in that history—is not immune from mythologizing and carefully circumscribed "official" narratives. As Diane Pecknold has argued in a recent essay, the CMA has played a key role in telling country music's "official" history through the establishment of the Country Music Foundation and the Country Music Hall of Fame and Museum, a history that is intimately linked to the CMA's broader goal of capitalizing on country music and building an industry in Nashville.[29] As a consequence, the story of the Nashville A Team has been one that focuses on the musicians' ability to produce arrangements on the spot and that supposes that these musicians were largely untrained, "natural" talents.

Furthermore, in a city that continues to capitalize on the iconography of major recording artists such as Patsy Cline and Johnny Cash (both of whom have been the subject of major exhibits at the Country Music Hall of Fame and Museum and who have had individual museums dedicated to their memories opened in the last decade), it is probably not surprising that the contributions of the Nashville A Team have not been widely recognized by either the guardians of Nashville's official narratives or by fans and scholars of the music that was created there. Stars—especially ones with tragic flaws or short lives—lend themselves easily to mythologizing, but journeymen musicians who showed up day in and day out for decades seldom do. As a consequence, the overwhelming majority of the original Nashville A Team have not yet been inducted into the Country Music Hall of Fame, despite their contributions to the recordings of dozens of recording artists who are members.[30] In fact, the current induction criteria at the Country Music Hall of Fame—which allow a "sideman" to be inducted every third year—will make it nearly impossible for the original A Team's *grandchildren* to see their ancestors honored in this manner.[31] By contrast, in 2007, the Musicians Hall of Fame, located just a few blocks from the Country Music Hall of Fame and Museum, inducted the entire A Team as a group; their focus on the broader US popular music industry and the nameless and faceless veterans of the music industry has led them to include several groups of session musicians, including Motown's Funk Brothers and the L.A. Wrecking Crew.[32]

Such omissions are not surprising given the ways that the A Team was credited during the height of their careers. With rare exception, session musicians received absolutely no credit on album sleeves—the majority of which were dedicated to brief essays written by other recording artists, producers, publicists, or disc jockeys to promote the artist's recording.[33] And, given the impossibly small space allocated on the label of a 45-rpm recording, session musicians simply couldn't be mentioned there, either. The record-buying public was, therefore, generally unaware of the Nashville A Team, even as journalists showed increasing interest in the studio scene through the 1960s. As a consequence, any attempt to recover the contributions of the Nashville A Team is an inherently challenging one, and, even when discographical information tells us which musicians played on a recording, we cannot be guaranteed that we know specifically what contributions they made to the final product because available documentation often lists only what instrument each musician played. But a musician listed as "guitarist" may have played multiple roles in a single session; how the lead, rhythm, and bass duties were split requires consultation of oral testimony or careful attention to the particular stylistic tendencies of a particular session musician.

Sometimes, research into the session musicians who helped drive the popular music industry in the 1950s and 1960s can be presented in such a manner as to suggest that the record-buying public have been the victims of a fraud. In particular, discussions of Los Angeles's Wrecking Crew often focus on the ways that these musicians actually substituted for beloved bands, as was the case when the Byrds made their debut recording with them in 1965.[34] Looking to the rock *auteurs* of the 1960s (including the Beatles, Jimi Hendrix, and others) as models, popular music critics have, since the mid-1960s, placed a great deal of value on those musicians and bands that appear to do the work themselves, from writing the songs to playing on the tracks and even producing their own albums.[35] So when it is revealed that a beloved rock band might have had the assistance of a team of professional session musicians, their work might be heard as a less authentic—and, using a troublingly masculine definition of authenticity, less virile—form of musical expression; after all, what is the difference between the obviously contrived marketing campaign that led to the formation of the Monkees and the powerful musical expression of the Byrds when the same musicians played on their recordings?[36]

That is not the point of this book. In fact, this book takes it as a given that the country music industry requires the contributions of session musicians in order to make marketable and aesthetically interesting recordings. It also accepts that recording work is a different kind of work than road work, so it simply makes sense that musicians have specialized in those areas. Someone who can play a flashy solo to excite a live audience might not be able to restrain the impulse to play constantly during a recording session. Similarly, an exceptional session musician might struggle to play something brilliant and flashy in a live setting after years of learning how to subtly fill the spaces between lyrics. (It's not terribly surprising that very few members of the Nashville A Team also found great success on the road. Pianist Floyd Cramer and multi-instrumentalist Charlie McCoy held down exceptional solo careers, and guitarist Grady Martin toured with Willie Nelson following his retirement from the studio scene in the 1980s.[37] But, generally, road musicians don't play in the studio, and studio musicians don't play on the road.)

Rather, this book draws attention to the unheralded contributions of the Nashville A Team in an effort to point to the significant role that these musicians played in shaping the sounds of the hundreds of recording artists with whom they worked and to shed new light on the particular talents that these musicians brought to their work. Rather than undermining the work of the recording artists whose names and faces grace the album sleeves that came out of Nashville during this time, acknowledging the talents and contributions of the Nashville A Team should add greater depth to our appreciation of their work. That an artist was able to walk into a room of musicians who had not survived the trials of road work with them, who had not learned to deal with every idiosyncrasy that the singer might have, and still produce iconic recordings is nothing short of remarkable. That the session musicians comprising the Nashville A Team were able to do that multiple times each day—with different recording artists in each session—is nothing short of miraculous.

As such, this book adds to our collective understanding of the ways that the Nashville A Team contributed to landmark recordings by the top country, pop, and rock recording artists of the 1950s, 1960s, and 1970s and to develop a better understanding of the lives and careers of those nameless and faceless musicians that we have heard constantly for the past six decades. In so doing, this book draws heavily upon recent insights from the musicology of recording, a field of study that has achieved greater prominence in popular music scholarship over the past decade or so. A broad and expansive field of inquiry, the musicology of recording explores many of the same concerns that traditional historical musicology has occupied itself with—musical aesthetics, compositional histories, economics, and so on—but also considers the place of specific recording technologies in these issues. Simon Zagorski-Thomas, a musicologist who brings a previous career in recording engineering and production to his scholarship, argues forcefully that the musicology of recording must connect "a production-based and a reception-based approach."[38] As such, in recent years, musicologists interested in recording have developed a variety of methodologies to better understand how recordings communicate meaning; how performers, composers, producers, and session musicians interact with various recording and playback technologies; and how listeners engage with various playback technologies.

From a "production-based" perspective, scholars have largely focused on the recordings themselves, treating them as primary texts that are ripe for further analysis. In popular music studies and jazz studies, recordings have long served as significant primary texts because written notation often falls short in its attempts to capture even the most basic elements of a composition, performance, or improvisation.[39] As such, scholars such as Albin Zak, Jay Hodgson, and Allan F. Moore, among others, have sought to build a common vocabulary to help scholars communicate what they are hearing to their colleagues, often focusing on the most common recording and production techniques.[40] Similarly, Moore, Ruth Dockwray, and Patricia Smith have developed techniques to analyze our spatial experiences of listening to a recording, offering a "sound-box" model that places all of the sounds that we encounter in a single hypothetical room.[41]

Yet, despite recording's prominent role in popular and vernacular music traditions around the globe, some of the most significant work in the musicology of recording has been focused on performers of Western art music, the traditional domain of historical musicologists and a body of music that was sure to facilitate wider acceptance of these methods into the "musicological toolbox."[42] Mark Katz, for instance, has argued that recording and playback technologies have exerted influence over the creation and reception of music since the earliest recording technologies were developed in the mid-nineteenth century. He calls our individual and collective responses to those influences "phonograph effects": "any change in musical behavior—whether listening, performing, or composing—that has arisen in response to sound-recording technology. . . . [I]n other words, any observable manifestation of recording's influence."[43] In particular, Katz has demonstrated that early twentieth-century concert violinists increasingly deployed vibrato in their recordings in order to overcome their "invisibility" to the audiences for their recordings.[44] Similarly, several musicologists—particularly those working on the notion of "historically informed performance practice"—have developed and deployed analytic methods to help scholars better understand how recording musicians have engaged with recording and playback technologies to convey their aesthetic ideas to their audiences.[45]

One of the most significant contributions made by scholars engaging with the musicology of recording has been an increased engagement with the work of those figures who do not always receive credit on the label, sleeve, or liner notes of a particular recording: engineers, producers, arrangers, and session musicians. Since recording is inherently collaborative, the products of recording sessions often resist musicological analysis because musicology is poorly equipped to deal with collaborative work.[46] Perhaps not surprisingly, then, musicologists have overwhelmingly gravitated toward those figures who functioned as impresarios and left their own indelible mark on the final product, such as producers Sam Phillips, Sir George Martin, Phil Spector, and Brian Eno. Virgil Moorefield, in his book *The Producer as Composer*, suggests, for instance, that Martin, Spector, and Eno "expanded the purview of the modern producer by introducing radical new concepts such as the Wall of Sound (Spector), the confluence of classical, commercial, and experimental techniques (Martin), and the studio as a musical instrument in its own right (Eno)." As a consequence, he argues, "the contemporary producer is an *auteur*" whose creative vision trumps all others.[47]

Scholars who approach the production of recordings from a social science perspective have also highlighted the significant contributions of those lesser-known figures who are involved in their creation. Ethnomusicologists Louise Meintjes and Eliot Bates, in their respective work on recording studios in 1990s South Africa and early 2000s Turkey, have highlighted the ways that session musicians, recording artists, producers, and engineers must navigate the complex politics of the outside world in the intensely political world of the recording studio.[48] And, extending the phenomenological work of Alfred Shutz, Thomas Porcello has argued that recording sessions can be particularly powerful moments during which individuals come together in "strategic, intentional, deeply felt forms of performed cultural activity" and create "living embodiments of multiple local epistemologies enacted in the flow of internal and external time in and out of the recording studio."[49] As a consequence, this book considers recording sessions as important moments during which individuals with different backgrounds, ideologies, and agencies come together for the purpose of creating something collectively, and it acknowledges—and perhaps even celebrates—the very courage that each person involved in a session needed to find in order to offer their greatest talents to the collective work.

As a consequence of this exceptional production-oriented scholarship, the table has been set for a deep examination of record production from a variety of perspectives. But a production-oriented approach is necessarily a limiting one, as it does not adequately consider what happens on the other side of the tracking room and control room doors. As such, any study of record production must also consider how recordings are received by record buyers, radio listeners, and other people who engage directly or indirectly with recorded sound. For example, historian William Howland Kenney has argued for the powerful influence of recording on collective memory during the first decades of audio recording, noting that, "[m]ore than we used to realize, the phonograph and recorded music served to stimulate collective memories among Americans of different social and ethnic backgrounds, who were, like the few large recording companies that survived the Depression, caught up in the swiftly changing patterns and politics of national life."[50] As Kenney and others have documented thoroughly, record buyers interact with the products that the recording industry releases, selecting those songs that speak to their individual and collective interests and leading recording companies to adjust their catalogues and marketing strategies to accommodate those needs.[51] Such uses of recorded sound have been extensively documented in the academic literature—although, undoubtedly, there are any number of examples that merit further investigation. Scholarship on record collecting, bootlegging, and audio archives has shown the power of physical recordings in providing access to a collective memory and in demonstrating the cultural value of a particular genre, form, or aesthetic practice.[52]

Although much of the reception-oriented scholarship on recorded sound has focused on recordings as physical objects (and fetishistic collection and engagement with them), recent scholarship has also begun to examine the ways that people engage with recorded sound and music aesthetically. Some of the most provocative work in this area has emerged from hip hop studies, where scholars are investigating an entire cultural form that has been developed around the recycling, repurposing, and reframing of snippets of recorded music and sound. In his book *Making Beats: The Art of Sample-Based Hip-Hop*, Joseph G. Schloss drew upon extensive ethnographic work with hip hop producers to, among other things, document the ways that they mine preexisting recordings for the raw materials that they use to produce their own unique beats. Schloss's work is particularly provocative in its investigation of both the aesthetics and the ethics of these borrowings.[53] Furthermore, Mark Katz has offered an historical investigation of hip hop borrowings in his extensive research on hip-hop DJs, showing how these borrowings were also inevitably shaped by the social, economic, and geographic contexts in which hip-hop emerged.[54] Recent insights from the field of sound studies, too, aid our efforts to understand how people interact with recorded sound. Although the field of sound studies is concerned with sound on the broadest scale (including the natural, human, and interstellar realms), recorded sound has been a central concern for these scholars. Sound studies, in its efforts to document and recover the ways that people interact with the sounds around them, has proven to be particularly interested in such things as radio broadcasts, personal listening devices, jukeboxes, and other technologies that allow people to shape the sounds of their environments.[55]

This study of the Nashville A Team and its contributions to popular music in the post–World War II era necessarily draws upon many of the insights provided by the musicology of recording and sound studies. In its focus on record production, this book necessarily deploys a production-oriented approach drawn from the musicology of recording, examining the various components of a completed production—songwriting, arranging, performance, and recording engineering—in great detail. Using the finished recordings these musicians produced as a major archive, this book will draw as many insights from the recordings themselves as from the written and oral archives that are being deployed here. At the same time, this book draws heavily upon oral testimony and previously unexplored

archival evidence to get a better sense of the ways that a routine recording session might have unfolded. Considering the pace that the Nashville
A Team was working at during the heights of their careers, sessions needed
to be routine. Any anomalies would have made it difficult to complete
their assigned tasks, and those rare instances when a session was more
challenging than normal do appear prominently in the memories of the
musicians who were there. These routines also offer useful insights into the
social interactions between musicians, the various hierarchies that were at
work in the studio, and the broader economic and political pressures that
musicians faced as they entered the studio for work each day. Moreover,
by drawing upon insights from producers, engineers, arrangers, and the
descendants and colleagues of the Nashville A Team, it is possible to get
an even more complete picture of the ways that these musicians fit into a
broader musical environment in Nashville and beyond.

A reception-oriented approach, drawing upon insights from sound
studies, will push this study beyond the boundaries of the recording studio and into the cars, homes, and social gathering places where people
encountered the music that was created on Music Row during the height
of the Nashville Sound era. These recordings were, after all, not art objects,
but commercial products intended for public consumption, and some of
the production standards were shaped as a response to the chart success (or failure) of a particular track. As such, radio and jukebox play
and record purchases, as forms of reception, also influenced production.
Moreover, as the Nashville A Team became more and more accustomed
to working with one another, they also became accustomed to referring
to earlier hit recordings as a sort of insider shorthand to communicate
particular arranging practices or sonic signatures to one another, showing
how their own reception influenced their production practices.

Nashville Cats: Record Production in Music City also rectifies a significant oversight in the broader field of popular music studies: the general
exclusion of country music from its primary discourses. As I have traced
elsewhere, country music studies has been a thriving and interdisci-
plinary field of study for more than five decades at this point, drawing
heavily from the insights of popular music studies, more generally.[56] Yet,

in spite of the efforts that country music scholars have taken to integrate the findings and insights of popular music scholars, the same cannot be said for popular music studies' engagement with country music studies. Country music is often referenced as an influence on early rock and roll, or as a retreat for rock artists who are seeking to return to their "roots," or as a musical form that even the most adventurous popular music aficionados should turn their nose up to.[57] Several scholars have observed that country music's affiliations with the white working class of the US South may encourage such attitudes and oversights, as that particular population's long association with racism (both real and presumed) and "backwardness" (thanks to narratives of "hillbilly" and rural otherness) have made country music an object of derision, not celebration.[58]

Yet country music—in a variety of forms—has been present alongside other forms of US popular music almost since the advent of commercial recording in the late nineteenth century. A number of scholars have shown that country music—known in the 1920s through a variety of names intended to connote tradition, rurality, and whiteness (such as "Old Familiar Tunes" and, more generally, "hillbilly music")—was the result of conscious recording industry efforts to develop new markets for their recordings.[59] Western swing music, which flourished in the 1930s and 1940s and is generally accepted as a genre of country music, is also deeply connected to the mainstream popularity of swing music during that time, although jazz historians have generally ignored the tradition altogether, despite the fact that many western swing pioneers considered themselves to be *jazz* musicians, not *hillbilly* musicians.[60] And contemporary country music—perhaps best represented by the recent "bro country" trend—is similarly linked aesthetically, commercially, and socially to other forms of US popular music, as it is often distributed by record labels that, in their overall work, attempt to reach all market segments and by radio stations that often own multiple stations in a single market, each of which attempts to address the needs of a particular niche in the communities that can pick up their signals.[61]

The era in which the Nashville A Team worked, known generally as the Nashville Sound era, offers a case study that is particularly ripe for acceptance (perhaps even canonization) into the broader realm of popular music studies. As Joli Jensen and Diane Pecknold have shown in their respective work on the emerging Nashville industry in the 1950s and 1960s, the leaders of the industry attempted to respond to the overwhelming—and, in many ways, unpredictable—popularity of early rock and roll, which drew audiences from live concerts of country music, record buyers from country music catalogues, and radio listeners away from the decades-old barn dance programs that had been so essential to the national (and international) success of the genre. As such, the Nashville Sound has often been viewed as an effort to use musical practices drawn from mainstream popular music—particularly the work of the pop crooners that were exceptionally popular from the 1940s onward—to reshape country music in a more palatable form.[62]

But, even more to the point, the musicians who contributed to the thousands of recording sessions held in Nashville came to the city from a variety of musical traditions. Some of them were long-standing members of the Nashville music scene, playing in society dance bands where they had learned to play in the primarily pop styles of the day. Others were conservatory-trained musicians who played with the Nashville Symphony and taught music at local colleges and universities. Some musicians, like Charlie McCoy (who came to the city in 1961), were dyed-in-the-wool blues and rock and roll aficionados, while others came through the ranks of the barn dances, schoolhouse concerts, and honky-tonks that had supported country music since the beginning. As such, the recording studios of the Nashville Sound era can be seen as points of confluence, where musicians with many different backgrounds were expected to come together, share their individual talents, and create new recordings that, while primarily marketed as "country" music, bear the traces of many forms of US popular music.

Rather than offering a strict chronological history of the Nashville Sound era and the role of the Nashville A Team in that history, this book offers a somewhat more thematically organized exploration of specific aspects of the Nashville A Team's history and its contributions to recorded popular music in the post–World War II era. *Nashville Cats* also attempts to tie the work of the Nashville A Team to the broader domain of US popular music during that time.

Chapter 1, "The Birth of the Nashville Recording Industry," traces the development of Nashville's recording studio infrastructure from ad hoc facilities used in the decade following the end of World War II to the mid-1970s, when the city was home to several state-of-the-art permanent recording facilities. This chapter not only explores the business of recording in Nashville, but also examines how new technologies that were deployed within the city's recording studios changed how musicians created their work. Finally, this chapter considers how trade publications, the mainstream press, and films promoted Nashville as both a state-of-the-art recording center and a relaxed, small-town alternative to urban recording industries in New York, Chicago, and Los Angeles.

At the height of the Nashville Sound era, the city's session musicians were widely celebrated for their ability to hear new musical compositions, construct head arrangements of those songs, and execute improvised arrangements with great precision. This story—although certainly true in the broadest sense—obscures valuable detail about the musical backgrounds, abilities, and tastes of Nashville's session musicians, in effect normalizing their diverse skill sets by treating them as interchangeable cogs in a record-production machine. Chapter 2, "The Musicianship of the Nashville Cats," examines the musicianship of Nashville Sound–era session musicians, following ethnomusicologist Henry Kingsbury's observation that discourses about musicianship reveal the values and ideologies that a given music culture celebrates and replicates.[63] This chapter, therefore, explores the myriad ways that Nashville Sound–era session musicians learned the fundamentals of music theory, utilized existing notional traditions and developed new ones, and negotiated work in recording sessions in which multiple kinds of musicianship were at play.

Many writers have treated the Nashville Sound as a single, monolithic style characterized by smooth background vocals, reverberant lead vocals, and sparing instrumental accompaniments. Yet, in a 1991 interview, prolific Nashville session guitarist Harold Bradley observed that "[w]hen people say the Nashville Sound, you know, singularly, I think they're wrong, because it should be plural. Everybody that's heavy has had their sound. . . ."[64] Drawing upon Mark Samples's work on musical branding, Chapter 3, "Musical Branding, Artist Identity, and the Nashville Sound," examines the ways that record producers, session musicians, and recording artists used the musical resources of Nashville's recording studios to develop signature sounds that helped listeners identify their favorite singers on recordings and radio.[65] Moreover, building upon recent work on the development of all-country radio during the 1960s, this chapter argues that musical brands may have played an essential role in maintaining listener attention, thereby ensuring the success of the new format.[66]

Many of the most iconic recordings of the Nashville Sound era gained popularity not simply because of the recording artist whose name appeared on the labels of the singles and the albums that contained them, but because of the contributions of Nashville's session musicians who crafted arrangements and "hook" motifs. Yet, for the most part, these session musicians were never credited and received only a seemingly small one-time fee for their efforts. Chapter 4, "Musical Labor and the Nashville Studio System," considers the creative impact of Nashville's session musicians through a careful examination of several chart-topping Nashville Sound–era recordings, exploring the ways that the arrangements and "hook" motifs that they created shaped the works. Moreover, this chapter suggests that, although session musicians were seldom credited for their work, many of them presented clear artistic identities that are anonymously visible across a wide spectrum of recordings.

The book concludes with a brief Afterword that considers the impacts of the Nashville Sound era's recording industry on the city's role as a major center for the production of not only country music, but a wide range of commercial popular musics, in the late twentieth and early twenty-first centuries.

The Nashville Sound era was an important time not only in the history of country music, but also in the history of popular music, more generally. A detailed exploration of the ways that country recordings were created can help us develop a better understanding of the dynamics of the mid-twentieth-century popular music industry and the flows of ideas, musical or otherwise, between Nashville and other cities. Moreover, by taking the work of session musicians seriously, we can begin to recover a remarkable history of creativity, collaboration, and collegiality that deserves to be both celebrated and problematized. To understand how this community of session musicians became established, however, it is essential first to consider how Nashville became a recording center in the first place.

The Birth of the Nashville Recording Industry

Despite its current prominence as a major popular music production center and its reputation as the home of country music, Nashville was a relatively minor music center prior to World War II. Instead, the city was primarily known as a center of education—the home of Fisk University (founded in 1866) and Vanderbilt University (founded in 1873), among many others—and religious publication, as well as the home of a nationally successful, but not singular, barn dance program, the *Grand Ole Opry*.[1] And despite the *Opry*'s national presence, Nashville was only one of several cities around the United States that could have laid claim to being country music's principal home.

In its highly racialized marketing, country music—known in the 1920s as "old familiar tunes," "old time tunes," and in the broadest sense, "hillbilly" music—was marketed as the music of rural whites. As part of a broader effort to capitalize on ethnic musics of all sorts, producers of hillbilly music attempted to capture, commodify, and market the songs and tunes that were already popular among white working-class audiences to those very

Nashville Cats. Travis D. Stimeling, © Oxford University Press (2020). Oxford University Press.
DOI: 10.1093/oso/9780197502815.001.0001

same audiences and to release recordings of new compositions in a similar vein.[2] Recording companies—of which there were several dozen active in the United States during the 1920s—sought to expand their offerings of classical and Tin Pan Alley pop songs to reach new markets that were supporting live musical performance in a number of varieties, a phenomenon that music industry historians Russell and David Sanjek have described as a "process of 'democratization' of American music."[3] A survey of recording catalogues from the 1920s reveals a remarkably wide range of musical offerings from various ethnic communities in the United States and Canada, as well as offerings from around the globe.[4] Hillbilly music was, therefore, just one segment of a vast and varied output of commercially recorded music that was intended to engage as much of the market as possible in the purchase of recordings.

At the dawn of the hillbilly era of the 1920s, recording sessions were typically held in one of two settings: (1) professional recording studios located in New York and New Jersey, where the recording companies had hired skilled recording engineers to create high-quality recordings in a relatively short amount of time; and (2) "location recording" sessions, held in impromptu studios set up in hotel ballrooms and other such spaces in cities located far from the record companies' home offices.[5] Hundreds of hillbilly recordings were made in New York and New Jersey during the 1920s, with musicians from rural communities traveling by train to commit their repertoires to wax.[6] But, as discographer Tony Russell has shown, location recording was also a popular tool to record country music as early as June 1923, when an executive from Okeh Records, Ralph Peer, traveled to Atlanta at the suggestion of local artist-and-repertoire (A&R) man Polk C. Brockman to record a number of artists who were popular in the area. Those sessions generated the first recordings of future hillbilly star Fiddlin' John Carson, whose "Little Old Log Cabin in the Lane" channeled the racial anxieties of the modern southern city through the lens of minstrel romanticism.[7] Russell has documented record company travels to several of cities throughout the US South in an effort to discover new, previously unrecorded talent, an effort that yielded more than two thousand recordings in a roughly four-year period between June 1923 and

July 1927.[8] Perhaps most significant to the history of country music were those sessions held in July and August 1927 in Bristol, Tennessee/Virginia, where Jimmie Rodgers and the Carter Family made their first commercial recordings.[9] Nashville, on the other hand, was only marginal to location recording; as Charles K. Wolfe has noted, Victor came to the city in 1928, producing sides that were "commercially unsuccessful."[10]

Location recordings were often done quickly, with only one or two takes per song, leaving a great deal of room for mistakes. Recording engineers and A&R men were often more concerned about audio fidelity than musical accuracy, and it is quite possible that these producers believed that the mistakes were a quaint marker of ethnic authenticity.[11] On the other hand, studio recordings often exemplified higher standards of audio fidelity and musical accuracy. Recording professionals worked diligently throughout the 1920s and 1930s to develop new techniques to maintain sound isolation—primarily to keep extraneous noises, such as passing streetcars and passenger trains, out of recordings—and to accurately capture the sounds of the voices and instruments.[12] Many professional studio sessions were accompanied by session musicians who played with dozens, if not hundreds, of recording artists in all forms of popular music.[13]

The recording of hillbilly music in the 1920s and 1930s was, therefore, a decidedly decentralized phenomenon. Russell's extensive discography of pre–World War II hillbilly recordings reveals sessions held not only in major cities such as New York, Chicago, and Los Angeles, but also in such regional cities as Dallas, San Antonio, New Orleans, Charlotte, and even Nashville.[14] A number of scholars have suggested, then, that although Nashville may have cornered the market on country record production by the 1950s, any of a number of cities could claim to be the home of country record production in the prewar era. Wayne Daniel, for one, has suggested that Atlanta might be fruitfully considered a leading producer of country recordings in the prewar era, not only because it was the site of an important early location recording session, but because of the extensive pool of talent that recorded there, including such hillbilly favorites as Fiddlin' John Carson and Gid Tanner and the Skillet Lickers.[15] Others have argued that Charlotte, North Carolina, which boasted a strong group of radio performers associated with station WBT, deserves to be considered the center of country production in the prewar era, especially during the 1930s, when such artists as J. B. and Wade Mainer and Charlie and Bill Monroe called Charlotte home.[16] And, challenging the southern chauvinism of many country music historians, Lisa Krissoff Boehm and Paul Tyler have made strong arguments in favor of Chicago, which was the location of the immensely popular *National Barn Dance* program.[17]

What all of these cities had in common was a contingent of professional musicians who were active as radio broadcasters. Radio stations were, in many ways, more important than recordings to the lives of professional hillbilly musicians, especially during the 1930s, when consumers increasingly chose to invest in radios, a new technology that provided unlimited free content, unlike phonographs, which required extensive new purchases to create a similarly diverse listening experience.[18] Throughout the 1920s and 1930s, radio stations—even with a wide range of recorded music available for them to play over the air—hired a variety of musicians to provide live entertainment.[19] It was quite common for hillbilly musicians to "barnstorm" or "wildcat" from one station to another, spending only enough time in any given location to exhaust the community's interest in booking them for live performances.[20] These stations provided an important venue to advertise an artist's upcoming performances, to attract potential sponsors who could capitalize on the artist's popularity, and to sell songbooks and other assorted products that could promote the artist's image and music.[21] And, in the absence of proper recording studios, these radio stations—which were outfitted with state-of-the-art broadcast microphones and acetate disc cutters—often served as important sites for the production of hillbilly recordings.[22]

Radio barn dances proved to be a particularly useful tool for record companies to discover new talent as well. These programs, which drew heavily upon geographic, ethnic, and racial stereotypes refined in the nineteenth-century minstrel theater, proliferated throughout the United States, starting in Fort Worth and quickly spreading to Atlanta, Chicago, and Los Angeles, among other cities.[23] These programs frequently required a broad range of musical and comedic talents, and they became hotbeds of musical and theatrical creativity that drew some of the best and brightest professionals of their era.[24] Not surprisingly, performers who worked on such significant programs as WLS's *National Barn Dance* in Chicago, WLW's *Renfro Valley Barn Dance* from Cincinnati, and WSM's *Grand Ole Opry* in Nashville came to be very well represented in the recording catalogues of record companies by the start of World War II.

Nashville's status as the home of the *Grand Ole Opry* was undoubtedly a significant reason that the city came to be known for its connections to country music. The program began on November 28, 1925, as a rather humble affair, like most barn dance programs in the 1920s. WSM station manager George D. Hay, who had distinguished himself on WLS's *WLS Barn Dance* (later the *National Barn Dance*), encouraged local fiddler Uncle Jimmy Thompson to play on the station, which had only been on the air for less than two months at the time. Thompson's performance was well received by the WSM audience, what *Opry* historian Charles K. Wolfe has described as "part of a pattern" of "a 'vox populi' phenomenon [encountered at other stations], with the stations being apologetic about broadcasting such music but caving in to public demand."[25] Initially drawing talent from a pool of local string band musicians that included Dr. Humphrey Bates & His Possum Hunters, the Gully Jumpers, and Uncle Dave Macon, as well as African American harmonica virtuoso DeFord Bailey, WSM's *Barn Dance*, as it was initially known, drew the attention of listeners not only in Middle Tennessee, but across the United States.[26] In its first two years, much of the program's success could be traced not only to the musicians featured on it, but also to the station's infrastructure itself. In the increasingly cluttered airwaves of the 1920s United States, WSM was fortunate to be a "clear-channel" station, a status that prevented other stations from broadcasting on the same frequency and interfering with its signal.[27] Additionally, the station was one of the most powerful stations in the nation; as Wolfe has documented, WSM "began broadcasting with one thousand watts of power, making it one of the two strongest stations in the South, and stronger than 85 percent of all other broadcasting stations in the country at the time."[28] In its first two years, then, WSM's *Barn Dance* was able to garner attention from a broad national audience, as well as the occasional international listener, especially on a clear night.[29] The program's audience grew even more in late 1927, when a segment of the program began to be broadcast over the new NBC radio network, carrying it to listeners nationwide. It was at this time, too, that the program's name changed, becoming the *Grand Ole Opry*.[30] By the mid-1930s—at the height of the Great Depression—the *Opry* could boast a great national audience that was willing to spend their hard-earned dollars to travel to Nashville to see the program in person. As WSM historian Craig Havighurst has noted, by the mid-1930s, "about a quarter of the cars parked outside [the Dixie Tabernacle, then home of the *Opry*] were from out of state. Visitors would approach him [Hay] and tell him they were from Illinois, Florida, or Minnesota, hoping they could coax him to pass on greetings home over the air. But there were too many out-of-towners in the crowds of three thousand to do so."[31]

By the end of the 1920s, then, the *Opry* was one of Nashville's most iconic musical exports, and musicians who were hoping to reach a national audience came to see the program as a potential venue for their work. Local and regional barn dance programs, along with sponsored radio programs on a variety of radio stations, provided a training ground for these musicians to develop their repertoire and stage personas, to learn how to work with broadcast microphones, and to respond to their audiences' musical and dramatic tastes. The *Opry* and other major barn dance programs, then, represented the highest form of the art and became a significant goal for those musicians who aspired to national success. As a consequence, the *Opry* attracted musicians from throughout the South—and later from around the entire country and Canada—to Nashville, in the process creating a concentrated pool of musicians that talent scouts, A&R men, and booking agents could audition and market. Not surprisingly, then, many of the musicians who performed on the *Opry* were also offered the opportunity to make commercial recordings, appear in films, and tour widely, while still other musicians were more than happy to work in the city in the hopes that they would get the chance to work on the *Opry* stage.[32] *Opry* membership, then, came with a number of significant benefits, perhaps none as significant as membership in the WSM Artist Service Bureau. Created in 1933, the Artist Service Bureau functioned as a vital booking agency for *Opry* acts well into the 1950s, just as the music industry in Nashville was beginning to expand significantly. The Artist Service Bureau initially promoted package shows that included several leading *Opry* acts, but it also booked tours to smaller communities that could not sustain a large package show, bringing artists to "school houses, lodges, and county fairs between Saturdays, when they were required to be back in Nashville to perform on the radio."[33] Not only did the Artist Service Bureau serve to promote *Opry* artists and allow them to make a solid living as entertainers—rather than simply working as an entertainer on the weekends while maintaining day jobs—but it also played a key role in making the *Opry* a destination for top talent. As Wolfe observed, "Such bookings were necessary if the station was going to attract any full-time professional talent."[34] And, as Jeffrey Lange has observed, during World War II, "artist service bureau-assembled package shows . . . [were] a means to continue touring in a wartime atmosphere of gas and tire rationing."[35]

By the start of World War II, the *Grand Ole Opry* was a major destination for fans of hillbilly music and for artists who aspired to national commercial success. The *Opry* had made household names of Tennessee fiddler, singer, and entertainer Roy Acuff—who had parlayed his musical success into a couple of failed campaigns for statewide political office—and comedian Minnie Pearl, who developed her iconic character on the *Opry* stage.[36] The *Opry* had cornered the market on concert promotions by booking *Opry* artists for live performances throughout the southeastern United States and portions of the Midwest. But the broadcasts and bookings were not enough to transform the city into a major music industry center. Rather, Nashville was only one node in a large and decentralized network of country music production. *Opry* artists needed to travel to other cities to cut their discs in the prewar era and to Los Angeles to participate in the film industry. Song publishers, too, were largely absent from Nashville, with long-established music publishing centers such as New York and, to a lesser extent, Chicago handling most of the business. But, if Nashville was only one of many country music centers in the prewar era, World War II and the decade immediately following proved to be a transformative time for the city's music industry as a number of factors— including the establishment of publishing houses and the construction of the city's first permanent recording studios—helped to launch Nashville into the national music production spotlight.

As it was in many aspects of life in the United States, World War II was a disrupting force that led to a wide array of significant cultural shifts in the decade following its conclusion. For country music, more gener- ally, the war played a powerful role in building an audience. As Lange has convincingly argued, rural-born GIs brought their music with them to military installations, and broadcasts over the Armed Forces Radio Network helped to popularize the genre among a more diverse population of men.[37] (This process continued well into the Vietnam War era as young men were subjected to the draft and mandatory military conscription.)[38] Furthermore, as historian Peter LaChappelle has documented, defense workers on the West Coast flocked to dance halls that featured western swing.[39] WSM, too, packaged *Opry* artists in the *Camel Caravan* and pre- sented performances at military installations across the country.[40] And, at the war's end, honky tonk songs gained popularity among white working- class men and women as they struggled to renegotiate their domestic roles after extended periods of separation.[41] Country music, then, emerged from the war as a major cultural force, not as a niche musical genre that catered to a presumably small population.

As country music's cultural significance seemed to be reaching new levels, the music's production was still scattered around the same musi- cal centers as it was before the war. But, as a number of scholars have documented, a number of factors led to the coalescence of a country music industry around Nashville in the decade immediately following World War II. At the end of World War II, the *Grand Ole Opry* remained Nashville's greatest country music export, drawing a highly talented pool of entertainers to work on the nationally broadcasted program. Yet, aside from the station and its associated Artist Service Bureau, there remained relatively little infrastructure in the city to support a music industry. But an increased demand in recorded song in the postwar decade created new opportunities for enterprising and creative people to build a music industry in Nashville. For the people involved in the Nashville recording industry, then, the war proved to be a particularly transformative force that created new spaces for emerging technologies, companies, and business leaders to develop. At the same time, as Lange has documented, the emergent country music industry was also concerned with a "struggle for respectability," trying to prove that country music was, in fact, big business that deserved to be taken seriously.[42]

One of the earliest developments in the postwar Nashville music industry was the establishment of a core group of music publishers with a dedicated interest in country songwriters. Song publishers, based primarily in New York and Chicago, had largely ignored Nashville altogether, occasionally selling songs to *Opry* artists and collecting royalties on the songs that other, non-hillbilly acts played on WSM and other radio stations.[43] But, as Brian Ward and Patrick Huber have noted, prewar hillbilly musicians frequently maintained a large repertoire of original songs that were not producing royalties for the artist—or for anyone. "Much of the country blues and hillbilly music heard on interwar roots recordings," they observe, "came directly from the artists themselves, whether the songs and tunes already comprised part of their live repertoires, or were located, purchased, or written by them."[44] As such, Nashville was a potential gold mine for song publishers who were interested in collecting copyright-eligible material and in finding ways to monetize those songs by putting them in the hands of a wide range of recording, broadcasting, and touring artists.

Despite the potential opportunities for song publishers, they were slow to find their way to Nashville. Often, this reluctance to engage with Nashville's hillbilly musicians—and country music, more generally—is attributed to the musical tastes and attitudes of New York–based song publishers and the performing rights organization that collected royalties on their behalf, the American Society of Composers, Authors, and Publishers (ASCAP).[45] To be sure, these attitudes were to blame in part; as Lange has observed, for instance, "ASCAP excluded country music songwriters as members," an exclusion that caused "many of those songwriters . . . [to never take] their profession seriously." Lange cites the remarks of honky tonk songwriter Floyd Tillman, who commented that his songwriting was "just . . . for my own amusement. I never heard of anyone in Texas writing songs. I always thought they all came out of New York, which most of them did."[46] And, as Huber has shown, Tillman's impressions of the New York songwriters could be supported by evidence from the earliest days of the hillbilly industry, as "citybilly" artists such as Carson Robinson, Bob Miller, and Vernon Dalhart recorded songs written by professional Tin Pan Alley composers in the 1920s and early 1930s.[47] Some of the most prolific writers of hillbilly songs in the prewar era were musical polyglots who wrote in whatever style was commercially advantageous at the time, while others who wrote primarily in the country vein struggled to gain a foothold in the New York and Chicago publishing industries.[48] So, if ASCAP and the New York publishers were willing to capitalize on hillbilly music's popularity, but they were not as interested in engaging songwriters living and working outside their immediate geographic and cultural orbits, it may very well have been the case that taste was only one reason— and perhaps not even the most compelling reason—that ASCAP ignored Nashville for several decades.

Rather, as the literature on deindustrialization demonstrates, industries that emerge in one place are likely to remain in that place unless there is a sufficient draw that pulls them to another location.[49] By the end of World War II, New York had been a major center for theatrical productions and related music-making for over a century, and an extensive infrastructure had been built up to support the creation and performance of music, as well as the marketing of artists and songs, the collection of royalties on those songs, and the production and distribution of recordings.[50] As a consequence, it was highly unlikely that a relatively small cadre of songwriters and performance venues located elsewhere was going to be sufficient enough to encourage business leaders to move their well-established industry infrastructure elsewhere. Rather, much as recording artists needed to travel to New York and Chicago to make their recordings in the prewar era, so, too, did they need to go there to sell their original songs.

Perhaps not surprisingly, then, some of the first forays into music publishing in Nashville were made by people who were interested in taking a risk on the hillbilly market. It has been politically and economically expedient for Nashville songwriters and publishers—as well as country music historians—to write about ASCAP's neglect of country music as one based on taste. New York, after all, serves as a useful, hoity-toity foil for people promoting a musical genre that is so deeply rooted in a white, working-class, Southern identity. If country music reflects the lives of "real" people, Tin Pan Alley song represents fabrication and artifice, which these "real" people have learned to distrust deeply. Yet, closer examination of the song publishing business's development in Nashville reveals that these early publishers were deeply involved in the broader industry as well. Again, this should not come as a surprise, especially considering that, as fledgling efforts, they needed the support of the New York–based industry to circulate their songs more widely and to provide other infrastructure that simply was not yet in place in Nashville. Such was the case for the most substantial publisher of hillbilly songs in the prewar era, the New York–based Southern Peer Music. Founded in 1928 by Kansas City native Ralph Peer—the same Peer who led the location recording movement during the 1920s—Southern Peer held a number of lucrative hillbilly catalogues, including that of the Carter Family.[51]

The first significant popular song publisher to open its doors in Nashville was Acuff-Rose Publishing, formed in October 1942 when *Opry* star Roy Acuff teamed with veteran pop songwriter Fred Rose.[52] Assessing Acuff-Rose's broad impact on the Nashville music industry, country music historian John Rumble has observed, "More than any other individual of his time, [Rose] helped to make songwriting a viable profession in the southern states. No longer would musicians in the region have to rely so exclusively on northern interests to market their compositions."[53] When Acuff-Rose was founded, Acuff was nearing the height of his popularity, which would peak by the end of World War II, making him an ideal person to promote songs to a wider audience. Moreover, Acuff had long been concerned with securing the rights to the songs that he recorded, so he already maintained a personal interest in the economics of songwriting.[54]

Rose, too, brought a wealth of experience to the partnership, having worked in many aspects of the music industry—including as a performer—prior to moving to Nashville in 1933.[55] As a result of his varied career, Rose had become intimately familiar with the workings of the New York and Chicago publishers, as well as the Hollywood film industry, and he had a keen sense of the ways that one could go about writing a hit song.[56] By the time that Acuff and Rose entered into their business partnership, Rose had already been working at WSM for nearly a decade, where he strove to make country songs more like mainstream pop songs and to promote hillbilly recording artists to a wider listenership.[57] Initially publishing songs written by Acuff (or, in at least one famous case, that may have been stolen by Acuff), Acuff-Rose had its first major success in 1946, when they signed emerging songwriting talent Hank Williams, a lonesome-sounding songwriter with a particular talent for writing short, powerful songs about love, loss, and loneliness.[58] Acuff-Rose's success quickly drew the attention of other entrepreneurs who were interested in cashing in on Nashville's songwriters. By the early 1950s, several new publishing companies joined Acuff-Rose, many of them gathering along Sixteenth Avenue South, a street that offered low-rent office space in the old houses that lined it.[59] Companies such as Cedarwood Publishing (started by former *Opry* manager Jim Denny) and Hill and Range Publishing competed to attract the best songwriters to their companies, offering them regular salaries in exchange for a guaranteed quantity of songs that the company could publish and then convince *Opry* artists to sing on the air and to record.[60]

Key to making this new publishing system work in Nashville was a way to collect royalties for the songs that they were publishing. ASCAP had been established in 1914 with the primary purpose of collecting songwriting royalties from stage performers and recording artists who used the songs owned by its member publishing companies. Focused primarily on publishers based in New York and Chicago and on the popular and art music markets, ASCAP showed little to no interest in country music and other forms of vernacular music that were being popularized on radio and recordings during the 1920s and 1930s. Although some of the early publishers in the country music business—Ralph Peer and the Aberbach

Brothers at Hill & Range, for instance—had offices in New York and were members of ASCAP, the performing rights organization's decision to ignore country music and other forms of vernacular music that were being popularized across the United States (and globally) led to the formation of a rival organization, Broadcast Music, Inc. (BMI), in 1939.[61] Also based in New York, BMI focused principally on signing publishers whose catalogues had been overlooked by ASCAP. Not surprisingly, BMI found allies in Nashville, where a steady stream of *Opry* artists brought new songs and arrangements of traditional material that could be copyrighted, controlled by a Nashville publisher, and capitalized on through radio and recordings.[62] BMI also hired Frances Preston, then a receptionist at WSM, to serve as BMI's Nashville representative in 1955, where she played a pivotal role in the promotion of Nashville's songwriting and publishing industry.[63] With the growth in publishing in Nashville during the late 1940s and early 1950s, the city began to attract a wide range of people with an interest in the music business, including clerical staff, accountants, journalists, and promoters, as well as other professionals who could meet the needs of the folks who were coming to the city.

Publishing took off in Nashville in the years after World War II, but the recording industry was slower to establish a presence in the city. Since major labels had already invested resources in building their own professional recording studios in large cities, they frequently encouraged their recording artists to travel to a central location to make their recordings. Red Foley, for instance, who had been making recordings since 1933, traveled to New York for one session and to Chicago for three sessions in the year following his arrival at the *Opry* in April 1946.[64] Similarly, bluegrass pioneer and barn dance veteran Bill Monroe took his Blue Grass Boys to Chicago for eight sessions between February 1945 and October 1949.[65] This practice makes a great deal of sense, as it was in these studios that label A&R men could closely supervise the performances and engineers could more carefully control the quality of the recordings. Moreover, it was often cheaper to bring a recording artist from Nashville to Chicago or New York than it was to bring the recording studio—with all of its assorted gear—to them. As such, the economics of recording simply made it difficult to justify such expenses, especially when makeshift studios could not guarantee the same audio quality as a professional one.

Radio stations and transcription services such as Nashville's Brown Radio Productions (opened around 1945 on Fourth Avenue North) offered studio facilities that were sufficient to produce test recordings for major labels, and many labels made use of these facilities on a contract basis to audition new talent.[66] Such was the case with the first RCA Victor sessions for Eddy Arnold, who would go on to become one of the leading country artists to emerge from the postwar Nashville scene. Arnold's two earliest sessions were held in these functional studios, his first at WSM on December 4, 1944, and his second at the Brown Radio Productions studio on July 9, 1945. The first session generated Arnold's first hit, "Each Minute Seems a Million Years," which was released with what would become his signature song, "Cattle Call," as the B side, in June 1945. As Arnold had proved himself to be a viable recording artist, new RCA Victor A&R man Steve Sholes decided to bring Arnold to Chicago for additional sessions in November 1945 and March 1946. In fact, none of Arnold's fifteen RCA Victor sessions between November 1945 and April 1950 was held in Nashville.[67] As a consequence, it seems that WSM and Brown Radio Productions were suitable as places to audition, but not to make a series of professional recordings.

At the same time, though, it is worth noting that the postwar recording industry, more generally, was undergoing a rapid transition of its own. Shellac shortages during World War II hindered record labels from pressing copies of their latest hit discs.[68] Compounding these supply shortages was a nationwide musicians' strike against the recording industry, led by American Federation of Musicians (AFM) president James Petrillo, that started in August 1942 and continued until November 1944. Long concerned with the impacts of recording and radio broadcasting on the employment opportunities and wages of working musicians, Petrillo effectively put a halt to the recording industry's work and, ironically, put a number of musicians out of work.[69] As Sanjek and Sanjek have noted, some of the major labels "expected the threat and stockpiled against it, awaiting White House intervention in the interest of the war effort" and even enjoyed rather significant sales records "with half-million—and million-copy sellers . . . common."[70] But record buyers undoubtedly heard the changing sounds of popular music over the radio and clamored for access to recordings of the latest bands and dance styles, and, with the majors out of play, popular music leader Decca, as well as a number of small independent labels, began to settle with the AFM as early as late 1943.[71]

In the wake of World War II and the AFM recording strike, independent record labels were quick to seize on some of the more exciting musical trends of the age, capturing a wide range of performances and pushing them out to jukeboxes, radio stations, and fans of genres that were not widely represented by artists who had been recording for the major labels.[72] As historian John Broven has suggested, "from the end of World War II in 1945 until the disc jockey payola scandal emerged in 1959, the independent record companies led the way in showing the major labels how to mine and exploit the rich, deep resources of American music."[73] These "rich, deep resources" included a wide range of musical practices, from rhythm and blues to hillbilly music, and from bebop to folk song.[74] And they also included a fascinating array of artists who had been laboring in local and regional markets but who might never have gained national attention without the benefit of the marketspace that the war, the shellac shortage, and the strike created. In a sense, one could easily argue that the postwar boom of the independents represented a new take on the location recording sessions that the major labels held during the 1920s, the major difference being that the independent labels did not need to travel as far to find talent.

The rise of the independent record labels was a particular boon for hillbilly music, both in Nashville and elsewhere. One of the leading labels to emerge from this independent boom was Cincinnati-based King Records, established by Syd Nathan in 1943.[75] Radio station WLW was practically in its backyard, blanketing much of the United States with a 500,000-watt signal and carrying a wide range of rural-oriented programming with it.[76] Among the artists working on WLW's programs were the Delmore Brothers, who had worked at the *Opry* during the 1930s, as well as veteran barnstormer Louis Marshall "Grandpa" Jones, thumbpicker Merle Travis, and western swing musician Hank Penny.[77] As King Records historian John Hartley Fox has observed, Nathan not only recorded these WLW stars as individual artists, but he also recorded them as a supergroup, the Brown's Ferry Four, a gospel group formed by the Delmores, Jones, and Travis to sing gospel songs on WLW.[78] Additionally, Nathan drew talented musicians from the surrounding region, including Wheeling, West Virginia's *Wheeling Jamboree*, which turned its powerful signal toward New England and exerted a strong influence on country music culture there.[79] As such, Nathan had access to a strong pool of musical talent who could make quality recordings and were willing to record a wide range of their musical output in the hopes that, because of WLW's powerful signal, their large radio audience would be interested in purchasing King's releases.

Many of King's earliest sessions were recorded in a home studio built by WLW engineer Earl Herzog. By 1945, King sessions were held in the E. T. Herzog Recording Studio, a permanent facility opened at 811 Race Street in Cincinnati, and after professional disagreements between Nathan and Herzog, Nathan opened his own studio facility at the label's headquarters on Brewster Avenue in 1948, possibly "the first for an independent label," as King historian Fox suggests.[80] The presence of this studio infrastructure proved to be particularly valuable for Nashville musicians, as well as the artists performing on WLW and other stations. As Herzog recalled, the studio facility and the excellent team of sidemen from WLW encouraged a number of A&R men to bring their Nashville acts to Cincinnati to record: "They [sidemen] were here before Nashville ever knew what it was all about. Over at our studio there, we had Capitol, Columbia, [and] RCA bring talent to Cincinnati for the sidemen."[81] The Nashville recording industry, which came to rely on a specially trained group of session musicians by the end of the 1940s, might then be seen as a direct response to Nathan's work at King. Simply put, if the musicians who were active on the *Opry* did not need to travel to make their recordings, they would have more time to perform throughout the region, and the labels would be able to increase the profitability of each recording session.

The independent record label boom that was moving throughout the United States was also taking root in Nashville, recording a wide range of musical styles in an effort to reach a broad consumer base. Bandleader Pee Wee King, for instance, recalled that he wanted to get into the record business because he wanted to sell directly to the people who came to his live performances:

> The Golden West Cowboys and I made our recording debut in 1945 when we started our own Nash label. We planned the company to sell not only my records but those of Minnie Pearl, Cowboy Copas, Bradley Kincaid, and other artists who were on the road with us. We would sell our records as a package during personal appearances. They wouldn't be in record shops.[82]

Direct-to-market sales had long been a key source of income for traveling hillbilly musicians who sold songbooks and autographed pictures to audiences over the radio airwaves and at live performances. Direct-to-market sales permitted artists to build important personal connections with fans—the lifeblood of a genre that thrives on notions of authenticity and accessibility—and they also allowed artists to carve out income streams that circumvented some of the music industry's royalty and fee collection systems.[83]

Former WSM radio announcer Jim Bulleit, too, decided to form a record label to capitalize on the wealth of talent in Nashville and the surrounding area. As Nashville music industry historian Martin Hawkins has noted, Bulleit left WSM in October 1945 and formed a booking agency to compete with the WSM Artist Service Bureau, focusing especially on those WSM-affiliated artists who were not, as Bulleit himself described, "real stars like Uncle Dave and Roy Acuff."[84] By April 1946, Bulleit had abandoned his booking agency to focus his attention on his new record label: Bullet Records.[85] Hawkins notes that early publicity materials for Bullet Records highlighted the label's connections to the *Opry*, citing a *Billboard* advertisement from April 1946 that proclaimed Bullet to be the source of "Hillbilly records from the home of [the] Grand Ole Opry."[86] This was likely an important marketing move for Bullet, as the *Opry*'s popularity was at its zenith, and any effort to attach the *Opry* brand to a product would undoubtedly help it reach a broader market. And these ties were borne out by the artist roster that Bulleit signed to the label; as Hawkins notes, "most of the early Bullet 600 series hillbilly discs showcased Grand Ole Opry artists who weren't under contract elsewhere," including "Bradley Kincaid, Minnie Pearl, and Pee Wee King, all backed by King's band, the Golden West Cowboys."[87] Throughout the next decade, Bullet was one of the leaders in the Nashville independent record scene, offering content by white and African American gospel groups, rhythm and blues musicians, and even pop artists, reflecting both the musical diversity of the Nashville music scene and the important role that diversification played in helping a record label stay afloat.[88]

By 1948, other Nashville-based independent record labels followed in the wake of Bullet's efforts, each seeking to distribute the music of the many talented performers who were active in the city. As Hawkins has noted, these labels—including Cheker, World, Collegiate, and Select— "shared a belief that the way was open for Nashville to take the lead in bringing a unique blend of popular musicianship and down-south folksiness to the attention of the wider world."[89] What many of these labels had in common was leadership that was already connected to the Nashville music industry. World Records' Jordan Stokes III, for instance, had served as the AFM's lawyer since 1933 and was deeply knowledgeable about not only the musicians in the scene, but also the business leaders who were active there.[90] And Select Records' founder Eleanor Hankins "Hank" Fort had grown up around the society band scene that thrived because of Nashville's culture of country clubs, cotillions, and other Southern social traditions and, as a "society woman" herself, had been involved in theatrical productions and a dance class for young people.[91] As a consequence of these various musical and social connections, then, these early label founders were able to leverage their own personal connections to build significant—if, at times, financially tenuous—organizations that marketed Nashville's musical vibrancy to a broader audience. Hillbilly music was a part of this equation, but it was not the only part—nor, in the case of some labels, was it a significant part—of their operation.[92] It is worth noting, too, that, just as Bullet Records expanded its offerings to include music by African American musicians, so, too, did other labels distribute recordings by local and regional African American musicians, providing a valuable outlet for the city's thriving black gospel and rhythm and blues communities, while also implicitly reinforcing racial segregation in the city through their racialized marketing strategies.[93]

At the same time that these independent record labels were beginning to spring up in Nashville, the major labels descended on Nashville at the conclusion of the AFM recording strike. Most notable among them was Decca Records, which had been involved in the country field since 1934.[94] The label was the prewar home to such artists as Ernest Tubb, the Sons of the Pioneers, and many others, and they were eager to continue their success in that field after the war's conclusion. Paul Cohen, who was in charge of country recordings for the label, made Nashville a major center of his operations, likely because many of his country artists were already associated with the *Opry*.[95]

With the postwar record label boom in Nashville came an increased demand for professional recording studio space to capture these performances and to create quality recordings that could match the sound quality of those made in the professional studios of New York, Chicago, and Los Angeles. The Herzog studios in Cincinnati proved to be a particularly valuable space for many Nashville recording artists to use, and some of the most significant recordings of artists such as Hank Williams—including "Lovesick Blues" (1948) and "I'm So Lonesome I Could Cry" (1949)— were made there as a result.[96] Moreover, major labels often called their Nashville artists to permanent studios in major music production centers. But, much as label owners and song publishers began to explore ways to exploit the city's musical talent, enterprising electronics experts began to construct facilities that could meet the city's production demands. By 1950, several makeshift studios had been constructed, churning out dozens of sides each month to the local, regional, and even national market.

The emergence of these makeshift Nashville studios was paralleled throughout the United States. As recording historian Susan Schmidt

Horning has noted, the postwar US recording industry benefited from "a new generation of audio engineers, many of whom gained their technical training as signal corpsmen during the war and after the war pursued careers in radio, television, film, and recording."[97] Moreover, engineers who had been developing their craft at radio stations also seized on the postwar boom to build their own studios to meet the needs of independent record labels. For many of these engineers, Horning suggests, the "excitement . . . [of] technical tinkering" often led to the creation of interesting new recording standards, novel effects, and recordings that stood out in the marketplace.[98] One such studio was that built by Alan Bubis, who, according to Hawkins, "upgrad[ed] the former Tennessee [Records] studio on Fourth Avenue South."[99] With the assistance of Ed Bowen, who served as Nashville radio station WLAC's lead engineer, Bubis made a number of significant technological innovations, including bringing magnetic tape, direct injection, and overdubbing to the city.[100] Even more makeshift, though, was the home studio of Maurice Likens, located at 726 Benton Avenue. Likens's studio was a far cry from professional. Rather, as Hawkins has documented, it was not really a studio at all. Instead, Likens—who had professional experience as an electrician—"dabble[d] in sound recording and . . . bought equipment to record either on location or at home."[101] As such, Likens could travel around Nashville and the surrounding area to capture a variety of live events, and, if a studio setting was necessary, he could invite people to his home to make their recordings, where, as Hawkins noted, "he extended the studio into the living room, where he balanced guitar amplifiers or other equipment on the baby chair and allowed his sons, Donald and Jere, to sit in on recording events as long as they kept quiet."[102] Recording singles for his own Cheker Records, as well as World Records, Likens carved out a niche recording a variety of local groups and, given the thin margins in most production budgets for lower- and middle-tier acts, likely delivering reasonable quality at a reasonable cost.

Compared to Likens's recording facilities, the Castle Recording Company was a slick professional operation. Founded in 1945 or 1946 and, by 1947, located in "a former dining room on the second floor of the

Tulane Hotel" on the northeast corner of Church Street and Eighth Avenue North, the studio was established by three engineers from WSM: Aaron Shelton, George Reynolds, and Carl Jenkins.[103] As Shelton told historian Craig Havighurst, the facility was spacious enough to hold sessions, but it certainly lacked both the character and technical requirements that a professional studio in New York or Chicago might have boasted:

> The windows in the control room and cutting room facing Eighth Avenue presented quite a problem. . . . The noise from the heavy duty trucks pulling up the hill from Church Street to Union Street was particularly annoying, and the late afternoon sun beaming through these windows caused a heat problem in both these technical areas.[104]

Moreover, as Rumble has documented, the Tulane space was made serviceable for recordings only after a "substantial remodeling of a dining room . . . and the conversion of a bathroom into an echo chamber."[105] As was widely the case in the postwar years, early recordings at Castle were made using "direct-to-disc" manner, meaning that what was captured by the microphones in the recording studio was immediately transferred to the surface of an acetate disc. That acetate would then be used in the manufacturing process to create a negative image of the disc's grooves that would be then used to press shellac—or later polyvinyl chloride—into playable recordings for home and jukebox play.[106] As Rumble has documented, for instance, the earliest Castle sessions took place in the WSM studios, but "the electrical impulses [from the session] were fed via telephone line to WSM's back-up transmitter site at Fifteenth and Compton, where the three men set up their first cutting lathe."[107] Within the first year of operation, Castle upgraded its recording equipment to include a Scully master cutting lathe and an Ampex tape recorder.[108]

Along with the improved hardware, Castle developed a number of technological improvements that, in some cases, actually surpassed the major-label studios elsewhere.[109] In both the direct-to-disc process and early tape recording, a flawed performance could not be edited or tweaked in any appreciable way in post-production. In fact, as Rumble has noted in his study of the Castle studio, "when Shelton, Jenkins, and Reynolds built a mixing board that would take eight inputs, they made an improvement considered remarkable at the time. More importantly, there was only one output channel, so that mixing had to be done during the recording itself. . . . [A]n acceptable take had to be produced then and there— on the first try, if possible."[110] As a consequence, the engineers at Castle could focus on the careful placement of microphones around the room and near the instruments to gain the clearest recording possible, even if it meant that they had to improvise a mix as the performance was unfolding before them.

Despite all the limitations and challenges that engineers, recording artists, and session musicians faced while working at Castle Recording's Tulane Hotel studio, the engineers there were successful in producing some major hit recordings and in creating innovative sounds that have come to define the postwar country sound, as well as major contributions to the pop hit parade. As Rumble has noted, the Castle studio was an exceptionally busy facility, booking sessions for local labels; church, educational, and civic organizations; and such national labels as Decca, Columbia, Capitol, Mercury, and MGM.[111] Havighurst, too, observes that, "according to Shelton's records, Castle made half of 1952's thirty top-sellers on *Billboard*'s country and western chart, including landmarks like Hank Williams's 'Jambalaya,' Kitty Wells's groundbreaking 'It Wasn't God Who Made Honky Tonk Angels,' and Webb Pierce's 'Back Street Affair.'"[112] Not only did chart-toppers record at Castle, though; it was a hub for a wide range of recording artists to cut discs between performances on the radio and personal appearances throughout the region. Others, such as songwriters Charlie and Ira Louvin, slated their early sessions in a schedule of intensive songwriting. In fact, as Charles K. Wolfe has documented, the Louvin Brothers made their first recordings during an Apollo Records session for Eddie Hill's band in 1947 and auditioned for Decca during a 1949 session there when their publisher, Fred Rose, arranged for them to record during half of a Decca session at Castle.[113] As Charlie Louvin recalled of their Decca audition:

We cut that session in eight or nine minutes. We'd waited out in the hall [of the Tulane Hotel]. Lonzo and Oscar [an *Opry* comedy duo] were in there recording and having all kinds of trouble getting their song all together. And we went in, after waiting until three o'clock in the morning for the studio. Went in and started the session and went straight through it. We were cutting from a microphone straight onto a disc. The first one we cut, they accepted. Of course, I'm not saying it couldn't have been better. But we cut it on the first take, then went on and did the same thing for "Seven Year Blues." Ira and I had been singing it so much we knew it forwards and backwards and sideways.[114]

But, as country music historian Ronnie Pugh has suggested, much of Castle's success depended on honky-tonk star Ernest Tubb, whose recordings for Decca had been leading the country hit parade since the mid-1930s; as Owen Bradley told Pugh, Tubb's pleasure with the Castle situation likely led to Decca's later decision to move its country operations to Nashville.[115]

One reason that Castle Recording was such a successful studio during the roughly ten years before its closure in 1955 was that it was the only significant studio in town.[116] Rumble has noted that the Castle staff "supplied much of the engineering know-how for Bullet Records . . . and for Dot Records" and that Nashville's Monogram Radio Programs "was another firm that employed the services of the Castle engineers for a time."[117] Castle's connections to the *Opry* and to WSM surely made the process of creating technically sound and musically interesting recordings easier. The engineers at Castle were primarily employed as engineers at WSM, where they were responsible for creating broadcasts that sounded clean and clear at long distances from Nashville. As a consequence, they not only had an intimate knowledge of contemporary broadcasting microphones (which were the gold standard for recording in those days), but also had already worked with the musicians who recorded at Castle.[118] As such, they knew most of the musicians' strengths and weaknesses and could help to circumvent potential issues in the studio through careful microphone placement, managing the input levels from those microphones, and even through managing the artist's personality. Thus, although Castle was not the only game in town, it was definitely the best. It was intimately linked to the city's music scene and provided an important venue for the city's recording industry to take shape.

With the advent of several independent Nashville-based record labels, the Castle Recording Company's studios at the Tulane Hotel, and increasing attention from the national major labels, the city's nascent recording industry emerged as an important sideline for many of the city's musicians. With a host of talented musicians at the *Grand Ole Opry*, the city's universities, and the clubs that served the city's African American community, recording artists were in abundance, and many musicians made a bid for stardom as a result. But, for all of the top-line talent that the city had at its disposal, there was still one major challenge that stood in the way of turning Nashville's limited studio space and time into a profitable enterprise: the need for a professional corps of musicians who could provide capable accompaniment in a timely fashion. It simply was not profitable for recording artists to bring their road bands into the studio every time they wanted to record a few sides. Road bands were not typically rehearsed for session work, and road work required a different set of skills than did studio work. This is not to say that musicians in Nashville didn't use their road bands in the studio. But, to get high-quality recordings on a regular basis, the labels needed to hire a team of musicians who were capable of playing into a microphone, able to take direction from a producer, consistent in their playing, and willing to work with little to no rehearsal time.

The wealth of musical talent in Nashville made the formation of a group of session musicians a tangible possibility as the city's music industry began to emerge in the late 1940s. Many of the musicians involved in the early session scene were, not surprisingly, drawn from the ranks of the WSM staff. Although the station was best-known for the *Opry*, country music comprised only a fraction of the station's musical programming (as was typical of radio stations in a pre-format radio era). Some WSM musicians provided music for multiple programs, and they were often fluent in multiple musical vocabularies and could accompany someone who wanted to sing a gospel song and later accompany someone on a honky-tonk hit. For example, Owen Bradley—who would later be much more widely known as a leading studio owner and producer during the height of the Nashville Sound era—was a staff pianist at WSM, where he was also responsible for writing musical arrangements for the station's programming. Additionally, he led a dance band that performed regularly at Nashville's Belle Meade Country Club, where he played popular songs of the day with a stellar group of sidemen. As a consequence, Bradley was more than capable of recording alongside a diverse roster of recording artists.[119]

The first core group of Nashville session musicians was a remarkably diverse one. From the *Opry*, guitarist Jack Shook and fiddler Tommy Jackson provided regular accompaniment. Guitarist Harold Bradley, who had played on the *Opry* but had also studied jazz and played guitar with his brother Owen's society dance band, quickly rose to prominence as one of the most versatile guitarists of the era. Ernie Newton played bass, as did Joe Zinkan, a bassist who had been recording in Nashville since the 1930s, when he cut sides with the Delmore Brothers. Owen Bradley played piano, and Farris Coursey, a versatile drummer who was capable of slimming his drum set down to the bare minimum to prevent distortion in the recordings, was the city's top session drummer.[120]

This first iteration of the Nashville A Team worked under what would today be seen as primitive conditions for recording. To begin, Nashville recording sessions typically used only a couple of microphones in the late 1940s and early 1950s. As a consequence, vocalists—whose work was of paramount importance—were often given sole access to one of those microphones, while the accompanying musicians were expected to gather around the second. Skilled vocalists were able to manipulate the microphone to advance the expressivity of their vocal performance, moving closer or further away from the microphone to increase the dynamic fluidity of the take. For vocalists who were accustomed to performing on the radio, these skills were likely well-honed and deployed to great advantage. The accompanying musicians, however, were at a great disadvantage when it came to expressivity. Electric guitars (including electric steel guitars) and drums were tied to a single space because of the size of their instruments and amplifiers. (No matter how close an electric guitarist stands to a microphone, what matters is the distance between the *amplifier*—not the guitar—and the microphone.) Moreover, acoustic guitars and double basses are comparatively quiet and are easily overpowered by electric instruments and drums, and therefore must be placed closer to the microphone than the electric instruments. What resulted was an often-awkward physical arrangement of musicians around the microphone that permitted the musicians to be heard clearly and in a balanced fashion in the final recording. Such had been the case since the earliest days of recording in the acoustic era, though, so musicians, engineers, and other technicians were accustomed to changing the physical arrangements of the room to get the clearest and most well-balanced recording possible.

After nearly a decade in operation, a number of factors conspired to bring about the closing of Castle Recording Company in 1955. To begin, the demands on the Castle staff were beginning to get out of control, because the staff was working there after hours and on weekends, trying their best to cram as many sessions as possible into the hours that they weren't already working at WSM. Havighurst has also noted that WSM's management was not terribly pleased with the amount of time that its engineers were spending on their side project and demanded that they shutter the business to keep their jobs at the station.[121] And perhaps most devastating was the decision to tear down the Tulane Hotel in 1957, a decision made by city government in an effort to redevelop part of the city's downtown.[122] With these forces pushing for Castle's closure, Shelton and his partners decided to close the studio, leaving a legacy of hundreds of excellent recordings in jukeboxes and record stores around the United States and, with the help of American GIs involved in the reconstruction of Europe and the emerging Cold War, the entire globe.[123]

The Castle experiment was wildly successful by just about any metric. It had proven that Nashville could support a substantial community of recording artists and produce recordings that were acceptable for the national and international marketplace. It demonstrated that the city's pool of talent—primarily in country music, but also in rhythm and blues, jazz, light classical music, and other forms—had a significant interest in and ability for creating recordings for that marketplace. It revealed that new independent record labels and the major national labels alike were willing to make recordings in Nashville and that the sizable pool of recording artists and songwriters based there could prove to be commercially viable. And it showed entrepreneurial Nashvillians that money could be made in the recording industry. With Castle in the rearview mirror and demand for Nashville recordings at an all-time high, the market was wide open for a new studio (or studios) to come to town to replace it.

Among the first entrepreneurs to see the potential for a new studio in Nashville were the Bradley brothers, Owen and Harold. Both veterans of the city's live and recorded music scenes, the Bradleys were known for their high musical standards and had developed extensive networks of contacts in Nashville and the broader national music industry by 1950. By 1947, Decca executive Paul Cohen had hired Owen Bradley to supervise all of the label's Nashville productions, which included work with such significant recording artists as Ernest Tubb, Bill Monroe, and Kitty Wells, and the Bradleys undoubtedly saw the opportunity to capitalize on Castle's demise.[124] The Bradleys had maintained a small recording studio operation prior to 1955, the year that they opened a permanent facility in a house on Sixteenth Avenue South, a residential neighborhood that had fallen into some disrepair.[125] The property included an older home that faced the street, as well as a large lot in the rear of the building and ample street parking—a necessity for session musicians who needed to carry their instruments and amplifiers. The Bradleys began construction of their studio in the basement of the house, likely because the open space provided enough room for all the musicians and because its subterranean location would help to shield the studio from street noise that could corrupt the recordings made there. The top floor of the Bradley facility was dedicated to a new innovation: echo chambers. Using curves and nonparallel planes, the room would reflect any sound that was played into it from a variety of different angles, in essence giving it a sense of "soft-focus" or "atmosphere." The sounds from the basement studio were pumped into the echo chamber via a speaker that was placed at one end of the chamber, and a microphone located in the chamber then picked those reflected sounds up and returned them to the basement, where they were added to the recording.[126] By mid-1956, the Bradleys needed to expand their facilities, erecting an army-surplus Quonset hut on the lot and moving sessions to the larger space (Figure 1.1). The "Quonset Hut," as it would be known, continued to host sessions well into the early 1980s, including two decades as Columbia Records' primary Nashville studio.[127]

New York–based RCA Victor, a label with a significantly smaller share of the country music marketplace than Decca, also sought out professional recording facilities in Nashville in the 1950s. RCA Victor established a significant contact with the Nashville music scene by sending Steve Sholes, a veteran A&R man for the label, to Nashville on a regular basis in the years

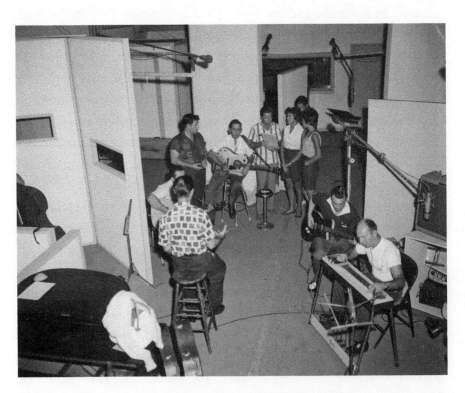

Figure 1.1. A session at Bradley Studio (the Quonset Hut), early 1960s.
Photo by Elmer Williams, courtesy of the Country Music Hall of Fame® and Museum..

immediately following the war.[128] But, like the other major labels with an interest in the country field, RCA Victor artists frequently visited studios in Chicago and Cincinnati to cut their discs, in large part because of the dearth of available studio time in Nashville. Leasing studio time and traveling to distant studios was not, however, the most cost-effective approach to making recordings, and Sholes sought out Nashville venues that might make suitable studio spaces for the label. One of the first studios to address RCA Victor's needs was located on MacGavock Street in a building owned by the United Methodist Church. RCA Victor used a studio that the church had built to produce film and audio materials to further their ministry.[129] Known as TRAFCO (short for Television, Radio, and Film Commission of the Methodist Church), the facility was RCA Victor's principal Nashville facility between 1955 and 1957.[130] By that point, though, Sholes had demonstrated the value of maintaining a Nashville base of operations for its country recording work, and, in the wake of the label's 1955 acquisition of Elvis Presley's contract, he made a strong case for the construction of a permanent facility that could host sessions for their new star, who lived in Memphis, as well as the coterie of RCA Victor recording artists already working in Nashville.[131] With that in mind, then, RCA Victor set out to construct a permanent recording facility on Seventeenth Avenue South, just one block away from the Bradley brothers' studio, which began operation with a test session for Don Gibson in December 1957.[132] The studio quickly began booking sessions for RCA Victor recording artists, as well as for other record labels that needed studio time, including Monument Records, which had a contract with Roy Orbison, and Cadence Records, which had a contract with the Everly Brothers.[133]

By the mid-1950s, then, Nashville was a bustling music industry center with a variety of opportunities for a wide range of professionals. The *Opry* continued to lead the way as the premiere barn dance program in the southern United States, and programs such as the *Louisiana Hayride* on KWKH in Shreveport, Louisiana, and the *Wheeling Jamboree* on WWVA in Wheeling, West Virginia, were training artists who were shooting for stardom on the *Opry*.[134] Music publishers such as Acuff-Rose and Hill and Range were cultivating songwriting talents in the city and leading the charge in capitalizing on the performance and mechanical royalties that their intellectual property generated.[135] BMI, the performing rights organization responsible for collecting those royalties, had established an office in Nashville and was helping to advocate for the writers and publishers on their roster.[136] Independent record labels were capitalizing on the significant musical talent that could be found in the city's highly stratified and segregated communities.[137] Major labels were attempting to expand their own offerings in country music, often signing the artists who had first broken through on the independent labels and aggressively marketing some of their most popular artists to the crossover market.[138] And, with the construction of new permanent recording facilities, those labels were increasingly able to utilize local musical and technical talent to cut their discs and get them to market.

It was undoubtedly an exciting time to be involved in the nascent Nashville music industry, and that chaos could have easily led to a quick and precipitous decline after a brief period of glory. But one of the things that helped to prevent the collapse of the Nashville music industry was an effort to set some guidelines for how business would be conducted there, particularly as it related to session work. Before the mid-1950s, sessions were organized in a relatively haphazard manner and were scheduled to accommodate studio availability, musician schedules, and the prime working hours of the artist to be recorded. Sessions could be as short as ninety minutes or as long as several hours, and there were no consistent expectations regarding the number of sides that should be finished during each session.[139] As more studios were established in the mid-1950s, the recording scene in Nashville could have fallen into scheduling chaos. Sensing that growth in the recording industry could be stunted without deliberate efforts to organize it, Nashville musicians' union president George Cooper used his power as union president to convince the city's studios to adopt a uniform session schedule that would govern all union sessions in the city. Considering that the top two studios in town were owned or operated by members of the Nashville musicians' union—Chet Atkins and Owen Bradley—it was likely fairly easy to convince them to join his effort to regularize the studio schedules.[140] Beginning in the mid-1950s, union recording sessions began to operate around a standard daily schedule. Sessions were three hours in length, followed by a one-hour break to allow musicians to pack up their equipment, grab a quick bite on their way to the next session, and be set up in time for the next session to begin. The recording day began at 10:00 a.m., with additional sessions starting at 2:00 p.m., 6:00 p.m., and 10:00 p.m. Additional sessions could be held during the overnight hours, but the vast majority of the major labels' business was conducted during the earliest three sessions.[141] Late-night sessions were often set aside for boutique projects or projects by some of the labels' brightest stars; Elvis Presley, for instance, frequently recorded during the overnight hours.[142]

In addition to cutting commercial recordings, Nashville's growing studio scene was also involved in the production of demonstration recordings for the city's music publishers. In stark contrast to the mainstream popular music industry, which relied heavily on printed sheet music to communicate the melody, form, and lyrics of a song, the Nashville recording scene was a largely oral-aural one. Publishers hired musicians to create printed sheet music—often consisting of little more than a melody, chord changes, and lyrics—for copyright purposes, and singers would often use the sheet music in sessions to help them remember the lyrics.[143] But demonstration recordings were used to convince musicians that they should record a particular song. These demos were not intended for commercial distribution, and only recently have demonstration recordings from this period begun to find their way into the popular music marketplace.[144] As a consequence, session musicians were paid a lower rate for demos than they were for commercial sessions; in those rare instances when a demonstration recording was later released as either a single or an album cut, labels were expected to pay the musicians on that session the difference between a standard studio rate and the demo rate.[145]

Another factor in the survival of Nashville's music industry was the deliberate effort of several local music industry leaders to create a music production district in the neighborhood around the Bradleys' Quonset Hut and the RCA Victor studios on Sixteenth and Seventeenth Avenue South. Recent scholarship by historian Jeremy Hill has convincingly shown that music industry leaders sought out cheap real estate in a residential neighborhood and worked with local government leaders to try to prevent the expansion of affordable housing (and housing for African Americans) and the Vanderbilt University campus into the neighborhood.[146] The centralization of Nashville's music industry along Sixteenth and Seventeenth Avenues South was key to making the production system work. Aspiring songwriters could audition for multiple publishers in a single day simply by walking down the street, and aspiring recording artists could audition for the city's top producers in the same manner.[147] When recording artists were preparing to go into the studio, they, too, could visit the Music Row publishers to find new material, although it was just as common for songwriters to visit the artists in a nearby hotel room.[148] Session musicians could move quickly from one session to another without needing to get in their cars (for the most part). And as studio facilities expanded to include mastering facilities in the mid-1960s, recording and mastering engineers could create pressing-plant-ready material without leaving a dark, soundproof room for hours on end.[149]

None of the work that was happening along Music Row would have mattered, however, if audiences were unable to connect with the music that was being produced there. Nashville studios were turning out thousands of commercial recordings each year by 1960, the overwhelming majority of them firmly situated within the country genre. As Joli Jensen, Diane Pecknold, and other chroniclers of the 1950s and 1960s Nashville music industry have indicated, country music—always a relatively small part of the overall popular music landscape in the United States—was struggling for market share by the mid-1950s as rock and roll began to take the country by storm. Country music had been an intergenerational popular music before World War II, but, by the mid-1950s, it was anathema to many young people, a population that was finding itself with increasing freedom to choose its entertainment and more cash to spend on it. Radio stations devoted more of their airtime to rock and roll programs, pushing country product to the margins. And the package shows that had sustained country musicians for a couple of decades increasingly programmed rock and roll musicians in place of country artists, making it even more difficult for country musicians to get their work heard.[150]

At the same time that young people were turning toward rock and roll, country music was increasingly problematic for men and women in their twenties, thirties, and forties to claim as their music of choice. The United States—and especially the US South—was becoming an increasingly urban and suburban country, and the residents of those new suburbs and expanding cities frequently had roots in rural communities. For these rural-to-urban migrants, conspicuous consumption of rural-themed music—or any music that might betray their rural origins—could be seen to undermine their urban and suburban middle-class aspirations.[151] Country music's string band–oriented sound and hard-edged lyric themes were often seen as being too raw and unrefined for an increasingly urban—and suburbanized—middle-class white audience. Although country music might provide nostalgic reminders of the old home place, few people wanted to be considered rubes, so they often hid their interest in country music or developed new musical tastes.[152] Importantly, the national popular music industry continued promoting recording artists whose style evoked the big band and crooner sounds of the 1940s, offering images of musicians in tuxedos and evening gowns and a sense of urbane sophistication through song lyrics and record jacket imagery, and so-called "easy listening" music, which frequently deployed string orchestras and concert pianists to play wordless versions of the latest pop hits, the standards of the so-called "Great American Songbook," and arrangements of light classical music. Listening to this music, which formed much of the basis of mainstream radio airplay as well as record sales, provided listeners with an opportunity to demonstrate sophistication, education, and upward economic and social mobility.[153]

Thus, many factors threatened to undermine the work of the Nashville recording industry as it was starting to grow. Although many early rock and roll recordings were made in Nashville's studios and were accompanied by the city's leading session musicians, country music was still the city's bread and butter. And the city did not have a large enough community of orchestral musicians to compete effectively in the easy listening market in the mid-1950s, nor did it have ready access to the large team of mainstream pop songwriters that the New York studios did. Although Nashville studios were frequently working with major national labels to record and distribute country music, the national labels were long accustomed to shifting their production priorities to the most lucrative sounds of the day, so country music did not *need* to be a major part of a label's portfolio. Much as guitar-driven blues music had been pushed to the side in the 1930s, so, too, could country music have found itself in a marginalized position to other, more popular musical styles, and the Nashville music industry could have collapsed almost as soon as it emerged.[154]

It was into this environment that Nashville musicians began to develop what came to be known as the "Nashville Sound." Session musicians, producers, journalists, and scholars tend to agree that it was a deliberate effort to try to engage rural-to-urban migrants with a more modern country music sound by blending adult lyrical themes with pop instrumental accompaniments. As Lange has shown in his work on efforts to build "respectability" in country music during the postwar era, country music had been changing sonically since the end of the war, with many musicians adopting a smoother vocal delivery and seeking out songs with less overtly rural themes.[155] Most commentators on the Nashville Sound observe that the changing musical aesthetic of country music in the mid-1950s deliberately eschewed string band instruments, such as the fiddle and the steel guitar, and replaced them with backing vocal groups and string orchestras.[156] Many of the leading country recording artists to break through during the mid- to late 1950s certainly did find their musical style changing to varying degrees over the course of the decade, but others maintained their allegiance to the honky-tonk ideal (although many of them recorded with independent labels such as Starday and not with RCA Victor, Decca, or Columbia).[157]

Regardless, these radical changes to country music did not come without controversy. In fact, it can be argued that it was this particular moment in country music that marked one of the very first "authenticity crises" in the genre's history.[158] For all of its rhetoric and imagery about rurality, the US South, and tradition, country music had long been a large tent genre that held many different musical styles. String band sounds had dominated much of the country music genre, but pop singers had also made significant inroads in the genre as early as the 1930s. And, as sociologist Richard A. Peterson indicated in his landmark study of country music authenticity, the genre had also been widely accepting of what he described as "hardcore" and "soft-shell" musics, recognizing that no single musical sound would appeal to all listeners.[159] Yet, as Joli Jensen first demonstrated in her pioneering study of the Nashville Sound era, the rise of the Nashville Sound in the mid- to late 1950s heralded a sort of paranoia about the imminent demise of country music.[160] As Jensen and many scholars following her lead have suggested, country fans began to separate themselves into two large groups, each of which has maintained its own discourse about country music's identity since the 1960s. On the one hand are traditionalists, who believe that the efforts that the Nashville music industry took to create music that could appeal to a pop crossover market were a deliberate attack on the genre's core musical—and cultural—identity. This group tends to believe that such broad efforts to rebrand country music sonically and visually are a deliberate betrayal of the music's rural—and presumably southern—origins and the people who preserved the music for the generations prior to recording. (Later generations of traditionalists tend to have a moving wall before which country music was "real" or "authentic." Interestingly, the Nashville Sound era is now widely considered to be one of the genre's zeniths.) On the other hand is a group that might be described as musical "progressives," who are attracted to whatever commercial country music sounds and images are being marketed at any given moment. This group may not have as deep a commitment to the genre and may not always look the part of a stereotypical country music fan, but they still figure as a substantial contributing group to the overall country music economy. In this traditionalist–progressive dichotomy, progress is almost always construed in a negative light by traditionalists, while progressive fans tend to show little interest in the debate in the first place.[161]

If country music was going "uptown" musically during the 1950s, it was moving there financially, as well.[162] Country music had long been a source of embarrassment and shame for some of Nashville's business leaders and government officials, despite the interest that the *Opry* brought to the city and the revenues that it generated for restaurants and hotels there. The music's backwardness and minstrel show rurality were not in line with the image of a progressive city built around a strong foundation of educational institutions and research. But the increasing financial power that the nascent country music industry brought to the table turned the heads of even the most reluctant civic boosters by the end of the 1950s. By 1960, Nashville's government and business leaders simply couldn't deny that country music was going to be a vital part of the city's ongoing economic development, and they needed to figure out ways to support the industry. In particular, Tennessee governor Frank Clement was a very public supporter of the industry, often meeting with out-of-town reporters to celebrate the contributions that the city's music industry was making not only to Nashville but to the entire state of Tennessee.[163]

Key to these developments was the establishment of the Country Music Association (CMA), a trade organization devoted to the promotion of country music to a variety of cultural and commercial outlets. Emerging from the annual convention of the Country Music Disc Jockeys' Association, which was first formally hosted by WSM in 1952, the CMA was formed in November 1958 and quickly began to cultivate interest in country music among the radio stations that served specific localities, to promote country music and its audiences to marketers, and to craft historical narratives for the genre. As Diane Pecknold has meticulously documented, the CMA's project ultimately came down first to convincing both broadcasters and advertisers that there was a substantial audience for country music (which had long been seen as a niche format, remember) and that the country music audience was not just a bunch of penniless rural farmers. That is, the CMA needed to rebrand the country audience as one that was sophisticated, urbane, and moneyed. Pecknold's research reveals that the CMA undertook a multipronged approach to this work. For radio station owners and disc jockeys, the CMA continued to hold special events that created opportunities for face-to-face contact with the recording artists whose work they were playing. The annual disc jockeys' convention continues to the present day in the form of the Country Radio Seminar. Using nice dinners, tickets to the *Opry*, meet-and-greet events with artists, and behind-the-scenes tours of studios and publishers, the CMA was able to win hearts and minds for country music. For advertisers, special seminars were held to demonstrate the economic power of the country music audience and to convince them that they should spend a portion of their limited advertising dollars on country programming. And, by the late 1960s, the CMA was also involved in telling the genre's official history—a decidedly Nashville-centered one, in their telling—through the work of the Country Music Foundation and the Country Music Hall of Fame and Museum. And, as Pecknold has demonstrated, when officially organized events and structures failed to convince a station owner or an advertiser to support country music, they often received hands-on support from CMA, most commonly in the shape of a personal office visit from veteran radio disc jockey and early country music supporter Connie B. Gay or a phone call from CMA official Jo Walker-Meador.[164] As a consequence of these deliberate actions, country music became a powerful cultural and economic force that led to increased demand for country music product and, therefore, increased demand for the work of Nashville's session musicians, arrangers, engineers, and producers.

Between the end of World War II and 1960, then, all of the major components of the country music industry had coalesced in Nashville, a city that had been known principally as the home of a leading barn dance program before the start of the war. By 1960, Nashville was a music publishing center, and songwriters from around the United States and Canada were flocking to the city to get their songs to a wide range of recording artists. Booking agents and talent promoters were thriving as an endless array of new talent came to the city in search of recording and personal appearance contracts. Journalists flocked to Nashville to cover the industry, some of them making Nashville their home. And the CMA worked to make Nashville the physical and spiritual center of the bustling country music business. But almost all of this business and energy was dependent upon the work of a relatively small and hard-working team of session musicians, arrangers, engineers, and producers who spent endless hours helping to shape the sounds of contemporary country music. Yet, unlike the business leaders who helped to make Nashville such an important music center, many of the people who worked in the city's studio scene have not been treated in the scholarly or popular literature. As such, the remaining chapters seek to understand how these musicians found their way to session work, how they contributed to the sonic identities of specific recording artists, and how they differentiated themselves from one another.

The Musicianship of the Nashville Cats

I n his 1966 song "Nashville Cats," Lovin' Spoonful frontman John Sebastian extolled the virtues of the Nashville A Team. From his perspective in the folk clubs of New York, Sebastian heard a sort of natural musicianship among the people who play on the country recordings that his record dealer claims are unpopular among urban sophisticates, guitar players who seem to grow out of the Nashville landscape and who can play "more notes than the ants on a Tennessee ant hill . . . as clean as country water."[1] This song was taken up most recently by Del McCoury, who recorded it in 2001 with his own sought-after session musician sons.[2]

In the more than five decades since the release of Sebastian's encomium, the folklore around the Nashville A Team has been reified in the popular and scholarly literature on the Nashville recording industry. A characteristic summary can be found in a piece by author Morris Levy:

A typical recording session in Nashville lasted three hours. It was expected that four songs would be completed by the end of the session.

Nashville Cats. Travis D. Stimeling, © Oxford University Press (2020). Oxford University Press.
DOI: 10.1093/oso/9780197502815.001.0001

The songs were chosen by the producer and the artist beforehand, but the studio musicians only heard them for the first time at the session. Sometimes the songs were played for the musicians on demonstration discs or tapes supplied by the publishing companies controlling the rights to the song or by the artist on the guitar or piano. The players would then sketch out the melody and song structure on scraps of paper and work out an arrangement between themselves, sometimes with input from the artist or producer. After a few run-throughs of the song to solidify the arrangement and allow the engineers to balance the sound levels, the song would be recorded. For most of the 1960s and certainly before then, Nashville's studios did not have the equipment necessary to do a lot of overdubbing, so any mistakes that were too big to be ignored would require the song to be redone.[3]

This story—although certainly true in the broadest sense—obscures valuable details about the musical backgrounds, abilities, and tastes of Nashville's exceptional team of session musicians, in effect normalizing their exceptional skill sets and diverse experiences by treating them as cogs in a record-production machine.[4]

Contrary to Sebastian's suggestion that Nashville session musicians were naturally gifted and could play with relatively little effort, the Nashville A Team brought a remarkably wide variety of musical backgrounds and pedigrees into the studio every day, having worked hard over a period of many years to develop skills that they could use in the creation of the perfect recording. Prior to becoming session musicians, many members of the Nashville A Team distinguished themselves as valuable backing musicians through apprenticeships with other musicians, engagement with the rich sacred singing traditions common to many white Protestant Christian denominations, and formal training in conservatories and schools of music. In fact, as this chapter documents, many members of the Nashville A Team came to the city's recording studios not with a deep background in country music, but in pop, rock and roll, jazz, and even classical music. Each session, then, drew upon the various skills and musical vocabularies that these musicians brought into the studio, requiring the constant negotiation of musical values and the development of common vocabularies with which to discuss the work that was in front of them. Far from being natural, then, the apparent polish of Nashville's session musicians was the consequence of intensive effort, both individually and as a group.

This chapter explores the ways that the many members of the Nashville A Team were trained and considers the impacts that those pedagogies may have had on their daily work in the studios along Music Row. Drawing upon extensive new oral histories with Nashville Sound–era session musicians, as well as their descendants and associates, and oral histories deposited in the Frist Library of the Country Music Hall of Fame and Museum, this chapter presents a more detailed and nuanced examination of the musicianship of Nashville Sound–era session musicians than has been captured in the myth-making that has surrounded them since the 1950s. This is not, however, simply an exercise in searching for obscure and arcane information about musicians whose work has emanated from radio and jukebox speakers for six decades (often without appropriate credit). Rather, as ethnomusicologist Henry Kingsbury has observed, the ways that we discuss musicianship reveal a great deal about the values and ideologies that a given music culture seeks to celebrate and replicate.[5] Moreover, discussions of musicianship in the US South are often laden with additional racial, classed, and gendered assumptions.[6] This chapter, therefore, uses new primary sources to reveal the variety of ways that Nashville Sound–era session musicians learned the fundamentals of music theory, utilized existing notional traditions and developed new ones, and negotiated work in recording sessions in which multiple kinds of musicianship were at play.

To accomplish this task, this chapter focuses on three core topics that have emerged from my ongoing research on record production in the Nashville Sound era. First, this chapter considers the myriad ways that session musicians received their musical training, including not only rhythm section players but also background vocalists and orchestral musicians. Second, this chapter discusses the variety of notational systems that were used in sessions during the Nashville Sound era, revealing that the typical session was a notationally diverse ecosystem.[7] Finally, this chapter will use oral testimonies to explore how session musicians came together—despite their varying musical backgrounds—to create some of country music's most iconic recordings.

TYPES OF MUSICAL TRAINING IN THE NASHVILLE STUDIO SYSTEM

The musicians of the Nashville A Team—across more than thirty years of collaboration—came to the studio through a variety of routes. Some began their careers as backing musicians in road bands and on barn dances, while others learned to read shape notes in the church choir. Still others were the products of years on the bandstand as jazz musicians or endless hours in the practice room learning to play classical concertos. This section, then, will trace some of the more common pathways through which musicians found their way to the Nashville recording scene.

Musicians with Informal Musical Training

Not surprisingly, many of the musicians who contributed to Nashville's studio scene during the Nashville Sound era could not claim to have had any formal musical training prior to their work in the studios. Country music, after all, has roots in vernacular culture, where informal methods of instruction tend to dominate. Much as the *Opry* and other barn dance programs that thrived in the 1930s and 1940s promoted their rustic authenticity through stagecraft, scripts, costumes, and song selection, the musicians who played on those programs derived a certain amount of their country music authenticity from their decidedly unlearned and unstudied approach to playing fiddle, guitars, banjos, and other instruments on stage.[8] These instruments, which could be found in homes throughout the United States from the end of the nineteenth century onward, have a low barrier for entry, making it possible for musicians of all skill levels to play them, and that may very well have been a contributing factor to the popularity of country music: the sense that anyone with even limited musical abilities could play it and have some fun with it.[9]

But possessing an unlearned approach to playing an instrument does not preclude the possibility that musicians received some sort of instruction from more knowledgeable musicians along the way to achieving their own career success. What differentiates a professional musician from an amateur, in many ways, is a willingness to dedicate endless hours to the practice of minute physical gestures that will make for performances that are both more efficient and more precise. The overwhelming majority of this time is spent in solitary study, reflecting upon and repeating licks and other musical ideas that one hears on recordings, sees someone play in person, or invents on one's own.[10] Just as vital to this process is the informal passing of musical ideas from one musician to another, often in backstage encounters and jam sessions. All of this is to say that, despite their lack of formal musical training, some of the most successful Nashville session musicians developed their remarkable facility on one or more instruments through careful practice and an informal system of pedagogy that prepared them to take new creative risks and to feel confident in their abilities to perform at a high standard day in and day out.

Although it might be comfortable to assume that the musicians who played on Nashville Sound–era recordings were untrained, the truth is that even those musicians who could not boast a formal pedigree possessed a musical education that was hard-won through years of work on the road. That is to say that many of the musicians who worked in the Nashville studio scene developed their skills through informal—but often quite lengthy—apprenticeships. Many of the leading instrumentalists who appeared on Nashville Sound–era recordings worked their way from local and regional venues to featured acts and members of the *Grand Ole Opry* backing band. Through this work, these musicians developed a variety of skills that would prove to be exceptionally useful in the recording studio. For instance, working on a staff band required an ability to learn a featured artist's repertoire, often at the drop of a hat and just minutes before a live, nationwide broadcast. Not only did that mean that the musicians had to develop a good ear for chord changes and song forms, but that they also

needed to have a deep understanding of the more common forms and harmonic progressions that underpinned the genre. Using references to more
familiar hit recordings, these musicians could even draw out the general
"feel" or attitude needed for a performance, from the nature of its rhythmic pulse to the timbre of the instruments. And of vital importance to
their future work in the studio was the formation of a deep understanding
of the microphone and its ability to both capture and modify the sounds of
their performances. Many talented musicians are incapable of recording
because they do not understand or are intimidated by the microphone, so
this knowledge helped radio musicians stand apart from those musicians
who could play well but had little face time with a microphone.

Perhaps not surprisingly, many of the musicians who came through this
less formalized training pathway played stringed instruments that were
commonly found in a wide range of rural vernacular musical styles. Among
them were the guitar, banjo, fiddle, and upright bass. These instruments
were often readily available in even the most impoverished homes—often
in homemade varieties in those cases—and aspiring musicians could often
find willing teachers in their home communities. Furthermore, although
formal pedagogical materials for these instruments—using Western-style
notation—had been available for decades prior to World War II, musicians could learn to play them without needing to read musical notation,
instead developing their aural skills and learning to translate what they
heard other musicians play into physical gestures in their hands and arms.
Fiddler Buddy Spicher, who began to make significant contributions to
the Nashville recording scene during the second half of the 1960s, recalled
that long hours in the car provided him the opportunity to develop his ear
and his dexterity. He told interviewer Jim Christian that, during his tenure
with Canadian singer Hank Snow's road band in the late 1950s, he worked
hard to develop a distinctive style of fiddling that used two notes at the
same time, known as "double stops":

[T]here were a lot of long trips into Canada[,] and there would be
many hours of just sitting in the car. So what I would do to pass
the time was take my fiddle out and just practice those double

stops pizzicato. I'd take any melody that I liked[,] and I'd figure out what the harmony was. And just for the challenge of it[,] I wanted to be able to play in any key. So I would just take several melodies, country tunes in the early days, and figure out a third above or a third below. In those same days, the first time I was with Hank, Chubby [Wise] was playing the lead[,] and I would try things out with Chubby. Chubby would say, "That don't sound quite right," and I'd try something else[,] and Chubby would say, "That's it, that's the way Tommy [Vaden] used to do it."[11]

As Spicher's recollections indicate, the long road trips that most road bands undertook as they served their fans provided not only long blocks of practice time (undoubtedly accompanied by many other activities), but also opportunities for mentorship from older musicians who could help the younger musicians learn to play within the country tradition.

Many of these musicians, too, often learned to play more than one instrument to accommodate the needs of family bands and, later, professional demands. Such was the case with rhythm guitarist Velma Williams Smith, who played on many RCA Victor sessions in the 1950s and 1960s. Although Smith was a regular member of the RCA session team, her participation in the Nashville recording scene has been largely overlooked and has only recently been documented by her niece, Suzi Burgher Payne, who interviewed Smith in her final years and has traced her contributions to sessions by such leading RCA Victor artists as Jim Reeves and Dottie West. Payne noted that Smith's entire family—including a number of cousins—lived in the small rural community of Eply Station, Kentucky, and were intensely close with one another.[12] Like many people living in rural areas, the Williamses needed to provide their own entertainment because traveling shows and technological amusements were hard to come by.[13] For the extended Williams clan, music and dancing were a major part of these entertainments; as Payne recounted, "the whole family just seemed to get together for what they called 'moonlight dances,' which were just little community gatherings on Saturday nights. The whole little rural community would come together and have picnics or, you know, and potluck and would have music."[14] In these dances, the children often provided the music; Payne noted that "[Velma] played the bass fiddle, and her older sister Mildred played the guitar."[15] Family bands provided an opportunity for musicians like Velma Smith to develop their musicianship in a familiar context. In the absence of formal music instruction, children often turned to older and more experienced family members or other more knowledgeable musicians in the community to learn basic skills, such as how to tune their instruments. And, for the most part, written notation often played a very small role in the ways that these musicians learned to play, so aspiring musicians needed to learn how to play by watching and listening to other musicians in their community. These aural skills would have proven to be of exceptional value in the Nashville recording scene, which also used standard Western musical notation in only limited ways and relied heavily on musicians' abilities to hear a song from a demonstration record or a live performance in the studio and transform it into a solid arrangement with commercial potential.

Although the overwhelming majority of family band musicians never aspired to professional careers in music, the 1930s of Smith's youth was a particularly good time for those few who did. Born in 1927, Smith came of age in a golden age of live local radio, and it did not take long for her and Mildred—performing as the Williams Sisters—to find their way to radio station WHOP in Hopkinsville, Kentucky (a nearly eighty-mile round trip from Eply Station) and other venues in the region.[16] Through their public performances, they met another musician from nearby Rosine, Kentucky, who was on his way to stardom as a member of the *Grand Ole Opry*: mandolinist Bill Monroe. Monroe, who had himself built his career through the work of a family band, was apparently quite impressed with the Williamses and invited them to audition for the *Opry*.[17] As Payne noted, "I believe this was about 1939. And so they auditioned and were allowed to appear that Saturday night as their first appearance on the *Opry*, and they were invited back with somewhat regular frequency to come and sing and perform on the *Opry*. And they did that for a couple of years."[18]

The Williams Sisters' stint on the *Opry* ended in 1941 or 1942, when Mildred married and moved to Louisville.[19] But that was just the beginning of Velma Williams Smith's career, which really began to take off following the dissolution of the Williams Sisters. Payne recounted that Williams's talents as a bassist were noted by *Opry* star Roy Acuff, who offered her a position in the Smoky Mountain Boys and Girls, where she filled the stage role of "big sister" to "Bashful Brother Oswald" Kirby. During her approximately seven-year tenure with Acuff, Williams played bass and guitar and joined the group in its various jokes and skits.[20] It was in this group that Williams met the man who would become her husband, the multi-instrumentalist Hal Smith, who was playing fiddle with Acuff at the time.[21] Velma and Hal played with many of the leading country recording artists of the late 1940s and early 1950s, including George Morgan, Carl Smith, and Hank Williams, with Velma contributing primarily as a guitarist and Hal contributing primarily as a fiddler and bassist.[22]

Along with Velma Smith, many of the musicians who came to Nashville's recording studios with a wide range of informal professional training on their instruments became some of the most successful and most admired guitarists of their generation. Chet Atkins, who later went on to be one of the leading producers at RCA Victor and a renowned solo guitarist, got his start playing the radio barn dances with such acts as Homer and Jethro and the Carter Sisters, performing on the *Old Dominion Barn Dance* in Richmond, Virginia; Cincinnati's WLW; and the *Midday Merry-Go-Round* in Knoxville, Tennessee.[23] Grady Martin—a guitarist whose work was widely heralded by his A Team peers as some of the most important and inventive guitar work ever captured on records—also began his career accompanying other musicians, most notably as the leader of Springfield, Missouri, nationally televised *Ozark Jubilee*, a significant breeding ground for aspiring country talent.[24] And guitarist Hank Garland, whose career as a session guitarist was cut tragically short following a near-fatal car accident in 1961, worked his way into studio work not only through apprenticeships in country music, but in jazz, as well.[25]

One noteworthy example to emerge from this informal system of learning and apprenticeship was rhythm guitarist and multi-instrumentalist Ray Edenton, who is perhaps best known for his development of the "high-strung" or "Nashville-tuned" guitar. He recalled: "I started playing music . . . when I was a kid at home with my brothers. I was playing four-string guitar when I was five, six years old at square dances. My grand-daddy already taught me to play some fiddle tunes. He was an old-time fiddle player."[26] He told country music journalist and critic Rich Kienzle that "he did learn from his relatives. One uncle showed him a two-finger (thumb and index finger) roll on the 5-string banjo that became the basis for his guitar roll."[27] After completing a stint in the US Army Radio Signal Corps in Luxembourg and Germany after World War II, he played lead guitar with the Rodeo Rangers and, by 1948, with Joe and Rose Lee Maphis's Corn Crackers on the *Old Dominion Barn Dance* in Richmond.[28] By 1949, he had begun working as a bassist with Homer and Jethro and Chet Atkins out of Knoxville radio station WNOX, playing on the *Midday Merry-Go-Round* and traveling to coal camps in Kentucky, Virginia, and West Virginia on what he called the "Lamp Lights Circuit."[29] After a bout of tuberculosis sidelined him for several years, Edenton moved to Nashville in 1952, where he played lead guitar for Jamup and Honey, became a regular backing musician on the *Grand Ole Opry*, and worked periodically as a road musician.[30] This work required backing musicians to learn songs quickly, craft simple arrangements on the fly (often backstage at the *Opry*), and perform accurately. As he recounted:

> Me and Lightnin' [Chance], we worked for a year and a half. We worked for every show on the Opry, and we never rehearsed after the first three or four months. We never rehearsed with anybody. We know all their songs. That's why they had me there. Me and Lightnin' and Don Slayman, fiddle player. We didn't rehearse with nobody unless they had a new song that was just out and then we'd slip backstage for five minutes and hear it and that [would] be about all we needed.[31]

When Edenton began recording regularly in the mid-1950s, then, he was already accustomed to the spontaneous ad hoc arranging practices that would come to dominate the Nashville studio scene, and his fluency on a variety of instruments—developed from as early as his primary school years—made him an indispensable resource for Nashville producers.

Not all of the musicians who came to a professional session career through the apprenticeship route came directly through country music. For musicians who came of age in the 1930s, it was almost as common to find work in the many traveling shows that served what was widely known as the "vaudeville circuit." Making use of the nation's railroads and steamboats, the vaudeville circuit was one of the leading sites for cross-cultural musical exchange, providing thousands of opportunities for musicians—both European American and African American—to learn to play a variety of popular and vernacular musical styles, to develop the ability to accompany a number of different kinds of acts (including not just vocalists, but a variety of theatrical acts), and to perform with great showmanship (often deploying what might be described as a "hokum" style of playing).[32] One such musician to have come to country recording sessions through vaudeville was bassist Joe Zinkan, who began his career as a bassist on a riverboat traveling between New Orleans and Cincinnati before joining the Acuff organization in 1943.[33] As Zinkan's friend and Nashville bass historian Kent Blanton recounted, it was on this job that an unnamed African American bassist from Paducah, Kentucky, taught him to play the slap bass style for which Zinkan would be best known.[34]

Bassist Ernie Newton, too, came up in the exciting creative realm of vaudeville before finding his way to Nashville. In a 1974 interview with Douglas Green, the Hartford, Connecticut, native recalled, "my mother was an opera singer, and my dad, he was a pantomime comedian. I mean, just, you know, the opposite of one another. . . . [A]ll my people back there, they were my uncles and cousins and all that, they were in show business, too. . . ."[35] Following his parents' death, Newton moved to Vermont, where he lived on a farm with his aunt and uncle and discovered that he had some musical talent of his own.[36] By the time he was fourteen or fifteen years old, Newton could play the trumpet and fiddle, and he moved to California, where he developed a reputation among his classmates as a blackface comedian:

I got out there and started going to school, and every time there was any kind of a play or anything like that, I was always in it. I was always a blackface comedian. I don't know why, but blues, and colored music I'd play, was very definitely, very strong in me all my life. I always liked it. . . . [I]t seemed it was more a rhythmic thing, and that's what I loved.[37]

He also joined a vocal group that specialized in barbershop music, sing-ing tenor and playing a banjo-ukulele on the Pantages vaudeville circuit.[38] Newton and two of his friends also spent their weekends in Hollywood, riding their bicycles the nearly forty miles from their home in Ontario, California, to find work as extras and stagehands.[39] Through this work, Newton interacted with some of the leading cowboy stars of the day, including Tom Mix (whom he recalled having "talked with" while on the lots), and he reflected that he "could have moved right into pictures in those days and grew up in it, like a lot of the kids did. . . ."[40] But he chose instead to follow his passion for music and to work with the vocal group on the Pantages circuit, something he did until his school schedule got in the way.[41]

After leaving the vocal group, Newton began to explore his interest in country music, but through a path that might seem unconventional to modern country fans: Hawaiian music. As John Troutman has demon-strated, Hawaiian music was extraordinarily popular in the 1920s and 1930s and provided many aspiring musicians from the mainland their first opportunities to learn the guitar (played in the Hawaiian style) and to perform in front of an audience. Its influences can be heard throughout the early recorded output of country musicians from Jimmie Rodgers to Roy Acuff, as well as in a variety of steel guitar traditions throughout not only the United States but the entire world.[42] Newton, it seems, took to Hawaiian music quite quickly and worked diligently to learn to play and sing it:

So I started back and I just went to country music. I don't know why, but I just loved it. Well, I went to Honolulu and I worked on—of course, I could play the ukulele. I got to working in a Hawaiian trio, and one of them was Lefty Shaffer [phonetic]. He was half white. He played the guitar. The steel player, he was all-Hawaiian. And we worked on the boat *Malola* [phonetic], going from Honolulu to Frisco. I met them in Frisco. . . .

It was a great job. I learned to sing Hawaiian and everything. I didn't know what I was saying, but I learned to sing it, and played ukulele in the trio. Then when we came back, why, we'd work at . . . Puffy Dan's [phonetic] in San Francisco, where all the people, the show people, used to come in after they'd get through the shows. They'd come in there, and we worked in there down there when we was in town in Frisco. I went through that phase of Hawaiian music.[43]

After that stint, Newton moved to Spokane, Washington, where he "worked . . . as a single" on radio station KXQ and played banjo in dance bands. There, he met Bob Crosby, brother of the now more famous Bing and a popular bandleader in the 1930s. As a soloist, and later as a member of a trio, Newton specialized in the popular hits of the 1930s, as well as country songs that could move his audience to tip him well.[44]

By 1930 or 1931, Newton was infatuated with country music, thanks in large part to Carson Robison's hit "Going Back to Texas," which was recorded for Edison in June 1929.[45] Around that time, he found himself in Phoenix, Arizona, where he joined up with a group called the Arizona Wranglers, playing guitar.[46] Upon returning to Ontario, California, he joined the Texas Ramblers as the group's bassist, despite having no prior experience playing the instrument.[47] Newton left the Texas Ramblers after "a long time," joining Bob Gardner, one half of the popular blind singing duo Mac & Bob. Newton's connection to Gardner led him to the national stage:

[W]e called WLS out of Chicago on the phone and told them to listen to us, see if they would take us back and take us up there. All I wanted to do, I wanted to get back up there and get to go to work at WLS and get Mac & Bob back together, because, see, Mac & Bob, they were a blind team, and they needed to be together. All I was, I was a seeing-eye dog for—you know, although I sang with him, but I wasn't the real McCoy.[48]

WLS invited Gardner and Newton to return to WLS, and, after a brief stint as Gardner's guitarist, Mac & Bob reunited, leaving Newton "out of a job." Fortunately, WLS decided to continue employing Newton as a staff musician, a position that allowed him to play with a number of the leading acts on the *National Barn Dance* and WLS, including the Hilltoppers (with Chet Atkins's half-brother Jimmy), the Hoosier Hot Shots, and George Gobel. "[W]e were staff," he recalled. "Everybody was staff on WLS—everybody. Everybody [who] worked there was on staff, and everybody got the same pay, no difference. I mean it was all the same money. Of course, when you went out on the road and done the road shows, why, then, the money was different. Then we got extra money for working the *National Barn Dance*, which was [broadcast from] the Eighth Street Theater."[49]

Newton's time at WLS undoubtedly afforded him the opportunity to play with a wide range of musicians in an equally diverse variety of musical styles, including not only the jazz-inflected popular music coming out of Tin Pan Alley, but also the variety of country music forms that were popularized on the *National Barn Dance*. The *National Barn Dance* was a particularly eclectic barn dance program in that it blended many of the central and eastern European vernacular forms that were popular among immigrant communities of the Upper Midwest and the prairies of Indiana and Illinois with Appalachian folk songs and string band sounds popular among the Appalachian migrants who came to Chicago and other industrial Midwestern cities in search of wage labor.[50] Moreover, WLS was the home to several significant specialists in cowboy singing, particularly the Tin Pan Alley–influenced version that was beginning to take the film world by storm.[51] As a consequence, the WLS position likely helped Newton become even more fluent in a variety of musical vocabularies and to nuance his stage presentation through the addition of microphone techniques.

Newton's work in Chicago led him to a young guitarist who would go on to be one of the most significant guitarists, luthiers, and recording pioneers of the second half of the twentieth century: Lester Polfuss, then known as the radio performer "Rhubarb Red" and later as Les Paul.[52] When Newton left WLS around 1936, Newton, Paul, and Atkins "formed a trio and called it the Les Paul Trio and went to New York and joined [popular big band leader] Fred Waring."[53] Newton, who had spent his entire career to that point as an "ear" musician who had used his ability to pick melodies and harmonies out without the need for written notation to further his career to that point, needed to learn to read music to work with Paul and Waring. But like many musicians who find themselves in need of additional training, he decided to learn how to read musical notation on his own. "Well, I taught myself," he remembered.

[L]ike I told Fred, he said, "Do you read [music]?"

I said, "Well, I don't read enough to hurt me," you know. But the thing of it is, I could get by. I could get by with the way I did—to read enough so I could get by, but I couldn't take a thing right then and just sit [sic] it up and just play, you know. But I taught myself enough so I could read.[54]

Similarly, Newton's gig with the Waring band required that he learn how to construct musical arrangements more or less on the fly, a skill that would come in handy later on as he began recording in Nashville. He told Douglas Green that the Waring orchestra would

do a thing like they'd call a montage, and they'd take tunes like— well, I mean you'd take a tune like "Jingle Bells," see, and the band would do it. I mean, the band would start it off and then the different groups in the band would do it. Then we'd do our version. Everybody would do our own version of it[.] We'd go one right in, segue right into another, you know, and we'd all do this thing. Then it would end up in the last—now, when we'd come on, I mean, Fred would say, "Make your arrangement a minute and ten seconds long, no longer."

I mean we had cut ours in a minute and ten seconds. So then he'd come around and when he'd come to ours, he'd just—you know, he'd throw it to us. Les'd be sitting on a stool, and Jim could sing. Jim sang very much like [Bob] Crosby. He had a great voice, great voice. Then we'd be on stage in the front, and we'd do our little minute and ten seconds, and zing right out of there into another group and then end up—then the glee club would do "Jingle Bells" the way it was supposed to be done, at the end. Then, of course, then we would sign off and go off with "Sleep," and that was the theme song.[55]

Newton recalled that these experiences were significant in expanding his musical creativity because he had to think of new ways to play familiar songs at a relatively quick pace:

It was a great experience, because then I really got to know—I don't say better, because music is music. I don't care if you do "Turkey in the Straw," if it's done right—I mean, you could do it with a three-string group here, and if they don't jazz it up, which I don't like to do on any tune, unless you take one chorus or something like that—but if it's done right, then it can be done with a three-string group or it can be done with a concert orchestra.[56]

Working in the New York scene forced Newton to develop additional skills and abilities that were already rudimentarily present in his work from the time that he was a kid playing the vaudeville circuit. But in the high-pressure situation of working with the Les Paul Trio and the Fred Waring & the Pennsylvanians, he was expected to push those skills to their maximum potential, which would hold him in good stead in the Nashville recording scene of the postwar era.

New York, as the hub of the big bands that were taking the American popular music scene by storm in the 1930s, provided numerous opportunities to play with and learn from some of the top musicians in the nation, and Newton took full advantage of them. After their regular gigs were over, musicians gathered in clubs in midtown Manhattan and in Harlem to show off their improvisational abilities to one another.[57] Newton recalled that he first encountered members of Benny Goodman's famous quartet in these jam sessions.[58] Newton noted that, although he was not the most confident improvising bassist on the scene, renowned jazz bassist Slam Stewart complimented his improvisations after a particularly strong performance, telling him, " 'Man,' he said, 'you're coming on.' He said, 'I heard you tonight.' He said, 'Man,' he says, 'you're there. You're getting there.' That was one of the biggest compliments I think I ever had, you know, because this guy played so much bass fiddle."[59]

With the coming of World War II, the big band scene in New York declined dramatically, and Newton's position with the Waring orchestra ended, leaving him an opportunity to seek out new opportunities in country music.[60] He found that his connections to the *National Barn Dance*—and particularly to one of its biggest stars—helped him forge a path in the postwar country music industry. Newton worked a short stint in Alabama with the Slow Easy Singers before moving to Jackson, Mississippi, radio station WRBC, where he was commissioned to build a barn dance program that he intended to call *Crossroad of the South*.[61] But sometime between 1946 and 1948—the oral testimony is unclear—Newton was summoned to Nashville by Red Foley, who thought that Newton could find steady work there.[62] Newton remembered that he had sung quite a bit with Foley and his wife Eva back in Chicago and that he had even written a hymn that Foley used in his *Opry* audition, but opportunities in Alabama had led him away from Foley after their successful audition in 1946.[63] But when Foley called a second time, Newton moved to Nashville, where he found that WSM welcomed his musical talents.[64] In addition to being able to use his diverse musical skills on WSM, Newton quickly found himself in a position to begin recording in the nascent Nashville studio scene thanks to his connections to the A&R men who had been vital in promoting the *National Barn Dance* cast to a national and international record-buying audience. Newton recalled:

> Everybody came down here. Like, I knew [Columbia Records country producer] Art Satherley, because I'd worked with Art Satherley in

1935, you know, when he was in Chicago. Then I knew Steve Sholes at RCA; and I knew Capitol, Lee Gillette; and I knew them all when we were kids together. So when they came in town, they said, "Ernie, what are you doing here?"

I said, "I'm playing on the Opry."

They said, "Well, we're going to do some recording."

I said, "Well, fine."

They said, "Well, you're our boy." So then, they wasn't going to go out [and recruit many other bass players] because every bass player in town—most of the bass players, they work in these groups, was the last guy they hired in the band. He was a sort of halfway comedian.[65]

That is to say that Newton's demonstrated experience as a professional musician in a wide variety of fields differentiated him from other Nashville bass players, who were often hired at the last minute to join a tour and who often learned to play the instrument on the job. Moreover, as *Opry*-based string bands continued to play on minstrel routines from the nineteenth century as a way to provide a program that was entertaining to a wide range of audience members, the bass player often filled the "Toby" role, appearing with blacked-out teeth and in clown-like rural clothing that differentiated him (and sometimes her) from the rest of the band.[66] Newton's professionalism eschewed such efforts to stereotype him comedically (despite his prior experience as a blackface comedian), and his connections to leading creative and business leaders in the country music industry helped to assure him steady work as a session musician.

Newton observed that his fluency in many musical styles and his efforts to develop a well-rounded musicianship stood him in good stead in comparison to even the best bass players in the Nashville *Opry* scene. He noted that, unlike Joe Zinkan, who "just tore that bass fiddle up" when slapping, he was able to vary his style to meet the needs of recording artists:

Joe was great. He was super. But when it come [*sic*] to playing bass like in a group—Joe would go along for a while and then he'd slap for a little while, you know. He couldn't do that on record, see. So they wanted somebody to play true notes.

They had bass players in town that played good bass, but they thought that playing country music, all you had to do to play country was play bad. This was the sort of thing that, I don't know, it just used to make me so mad when I'd hear people say that. I just wanted to slap them, you know, because country music had a heart in it and had a soul in there.[67]

Newton's commitment to playing the right kind of notes to fit a song helped him win over bluegrass pioneer Bill Monroe, who frequently hired Newton to replace Monroe's brother and road bass player Birch for his Decca sessions:

Birch was playing with Bill. See, Birch came in one time. When they came in, you know, I said, "Birch, go on, go on, play with Bill on the show [presumably the *Opry*]," so he could make some money, see.

So Birch went up and Birch just started playing. Bill got him over to the side, and he said, "Birch, look," he said, "you're playing not very good." He says, "There's notes that you play, certain notes you play for certain things." [Green laughs.]

Birch says, "What do you mean?"

He says, "Well, like Ernie. Ernie plays certain notes," and he said, "they all mean—they go with what I'm playing." He says, "The notes you're playing is bad."

Birch says, "Look, there's no bad notes on a bass fiddle." [Laughter] This is the way the bass players were in those days. . . .

I played all of Bill Monroe's stuff [recordings] because, see, I was country enough.[68]

Newton noted that his musicianship was a major contributor to Monroe's deep respect for him. Monroe was a notoriously difficult bandleader who pushed his accompanying musicians to play at their absolute best, and, as a consequence, even Nashville's most skilled musicians were sometimes intimidated by him. But Newton was afforded a degree of candor with Monroe that other musicians were not. He recalled that Monroe

was on Decca and Paul Cohen was head of [country recording for] Decca, and so Owen Bradley, [who was Cohen's assistant], Owen would say, "Ernie, I'm scared to work with Bill Monroe."

I said, "Well, Bill Monroe's all right."

He said, "Well, they're funny kind of people."

I said, "There's nothing wrong with Bill." I says, "He's from Kentucky. He's just country."

He said, "Well, can you handle it?"

I said, "I can say anything I want to."

So we'd go in there, and he'd say, "All right." He'd sit at the [mixing] board, and he'd say, "Ernie, you handle it. You tell him what to do. You tell him. I can't tell him." His [Monroe's] fiddle player would play, and I mean he just played up and down, you know, just played. He played straight across with his finger, but it would be weird arming [bowing], see. It would be real weird, but it was great. It made a bluegrass sound, see, something different. Of course, Bill played good on mandolin, played great. But his fiddle player just played up and down, see.

Then they'd sing, and you couldn't understand what they were singing, but people in Kentucky could, see.

Anyway, so I get in there. I knew Bill real well, see. I could say anything I want[ed] to. I'd go in there, and I was the only guy that every played on Bill Monroe's records, just like a bass fiddle. I slacked on some of it because it went with the thing we were doing, see. I played on all those things, and I'd tell those guys, you know—Bill would say, "What did it sound like?"

I says, "It didn't sound good, Bill." I said, "The guitar player's off."

OK. Then he'd eat them out. Bill never said diddly squat to me. Never. Bill and I just got along. He'd [sic] just a great guy, you know. Bill used to say, "Ernie, you tell them how to play. You tell them. You tell them," you know.[69]

Newton, therefore, earned the respect of other musicians in large part because he could play well and communicate with musicians with diverse backgrounds—skills that he had honed over the course of more than two decades of work on the road and on the radio. (It is also worth noting that he was replaced in the studio by Bessie Lee Mauldin, a bassist who is most often framed through her romantic relationship with Monroe, but who was obviously exceptional enough to have replaced the experienced work of Newton in the studio.)[70]

Rather than being naturally talented musicians who had the potential to craft memorable arrangements and play with minimal errors in a high-pressure environment, then, these barn dance and radio veterans brought a hard-won musicianship drawn from practical experience into the recording studios, a musicianship that should be celebrated for its own distinctive histories and not simply glossed over as an apparent outgrowth of an organic Nashville environment.

Musicians with Formal Training

Although many of Nashville's session musicians came to their work with little to no formal musical training, still others were involved with some sort of formal musical training as children or young adults. Members of the Nashville A Team and the other session musicians who worked in the Nashville studios sometimes bragged, like Ernie Newton, that they might read music, but "not enough to hurt my playing." But closer investigation of their musical backgrounds reveals that several key musicians had participated in school choir, band, and orchestra programs, which were an essential part of many public school curricula throughout much of the twentieth century.[71] Others found their way to musical notation through engagement with Christian church music, which—especially in the US South—embedded music pedagogy in its broader efforts toward religious education.[72] Still others developed their musical skills through formal piano lessons, in the home of a local woman who may have been disappointed by their students' love of popular musical styles.[73]

Therefore, although many Nashville session musicians claimed relatively minimal musical training, it is worth remembering that such denials of formal training often obscure their early musical biographies.

The presence of formal musical training in the biographies of some Nashville session musicians runs counter to many of the prevailing narratives of country music authenticity. If country music culture values rural rusticity, working-class identity, and a certain unpretentious musical affect, formal music education often symbolizes a more urban (or at least small-town) setting, middle-class virtue, and pretentiousness. School and church music programs, for instance, were part of a broader effort to encourage civic engagement in the twentieth-century US, building in the process an ideal of American citizenship that celebrated conformation to a deeply Christian American patriotism. The militaristic nature of many band programs might be seen as the greatest embodiment of this conformist culture, with all-male Reserve Officers' Training Corps (ROTC)–oriented programs that required students to march in formation, wear military-style uniforms, and maintain close-cut hair styles.[74] And church music programs—particularly those emerging from mainline Protestant churches that might be found located on a "Church Street" in any given Southern town—were intimately linked with efforts to build a Christian-oriented (and often white) majority to lead business, government, and civic life.

Formal music education is also intimately linked with women, another harbinger of inauthenticity in an authenticity regime that privileges masculinity.[75] Numerous scholars of early twentieth-century musical life have noted that music education's deep ties to women were often seen to undermine (or at least complicate) white masculinity.[76] Put another way: every hour spent in the house playing the piano under the supervision of a woman was an hour that wasn't spent playing baseball, one of the primary ways that boys developed their physical prowess in the prewar era.[77] The piano was a decidedly domestic instrument, located in the front rooms of many white middle-class homes and associated with women's music-making since the mid-nineteenth century.[78] Thus the piano—although an exceptionally important instrument in the formal musical training of so many professional and advanced amateur musicians—might have been read as a tool of domestication that restricted a young boy's ability to go out into the world of homosocial masculine activity. Even if a boy thoroughly enjoyed and appreciated the opportunity to learn to play the piano, then, the attitudes of his friends (and perhaps older male siblings and uncles) may very well have led him to believe that he needed to mask that part of his life to present a proper white middle-class masculinity to the world.

At the same time, music educators were not known for being the most progressive musical minds of their generations. In the oral testimonies of many Nashville session musicians, it becomes clear that their music teachers perceived their interest in popular music—whether jazz, rock, country, or mainstream pop—as a distraction from their studies of the great European composers of the eighteenth and nineteenth centuries. For aspiring musicians interested in creating their own musical pathways, a classically oriented musical training may have felt somewhat chaffing, at best, and downright restrictive, at worst.[79] That these restrictions were often presented by militaristic band leaders or domesticated women only amplified the students' protests against classical training. In the former case, an embrace of rock, pop, jazz, and country could be cast as a resistance to the broader civic project of the first half of the twentieth century and a general rejection of middle-class white austerity; in the latter, rock, pop, jazz, and country could be read as too wild for the average white middle-class woman to be able to handle, often with implied sexual and alcohol- and drug-induced overtones. In either case, if musicians were to embrace formal musical training as a part of their public professional biography, it might very well undermine their cultural capital in the popular music scene. If the barn dances and schoolhouse shows that formed the training ground for informally trained session musicians granted them a degree of authenticity, formal musical training could easily be seen as a liability. Formal musical training was a marker of middle-class affluence that stood out in a recording scene that frequently celebrated recording artists and songwriters with humble origins.[80] But, by the same token, even the slightest amount of formal musical training offered musicians the opportunity to communicate with the wide variety of musicians who came into the Nashville recording scene during the 1950s, 1960s, and 1970s, and the ability to read limited musical notation and to think in terms of elementary harmony and form could make session work go much more smoothly. As such, formal musical training may have been a liability when attached to one's personal biography, but it was also a vital asset for many musicians who were contributing to the Nashville recording scene.

Many session musicians received their initial formal musical training through their associations with Christian churches. Notably, the Jordanaires, renowned for their contributions as backing vocalists on Nashville recording sessions from the 1950s through the 1980s, reported extensive engagement with shape-note singing traditions, particularly the seven-shape gospel convention styles that were commonly deployed in Protestant churches throughout the southern United States.[81] Shape-note singing—and the gospel quartet tradition that emerged from shape-note singing conventions—was a widespread popular entertainment in the US South in the late nineteenth and early twentieth centuries, particularly among white Christians associated with the Pentecostal and Holiness traditions. Shape-note singing emerged from a broad effort to improve the quality of singing and musicianship in Protestant churches across the United States and can be traced to a group of New England–based composers and publishers who worked in the mid-eighteenth century. Shape-note systems assigned specific shapes to each of the degrees of the major and minor scale, thereby making it easier to discern the relationships between individual pitches than the familiar "round-note" system that has been in widespread use in the Western art music tradition since the beginning of the seventeenth century.[82] Prior to the advent of shape-note systems, many American Protestant churches relied on a singing style in which a song leader would sing a portion of each line of a hymn to guide the congregation, after which the congregation would sing the melody collectively. Although still maintained in a few denominations still today (such as the Old Regular Baptists of central Appalachia), this "old way of singing" was largely supplanted by the collective singing of hymns published in shape notes by the end of the eighteenth century.[83]

Shape-note singing was out of fashion in New England by the beginning of the nineteenth century as church music reformers such as Lowell
Mason encouraged an embrace of more European-based models for
church music.[84] But it was widely maintained by people who moved
southward down the Great Wagon Road that ran through the Shenandoah
Valley of Virginia and the Cumberland Gap.[85] South Carolina publisher
and singing teacher William Walker helped to spread shape-note singing throughout rural communities in the southern United States with the
publication of *The Southern Harmony and Musical Companion* in 1835.[86]
In churches that did not adhere to a formal liturgy and relied on itinerant
preachers, the communal singing associated with *The Southern Harmony*
(and other similar books such as B. F. White's even more popular com-
pilation *The Sacred Harp*, first published in 1844) served to forge bonds
among the worshippers, and shape-note singing events were often held
as major community gatherings that featured full-day singing, communal
dinners, trading, and courting.[87]

By the end of the Civil War, shape-note singing was beginning to
gain widespread popularity throughout the US South, thanks in large
part to the work of enterprising publishers who found ways to integrate
their interest in publication with the need to educate the singing public
about the fundamentals of music-making.[88] One of the leading publishers
to emerge after the Civil War was Ruebush, Kieffer, & Company, organized by Ephraim Ruebush, Aldine Kieffer, and John W. Howe in 1872.
Ruebush-Kieffer published an extraordinary amount of material, flood-
ing the market with original musical content composed by an increasingly broad range of composers and lyricists. To develop a market for their
growing library of songbooks, Ruebush-Kieffer began to offer instruction
in singing and singing pedagogy at "normal" schools and to organize gospel singing conventions that allowed singers to come together to sing the
latest product that they were putting on sale.[89] Normal schools provided
opportunities for aspiring music pedagogues to develop a foundation
in singing technique, notation, composition, and diction, among other
things, and eventually led to the creation of an entire community of singing school teachers who serviced communities throughout the US South.

By the turn of the twentieth century, then, congregations throughout the region were singing gospel songs spelled out in seven shape notes and performed in full four-part harmony, and non-believers were attending gospel conventions for social purposes and getting an introduction to gospel music in the process.[90]

As new technologies were developed in the first decades of the twentieth century, gospel music publishers exploited them as tools to spread their religious message and to expand the market for their publications, their normal schools, and their conventions. As southern gospel historian James Goff has demonstrated, such publishers as James D. Vaughan and V. O. Stamps of the Stamps-Baxter Publishing Company assembled professional quartets to make appearances on radio broadcasts and to record material for home consumption in the growing middle-class phonograph market.[91] By the end of the 1930s, gospel quartet singing was commonplace on radio, on records, in churches, and even on the popular stage (sometimes to the consternation of the religious congregations that had supported the rise of gospel music in the first place). Aspiring young musicians who were willing and able to take to the road often did so, performing for a wide range of audiences throughout the US South and, by the start of World War II, across the entire United States. Thanks in large part to nationwide radio broadcasting, such groups as the Blackwood Brothers and Wally Fowler's Oak Ridge Quartet—which broadcast over WSM, the home of the *Grand Ole Opry*—popularized shape-note gospel songs in all corners of the nation.[92]

As Goff has discussed, the gospel quartets that rose to fame in the postwar years often drew heavily upon African American singing traditions, particularly in their approach to rhythm and timbre.[93] Lynn Abbott and Douglas Seroff, in their expansive book on black gospel traditions, have shown that African American quartet singing frequently eschewed written notation, favoring instead a community of skilled "trainers" who would teach four-part harmony to a quartet by rote and who could use their well-developed aural skills to identify incorrect pitches, troublesome harmonies, and conflicting vowel sounds.[94] Growing out of the jubilee singing tradition that was developed by John Wesley Work II at Fisk University, this form of pedagogy became the standard for African American quartets not only in Tennessee, but in Birmingham, Chicago, and New Orleans, as well.[95] Many of the quartets to train in this method were, by the 1930s, embracing rhythmic accompaniments to non-lexical phonemes, generating a degree of rhythmic excitement among their audiences through the use of looping rhythmic ostinati.[96] Songwriters working in the white shape-note publishing industry tried to capture this carefully developed but seemingly improvisatory accompaniment in many of their compositions of the 1940s and 1950s, leading to the widespread notation of call-and-response and ostinato techniques that had been previously developed in an almost entirely oral/aural context among African American gospel quartets.[97]

It was into this world that the Jordanaires were formed. The group was founded in 1948 and quickly became a leading white gospel quartet, performing on radio and even touring with pioneering African American gospel singer and guitarist Sister Rosetta Tharpe for a bit in the late 1940s.[98] The group's personnel changed frequently in the group's early days, but by 1950, the Jordanaires were a more or less fully formed and stable group: Neil Matthews, Jr., Gordon Stoker, Hoyt Hawkins, and Ray Walker. As Stoker noted in an interview with Douglas B. Green, his early musical background could be traced to gospel music, even before he joined the Jordanaires. During his youth, he

started playing piano for conventions, quartet conventions, and church gatherings, and all that type of thing when I was ten years old. . . . Then I started playing for many quartet conventions and just various gatherings around here, there, and everywhere. Then John Daniel, who was on WSM, called the Daniel Quartet, heard me play, and he said, "The moment you get out of high school, I'm going to call you. You're going to come to Nashville, and you're going to be in the Daniel Quartet. . . ." [T]he moment I got out of high school, John called me and said, "All right, you're out of high school. Come to Nashville." So I came to Nashville in 1942.[99]

Hawkins, too, had a gospel quartet background before joining the Jordanaires, singing with his brothers as the Hawkins Junior Quartet on Paducah, Kentucky, radio station WPAD.[100] Neil Matthews, too, was at the forefront of the white southern gospel movement of the 1940s; as a published biography indicates, "After graduating from Hume Fogg High School in Nashville, he sang and played guitar with 'Wally Fowler and the Oak Ridge Quartet' [sic], which eventually evolved into the present 'Oak Ridge Boys.'"[101]

The white gospel quartets in which the Jordanaires sang during their youth provided valuable training in sight-reading, vowel matching, timing, and intonation that would serve them well as they ventured into more public venues. Moreover, their work as radio performers undoubtedly allowed them to develop the increasingly important microphone skills needed to improve their overall musical effects. That is, radio broadcasts could provide hands-on (and paid) training on how to use the microphone for dynamic effects by stepping away or stepping closer to decrease or increase the group's volume, to stand slightly off-mic or stand in the center of its pickup field to balance the ensemble's sound for the listeners, and other microphonic tricks of the trade that would prove to be particularly useful in the recording studio later in their careers.[102]

Each of the group's members also expanded his musical horizons by enrolling in formal music instruction at the university level. Stoker, for instance, served in the Army Air Corps during World War II and enrolled at Oklahoma Baptist University in Shawnee, Oklahoma, upon his discharge. Later, he recalled, "I came from there back to Peabody [now part of Vanderbilt University], because Peabody had some things . . . that I wanted to get. . . ."[103] It was in college that Stoker "took tenor range," a voice type that he would maintain for the entirety of his career. Neil Matthews, Jr., trained in music at Belmont College, located near the end of what would become the Music Row neighborhood, and Ray Walker held a degree from Nashville's Lipscomb University.[104] As Stoker noted, "All of us have three to four years in college."[105]

Because their musical training came from a variety of formal and informal sources, the Jordanaires were able to function effectively on stage and in the recording studio. Their gospel quartet singing experience forced them to be fluent in shape-note singing, which prioritized sight-singing and the ability to read entirely new material flawlessly. Their experience in university music programs would have also emphasized sight-singing, but in the "round note" tradition that dominates much formal music education, as well as the fundamentals of voice-leading and part-writing for a four-part ensemble. Such coursework in harmony, musicianship, and counterpoint was grounded in four-part singing.[106] At the same time, though, the Jordanaires also drew heavily upon the singing and arranging styles developed by the African American gospel quartets that were enormously popular at the time that the group began to gain some fame. As Ray Walker noted in an interview, "[W]e sang spirituals. We sang very few gospel-type songs, and when we did, it had a different feel."[107] A film clip showing the Jordanaires singing "Dig a Little Deeper" in the mid-1950s reveals the use of the riff-based accompaniments, call-and-response technique, and padded "oohs" and "aahs" that were commonly heard in the music of African American gospel quartets of the time such as the Golden Gate Quartet.[108] Similarly, a performance of "Workin' on a Building" recorded with members of the *Grand Ole Opry* cast in the late 1950s shows the group using many of these same techniques in their arrangements.[109] Thus Walker's distinction between "gospel" and "spiritual" songs in the Jordanaires' repertoire is a significant one, because it demonstrates that the group was not only capable of reading music from shape-note hymnals and convention songbooks, but also used their ample ear-training skills to create their own interesting arrangements in the style of the African American quartets that used similar "faking" techniques to create their arrangements.

The ability to "fake" their way through an arrangement would prove to be of vital importance to the Jordanaires as a recording group. As Stoker told interviewer Morris Levy, "The secret . . . to being a successful background quartet. . . . If you couldn't do it quick, they couldn't use you. If you couldn't fake harmony real quick, they couldn't use you. In that, you tied up too much money."[110] Ear training and voice leading courses, combined with years of professional experience, revealed the relatively few combinations of tones that were necessary to create a smooth-sounding and relatively unobtrusive vocal accompaniment for songs that only used three or four chords (principally the tonic, subdominant, and dominant triads), and training in counterpoint also allowed them to understand the effects that could emerge from spacing the voices far apart or close together or inverting harmonies to change a chord's voicing. At the same time, their working knowledge of two different (but related) forms of written musical notation also allowed them to use notation to communicate some of the more complex parts of their arrangements to one another and to remind them of what they were supposed to sing.

The Jordanaires pioneered the use of written notation to communicate the structure and harmonic underpinnings of a song arrangement in the Nashville recording scene. Matthews developed what came to be known as the "Nashville Number System," a shorthand system that used Arabic numerals to indicate the scale degree that a particular chord was to be built upon and a variety of other signs to indicate the quality (major, minor, diminished, augmented) of that chord. The system was essentially the same as that used in harmony textbooks on college campuses, although the Nashville Number System eschewed the Roman numerals commonly found there. The value of these chord symbols came primarily in their ability to reduce the amount of time needed to communicate a key change. For instance, if the band were using the letter names of the chords, a key change would require a whole new set of chord names. But the use of numerals allowed musicians to change keys with relative ease, as the musicians did not need to write completely new notated arrangements when the singer or the producer decided to change keys during a session.[111] The Nashville Number System was slow to catch on; Stoker noted, for instance, that the Jordanaires "used it for three or four years" before other musicians—including especially harmonica player Charlie McCoy—grew interested in it.[112]

The Jordanaires may have been able to fake their way through the backgrounds of many of their early recordings, but occasionally, more specific musical information was necessary to make the arrangement work. For example, if a particular line needed a lead-in or the singers were needed to create a melodic hook that would make the recording stand out in the crowded marketplace, the simple use of Arabic numerals did not communicate enough information to make the session run smoothly and efficiently. As a consequence of their shared training in the gospel convention tradition, it was possible for the Jordanaires to quickly notate the melodic lines and hooks of a vocal arrangement using shape notes.[113] Fortunately, Jordanaire Neil Matthews, Jr., left a series of lead sheets—likely written after the fact—to the Country Music Foundation Library, and these lead sheets reveal just how important shape notes were to conveying nuanced details about a vocal arrangement. For example, a lead sheet for Elvis Presley's 1959 recording of "(Now and Then There's) A Fool Such as I" highlights the voice-leading of the highest tenor voice in the first and third lines of the verse by using a round whole note for *do*, followed by a sharped whole note for *di*, and a square whole note for *re*. To indicate where the group is supposed to fake four-part harmony in the second line of the verse, Matthews simply writes the cue "4PT"; a root-position, closed voicing indicated from bottom to top as "1351"; and the syllables that the group is supposed to sing with an "OOO." In the chorus, however, an ascending melodic line created by the inversion of harmonies is indicated by a series of ascending round noteheads, suggesting that the overall contour of the line was more important to indicate than its pitch content was.[114] Similarly, Matthews's lead sheet for Presley's 1960 recording of "It's Now or Never" reveals still more use of shape notes to indicate specific pitch content (both in unison and in harmony) and round noteheads to indicate overall melodic contour. The use of specific chord voicings is even more important in this lead sheet, as indicated in the song's introduction, which finds Hoyt Hawkins's baritone moving in stepwise melodic motion while the remainder of the group holds their pitches.[115]

A firm background in written notation, then, seems to have given the Jordanaires the ability to work quickly in the studio, a skill that was of vital importance to a system that was increasingly focused on productivity as demand for country recordings and Nashville studio time grew through the late 1950s and 1960s. Not surprisingly, many of the singers who came into the Nashville system after the Jordanaires also brought similar backgrounds, which stood them in good stead with Nashville producers. Arranger and background vocalist Bergen White recalled the influence of the church choir—which did not sing from gospel convention books—in his acquisition of notational literacy.[116] Ray Stevens (born Ray Ragsdale) also took piano lessons as a child, which developed skills that he leaned on as a backing vocalist and pianist on many sessions in the mid-1960s.[117] And Joe Babcock, who went on to lead the Nashville Edition—one of the city's top vocal backing groups of the late 1960s and 1970s—and who substituted for Hoyt Hawkins in the studio, received formal musical training as a voice major at the University of Nebraska.[118]

Backing vocalists were not the only regular session musicians to have experienced some formal musical training prior to coming to work in the studio. For instance, the case of Charlie McCoy raises a number of questions about the role of formal musical training in the work of the Nashville session musicians of the 1950s and 1960s. Born in Oak Hill, West Virginia, and splitting his time between Florida and West Virginia after the first grade, McCoy began playing harmonica after obtaining a toy instrument from a cereal box top exchange.[119] Although his early efforts as an aspiring young musician were largely trial-and-error, he development reasonable proficiency on a variety of instruments, including the electric guitar, which he played in an audition for Chet Atkins and Owen Bradley during his first visit to Nashville in 1959. McCoy's prodigious abilities as a session musician and bandleader have obscured an essential part of his own musical training: high school and university course work in music theory. As McCoy recalled in a July 2014 interview:

> The state of Florida in 1958/59 decided to experiment with music theory on a high school level. Because my school had the right teacher for it, we were lucky enough that we had it at our school. And they said, "Anybody that's interested can take this class." And they gave you a test. If you knew where middle C was, you went in advanced. . . . So me and fourteen others went in advanced. And I'm gonna tell you, it was the most intense. . . . We were studying classical figured bass in high school.[120]

Later, as a freshman music education major at the University of Miami, McCoy took an additional year of music theory under the tutelage of Madame Renée Longy, previously one of Leonard Bernstein's teachers at the Curtis Institute, who drilled them in melodic, harmonic, and rhythmic dictation; as McCoy remarked, "When I came out of there, . . . I could take dictation of a bird up on a telephone wire."[121] McCoy's high school exposure to the fundamentals of music theory came in handy as early as his first visit to Nashville, when he struck up a conversation with Jordanaire Neil Matthews, Jr., who had a series of numbers scratched out on a legal pad using a system that would later be known internationally as the Nashville Number System.[122] As McCoy recounted, "[T]hrough the corner of my eye, I could see on his music stand like a yellow legal pad with numbers written on it. And . . . I was so distracted. I said, 'Excuse me. I want to look at this a second.' And I looked at it, and he said, 'You know what that is?' And I said, 'You know what? I think I do.' And he said, 'Well, you're the only musician around here that does.'"[123] McCoy's experience with Roman numeral analysis and figured bass was almost certainly influential in his decision to be an early adopter of the Nashville Number System and a key figure in its transmission to the rhythm section musicians in the city's studios.

One might expect that musicians who played melodic instruments or who sang may have had some formal musical training at some point during their careers, but it may be surprising to learn that one of the most significant drummers in the Nashville recording scene also took formal training before coming to Nashville to begin his career as a Nashville cat. Nashville native Murray "Buddy" Harman began working as a recording musician in the city during the early 1950s, and he contributed to recording sessions for artists not only in country music, but in rockabilly, rock and roll, pop, and jazz, during his tenure. Harman came from a musical family. His father was a bandleader of a small group with a "couple of horns," and his mother was the group's drummer. During his high school years, Harman took up the drums, playing in both the high school band and in several dance bands put together by his classmates. At the age of seventeen, he joined the US Navy, where he found himself playing with dance bands in NCO (non-commissioned officers') and officers' clubs. These early semi-professional and professional engagements undoubtedly provided him with an opportunity to learn to accompany a wide range of musicians with a fairly wide range of musical abilities, helping to make him a versatile drummer in the studio later in his career.[124]

Upon his discharge from the US Navy, Harman sought out additional musical training in Chicago. As he told interviewer Morris Levy in 1996, "After I got out of the Navy, I went to a drum school in Chicago called the Roy C. Knapp School of Percussion. And I had classes in everything: classes in theory, harmony, arranging, vibes [vibraphone], drums, to read properly, Latin drumming. . . . That made me a more well-rounded drummer."[125] The Knapp School must have been particularly good at educating aspiring percussionists, because it was able to boast not one, but two of the most widely recorded drummers in the history of recorded music. Harman was classmates with Hal Blaine, who made a name for himself as the top drummer in Los Angeles's Wrecking Crew during the 1960s and 1970s.[126] Blaine noted in a 2005 interview for *Modern Drummer* magazine that Knapp himself had an impressive pedagogical pedigree, having taught big band drummer and Benny Goodman bandmate Gene Krupa.[127] Like Blaine, Harman was a big fan of both Krupa and Buddy Rich—the two leading big band drummers of the 1940s—so the Knapp School made perfect sense for them both.[128]

Upon returning to Nashville, Harman recalled in his interview with Levy, he began to fill his schedule with club dates. Eventually, his reputation began to grow, and he was invited to join a recording session with Texas honky-tonk, western swing, and boogie-woogie pianist Moon Mullican.[129] Due to the limitations of the recording studios at that time, Harman could only use a snare drum and brushes, likely because sticks would overpower the microphones and tom-toms would not be captured clearly. Following that session, Harman began to get called for other sessions with such artists as Ray Price and Martha Carson, eventually replacing the first Nashville session drummer, Farris Coursey, when Coursey—who was also a member of Decca producer Owen Bradley's dance band—took a leave from session work to undergo much-needed back surgery.[130] Although drums were generally frowned upon in much country music of the 1950s, particularly on the *Grand Ole Opry*, Harman made significant inroads for drums in country music by adapting to the demands of the ever-changing country styles of the decade.[131] As he told Levy: "We got into that [the 'Ray Price shuffle'], and people started liking that, and they started liking hearing drums. Ones that never used drums on their record before started hearing what I was doing and thought, 'Hey, that'll be good on my record.'"[132] Fellow Nashville A Team member Harold Bradley noted that Harman's drumming stood out in comparison to Coursey's in that it was "more aggressive," which Bradley claimed was widely appealing to many Nashville recording artists.[133] In an effort "to please everybody" who came into the studio, Harman developed a wide-ranging drum style that was driving but unobtrusive and that used combinations of sticks and brushes (and sometimes one of each) to create the right sound for each artist.[134]

Like the rest of his A Team colleagues, Harman's incessant quest for formal and informal musical training and hands-on professional experiences led him to a career as a leading session musician. He was fluent in written notational traditions and harmony, and he could play both melodic and rhythmic percussion instruments, a skill that many drummers lack. As a drummer who was steeped in jazz and Latin traditions, he was able to provide a variety of rhythmic accompaniment to different kinds of singers without needing a lot of time to think of something new and original. And, as someone who had been responsible for providing the pulse for dance music, he had significantly strong timing, which he recalled was a strong point of the Nashville A Team band consisting of Floyd Cramer, Hank Garland, and Bob Moore: "Everybody had a good time feel. We didn't have hardly any rushing or dragging problems with this particular band."[135]

Formal musical training was far from a liability for the top Nashville session musicians of the Nashville Sound era. Rather, as the examples discussed here should indicate, it was a significant advantage for these musicians to have a variety of ways to talk about music and to communicate with one another. But, just as most of the Nashville A Team musicians came to sessions with a rich background in many different styles, still another very important group of musicians came into the studio with deep formal training in some of the nation's greatest conservatories: the string players. The orchestral string players who called the Nashville studios their home made some of the most lasting, if not also controversial, contributions to the Nashville sound, and with them came a deep and significant classical training. As media scholar Joli Jensen observed in her landmark book on the subject, "In the 1950s and early '60s, many believed that earlier forms of country music were more 'real' than the Nashville Sound. Yet defenders of the new Nashville Sound found a number of ways to argue that it was still 'really' country music, even if it sounded a lot like pop."[136] Jensen—along with such scholars as Barbara Ching, Aaron Fox, and Diane Pecknold—have argued convincingly that these notions of country music authenticity are intimately tied to honky-tonks, which serve as a locus of cultural expression among white working-class communities.[137] Needless to say, honky-tonks—often small, dimly lit, and full of men and women engaging in the many rituals of working-class sociability—are not necessarily hospitable sites for orchestral music, pragmatically or socially. But if we hear the string-laden country recordings that emerged from Nashville from the late 1950s forward not from the perspective of the country recording artist heard at the front and center of the mix but from the orchestral string musicians who provided necessary emotional context and amplification to these recorded performances, debates about honky-tonk authenticity become less important than those about the purity of the traditions of Western art music. As such scholars as Lawrence Levine, Ralph Locke, Christina Bashford, and Joseph Horowitz have demonstrated, the composition, performance, and consumption of western art music has been increasingly tied to racial and classed hierarchies since the mid-nineteenth century.[138] In Nashville—a city that fancied itself to be the "Athens of the South"—orchestral musicians brought the city a degree of cultural legitimacy that contact with country music culture could taint.[139] So how did Nashville's orchestral string players navigate the complex cultural landscape that was the Nashville music scene during the Nashville Sound era to establish themselves as leaders in a variety of musical settings?

The case of Sheldon "Shelly" Kurland provides some insights that might help us better address this question. Kurland, born in Brooklyn, New York, studied at Julliard and taught at Cornell University from 1956 to 1964 prior to moving to Nashville in 1964 to accept an associate professorship at George Peabody College for Teachers.[140] As concert programs from the Peabody College School of Music indicate, Kurland appeared with great regularity as a chamber musician on the Peabody campus. A program dated December 1, 1964—only months after joining the faculty—reports that he performed Beethoven's op. 9, no. 3 string trio and op. 16 piano quartet, along with a Bach sonata in A major for violin and harpsichord (likely BWV 1015). Over the next four years, he performed in several concerts sponsored by Peabody's Friends of Chamber Music, playing works by Beethoven, Bach, Mozart, Kodály, Schumann, and Brahms, among others.[141] Particularly noteworthy is a series of three concerts he offered between October 21 and 28, 1966, in which he performed all ten of Beethoven's sonatas for piano and violin.[142] Although the exact date of Kurland's first Nashville sessions is not available, Peter Cooper, in an obituary published in the *Nashville Tennessean*, notes that Kurland began playing sessions "soon" after his arrival in Nashville and that "in the late 1960s, he halted his teaching and worked full time in music."[143] Regardless, Kurland established himself as a country music session mainstay, eventually logging "thousands of sessions" as both a freelancer and as the leader of the Sheldon Kurland Strings, which he founded in 1970, and he is credited with improving the overall quality of string playing in the city's recording studios.[144] Yet, despite putting aside much of his classical playing to focus on studio work (and, later, on running the famous Bluebird Café in Hillsboro Village), he wore his classical training proudly, literally "wearing a jacket with 'Julliard' spelled out on the back, in sequins."[145] Whether worn ironically or as a symbol of pride, it is clear that Kurland understood the value of his training and took advantage of it to position himself as a leader of the Nashville session world. The recipient of several Nashville "Super Picker" Awards, Kurland is also the only orchestral string musician to be featured in Nashville's Musicians Hall of

Fame, recognition that has not been afforded some of his predecessors and collaborators.[146]

Kurland is only one of dozens of orchestral string players who brought some level of classical training to Nashville's studios during the Nashville Sound era, but he was perhaps the most entrepreneurial of them, as evidenced by his formation of the Shelly Kurland Strings. Other string players balanced a wide range of musical activities, as well as additional professional responsibilities, and saw recording as only one of many aspects of a successful life in music. Many of the city's first orchestral session musicians were drawn from the ranks of the Nashville Symphony, which was established in 1946 and which presented a regular concert series featuring orchestral warhorses and, by the early 1960s, pieces by contemporary US composers.[147] Violinist Lillian Vann Hunt, for instance, was a founding member of the Nashville Symphony Orchestra (NSO), along with her husband, clarinetist Charles Brownlow Hunt, Jr.[148] Born in Jasper, Tennessee, in 1914, Hunt was a graduate of the Cadek Conservatory in Chattanooga (now part of the University of Tennessee at Chattanooga) and studied in Nashville, Los Angeles, and New York.[149] She was also a member of the faculty of Peabody College, where she performed chamber recitals at Peabody as early as 1947 and continuing at least through 1960, and served as a staff musician on Nashville radio station WSM.[150] Hunt also served as principal second violinist in the NSO through the 1960–1961 season; from 1961 until 1967, Hunt was absent from the orchestra, a period that coincided with a demanding session schedule that found her accompanying such musicians as Jim Reeves, Patsy Cline, and other early stars of the Nashville Sound era.[151]

Similarly, cellist Byron Bach occasionally played as a chamber musician and was a regular member of the NSO beginning in 1959, drawing upon his childhood experiences as a scholarship student of Fritz Bruch, principal cellist of the Cincinnati Symphony, and, during his college years, as a member of musical ensembles at the University of Kentucky and the University of Louisville. Yet, unlike Hunt, who appears to have made a living exclusively from her music-making, Bach's early career achievements were principally in the field of chemistry, in which he held a degree from the University of Louisville. Prior to moving to Nashville in 1957 or 1958, he worked as a chemist for Goodyear in Akron, Ohio, taught high school chemistry, served as a county music director in a public school district near Cincinnati, and even as a vice president of a dental supply company.[152] In Nashville, he served as a warehouse manager for the Tobacco States Chemical Company and, within two years, was performing such works as Berlioz's *Symphonie fantastique*, Tchaikovsky's Fifth Symphony, and Howard Hanson's *Mosaics* as a section cellist with the NSO.[153] As Bach recalled in an undated typescript that appears to be his notes for a public performance and speech, it became increasingly difficult to balance his career in the chemical industry and his musical life:

> For strings, the players were either teachers or working at something else. [T]herefore the string sessions were mostly of a night.—I literally worked day and night.[.] I got to about 250 sessions a year for over 20 years—had to drop the Chemical [*sic*] business, and finally had to drop the Symphony.[154]

Yet, even with this demanding schedule, Bach managed to make time for his wife and four children. As his youngest daughter, Cathy Bach Guenther, recalled to me in a personal interview, "When I was young, he kept work—specifically session work—and home very separate. He was raised by devout Southern Baptist parents, and any of the really interesting stories, I did not hear until after I was an adult because he did not want anything . . . that was less than wholesome to sully his family. He was very much a family man."[155] As his personal ledgers show, however, such compartmentalization must have been intensely challenging, as, by the early 1970s, he was not only playing for recording sessions but was regularly appearing as a backing musician for events in the city.[156]

It is worth noting that, although the Nashville Symphony Orchestra was a primary supplier of orchestral talent to Nashville's recording studios throughout the 1960s and 1970s, many of these musicians were also deeply embedded in the world of academic music making, teaching at several of the institutions of higher education in Middle Tennessee. Violinist and Pittsburgh native Michael Semanitzky, for instance, earned both a Bachelor of Music and Master of Music from Yale prior to joining the faculty of the Memphis College of Music by his twenty-third birthday in 1952.[157] By 1957, he was an assistant professor of music at Ithaca College, a post that he left that spring to take a teaching position at Peabody College in Nashville; he later appeared on occasional Nashville sessions.[158] Similarly, violinist Solie Fott—a long-time Nashville session veteran—served on the music faculty at Austin-Peay State University in nearby Clarksville, Tennessee, from 1958 until his retirement in 2000; there, he conducted the university's orchestra, an ensemble that often included those session colleagues who played with the NSO.[159]

So, too, did violinist Brenton Bolden Banks come from the ranks of Nashville's music educators, but not from the predominantly white institutions of higher education in the city. Rather, Banks was a member of the music faculty of Tennessee State University, the Volunteer State's African American land-grant institution, from 1952 until his departure for Los Angeles in 1976.[160] Nashville historians P. J. Broume and Clay Tucker, in their book *The Other Music City: The Dance Bands and Jazz Musicians[,] 1920 to 1970*, note that Banks was appointed to teach theory, counterpoint, and form and analysis in addition to his duties as a violin teacher.[161] Tennessee State colleague W. O. Smith recalled that Banks played first violin in a faculty string quartet that toured throughout the region. As Smith reflected in his 1991 memoir:

> The quartet, which was the only string quartet associated with a black college, was [music department chair] Dr. Mells' personal pride and joy. Brenton Banks, a fine violinist and jazz pianist from the Cleveland Institute, was our first violinist, and Maureen Stovall played second violin. I played the viola, and Dave Kimbrell, a graduate student who had played bass with Duke Ellington, was our cellist. We were given rehearsal time as part of our teaching load. We had lots of fun even though our rehearsals were very serious and intense. Our repertoire was mostly Hayden [*sic*] and Mozart quartets, or the Schumann

piano quintet with a guest or faculty pianist. I will never forget the challenge of our feature selection, the Ravel Quartet in F major. . . .

As a business manager of the quartet, I booked a tour, which took us through Arkansas to Texas. We were a novelty, a black string quartet playing classical music. Later we were to play as much black music as we could get our hands on to break down the barrier between black audiences and classical music. . . . [T]o the general masses, classical music was a foreign subject. This is the point that Dr. Mells was trying to address on the TSU campus. Toward that end, we played monthly concerts on the campus, as well as appearances at Fisk University and some of the leading black churches.[162]

According to Smith, one of the pieces that the group played was a quartet written by Banks, which Smith described as "really jazzy."[163] This should come as no surprise, however, as Banks was a celebrated jazz pianist and violinist in the Nashville area, leading the Brenton Banks Quartet at the Gaslight Club.[164] Nashville jazz musician Beegie Adair recalled that, when she first encountered the Brenton Banks Quartet during the summer of 1959, she found "the first really 'grown up' group I'd ever heard, music that sounded like the records we bought. We spent hours listening to them that summer, and they would come next door to hear us . . . on their break."[165] Banks's prowess as a jazz musician was widely recognized around Music City, and in 1960, he accompanied Nashville session musicians Hank Garland, Chet Atkins, Boots Randolph, Floyd Cramer, Bob Moore, and Buddy Harman, as well as a teenaged vibraphonist named Gary Burton, to the Newport Jazz Festival for a performance that was canceled due to a riot.[166]

As a session musician, Banks was highly sought after, often performing as part of a string quartet that also included Lillian Vann Hunt. Even a cursory survey of session discographies from the 1960s reveals that Banks was an active contributor to the Nashville Sound, contributing to recordings by Jim Reeves, Patsy Cline, and Brenda Lee. Arranger, producer, and session vocalist Anita Kerr brought Banks into the session community, noting that she put him "in charge to tell them [the other string players] . . . when they are ahead of the beat or behind the beat."[167] Cline biographer Douglas Gomery has noted, as well, that Banks was particularly favored by producer and dance band leader Owen Bradley, who hired Banks to play on Cline's sessions, becoming "the de facto leader of a set of freelance players." Gomery also noted that Cline was particularly fond of Banks's work with the string musicians "because [it] . . . reminded her of the sweet Big Band [*sic*] music she had learned to love at W[ashington] & L[ee College]."[168]

Yet, as the only African American musician in Nashville's recording studios, Banks may have encountered some resistance as a consequence of his race. Leo Jackson, lead guitarist in Reeves's road band, recalled to Reeves biographer Larry Jordan that Reeves "always fussed and griped about" Banks: "He hated him. He said[,] 'the sonofabitch is never in tune. It's always one.'"[169] Banks served as the concertmaster in many of these sessions, and, Kerr told Jordan, the strings "had to do what he said. He played beautifully."[170] It is highly likely that Kerr's remarks are the more accurate description of Banks's musicianship, both because Kerr led one of the most sought-after and musically precise vocal backing groups of the Nashville Sound era and because she was also the product of extensive musical training.[171] As a leader of Nashville's African American musical community, Banks was also expected to demonstrate a high skill level in all of his work, perhaps an even higher level of mastery than his white counterparts.[172] Even more importantly, Banks served in a powerful role in the recording studio, serving as both the contractor who hired and fired string players and the first violinist on most sessions. As such, Banks's leadership and economic power may have rubbed some recording artists the wrong way, especially as Jim Crow's reign was being challenged by presumably "uppity" black Southerners.

Whether Banks was subjected to outright discrimination in the recording studio—most likely from recording artists who did not work with him on a daily basis—or not is hard to verify, but it is worth noting that one of my research consultants described Banks as looking "a little bit like Uncle Remus" from the Walt Disney film *Song of the South* and as someone who "was a really natty man about town" who could look "at the chart and finger sixteenth notes with the best of them." When pressed as to whether there was ever any awkwardness or confrontation during sessions that this consultant worked with Banks, I was informed that "racial problems, especially in Nashville, and especially in the music business, have been overblown by the Democrats, the liberals." Yet, as historian Charles Hughes has demonstrated in his recent study of race in Civil Rights–era southern recording studios, this rhetoric of racial equality and mutual affection often obscures a history of microaggression and overt racial antagonism that may be more commonly expected in the US South during the height of the Civil Rights era.[173] Moreover, Diane Pecknold has written of reports that, during a session at Shelby Singleton's Plantation Records, an African American recording artist "was confronted with a noose hanging from a microphone and a crowd of people in fake Klan hoods fashioned from pillowcases."[174]

Banks likely felt the impact of racial discrimination every time he received his pay for session labor. Leonard Morton, a fellow Nashville jazz pianist and public school music teacher and administrator, recalled that Nashville was a difficult place for African American musicians in the 1950s and 1960s because they were not permitted to join the American Federation of Musicians (AF of M) local; instead, they were required to affiliate with the black union local in Birmingham, Alabama, some two hundred miles away and had, in Morton's words, "no protection" economically.[175] Unfortunately, the records of the Nashville AF of M local from this period were destroyed, and it is unclear how well Banks was compensated for his labor and whether he received the same pay as his white colleagues. Moreover, as Nashville was the site of several significant sit-ins and other protests intended to desegregate the city, it is likely that Banks's constant travel between the worlds the Nashville jazz scene, Tennessee State University, and the Music Row studios made it nearly impossible *not* to keep race at the forefront of his mind as he participated in his own musical life.[176]

Although Banks's professional vita raises a number of questions about the ways that he negotiated the constantly shifting boundaries of race across several musical worlds, he and his fellow classically trained musicians also negotiated radically different musical expectations in various aspects of their work as freelance musicians. For instance, many of Nashville's orchestral session musicians had been rigorously trained in some of the nation's top schools of music, and, as concert programs from the NSO indicate, their participation in the orchestra often required a high degree of technical facility.[177] During the period 1955 to 1970, the orchestra performed a regular series of six concerts, as well as several summer pops series and periodic holiday performances of Handel's *Messiah*. Concert programs indicate that the NSO's repertoire was fairly typical of mid-twentieth-century orchestras, with works by Beethoven, Ravel, Debussy, Mendelssohn, and Wagner appearing regularly alongside the works of Copland, Bernstein, Hanson, Bloch, and Schuman.[178] Session work, on the other hand, could often be incredibly dull by comparison, with orchestral string players providing whole-note and half-note pads that thickened the textures of a recording, essentially playing the role of the background singers' "oohs" and "aahs." As fiddler and sometimes violinist Buddy Spicher recalled to me, he learned to read notation well enough to begin playing string sessions:

> [A]s the years went by and there were more and more strings out, people used to ask me if the fiddle's going to last in country music. And I had to answer, "I honestly don't know." It didn't look like it. So that's when I decided I got to learn to read. And so I did. . . . I was kind of in with Lillian Hunt and Brenton Banks. And so I would get the occasional session through them. . . . [T]hey were readers, but . . . it wasn't as hard back then. It was a lot of whole notes.[179]

String arrangements, too, were sometimes rudimentary because the arrangers were learning on the fly. As arranger Bergen White recounted:

> [L]earning the ranges [of the instruments] was a task for me. I remember when I was first starting, the first thing I ever wrote for strings, we were copying "Yesterday," the Beatles' "Yesterday," and I had a string quartet and a guitar. Anyway, I wrote the part just like

I heard them off the record. But anyway, when we got in to do the session, this little lady that was playing the viola, we were running through it, practicing it. I'm scared to death. She knows it, and she motions for me to come over. And I walked over, and she said, "Bergen," she pointed, she said, "I can't play that note." And I said, "Why not?" She said, "It's not on the instrument." And I said, "Well, how low can you go?" And she told me, and that's how I learned. I learned by people telling me.[180]

The "little lady . . . playing the viola," White later confirmed, was Lillian Vann Hunt, who seems to have treated White in the same way that she might treat her students at Peabody College, offering a gentle correction to an important orchestrational oversight.

Although the arrangements may have been particularly uninspiring (especially in the 1960s), session work undoubtedly taxed the classically trained musicians' musicianship. By the first years of the 1960s, most of Nashville's guitarists, bassists, pianists, and backing vocalists had adopted the so-called Nashville Number System to outline the harmonic progression and form of a song. Using Arabic numerals to signify the root of each chord, Nashville Numbers allowed rhythm section musicians to easily transpose a song to a different key to accommodate the range of the recording artist.[181] Yet the string parts for these sessions were written out in standard Western notation, a difficult notational tradition to transpose at sight. Arrangers were sometimes called upon to rewrite arrangements during a session, but it was even more common for the string players to transpose the arrangements at sight.[182] As Byron Bach's daughter Carole Ann recounted to me, Bach "had perfect pitch. . . . [H]e could adjust to the musicians who couldn't carry a note in a bucket. . . ."[183] As such, Nashville's classically trained session musicians often brought added value to the session simply by virtue of the extent of their musical training and their own pedagogical backgrounds, quickly solving problems using practical musicianship and saving the record label money in the end.

Recording sessions could occasionally be dangerous places for orchestral musicians, especially in light of the often-celebrated drug and alcohol abuse exhibited by some of the genre's biggest stars. One such instance occurred during a session with an artist who arrived at a session visibly under the influence and began to throw bottles around the studio. In protest, the musicians put their instruments in their cases and left the studio. Carole Ann Bach reflected: "[Y]ou know, the artist is the one paying for it, but, you know, these folks are, as you said, consummate professionals, and they're not going to put up with that nonsense."[184] Cathy Bach Guenther took it one step further, remarking that her father and his peers were upstanding citizens: "These were professionally trained musicians. And they were, for the most part, like anybody else, as far as having their families. They attended church. A lot of them had something on the side, maybe a music store or something else that they did."[185] That is, musicians such as Bach, Hunt, and Kurland did not necessarily *need* the session work to provide an adequate income for their families, and, in many cases, these sessions may have been aesthetically and kinesthetically unfulfilling by comparison to the complex works of the orchestral tradition they were playing with the Nashville Symphony Orchestra. As such, encounters like those with the inebriated artist suggest that orchestral musicians were able to demand respect, even from recording artists who may have enjoyed the excesses of stardom.[186] At the same time, it is important to note that the recording sessions featuring Nashville's orchestral musicians were not typically sites of class conflict; rather, one gets the sense from conversations with all of Nashville's session musicians from this era that there was a shared camaraderie among the people who were in the trenches every day and that, on occasion, bonds of friendship—or at least mutual admiration—were formed between the orchestral musicians and the recording artists whom they supported.[187]

NOTATIONAL AND COMMUNICATION CONSIDERATIONS

Considering the variety of musical experiences and backgrounds that Nashville's session musicians brought to each session (not to mention the varying skill levels and backgrounds that recording artists contributed to the work), it might be surprising that recordings could be made efficiently in Nashville in the first place. Added to the mix, as well, were recording engineers, who often brought extensive technical expertise with electronics and recording technology but who may have lacked terminology to talk about musical techniques and practices with the musicians in the room. Recording artists, too, often brought rather limited background in musical and electronic terminology, focusing their attention instead on writing and selecting repertoire that suited their voices and public personae and learning to express the meanings hidden in these songs vocally. And even more removed from the musical labor in the recording studio were the record label and publishing house executives who oversaw sessions to keep an eye on business matters (but who, nonetheless, had opinions of their own about the performances unfolding before them). Yet, as Ray Stevens recalled, these recording sessions normally unfolded as rather easygoing and collaborative affairs:

> The musicians play the song through once and discuss ideas. Someone standing in the control room can hear them "noodling" on their instruments as they work up an intro, [sic] or the lead instrumental on a break as players offer options and licks for the producer to choose from. The producer's role is to listen and decide which ideas to incorporate. The producer may say[,] "Hey, I like that—give me some more of it" or "Yeah, that's good, but try to lay back a little and let me hear it on the bridge." Most producers give the pickers an idea of what they have in mind and then the musicians give him their interpretations and the producer pulls it together.[188]

In this context, then, quick and free communication was absolutely essential, and the barriers that may have emerged as a consequence of the different kinds of musical training these musicians brought to the studio had the potential to slow the work to a crawl or to halt the production process altogether.

Photographic evidence from recording sessions seems to indicate that collaboration and shared responsibility were the norm among the musicians in the Nashville recording studios of the 1950s, 1960s, and 1970s. A photograph taken during an August 8, 1960, Roy Orbison session at RCA Victor's studio, for instance, shows a group of six orchestral string players crowded around a single microphone with their bows in playing position, while singer and arranger Anita Kerr, bassist Bob Moore, and Orbison himself stand behind them (Figure 2.1). Lillian Vann Hunt is making direct eye contact with Orbison, whose mouth is slightly open, perhaps in the middle of singing a line from one of the songs they were preparing to record. This nonverbal communication could help the string section mimic Orbison's phrasing, adding nuance to the written notation that is placed on the stands in front of them. Moreover, Moore—in his likely role as the bandleader for this session—is turned with his right ear

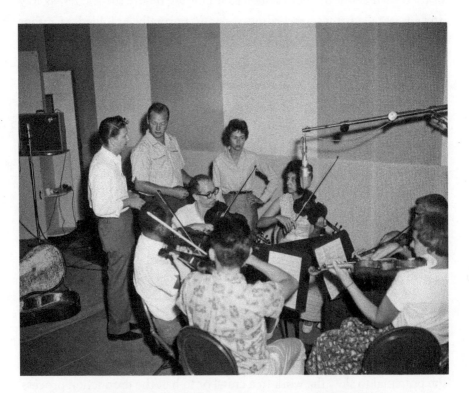

Figure 2.1. Roy Orbison session at RCA Studio B, C, August 8, 1960. L-R, standing: Orbison, Bob Moore, Anita Kerr. Lillian Vann Hunt (facing) and Brenton Banks (two seats away) are in the string section.
Photo by Elmer Williams, courtesy of the Country Music Hall of Fame® and Museum.

toward Orbison, as if to hear him better. As Moore does not have his bass in hand and no microphones are placed near Orbison, Moore, or Kerr, this photograph was most likely taken during an in-session rehearsal, when important musical ideas needed to be communicated quickly so that the recording could begin. As such, the deliberate effort to work out minute details with as few words as possible was vital to a successful session.[189]

Attitudes toward and fluency in various traditions of musical notation undoubtedly formed one significant communication barrier as musicians entered the studio. Many of the rhythm section musicians were unable to read musical notation and, prior to the widespread adoption of the Nashville Number System in the early 1960s, often struggled to convey chord changes using conventional letter names, while orchestral musicians, backing vocalists, and some—but not all—pianists could read musical notation fluently. Although some session musicians—including bassist Lightnin' Chance and fiddler Buddy Spicher—took music theory courses or worked through theory tutorials to learn to read musical notation (and gain access to session work that required notational fluency, as a consequence), Nashville session musicians communicated using different vocabularies for the most part. The Nashville Number System alleviated some of these issues, as well, as the Arabic numerals used in the system translate well into the Roman numeral system used in much classically oriented pedagogy.

Because they were responsible for scoring string and wind parts with a rhythm section, Nashville's arrangers were placed in the crucial role of mediating these multilingual conversations. Arranger Bergen White, for instance, recalled a Chuck Woolery session during which communications proved to be particularly challenging:

We were doing it at Columbia Studio B, and it's full rhythm section with strings. So in a case like that, I knew because I wrote the chart, I knew where I had strings doing things, but as far as writing licks, it's like I said a while ago, unless I had something playing with somebody, I'd let these guys kind of do what they do. So anyway, but I would write section A, I'd say electric guitar fill. Then section B,

I'd say steel, and then maybe piano later. . . . We're running through this [sic] things, where I've got the strings kind of busy doing stuff, Grady is picking just all over the top of it and in a place where I didn't have, where Grady's not supposed to be playing. He's supposed to be filling there. And it's just an absolute train wreck. Grady's playing electric guitar, and Buddy Emmons, who's a marvelous steel player, was playing steel, and they're sitting there right across from each other. So Norro punches the button and says, "Bergen, come here." So I went in the control room and he said, "Man, it's too busy in there." I said, "Well, Grady's not supposed to be playing right there." And he said, "Well, tell him." And I said, "Ok." So I went back out and said, "Hey guys, right here, Grady, the strings are doing this." And I said, "It's kind of busy right there." And I'm trying to say it kind of soft, you know. Anyway, [we] ran through it again, and Grady doesn't play anything, anywhere. The places where I said to play an electric fill, he doesn't play there and he doesn't play the other place. And Norro says, "What happened? There's nothing happening." So I went to Grady and said, you know, "Hey I need you to play in these places, but just kind of lay off right here." And Grady looks over at Buddy Emmons, and he says, "Buddy, we only *play* where it's *designated* to play."[190]

Arrangers were often forced to work quickly to rewrite string and wind parts for reading musicians when an arrangement was not effective and likely also rewrote some parts when singers needed to change keys to accommodate their voices, as well. After years of practical experience, however, it was just as common for the orchestral musicians to transpose their written parts on the fly, as well, and rhythm section musicians adopted the Nashville Number System to communicate about harmonies more clearly. [191]

Nashville's recording studios were sites in which session musicians, recording artists, producers, arrangers, and songwriters regularly negotiated the complex cultural politics of the mid-twentieth-century US South. As ethnomusicologist Louise Meintjes's research on South African recording sessions reminds us, musicians in the recording studio work within "two intersecting political planes": (1) "the micro-politics of studio interaction," which includes power structures that shape the sounds of a recording and "the division of labour in the studio," and (2) the "political dynamics of the historically specific moment and place," which includes broader concerns related to "social practices and values about race, ethnicity, class[,] and gender."[192] Nashville Sound–era session musicians may have collaborated on tens of thousands of recordings (several hundred of which went on to reach the *Billboard* charts), but the power afforded to each musician varied widely. For instance, the orchestral musicians— who were, by most estimates, the most highly trained contributors to Nashville Sound–era sessions—were typically directed to play the notation in front of them, while rhythm section players who learned their trade through long-term apprenticeships with road bands and radio programs were free to improvise parts as they saw fit. Of course, classically trained musicians—particularly orchestral string players—may very well have accepted their roles with no concern, as the experience of working under a record producer may not have differed much from responding to the aesthetic vision of an orchestra conductor.[193] At the same time, session musicians who were forged in the crucible of road and radio work may have also been intimidated by the cultural baggage that is often associated with classical training and offered a degree of deference to the string players who accompanied them in their daily work. In fact, all of the session musicians and arrangers that I have spoken with in my fieldwork have spoken very highly of the musicianship and professionalism that classically trained musicians such as Kurland, Banks, Hunt, and Bach brought to their work. But, at the same time, it is worth noting that orchestral musicians were, in some ways, interlopers in the recording studio, appearing on only a fraction of sessions during the long Nashville Sound era; the stable of guitarists, bassists, pianists, and backing vocalists worked together much more frequently, often for nine hours or more each day, five or six days a week.[194] Moreover, by the 1970s, string sessions were often conducted separately from rhythm section and vocal sessions, literally marginalizing orchestral session musicians to a different time and place. String sessions were, quite simply, not the norm and thus highlight the collision of musical cultures that must have occurred in these relatively infrequent events.[195]

By the same token, Nashville's session musicians were undoubtedly affected by the macro-political landscape of the mid-century United States and, in particular, the South. As members of the NSO, performers in various chamber music series, and educators in the city's institutions of higher education, orchestral session musicians were directly involved in teaching their audiences and their students about the values of art music and enculturating them into the decidedly classed world of music appreciation.[196] Moreover, as the cases of Lillian Vann Hunt and Brenton Bolden Banks suggest, the gender and racial politics of the South may also have exerted an influence on these musicians' daily activities.

Nashville Sound–era recording sessions were complicated events, drawing together musicians with a diverse range of musical skill sets, professional experiences, and vocabularies. Looking at discographies from this period, we can see radio barn dance veterans playing alongside members of the NSO to accompany a vocalist who learned to sing by listening to the radio. Although the legend and lore exemplified by John Sebastian's "Nashville Cats" suggests that these sessions unfolded effortlessly and the pervading "four sides per three-hour session" would seem to confirm such stories, Nashville sessions were anything but natural. Certainly, it is to the benefit of those who are in search of country music's Sasquatch-like "authenticity" to promote such legends, but these legends also work to obscure the significance of Nashville's diverse musical community in crafting recorded country music in the city. Moreover, while rhythm section musicians—for whom I have great respect and admiration—have been honored by the Country Music Hall of Fame and Museum and the Musicians Hall of Fame, their classically oriented colleagues have been ignored for such honors, despite extensive lobbying on the part of some of their family members (including the children of Byron Bach).[197] By accounting for their work, we can complicate our understanding of what happened in the tens of thousands of recording sessions in which this comparatively small cadre of session musicians participated. For it will only be when we consider the recording studio as a space in which complicated and often fraught relationships and ideologies are played out on tape that we can begin to understand the significance of their contributions.[198]

Musical Branding, Artist Identity, and the Nashville Sound

he mid-1950s emergence of the so-called Nashville Sound in country music is frequently described as the moment when country
music lost its innocence. According to the popular narrative, the
Nashville Sound era was a time during which country record producers
and other Nashville music industry executives were forced to save country music, which faced a rock and roll "onslaught," in the words of media
scholar Joli Jensen, or to use folklorist Bill Ivey's terminology, a "rock 'n'
roll crisis."[1] From this perspective, the emergence of a youth audience—
particularly a young, white, and southern audience—that was not interested in purchasing country recordings, playing them on jukeboxes, or
attending live performances featuring country recording artists had the
potential to destroy the still nascent Nashville country music industry.[2]
As the "rock 'n' roll crisis" narrative suggests, country music was only able
to survive by compromising the core values and audiences that had kept
it going since the 1920s. From this perspective, Nashville record producers and A&R men forced country recording artists to compromise their

Nashville Cats. Travis D. Stimeling, © Oxford University Press (2020). Oxford University Press.
DOI: 10.1093/oso/9780197502815.001.0001

musical values by pushing them to disavow the fiddles, steel guitars, and twangy vocals that had characterized the music of some of the genre's biggest stars in order to ensure that country music would remain a viable vehicle for cultural expression and a source of revenue for Nashville publishers as rock and roll drew away young people. (Of course, this narrative conveniently overlooks the remarkably successful pop-oriented musicians who also thrived in hillbilly music in the pre-rock 'n' roll era.)[3]

This narrative can be found in a wide range of sources, from scholarly histories of country music to the reflections of long-time Nashville music executives. As venerable country music historian Bill C. Malone remarked in his landmark history *Country Music, USA*, for instance:

> Country singers hoped to place themselves as well as their songs on the popular music charts. "Crossing over," as it would ultimately be called, would be achieved with great frequency in the following years, but not without radical changes in the stylistic structure of both instrumentation and singing. Country musicians and singers adapted their sounds to fit the tastes of popular music devotees who refused to accept the traditional country styles. These changes, which brought grief to many supporters and joy to others, made country music a billion-dollar industry and completely "revolutionized" the popular music world.[4]

Similarly, Nashville music industry executive Joe Allison critiqued singer Marty Robbins's sessions with the Ray Conniff Singers in a 1994 oral history for the Country Music Hall of Fame and Museum, arguing: "That's going too far, as far as I'm concerned. That's reaching, trying to get into the pop field. Now, his A&R people would try that. They'd try a lot of things to get him to cross over into the pop charts, and that was trying to reach for sales."[5]

This issue of "crossover" was one that fascinated leaders in all sectors of the music industry during the 1950s and, arguably, continues to be a significant concern for popular musicians in the present day. In the racialized and classed logics of the twentieth-century US popular music industry, the music of black artists and rural white artists were treated as idiosyncratic "Others" to a popular mainstream that reached a demographic that transcended socioeconomic and geographic—but not gender—boundaries.[6] In this state of presumed racelessness and classlessness, the popular mainstream was frequently cast as less vital, less authentic, and less expressive than its Othered counterparts, a white-bread mass product that, in catering to everyone, spoke to no one in particular.[7] And, perhaps even more importantly, this pop mainstream has frequently been seen as the province of women who presumably had no taste and were willing to consume whatever was put in front of them, further making crossover efforts suspect to critics and historians.[8] As a consequence, the class-inflected sounds of Hank Williams's MGM releases from the early 1950s and the racially inflected music of Little Richard's Imperial releases from the mid- to late 1950s have been treated as more virile and expressive than covers of those same songs made by pop artists such as Tony Bennett and Pat Boone.[9]

Contemporary reportage and music industry histories, on the other hand, often point to crossover appeal as one of the markers of great success, especially from the 1950s onward. Crossing over meant increased financial gain, as a song that might hit in the country field would undoubtedly sell significantly fewer copies than one that reached the pop mainstream, and pop crossover would have resulted in higher yields for music publishers (and sometimes artists and record labels, as well).[10] Certainly, there are numerous examples of white artists "covering" the sales of African American musicians by releasing their own recordings of a song and cashing in on the pop marketplace, an act that systematically disempowered black musicians and the labels that recorded their music.[11] (African American covers of country material, on the other hand, sometimes struggled to make sense to every market, as Diane Pecknold's discussion of Ray Charles's 1962 album *Modern Sounds in Country and Western Music* reveals.)[12] But, for music publishers and songwriters, covers and crossover hits generated additional royalties and provided an important source of revenue that allowed these businesses to grow.[13]

Of course, in the realm of popular music, commerce is seldom seen as a force that improves the expressive capacity of a musical work or style. In fact, commercial success is more commonly seen as a force that reduces the power of musical expression, a force that requires musicians to compromise their artistic vision for the sake of increased sales.[14] Undoubtedly, the dramatic changes that were made to the sounds of country music in the mid-1950s raised concerns among longtime fans of the genre, who sometimes expressed their frustrations and fears that country music would no longer speak to their experiences. But, as Pecknold has demonstrated in her remarkable study of the country music industry's centralization in this era, the country music fan base was also changing during this period, becoming increasingly urban and suburban, as well as increasingly middle class. As such, country music of the Nashville Sound era can be heard not simply as chasing a dollar, but as changing in parallel with its core audience, while also expanding its popularity regionally, nationally, and even internationally.[15]

Concerns about the changing musical aesthetics of country music in the Nashville Sound era have exaggerated the similarities between mainstream popular music of the 1950s and 1960s and Nashville country music productions, as well as the apparent homogenizing forces that pop crossover aspirations had on the genre. For instance, in a 1982 essay titled "Commercialization and Tradition in the Nashville Sound," former Country Music Foundation director Bill Ivey criticized writers who, like Malone, have focused primarily on "the graft[ing] of pop clichés onto country music," noting that Nashville Sound–era country is sonically distinct from much of its pop counterparts.[16] At the same time, though, Ivey casts the Nashville Sound as one that is fairly homogeneous and identifiable through "instrumentation alone."[17] Other writers, too, have pointed to the high profile that classically oriented string ensembles and backing vocal groups had in the recordings that were produced in Nashville during this time, suggesting that, in all cases, steel guitars and fiddles were replaced by less marked sound-alikes. Although numerous recordings do, indeed, support such assertions, a broader examination of country music recordings made in Nashville during the 1950s and 1960s reveals a remarkable heterogeneity of musical style that complicates—and, in many cases, undermines—this narrative of homogeneity.

Close listening to country music recorded in Nashville during the late 1950s and 1960s suggests that such broad characterizations of the Nashville sound obscure important distinctions between the styles created around individual recording artists. These differences were most likely the consequence of a deliberate effort to create identifiable musical brands for leading recording artists. Again, as Nashville session guitarist Harold Bradley reflected in a 1991 interview: "When people say the Nashville Sound, you know, singularly, I think they're wrong, because it should be plural. Everybody that's heavy has had their sound. . . . [I]f we had had only one sound, I think we'd have been out of business a long time ago."[18] Similarly, fiddler Buddy Spicher, who began playing in Nashville in the late 1950s, recalled that it was common to rehearse the session musicians in advance of the session for "the early artists who had their own sound like, for example, Ray Price or Kitty Wells. Maybe not Faron [Young], but Hank Snow, Bill Monroe. . . ."[19] Statements such as these challenge the notion that the Nashville Sound was a homogenous one, a belief that irritated long-time session multi-instrument instrumentalist Charlie McCoy, who remarked: "We used to get a bad rap in *Rolling Stone*. 'Oh, Nashville. It's a music factory. All day, it's like cookie-cutter music they turn out.' "[20] At the same time, these statements indicate that Nashville's producers and session musicians were aware that radio listeners and record buyers expected brand consistency from their favorite recording artists.[21] Responding to what Jensen has described as "the new radio-record environment" in national popular music, many country recording artists, producers, and session musicians appear to have turned toward what musicologist Mark Samples has described as "musical branding" to distinguish individual recording artists from one another while simultaneously balancing consistency and variety to attract radio listeners and record buyers to their product.[22]

To explore the role that musical branding may have played in Nashville Sound–era country music, this chapter explores the ways that Nashville session musicians crafted unique sounds for the recording artists they accompanied and considers the effects that these identifiable musical brands had on the marketing of those recordings to radio stations and record buyers during the Nashville Sound era. In so doing, this chapter considers session musicians as collaborators, co-creators, and co-authors in the production of musical brands and challenges the notion that session musicians were themselves little more than automatons working on an assembly line to produce music that all sounded alike. Following Jensen's examination of producer Owen Bradley's role in creating identifiable "Patsy Cline songs," this chapter focuses on the recorded oeuvres of several iconic Nashville Sound–era recording artists to demonstrate the ways that songwriters, backing musicians, and recording practices were marshaled to create a cohesive and iconic musical style that would distinguish one artist from another while ensuring some consistency of sound in the emergent all-country radio format.[23] Taken together, these case studies will provide important new insights into the ways that Nashville Sound–era musicians navigated the new commercial pressures of the 1950s and 1960s and will shed light on some of the specific ways that musicians displayed their creativity in recording sessions.[24]

Before doing so, though, it is worthwhile to take a moment to consider the role of jukeboxes and radio broadcasting in shaping the reception of country music during the Nashville Sound era. These two mediums were the principal venues through which country artists engaged with country music in the decades following World War II, with record purchases trailing behind. As Jeffrey Lange has noted, the war accelerated the jukebox's popularity, and in the immediate aftermath of the war, jukeboxes in cities in the Northern United States were increasingly filled with country records.[25] Jukeboxes offered club owners a cheaper alternative to live music, Lange argues, helping "coin machine operators . . . [to become] the country music industry's biggest consumers and suppliers of music."[26] Radio, which had been a significant venue for the performance of live country music in the prewar era, increasingly turned to commercial recordings to fill the broadcasting day by the mid-1950s, as well. Replacing the stars of live radio performances were "disc jockeys," a group of almost exclusively male broadcasters who played the role of entertainer and tastemaker, creating interesting promotions and gimmicks to keep people listening between the recordings that they selected to share with their listeners.[27] A number of authors have pointed to the significant role that disc jockeys played in popularizing rhythm and blues and early rock and roll in the late 1940s and early 1950s, and contemporary observers were so concerned about the role that these figures played in shaping the musical tastes of young people—and introducing them to "unacceptable" music—that disc jockeys were the subjects of numerous sermons, protests, and even congressional hearings.[28]

Even as radio stations began to embrace the disc jockey model, they were still, for the most part, broadcasting a remarkably diverse range of musical styles over the course of a single broadcast day—and certainly over the span of an entire week. Much as contemporary public radio affiliates divide their days between news programs, talk shows, and specialized musical programs, so, too, did these postwar radio stations maintain a diverse program schedule in an attempt to reach out to as many different audience segments as possible.[29] But, by the mid-1950s, a new approach to radio broadcasting was emerging: the format radio station. As Eric Weisbard has argued, format radio "created . . . multiple mainstreams: distinct, if at times overlapping, cultural centers."[30] Weisbard notes that these "formats did not idealize culture; they sold it. They structured eclecticism rather than imposing aesthetic values. It was the customer's money—a democracy of whatever moved people."[31] Similarly, Ron Rodman has suggested that "the format system has made radio a unique and distinctive medium in the United States and the world, enabling station owners and managers to identify, recruit, cater to, and even communicate with a well-defined audience."[32]

Format radio thrives in the tension between unpredictability and regularity. One of the earliest radio formats in the United States—Top 40—was developed by radio programmer Ted Storz after World War II, reportedly in response to watching waitresses fill jukeboxes with coins in order to hear the same songs over and over.[33] As such, the recordings that were played on format radio stations needed to retain a degree of musical interest (perhaps created by memorable melodies or interesting rhythmic hooks), while also providing a limited number of new recordings that could keep the playl-ists (known as "rotations") fresh.[34] As Rodman suggests, "as a contractual system, the radio format system is a nexus point where broadcasters and producers are both active in the formation and production of musical for-mats. Audiences are selective about what format(s) they listen to, while station managers, producers, and DJs all do their part to cultivate a loyal and attentive audience."[35] Country radio audiences—like radio audiences for the other dominant formats of the 1950s and 1960s—came to expect disc jockeys and program directors to select recordings that spoke to local and regional tastes while also introducing them to new material that was only moderately disruptive to the station's overall identity. As such, record producers became increasingly sensitive to these demands and worked to create music that met those audience expectations on both a broad level and on the level of individual artist identities.

Country record producers were rather sensitive to radio and jukeboxes on a more general level, as well, noting that the technological limitations of the playback formats required some adaptation in the studio. Harold Bradley, for instance, remarked that the creation of his iconic "tic-tac bass" sound arose in large part from the rather weak bass playback on transis-tor radios and the speakers mounted inside the doors and dashboards of automobiles. Heard prominently in the recordings of Patsy Cline, among many others, Bradley's tic-tac bass—played on a Danelectro electric bass—doubled the acoustic upright bass line to accentuate it, but not overtake it completely. As he told interviewer John Rumble:

> [W]e had the bass guitar, which Owen really loved, and I played that. He loved it because I played it. He'd already figured it out. The acoustic bass didn't record evenly. Some of the notes would drop out, and so, naturally, it would drop out on the radio, and that note would come out on the radio as a kind of a bass. So it reinforced whatever the bass was doing.[36]

He went on to explain that the doubling between the electric and acoustic bass was not always an exact doubling, but could instead be understood as a complementary doubling in which the two bassists worked together to fill in all the parts, as he noted in discussing his work on Cline's iconic recording of "Crazy":

JOHN RUMBLE: And you were doubling the acoustic bass?

HAROLD BRADLEY: Yeah, that's a great question, because what I was going to say, yes and no, I was doubling it. He [bassist Bob Moore] was only playing [beats] one and three. But I was able to play the in-between notes, [hums], stuff like that. With the click in that, it wasn't overwhelming. If you played that on the bass, the sound was like shooting off a cannon in the low end because it's so powerful and dominating, so I could keep the record interesting even when there were no fills, by playing a little connecting-up stuff. Also, I could give him [Owen] a note that would reproduce on the radio.[37]

Producer Billy Sherrill, too, recalled sending recordings to disc jockeys prior to releasing them so he could tell if they would sound good on the medium. As he remarked to journalist Marc Myers, when he was producing Tammy Wynette's 1968 Epic single "Stand by Your Man," he "sent an acetate disc to a disc-jockey friend at WKDA in Nashville and asked him to play it. He agreed to do that for me, and when the time came for it to air, I went out and sat in my black 1953 Buick to listen on the radio. When I heard the song, I loved its snap."[38]

Radio airplay and jukebox spins created opportunities for listeners to become intimately familiar with the musical brands of their favorite artists. In helping to create these brands, many session musicians found their datebooks filling with subsequent studio engagements with the same artists in the hope that they could recreate those sounds and ensure continued success. At the same time, when a particular brand began to grow stale and yield fewer spins on radio and jukeboxes, some of these same musicians were often called upon to create an entirely different musical brand, while still others were hired to forge new paths with established artists. The next section, then, turns to the role that Nashville session musicians played in shaping and reproducing musical brands, first by looking at

several artists who enjoyed extensive chart success and then by considering a recording artist who struggled to make commercial headway in the
Nashville system: Willie Nelson.

SESSION MUSICIANS AND THE MAKING
OF MUSICAL BRANDS

By the very nature of their jobs, session musicians must be exceptionally
knowledgeable of a wide range of musical styles and must call up a variety of techniques and sound concepts almost immediately. In talking with
session musicians of the Nashville Sound era, it became clear that they had
developed a refined and nuanced understanding of the intricate details
that distinguished one recording artist's work from another. But, rather
than focusing on lyrical themes or other characteristics of the songs that
each artist wrote or performed, they tended to home in on specific details
of instrumentation, arrangement, and performance practice. Buddy
Spicher recalled, for instance, that "Jean Shepard had her own sound. She
recorded mostly on the West Coast. Her sound was a muted fiddle, [devel-
oped by] Jelly Sanders. . . . He was kind of a Tommy Jackson out on the
West Coast. And I don't know who the guitar player was, probably somebody famous. But he would double that fiddle on his bass strings. Well,
that gave a very unique, special sound to Jean."[39] Just as commonly, session
musicians recalled sound concepts by invoking the names of the session
musicians who played on a specific recording, calling for a "Chet [Atkins]
sound" or a "Floyd [Cramer] sound." For instance, Charlie McCoy noted
that, in his 1965 debut session with Bob Dylan (which generated a recording of Dylan's "Desolation Row"), he "was playing a very poor imitation
of Grady Martin['s] classical guitar sound," a sound heard most prominently on Marty Robbins's 1959 hit single "El Paso."[40] Similarly, when
Billy Walker recorded "Cross the Brazos at Waco" for Columbia in 1964,
producer Don Law hired Martin to play lead in a clear effort to evoke
Robbins's chart hit.[41] Session musicians, then, maintained a remarkably
diverse stylistic vocabulary, often relating a particular technique or sound

concept to a specific recording and the musicians who played on it. At the same time, these musicians also maintained a core repertoire that would allow them to discuss their stylistic goals and objectives through shared reference points.

Discographical information for Nashville Sound–era recording sessions provides valuable insight into the different configurations of musicians who accompanied specific artists. Corporate records have provided much of the information that is found in these published discographies (many of which can be found in the extensive liner notes published with the German record label Bear Family's exceptional reissue box sets), but they often only tell the story of who played on the session, without documenting what exactly they contributed to each recording. This especially becomes an issue when several guitarists were hired for the same session, leaving it unclear who played lead, rhythm, and tic-tac (or another plucked string instrument such as the banjo, resonator guitar, or mandolin). Union timecards filed at the end of each recording session also provide documentation of the musicians who played on each recording session, but they, too, offer no insights into what specific musical contributions each made. Moreover, the Nashville Federation of Musicians regularly purged these timecards, leaving documentation of recording sessions only after 1970.[42] As such, scholars must also look to oral histories as a valuable data source to corroborate the details of specific recording sessions and to consider more fully the ways that these musicians contributed to the musical brands of individual recording artists.

That Nashville session musicians became so closely associated with the sound of a particular recording artist or style of playing reveals a great deal about the nature of their work. In fact, their success pairing with a particular artist—or even an entire roster of artists—often helped to guarantee them regular employment, maintaining several "accounts" (steady gigs) with different artists and producers. As the Nashville recording scene grew in the 1960s and an increasing number of labels brought artists from other fields to record there, those session musicians with established accounts often found it difficult to make time for new work, creating opportunities for other musicians to enter into the studio system. As these new musicians entered the field, though, they needed to be competent in the established country styles and capable of creating new sounds, as well. This tension can be witnessed firsthand in the dramatization of a Nashville recording session seen in Robert Altman's 1975 film *Nashville*, in which singer Haven Hamilton (played by Henry Gibson) calls for the producer to fire the pianist, "Dog," when he makes a couple of mistakes, saying, "When I ask for Pig [presumably Hargus 'Pig' Robbins], I want Pig. Now you get me Pig, and we'll ready to record this hit."[43] Recording artists are often at their most vulnerable while in the recording studio, and the musical competence and interpersonal skills of the session musicians often work to put them at ease as they venture out into new creative territory. It should not be surprising, then, that session musicians often maintained long relationships with specific recording artists, often cutting several albums over the course of many years together, simultaneously reinforcing their comfort in the studio and accentuating the artist's musical brand.

Among the more demanding recording artists to work in Nashville during the Nashville Sound era was Jim Reeves, a Texas native and former star of Shreveport's *Louisiana Hayride*.[44] Known among his fans and his colleagues alike as "Gentleman Jim," his resonant baritone voice and dapper fashion sense echoed the upwardly mobile class aspirations of many Southerners in the postwar years, and for a period of nearly fourteen years, he dominated the *Billboard* country charts, scoring eleven number-one hits and more than forty top-ten hits during that time. Five of those number-one recordings were posthumous releases, coming in the wake of his July 1964 death in a tragic plane crash outside of Nashville.[45] Much like his contemporary Patsy Cline, who also died in a plane crash in 1963, Reeves's music came to define the Nashville Sound for many listeners, not only at the time, but through reissue packages that continue to be sold on television infomercials to the present day.

Like many future Nashville Sound stars, Reeves's recording career began on a small independent label and in a number of studios, including one owned by Dallas, Texas, producer Jim Beck, who served as an important conduit to connect Texan musicians with Don Law at Columbia Records in Nashville.[46] As Colin Escott has noted, sessions for Reeves's first hit recordings for Abbott Records—including the number-one hit he had with Mitchell Torok's "Mexican Joe"—were held during the late-night/ early-morning hours at KWKH in Shreveport, a setting that allowed Reeves to develop familiarity with the leading broadcast microphone of the day. "The studio had a board with six inputs," Escott observes, "which didn't put it at the forefront of studio technology, but certainly made it serviceable for a hillbilly band without drums. Jim quickly learned to love the RCA 44BX ribbon microphones that KWKH used; he found they imparted a warmth to his voice, and he made a point of using them on future sessions."[47] Such an exacting attention to detail would become even more evident as his career developed and as he demonstrated the ability to generate record sales for a major label following his move to RCA Victor in 1955.

When Reeves signed with RCA Victor, he had already established a clear musical brand for himself. Recording with musicians living in the Shreveport area, Reeves played to a Texan identity, recording songs with western themes, such as Sons of the Pioneer songwriter Tim Spencer's "Padre of Old San Antone" and "Mexican Joe," which makes use of many of the border tropes heard in cowboy songs of the 1930s.[48] It is likely that Reeves was signed to RCA Victor on the basis of his success with western-oriented songs and that A&R man Steve Sholes had hoped to market Reeves in that manner. Not surprisingly, Reeves continued in this vein for two years after joining RCA Victor, cutting such tunes as the Bob Wills standard "Roly Poly" and Jimmie Rodgers's "Waiting for a Train" in 1956.[49] These early RCA Victor sessions were played by a rather eclectic group of Nashville session musicians, each of which brought strong honky-tonk and western swing influences to their work. Fiddler Tommy Jackson appeared on Reeves's first four RCA Victor sessions, where he was joined by Tommy Vaden and Dale Potter to create the twin fiddle sound that was so popular in honky-tonk and western swing. The steel guitar, too, was prominent in these recordings, played by a rotating cast of Bobby Garrett, Basil Burnette, Don Helms, and Jimmy Day. Lead and rhythm guitarists, bassists, and drummers were equally fluid in this work, making it obvious that, as Reeves was establishing himself as a recording artist, he did not have a consistent group of musicians with which to craft a distinctive sound.[50] At the same time, it could be argued that Reeves's musical brand at the time was rather interchangeable with that of many recording artists in the country field at the time. Honky-tonk and western swing were, after all, the bread and butter of the Nashville recording industry from the late 1940s through the late 1950s.

Reeves may very well have remained a solid jukebox favorite had he maintained his musical brand as a western-oriented singer, but his legacy as one of the genre's top recording artists of all time arguably would not have been cemented without a radical revision of his musical output and public image in 1957.[51] It was at this time that Reeves began to develop a pop-oriented approach to his recording practice, repertoire selection, and vocal production that helped him stand out from the crowded field of honky-tonk singers on jukeboxes and radio stations across the United States.[52] This new approach can be first heard in a February 7, 1957, Chet Atkins–produced session that included long-time Reeves sideman Floyd Cramer on piano and the Jordanaires as a backing vocal group. This session generated one single, "Four Walls" b/w "I Know (and You Know)" (RCA Victor 20/47-6974), which spent eight weeks in the number-one position on the *Billboard* country charts and reached the number eleven position on the *Billboard* pop charts in 1957.[53] "Four Walls," which Escott describes as "the first great Nashville Sound record," was recorded only sixteen days prior to Ferlin Husky's re-recording of "Gone," which has been widely considered the first recording in the Nashville Sound style.[54] Husky's recording was on the *Billboard* country charts for twenty-seven weeks in 1957, and Reeves's "Four Walls"—released on April 29, 1957—was there for twenty-six weeks. Both recordings reached number one, sharing the honor for a total of fourteen weeks that year.[55] Also on the charts was Patsy Cline's "Walkin' after Midnight" (Decca 30221), which peaked at number two and stayed on the charts for nineteen weeks.[56]

Reeves was actively involved in the decision-making process in preparation for the "Four Walls" session, hiring the musicians and expecting rehearsals in advance of the session itself. Rehearsals were not unheard of in the Nashville recording community in the first postwar decade, but they were not very common either.[57] Rather, as has been well documented here and elsewhere, sessions were quite commonly arranged on the fly in the studio in an effort to reduce the amount of time—and, therefore, money—spent in the production of the recording. Yet, Reeves not only rehearsed the group; he called for specific accompanists, as well. As producer Chet Atkins recalled, "Jim liked my guitar sound and wanted me to play the introduction and bridge. He also wanted the Jordanaires, and I called and couldn't get them. Jim said he wanted that sound, so we moved the session back to when we could get them. He also wanted to rehearse that song, and we were both working on WSM, and we arranged to rehearse 'Four Walls' one evening after the radio programme [sic]. The Jordanaires were there, too."[58]

Just as important as the accompaniment, though, was Reeves's own well-developed microphone technique—a technique he likely honed while working in the KWKH studio in Shreveport and most likely rehearsed in advance of the session—and his preparation of the songs to be recorded in any given session. Extensive photographic evidence indicates that Reeves often worked with the RCA ribbon microphones that were commonly used in broadcast settings, as well as several high-quality (possibly Neumann) condenser microphones.[59] As Atkins recalled:

> At that time, we had an engineer from New York who was from the old school[,] and he didn't believe in artists getting too close to the microphone in case they popped a "p" into it. Jim wanted an intimate sound and wanted to get real close and whisper the lyrics, and he had many arguments with this engineer. Then it so happened he left, and we recorded "Four Walls" with Selby Coffeen . . . [RCA Nashville head] Steve Sholes was amazed. He said, "How did you get that beautiful vocal sound?"[60]

Similarly, songwriter Tommy Hill, who observed the "Four Walls" session, recounted that Reeves "recorded roughly two inches from the microphone. . . . [H]e knew how to control the air hitting the mike. He would turn his head when he was hitting a 'p' or something that had the air-pressure. He would work that mike when he was recording."[61] We can hear this approach in many—but not all—of Reeves's recordings from 1957 until his death, including 1958's "Precious Memories," 1961's "Danny Boy," 1962's "Blue Skies," and, perhaps most famously, 1959's "He'll Have to Go."[62] Anita Kerr, who provided backing vocals and arrangements for many of Reeves's post–"Four Walls" recordings, recalled that Reeves was also always prepared for his recording sessions, noting that, even under time constraints, "He always knew his songs very well, [sic] and had wonderful vocal control."[63]

Unlike most Nashville vocal artists, Reeves is credited as the bandleader for his RCA Victor sessions, revealing the respect that he commanded in the recording studio—a result, in part, of his decision to dress in business attire and to address session musicians in a professional manner—and the control that he maintained over the recording sessions themselves.[64] As Kerr recalled, Reeves "was always very nice to work with, extremely quiet. He was a quiet man. He sang very softly[,] and he did demand quietness in the studio. He didn't like it if people were noisy. Maybe it messed up his concentration. He was always nice about it. I can't think of one time that I've ever heard him raise his voice or look like he was going to."[65] Such practices were not uncommon when Reeves was in the studio. As Royce Morgan—former guitarist for Reeves's road band, the Blue Boys—recounted to John Rumble, Reeves

wanted everything to be perfect, and he wanted the players to be perfect. He always used the best players he could get. Even some that thought they should be on there, they were not his choice, and I won't go into that, but he had his own ideas about who played what the best, and he always would have Chet to get these people to work.

Chet would just more or less turn Jim loose in the studio. If Jim got hung up on something, he'd say, "What do you think, Chet?" But that was very rare. Jim would do his thing, and did it quite well, as we all know. And the players, you know. In that, I'm saying that he was way ahead of his time, because he always had drums, light drums. Nice changes. Great choruses, if there was a chorus. If he needed a chorus, he would critique it to his own taste. He and Chet were a very dynamic duo at that time in the studio.[66]

Many of the musicians seemed to appreciate Reeves's taskmaster approach, including guitarist Velma Smith, who was called to play on her first Reeves session on September 4, 1958.[67] As her cousin Suzi Burgher Payne recounted:

> [S]he'd never worked with Mr. Reeves before, and so she wanted to make sure that she got to the studio early, that she was prepared, and had all of her ducks in a row. And she said she got there, and there was no one else in the studio except Mr. Reeves. And so she walks in to meet with him. . . . And he kind of looked at her and asked her who she was, thinking that she might be a secretary or just another staff member. And she said, "Mr. Reeves, I'm Velma Smith, and I will be your rhythm guitarist today." He just kind of looked at her and kind of mumbled something like "What has Atkins gotten me into?" Because it was at Chet's invitation that she play with Jim Reeves, and he was producer so she could tell there was . . . a little conflict there. And she said, "I'll tell you Mr. Reeves, I'm going to try my best to please you, and if there's anything that I do that is not up to par with what you would like, I only ask that you come and tell me. Don't go tell anybody else, you come to me and let me fix it." And so he agreed to that. . . . [T]hey did it in the first take, and after it was over with, he came up behind her and kissed her on the back of the neck, and he said, "Velma, I think we're going to get along just fine." And she said from that day forward there were never any problems.[68]

Reeves, then, appears to have appreciated Smith's professionalism, both in her playing and in her demeanor, and was excited to call her for session work through the remainder of his life.

Looking at the discographical record, it becomes fairly obvious that Reeves created a specific band to accompany him in the post–"Four Walls" era, drawing from the cream of the Nashville A Team. With rare exceptions,

Reeves recorded with guitarists Chet Atkins, Hank Garland, and Velma Smith; bassist Bob Moore; and pianist Floyd Kramer. Moreover, Reeves worked with three drummers, each for extended, multiyear stints: Farris Coursey, Buddy Harman, and Willie Ackerman.[69] As a consequence, the accompaniments for Reeves's recordings were quite consistent from one recording session to the next, and, apart from minor differences when an occasional substitute would be called for the session or when a bit of additional reverberation will be added to his vocal tracks, it would change little over the six and a half years between "Four Walls" and his death.

Reeves's musical brand, then, was characterized by intimate vocal deliveries, subtle instrumental accompanists, tinkling vibraphone and piano parts, and—after 1960—understated string arrangements written by Anita Kerr.[70] "Four Walls" marked the beginning of a period of great chart success for Reeves that would include three more number-one hit singles and twenty-four top-ten singles.[71] Additionally, mainstream pop artists such as Perry Como came to Nashville to record their RCA Victor sessions, likely in part because of Reeves's success with Nashville's A Team. Como, for instance, traveled to Nashville in February and June 1965 to record under the direction of Chet Atkins and Anita Kerr.[72] Of course, it would be little more than foolish speculation to assume that we know what Reeves's music would have sounded like had he lived beyond 1964, but there is little doubt that he would have maintained a strong sense of control over the session musicians who performed on his recordings.

A similar approach to the hiring of session musicians can be found in the work of Capitol Records recording artist Sonny James. After nearly eight years with Capitol Records, James landed only one single at the top of the *Billboard* country charts; his 1956 recording of "Young Love," which is often noted as an important early Nashville Sound single, was recorded at Bradley's studio on October 30, 1956.[73] This is not to suggest, however, that James was not maintaining a strong chart presence; rather, between February 1953 and July 1964, James placed sixteen singles on the *Billboard* country charts, eight of which reached the top ten.[74] But close examination of the discographical records from the first decade of James's recording career reveals a remarkable inconsistency of recording circumstances.

The overwhelming majority of his recording sessions were held in Hollywood at Capitol Records' studios or in Nashville at the Bradley studios.[75] In Hollywood, the group of studio musicians used on these recordings changed constantly. The Capitol studio pool was an exceptionally strong group of musicians, many of whom had honed their skills in the honky-tonk and dancehall circuits of southern California, including Joe Maphis and Buck Owens, among others.[76] In the year following the release of "Young Love," however, the "Young Love" band—guitarist Chet Atkins, bassist Lightnin' Chance, drummer Buddy Harman, and the Jordanaires—was used to play six consecutive sessions, held twice daily between April 15 and 17, 1957; the recordings made during those sessions were released on the LP *Sonny* (Capitol T 867) as an obvious attempt to cash in on the success he had enjoyed with "Young Love."[77] But the album did not generate a chart-topper, and it seems that producer Ken Nelson, who was trying hard to push James toward the pop market, sought to explore other possibilities by returning him to the West Coast.[78] After middling success in the years following "Young Love," James left Capitol for NRC, RCA Victor, and Dot Records, only to return to Capitol in late 1962 or early 1963.[79]

James's recording career took a remarkable—and record-setting—turn in late 1964, at which time he began an eight-year streak of number-one country hits. Between 1964 and 1972, James placed twenty-one recordings at the top of the charts—sixteen of them consecutively—and an additional four in the top three slots. Among them were "You're the Only World I'll Ever Know," "Born to Be with You," and "Don't Keep Me Hangin' On."[80] Despite their strong success on the country charts, these singles did not fare well on the *Billboard* pop charts, occasionally breaking into the "Hot 100" chart, but seldom moving higher than the mid-eighties.[81] The failure of these recordings to cross over into the pop charts is made all the more remarkable by the songs that James recorded during this streak, including previous pop hits "Need You" (made famous by Jo Stafford and Gordon MacRae in 1949), "Born to Be with You" (recorded by the Chordettes in 1956), and "It's Just a Matter of Time" (which reached the number three slot when Brook Benton recorded it in 1959).[82] It could very well be, though, that James's recordings might have spoken to country music's aging audience, an audience that had been enthusiastic about mainstream pop music in their teenaged years and that longed for new versions of the same songs as they settled into marriage, childrearing, and the workplace. The teen market, though, seemed to be relatively uninterested, as evidenced by the recordings' general absence from the *Billboard* pop charts.

What is clear from this lengthy streak of number-one singles, though, is the power of musical branding and the important role that session musicians played in shaping those musical brands. After more than a decade of working with random assortments of session musicians assembled by his producer, Ken Nelson, the mid-1960s witnessed James taking a more significant role in production decisions. A key component of James's mid-1960s sound came from his backing vocalists, a group known as the Southern Gentlemen. The Southern Gentlemen—composed of Milo Liggett, Gary Robble, Duane West, Lin Bown, and Glenn Huggins—began their career as the Parsons, a gospel group at Eastern Nazarene College in Quincy, Massachusetts.[83] According to Southern Gentleman Gary Robble, who sang baritone with the group, the Parsons honed their skills during extensive summer tours of New England that paid for part of their tuition. As he noted, the Parsons quickly became a favorite on the gospel circuit and were in such high demand that their travels began to have an impact on their grades:

> Our last year in college, as we became more popular and the churches started asking for us [specifically] . . . , my dad . . . found a limousine owned by a lady and bought it at auction for $400. . . . [W]e used it its last year when we were in school. We even brought it to Nashville when we transferred down here. But in our last year of college, we drove that car fifty thousand miles. . . . So we were used to singing and traveling, and that's where it started. And our grades became so bad . . . [that] the administration said that "these boys are not good representatives of the school because they don't have good grades." But we had a great sound, obviously.[84]

The Parsons were deeply embedded in the white southern gospel sound that flourished following World War II, and they were particularly influenced by the Weatherford Quartet of Arkon, Ohio, and the Jordanaires, who had been making their mark in the Nashville recording scene for a decade. As Robble recollected, the Parsons were especially excited about the Jordaniares album *The Land of Jordan*, an album of "Negro spirituals," not their pop music work: "We didn't know the Jordanaires were on the *Opry*. We didn't know they were part of Elvis."[85]

The Parsons moved to Nashville in 1962, where they matriculated at Trevecca Nazarene College. Before long, they found that the Nashville studios could make use of their skills as backing vocalists, and they made their entry into the recording field, perhaps in part through a personal connection to Ray Walker of the Jordanaires.[86] At least initially, the group picked up sessions for lower-tier artists and demonstration recordings, serving a vital niche that the Jordanaires and the Anita Kerr Singers were too busy to handle. As Robble noted, "We were recording and doing background vocals in garages with egg crates on the wall for soundproofing. . . ."[87] The group also sang wherever they could, including at the local car lot where Lin Bown worked, a performance that led to an audition for *Opry* comedian Archie Campbell, who was so impressed with their renditions of spirituals that he helped them secure work on the *Opry* when the Jordanaires left the group to become full-time session musicians.[88] The Parsons had already developed a keen sense of musicianship that allowed them to work out arrangements without the aid of sheet music, and they frequently found themselves in the position of doing precisely that on the *Opry*, especially since they had relatively little familiarity with country music as a genre.[89] As Robble observed, "We just backed them up. I don't know how we knew what to do. . . . I don't remember getting the records. Maybe we ran over songs with them in the back. I really don't know. . . . But there's one thing we had: we could blend. We could pick up real quick, and we didn't have to write it all down."[90]

By the summer of 1964, the Parsons were maintaining a busy schedule, cutting demonstration recordings for Southern Peer International, performing on the *Opry*, and filling in for the Jordanaires in live performances (including a trip to Madison Square Garden). In August 1964, they met Sonny James, who was just beginning his second stint at Capitol Records. As Robble recounted, James approached Jordanaire Ray Walker for help in finding a new vocal group to travel with him: "Ray and Sonny were a member of the same church, and maybe in that, Sonny said to Ray, 'Look, you're over at [David] Lipscomb [College], and you know people that sing there.' . . . [A]ccording to Ray, he told Sonny, 'You ought to get ahold of these boys.'"[91] Robble acknowledged that Walker may have had economic reasons, as well as musical ones, for recommending the Parsons to James: "[M]aybe there's two sides to it. At that time, we were starting to hedge in on the Jordanaires, some of their business. I don't know why they would have been worried, but then again, you do."[92] Regardless, James approached the group, expressly noting, "I'm trying to put together a second career, and I think the combination [of your voices with mine] could really work."[93] The Parsons, though, had no idea who James was, even thinking that Tab Hunter—the artist who enjoyed mainstream pop success in his cover of "Young Love"—was the artist who was best known for his trademark hit.[94] Regardless, James promised the Parsons that they would "never play in a place where you'd be embarrassed to have your family, your friends, your pastor to come hear you sing. . . . I don't work in places where they drink or dance."[95] For the religiously minded singers, the opportunity to explore new musical opportunities with a musician who shared their moral and ethical sensibility proved to be a powerful draw, and, on August 15, 1964, the Parsons joined James on the *Opry* stage, trading the name the Parsons for the Southern Gentlemen.

James, who exerted a great deal more control over his recording and performing career during his second stint with Capitol than he did during his first, was quick to highlight the Southern Gentlemen's contributions to his sound and image.[96] A September 1964 *Billboard* article announced that "Capitol's country singer Sonny James, after successful appearances on 'Grand Ole Opry' with a new group known as the Southern Gentlemen, has decided to retain the trio as a permanent fixture of his act."[97] Similarly, an October 1969 *Billboard* essay titled "The Boys in the Band" remarked that "Sonny James, whose greatness is attested to in his continuous string of number one [*sic*] records, is among the first to seek glory for his band, the Southern Gentlemen. Three of them not only play but sing, complementing every performance."[98]

For James, though, the Southern Gentlemen were not simply part of his traveling show; they were central to his sound on recordings, as well. At a time when it was quite atypical for road musicians to enter the studio with a recording artist, James included the Southern Gentlemen on his recordings from the beginning, thanks in large part to encouragement from Robble, who suggested to James that "you ought to sound on your records how you sound on stage."[99] The Southern Gentlemen were afforded their first opportunity to record with James in January 1965, cutting several sides for a gospel album that would not be released until 1966, *Till the Last Leaf Shall Fall* (Capitol T-2561).[100] But from that time until the early 1970s, the Southern Gentlemen were inextricably linked to James in live performance and on recordings. So important was the group to his sound, in fact, that James even lobbied to have their names included on the sleeves of his albums, a rare privilege normally afforded to only the Jordanaires and the Anita Kerr Singers (both of which had major-label recording contracts of their own) and to arrangers such as Bill Walker.[101] Both the sound and the public image of the Southern Gentlemen were important to James's brand, then, linking upstanding morals, a catchy group name, and an identifiable musical sound to each of his singles.

Key to this musical brand was what Robble described as a vocal "punch" that was built around the loud second tenor, which happened to be his part. As he recalled, "We'd have the bass singer and the baritone and first tenor . . . all up here [in front], and I'd stand behind them and sing loud. And even Duane . . . on occasion would say, 'You need to sing out more. We can't blend with you not singing loud enough. . . . Sonny said years later . . . , 'I've been listening to the records. Boy, Gary, when you left, it got too mellow.' "[102] This sound can be heard quite prominently on the closing syllables of "It's the Little Things" (recorded September 1, 1965), particularly the word "so," which features a particularly strident and bright vowel sound. Similarly, the hooks of "A World of Our Own" (recorded October 31, 1967) feature a particularly strident tenor vocal that, combined with the song's brisk tempo and James's flatpicked guitar lead, adds a sense of urgency to a song that depicts a man desperately trying to convince his beloved to stay with him to build "a world of our own." Occasionally, this "punchy" male vocal backing was augmented by soprano Millie Kirkham. As she did in such recordings as Ferlin Husky's "Gone" (1957), Kirkham offered soaring legato lines that dramatically expanded the recording's frequency range and added a sense of epic drama to many recordings, including "Take Good Care of Her" (recorded November 24, 1965), "Born to Be with You" (recorded July 18, 1968), and "Don't Keep Me Hangin' On" (recorded February 18, 1970).[103] On the road, Robble—who maintained a strong falsetto voice—sang Kirkham's parts.[104]

James's recordings maintained this energetic vocal sound through 1971, when Robble left the group to pursue a career in the insurance industry. For a period of nearly five years, however, the group led an unprecedented string of number-one singles that undoubtedly secured Sonny James's place in the Country Music Hall of Fame, to which he was inducted in 2006.[105] Although "Young Love" was a significant hit for him and a landmark recording in the development of the Nashville Sound, it is unlikely that James would have been recognized for his role without the hit streak of the late 1960s. Moreover, although James had been branded as "the Southern Gentleman" as early as 1957, his association with the late-1960s configuration of the Southern Gentlemen worked to confirm his identity as a recording and touring artist and helped audiences to know what to expect when they saw a new James single or album in the department stores or heard the introduction of a James recording on the radio.[106]

If James and Reeves represent artists who were proactive in searching out session musicians to support their work, they were, by far, the exception in the Nashville Sound era. Rather, it was far more common for the session producer to hire the session musicians in an effort to find a sound that would suit a particular artist on their roster. Recording artists could certainly voice their opinions about the musicians who joined them on sessions, but it was ultimately a producer's decision when it came time to hire them. As such, it is worth turning attention away from artists who exerted exceptional control over their work, and to focus on two artists who searched for musical brands with the help of their producers: Connie Smith and Willie Nelson.

Vocalist Connie Smith began recording for RCA Victor on July 16, 1964, only two weeks before the plane crash that took Reeves's life.[107] Working with RCA producer Bob Ferguson for a decade, Smith was one of the label's most popular recording artists, placing eighteen singles in the top-ten spots on *Billboard*'s country charts between September 1964 and December 1972.[108] That Smith enjoyed such chart success is all the more remarkable considering her relative inexperience as a musician. Unlike some recording artists who found their way to Nashville after years on the road and perhaps even a limited independent release or two, Smith brought no such experience to her work, marrying young and only coming to the attention of RCA Victor's Chet Atkins after winning a talent contest in Ohio.[109] As a consequence, Smith likely needed to rely more heavily on Ferguson's production instincts than more experienced artists did. As she told interviewer Colin Escott, Ferguson "knew how to get it [a performance] out of you, and how to get the most out of the musicians[,] too. He had fresh input every session, and he knew when to call a halt to it."[110]

One might imagine that a rather inexperienced artist like Smith would have required a period of acclimatization to the Nashville studio environment, but it seems that she took to the work quite readily, placing twelve consecutive top-ten singles on the *Billboard* country charts (and reaching the top twenty-five with a B-side, "Tiny Blue Transistor Radio").[111] A closer examination of her discography reveals that the singles she released during this period of time were shaped by consistent forces. Overwhelmingly, Smith's singles from the period 1964 to 1968 were written by Bill Anderson, who was also making a name for himself as a Decca recording artist at that time.[112] Furthermore, Smith worked with a fairly consistent group of session musicians, including guitarists Ray Edenton and Jimmy Lance, steel guitarist Weldon Myrick, pianist Hargus "Pig" Robbins, drummer Leonard Miller, and the Anita Kerr Singers.[113] Listening to these first hit singles alongside the album cuts recorded during the same sessions, it becomes increasingly clear that Smith and Ferguson's use of consistent personnel and continued reliance on Anderson's songwriting talents allowed for the creation of two core Connie Smith sounds, each of which were identifiably Connie Smith's within the first few bars of the record.[114] In the first, the recording began with treble-laden lead guitar—either Ray Edenton's high-strung acoustic guitar (an acoustic guitar that used banjo strings on the lowest strings to sound an octave higher than a standard guitar), Weldon Myrick's crying pedal steel, or both. In the second, Smith sang the song's title with the support of the Anita Kerr Singers, emphasizing the most important data for potential record buyers and radio listeners calling to disc jockeys on the request line.

The former approach can be heard prominently on Smith's debut single, "Once a Day" (1964). The recording's introduction features Myrick's steel playing the song's melodic hook, filigreed by Edenton's cross-picked high-strung acoustic guitar. As Edenton recalled, that cross-picked lead gave the recording a distinctive character, even if it is less audible than Myrick's steel lead:

> I did her first session, "Once a Day." And I did the intro and turnaround on the high string. And the engineer, when he remixed it, he said, "What the hell?," and he thought the steel did it. Weldon was the steel player, and he had Weldon play the chords [sings] do, do, do, do and I'm behind him going [sings]. And if you listen real close, you can barely hear it. See when he, different engineer remixed it, and he thought it wasn't a high string player play the lead, surely. But it was me. And turnaround, too.[115]

The recording shot to the top of the *Billboard* country chart, where it remained for eight weeks.[116] Her next single, "Then and Only Then," was recorded on November 18, 1964, nearly two months after "Once a Day" made its chart debut and ample time to gauge whether the "Once a Day" sound would be a success. Not surprisingly, her sophomore single was arranged in the same style as "Once a Day," with Myrick playing a lively lead, the Anita Kerr Singers reinforcing the hook in the chorus, and the tempo and shuffle feel remaining the same. Similarly, "I Can't Remember," her third top-ten single, maintained the same personnel, tempo, and feel as her previous two singles. It, too, was recorded after "Then and Only Then" had demonstrated its chart potential, following a pattern in which the decision to maintain a musical brand was made after the previous single had revealed its chart potential.[117]

Smith's second musical brand, in which she and the Anita Kerr Singers intone the song's title at the very beginning of the recording, first appeared on "Nobody but a Fool (Would Love You)" (released 1966).[118] Smith's fifth consecutive top-ten single, "Nobody but a Fool" maintains the same high-energy shuffle that was heard in her previous singles, but the arrangements place Smith's vocals in a more prominent place in the recording's timeline, indicating from the very first notes that listeners are hearing a Connie Smith recording. But it is worth noting that this second brand was presaged by an intermediate arrangement in which both the Wyrick steel guitar lead and the Smith/Anita Kerr Singers introduction are both present. In "If I Talk to Him" (released 1965), the recording begins with Wyrick's steel guitar lead, which is then followed by Smith and the Anita Kerr Singers presenting the last two lines of the song's chorus.[119] Additionally, Edenton's cross-picked high-strung acoustic guitar lead is heard in the second verse, echoing the introduction of Smith's debut. We might, then, hear this recording as an effort to prepare Smith's core audience for a subtle change to her musical style while also grounding the recording in a tried-and-true musical formula. The Kerr-led introduction was not as significant, however, as the Myrick-led introduction, which continued to appear in such recordings as "Ain't Had No Lovin'" (released 1966) and "I'll Come Runnin'" (released 1967).[120] Rather, the Kerr-led introduction was heard prominently only on the mid-tempo "The Hurtin's All Over" (released 1966), "Cincinnati, Ohio" (released 1967) and, with a nylon-string guitar introduction, "Run Away Little Tears" (released 1968).[121] As such, it seems that Smith's initial musical brand was so remarkably successful that it exerted a sort of gravity on Ferguson's production decisions, calling them back to the same well again and again.

By comparison to Smith, whose musical brand appears to have been so successful that it was hard to break free from, Willie Nelson—who is now a beloved country music star whose popularity transcends generic boundaries—was, by all counts, unsuccessful as a recording artist during his nearly ten-year tenure with RCA Victor because he and his producers could not find a musical brand to secure his place in country radio. Nashville insiders commonly cited Nelson as one of the most creative songwriters working in the city during the 1960s, and songs such as "Crazy," "Night Life," and "Hello Walls" were smash records for Patsy Cline, Ray Price, and Faron Young, respectively.[122] Yet, even armed with a wide range of excellent original songs and a deep catalog of country and gospel standards, Nelson was a chart flop until he developed his iconic hippie-outlaw image in the early 1970s. In fact, he scored no top-ten *Billboard* hits between his 1964 label debut and his departure for Atlantic Records in 1973.[123] Nelson's run of terrible results makes for a great story, as the master songwriter can be cast as a misunderstood genius whose work was simply too advanced for a conservative Nashville establishment to understand.[124] During his nearly decade-long association with RCA Victor, Nelson recorded dozens of his own compositions and, like Reeves, worked with only two producers: Chet Atkins and Felton Jarvis. It would seem, then, that Nelson should have been in a strong position to build a clear identity as a recording artist.

Yet even a cursory examination of Nelson's recorded output reveals that Atkins and Jarvis seem to have struggled to find an identifiable musical brand with which to market Nelson to the widening country market. He was marketed as a songwriter in such albums as *Country Willie: His Own Songs* (1965) and *The Party's Over and Other Great Willie Nelson Songs* (1967); as a stylist capable of offering interesting interpretations of country standards in *Country Favorites: Willie Nelson Style* (1966); as a suburban sophisticate in *Good Times* (1968) and *My Own Peculiar Way* (1969); as a Texan in *Country Music Concert at Panther Hall in Fort Worth, Texas* (1966) and *Texas in My Soul* (1968); and as a hippie in *Willie Nelson & Family* (1971). At the same time, these visual images were paired with a variety of string-laden pop orchestrations, the accompaniment of straight-ahead honky-tonk band, and a rock group complete with gospel choir backing vocals.

Closer examination of the discographical record from the period 1964 to 1968—the same period that witnessed Connie Smith's remarkable run of chart success for the same label—reveals that these shifting musical aesthetics were created by an ever-changing array of session musicians. In fact, between 1964 and 1968, Nelson was never afforded the opportunity to work with a consistent group of session musicians. He recorded with practically everyone involved in the Nashville session scene: guitarists Chet Atkins, Grady Martin, Wayne Moss, Velma Smith, Chip Young, and Jerry Reed, among others; bassists Bob Moore, Junior Huskey, and Henry Strzelecki; pianists "Pig" Robbins, Ray Stevens, and Jerry Smith; and drummers Buddy Harman and Jerry Carrigan. He also brought members of his road band—such as steel guitarist Jimmy Day and drummer Johnny Bush—into the studio with him, an act that one might imagine would help him project his own sound more effectively, but to little avail.[125] All the more remarkable is that the studio personnel even changed between consecutive days in a series of recording sessions. One such example can be found in a three-day stint between August 9 and 11, 1967. On August 9, the band comprised Grady Martin, Chet Atkins, Harold Bradley, Jimmy Day, Junior Huskey, Jerry Carrigan, Jerry Smith, and Ray Stevens. On August 10, Bradley was replaced by Ray Edenton, and Carrigan was replaced by Buddy Harmon; both musicians finished the stand, playing on the August 11 session, as well. These sessions, which produced fifteen cuts, generated only two sides for an unremarkable single and the entirety of Nelson's *Texas in My Soul* album.[126] Similarly, when one takes a longitudinal view of Nelson's recorded output from this period, it is clear that his producers tried a variety of combinations—at one time even hiring Ernest Tubb's Texas Troubadours as a session band—to find an ideal pairing for Nelson's idiosyncratic singing.[127] Yet none of these formations lasted beyond a single long-playing album, making it exceptionally difficult for radio disc jockeys and record buyers to know what to expect from a Nelson single.

Although Nelson's braids, worn-out nylon-string acoustic guitar Trigger, and off-kilter rhythmic phrasing are now iconic, it was not until after he left RCA Victor for Atlantic Records that he was able to find a musical and visual brand that would secure his place in the minds of country fans—and music fans, more generally—around the world. Perhaps not surprisingly, it was in his work with Atlantic that Nelson began to make even more extensive use of his road band—the Family—in his recordings, including his sister Bobbie on piano, drummer Paul English, and harmonica player Mickey Raphael. These musicians have continued to play a significant role in Nelson's recordings into the present day, helping to create and reinforce a musical brand that has maintained for more than forty years.

Music from the Nashville Sound era was inextricably bound to commerce. As radio stations turned to all-country formats, they increasingly needed a consistent and coherent sonic identity to reach audiences and to package those audiences for the advertisers that underwrote their stations.[128] Similarly, with the establishment of the Country Music Association in 1958, the industry as a whole responded to these needs, crafting songs and arrangements that were, in the words of Bill Ivey, "distinctive."[129] As the admittedly limited case studies presented here demonstrate, recording artists, producers, songwriters, and session musicians often worked in conjunction with one another to craft identifiable sonic brands that propelled some artists to the top of the *Billboard* country charts. For others, uncoordinated efforts fell flat due to inconsistency and constantly shifting priorities. Moreover, these case studies begin to provide insight into the noteworthy diversity of sounds that were developed in Nashville's recording studios during the Nashville Sound era. As Harold Bradley reminds us, there would have been little value in simply replicating a sound for all artists; rather, each artist developed a unique approach within the boundaries of the genre. Therefore, rather than being marginalized as a bastardized take on traditional country music—Joli Jensen's recorded "uptown" to the Grand Ole Opry's "downhome"—we might instead hear the Nashville Sound as an attempt to balance competing needs for consistency and variety.[130] When we do so, it becomes all the more possible to value the significant contributions that the Nashville industrial system made to the American musical landscape during the Nashville Sound era.

Musical Labor and the Nashville Studio System

One of the most common critiques leveled against the Nashville Sound and the studio system that helped to propel Nashville to a new level of success during the 1960s is that the musicians involved in the production were freely interchangeable and treated their work in the same manner as one might treat assembly line work.[1] Certainly, such comparisons are easy to make. Like an assembly line, Nashville recording studios were prized for their ability to produce large quantities of saleable material in a relatively short amount of time. Studio sessions were organized around a strict schedule, much as factory shifts are timed carefully to ensure that production never ceases. And quality control systems—put in place largely through the self-policing efforts of the musicians themselves—helped to guarantee that all of the products that came from those studios were consistent, with only a few cuts finding their way to the dustbins of history.

The rise of the Nashville studio system also coincided with the golden age of manufacturing in the postwar US economy, and it was through the

Nashville Cats. Travis D. Stimeling, © Oxford University Press (2020). Oxford University Press.
DOI: 10.1093/oso/9780197502815.001.0001

mid-century growth in manufacturing that much of the infrastructure
that supported the growth of the country music market came into being.
For instance, small-town car dealers could afford to spend money on
advertisements on all-country radio stations because the factories in those
communities could guarantee near-full employment. The constant supply
of new recorded product would also have been unnecessary without communities that could afford to spend money on it, another consequence of
full employment. And, for those people who found middle-class aspirations within reach in their new cash-flush personal finances, the Nashville
Sound's own middle-class aspirations may well have echoed their own.[2]

Nashville was not the only place with a thriving music industry that
often found itself compared to the factories that drove mass consumption in the mid-twentieth century. Motown Records, for instance, is perhaps the most common label to experience such comparisons, especially
with its connections to the thriving mid-century automotive manufacturing industry. But, as Andrew Flory has shown in his extensive work on
creative practices at Motown's Hitsville, U.S.A., studio and its later itera-
tions in Los Angeles, these comparisons often fall short of capturing the
full extent of creative agency that the musicians who worked there felt
as they collectively crafted their work.[3] Although eccentric originality is
something that we might expect of our leading recording artists, the session musicians who accompany them simply cannot afford the luxury of
eccentricity. One eccentric drummer could ruin the work of dozens of
other musicians on that same session. As such, we must listen for different
kinds of innovations to understand session musicians' creativity.

The emphasis that popular music studies—and, in fact, musicology,
more broadly defined—has placed on the eccentric, the rare, and the
exceptional has unfortunately clouded our ability to discern the unique
contributions of session musicians (and other musicians who contribute
in less obvious ways) to a musical product (be that a recording, concert,
composition, etc.). Although many scholars have reframed musical products as the result of many people's contributions, this broader and more
inclusive view of musical production has not taken hold in such a way as
to decenter the "great man/woman" model.[4] As such, musicians and other

figures who play "supporting roles" are often not treated with the same care that stars are, and their creativity often goes unnoticed or maligned as a consequence.

This phenomenon should not be terribly surprising, though. Despite efforts to cast assembly line workers as mindless drones who do little more than execute the orders of the designers, engineers, and plant managers, extensive literature in the field of occupational folklore suggests that assembly line workers often bring their own individual creativity to their work. Although they might not be radically redesigning refrigerators or developing flying cars, assembly line workers often demonstrate their creativity within the sharply defined boundaries of the project that is at hand. As such, they might develop a novel way of conducting their specific task to make the work easier and to speed up the process. And they may very well even sign their names to their work in ways that consumers are not able to decipher, but that communicate clearly to their fellow factory workers.[5]

Such is also the case with session musicians. In conversations, they frequently show great admiration for one another and for the very specific ways that they can point to their own contributions and those of their fellow musicians. It is quite common, for instance, for a session musician to discuss an interesting approach to strumming the rhythm guitar part that they witnessed one of their colleagues develop, or a particular way that a bassist was able to draw tone from an instrument that recorded rather poorly in the earliest days of the Nashville scene. They speak in great detail about the specific instruments that their colleagues owned and the ways that they were able to overcome their limitations and manipulate their strengths to create a unique sound that is virtually impossible to create with other gear.[6] They lovingly recall the ways that they could communicate with each other with little more than a head nod, or the ability that they developed to predict a particular move that someone was going to make and to sync their own moves with them. And, still to the present day, these men and women come together to reminisce about their collective work, talking less frequently about the artists that they worked with than about the remarkable contributions of the men and women who shared the studio space with them every day.[7]

When listening for creativity among Nashville's session musicians, then, we must listen to a great deal of music, much as someone looking for creativity among workers on a refrigerator assembly line would need to examine dozens, if not hundreds, of refrigerators. It might be easy to caricature the Nashville Sound as little more than a sterile accompaniment to an increasingly pop style of singing, but a close listening reveals that Nashville Sound–era session musicians developed idiosyncratic approaches to their instruments, created new techniques, and emulated the successful techniques of their colleagues to create memorable accompaniments and to draw listeners to a particular recording. Moreover, in interviews, Nashville session musicians frequently discuss the demands that an individual song might have placed on them; that is, each song had a special musical or lyrical element that they felt needed to be emphasized. As such, they had to develop strategies that allowed them to be creative within the boundaries of a song that was provided to them but that were not so creative as to slow the production schedule.[8] And, because each singer was different, they also needed to respond to the demands of that particular singer's voice, including particular key choices, phrasing idiosyncracies, and other things that changed each time a new singer stood before the microphone. As such, a Nashville session musician's creativity can not be heard simply through a cursory listening to one or two or even several dozen recordings, but it must be approached through a broad investigation of their musical contributions.

When we take these contributions seriously, it is possible to reconsider one of the major assumptions of this "assembly line": that these musicians were as interchangeable as the workers in a factory. As any assembly line worker will tell you, the basic premise of that suggestion is faulty; it often takes weeks, if not months or even years, to master the tasks associated with factory work.[9] And the same was true of Nashville's session musicians. Although there were dozens of guitarists working in Nashville during the height of the Nashville Sound boom in the late 1960s, each of them brought their own unique approaches to playing lead and rhythm, idiosyncracies regarding interpersonal communications with other musicians, and technological innovations. Other musicians certainly learned to imitate those contributions—and often found imitation to be a great pathway into session work—but there was simply no substituting one guitarist for another. In fact, this is precisely the challenge that producers and artists faced as demand for the A Team's services increased. Despite sometimes Herculean efforts to play twenty or more sessions a week, there was still unmet demand. As a consequence, some recording artists and lower-profile record labels were unable to access the top talent in the field.

This chapter, therefore, considers the contributions that individual Nashville session musicians made to the recordings that were produced in Music City during the height of the Nashville Sound era. As in other parts of this book, the examples presented here are not comprehensive, but they offer a broad survey that allows us to reach a deeper understanding of the specific contributions that individual musicians made to the overall sound of Nashville Sound–era recordings. Using discographical information, oral histories, and musical analysis, this chapter examines the ways that Nashville Sound–era session musicians innovated within the confines of a three-minute country song; a four-song, three-hour session; and a three- to four-session day. Necessarily, this survey will examine each significant instrument individually, considering the contributions of its leading practitioners and the ways that other musicians emulated their creative contributions. As a consequence of this focused listening, it is possible to develop both a more nuanced understanding of the specific contributions that musicians were making in the Nashville recording studios of the Nashville Sound era and a deeper appreciation for the ways that hard-working people innovate within the boundaries that are outlined for them.

DISTINCTION AMONG THE MASSES

One of the Nashville Sound's most notable stylistic changes to country music was the judicious addition of backing vocals to country recordings.

Although not uncommon in western-themed country music from the 1930s and 1940s, backing vocals were more commonly associated with mainstream popular music record production since at least the 1930s, when groups such as the Mills Brothers and others took the radio and records by storm. Background vocals often served to provide "pads," or soft and luxurious backdrops, for the lead vocals, often comprising little more than a series of "oohs" and "aahs" in the way that a string section might provide whole- and half-note accompaniment. As Jordanaire Gordon Stoker told interviewer Douglas B. Green:

> [T]he background singers are here to complement the vocalist, to complement the star, is actually what we call ourselves. We actually complement the star. We "ooh" and "aah." Like Dottie Dillard says, she's been oohing and aahing over a hot microphone all day. [Laughter] . . .
> What you do is you "ooh" and "aah" and pad the singer and try to make him sound better. A lot of times, we do it double tracking it to make it sound bigger. If we feel like it needs to be bigger, we double track it. A lot of times, you'll sing along with the artist to bring out a particular line or maybe the title line of the song. So it just goes on and on. [10]

Backing vocals have often been written off as little more than superfluous fluff that, like the soft-focus techniques used in film of the same era to make actresses seem more gentle, warm, and inviting, did little to amplify the emotional impact of a lyric. But, as Stoker noted, they were also essential tools in amplifying a song's emotional intensity, musical structure, and lyrical hook.

In country music, such backing vocals were not only superfluous, but perhaps dangerous to the emotional impact of a song. For honky-tonk artists who thrived in the immediate aftermath of World War II, backing oohs and aahs may have seemed to sap the hard-driven and often naturalized vocals of the lead singer of their emotional immediacy.[11] This concern speaks to Richard A. Peterson's distinction between "hard-core" and "soft-shell" trends in country music, a formulation that, despite its gendered implications, still has relevance for its relationship to country fans' criticisms against the Nashville Sound.[12] Backing vocals, with their connections to mainstream pop and their seeming softness, might be heard as an emasculation of the lead singer, tempering the singer's out-of-control aspect (and even madness) with a more restrained sense of control.[13] Similarly, as Joli Jensen's foundational work on the Nashville Sound suggests, the presence of backing vocals also contributed to growing country fan concerns about the music's increasingly "uptown" sound, a sound that some fans feared would take country music too far from its "downhome" roots.[14]

At the height of the Nashville Sound era, nearly all of the backing vocal work was done by only two vocal groups. The Jordanaires, which started its life as a gospel quartet and found its way to studio work through a regular engagement on the *Grand Ole Opry*, was an all-male quartet composed of Neal Matthews, Jr., Gordon Stoker, Hoyt Hawkins, and Ray Walker. The Anita Kerr Singers, on the other hand, was a mixed-gender group composed of Anita Kerr, Dottie Dillard, Gil Wright, and Louis Nunley. Because they were the only two vocal groups to work the session scene for more than a decade, the Jordanaires and the Anita Kerr Singers worked constantly, often finding their way to four or five sessions a day in order to keep up with the demand for quartet backing. Although some singers— most notably Ray Price—might ask a band member to provide a harmony vocal to complement their lead, it was just as common for these two vocal groups to shoulder the entire burden of harmonizing and providing background pads.[15] It wasn't until the mid-1960s, when Anita Kerr decided to move to Los Angeles and later to Europe, that additional vocal groups began to find their way into the major-label sessions along Music Row.[16]

Backing vocalists served three primary functions in Nashville Sound–era recordings. First, they provided the iconic background pads to fill out the texture of an accompaniment and to help build dynamic interest, particularly at the ends of lines of lyrics. For example, in Stonewall Jackson's "I Washed My Hands in Muddy Water" (1964), the second and fourth verses feature a backing group singing the syllable "ooh" behind Jackson's lead vocals, while a single male vocalist provides harmony vocals in the song's chorus.[17] In the third verse, the group sings a response to Jackson's vocals, emphasizing the verse's lyrics in the process. Second, they might help to emphasize the song's "hook," or the lyric from which the title of the song is derived. In a marketplace that requires listeners to catch on to the title of the song quickly so that they might know what song to request their local disc jockey to play on the radio or which recording they want to buy at the local five-and-dime, hook saturation and retention were essential.[18] In Don Gibson's 1961 recording of his song "Sea of Heartbreak," for example, the Anita Kerr Singers follow the song's chorus—where hook saturation is at its greatest—with the line "Sea of Heartbreak . . . Heartbreak."[19] This, along with the calypso-inspired instrumental accompaniment, immediately grabs the listener's attention and identifies the title of the song. This recording also provides evidence of the third key contribution that backing vocalists made to Nashville Sound–era recordings: musical hooks. If lyrical hooks were essential in embedding the title of a song into the memories of its listeners, musical hooks were essential in keeping a listener's attention. Jocelyn Neal, for instance, has pointed to the ways that metric quirks can serve as musical hooks.[20] But, as "Sea of Heartbreak" demonstrates, backing vocals can be just as effective, in part because they encourage singing along. Gibson's verses, which consist of relatively brief lines that leave a fair amount of space between them, made room for bass singer Louis Nunley to walk down stepwise at the end of the first line and back up at the end of the second, a simple melody that, thanks to Nunley's booming bass, begs for imitation.

Although they played similar functions within a particular recording, the genders of the Anita Kerr Singers and the Jordanaires were deployed strategically throughout the Nashville Sound era. Female vocalists, for instance, were seldom paired with the Anita Kerr Singers, but the Jordanaires could be found in a wide range of sessions, seemingly regardless of the gender of the lead singer.[21] The reasons for this apparent gender segregation are unclear, but there are a number of possibilities. Perhaps the most obvious one is that women's voices have always been somewhat marginalized in the broader country music industry, with female artists seldom making up more than a small fraction of the total recorded out-put on the *Billboard* charts at any point in time.[22] A more musical reason, though, might be found in the potential clash between the higher vocals that Kerr and Dillard provided and the vocals of their female counter-parts. They would have occupied the same general frequency space, and for some altos (such as Kitty Wells, for instance), the presence of round-voiced female vocalists could actually have caused some signal destruc-tion of Wells's vocals. Simply put, Wells's lead vocals may have been less prominent with other women's voices in the mix.[23] In fact, Kerr herself observed that Owen Bradley may have used the Jordanaires instead of the Anita Kerr Singers on his sessions with Patsy Cline because "he didn't want any female voices to clash with what she [Cline] was doing."[24]

In addition to their gender differences—and the resultant timbral and frequency differences—the Jordanaires and the Anita Kerr Singers dif-fered quite dramatically in their respective approaches to arranging and performing backing vocals. The Jordanaires, for example, tended to rely on rather close voicings, seldom spacing the notes of a chord across more than the range of a major tenth, a likely product of the all-male compo-sition of the quartet. The Anita Kerr Singers, on the other hand, had an expansive range thanks to the gender diversity of their group. As such, chords were often voiced in an open fashion, with bass singer Louis Nunley offering a deep bass to Kerr and Dillard's soprano voices. The con-sequences of these different approaches to chord voicing were quite strik-ing. The expansive range of the Anita Kerr Singers often allowed them to create a sense of grandeur and epicness, particularly when they emulated a church choir or a string orchestra.

Roy Orbison's 1963 recording of "Falling," for example, is one such example.[25] The narrator in this song finds himself falling in love with someone who had previously been little more than a plaything or a tool to chase the loneliness away. In an almost operatic emotional turn, the speaker grows concerned that "now that I'm falling for you," the object of his affection might not feel the same way about him. The arrangement starts small and quietly, with Orbison singing the line "I'm falling, I'm falling in love with you" to the accompaniment of a strummed acoustic guitar and a ride cymbal. With the start of the first verse, the drums and upright bass enter playing a Latin rhythm, suggesting a tropical location and channeling the exotic sexuality that was commonly heard in much easy listening and mainstream pop arrangements of the era.[26] The second line of the first verse marks the entrance of the Kerr Singers, offering textless "aahs" that add to the textural density, the frequency range, and the overall perceived volume of the recording, all while conveying a sense that the speaker is starting to feel new emotions. The addition of a string quartet, piano, and electric bass in the second verse continues this trend of increasing the sense of epicness that complements Orbison's increasingly tense vocals; the Anita Kerr Singers' rhythmically static backgrounds are contrasted by a more rhythmically active string part that effectively portrays the topsy-turvy nature of the speaker's emotional transformation. The song does not resolve with an affirmation of the beloved's mutual feelings for the speaker; rather, it ends on a question, so the arrangement builds to a climax that comes at the very last note.

Another example of the Anita Kerr Singers' ability to emulate choirs and orchestras can be heard in Ferlin Husky's 1957 Capitol recording of "A Fallen Star."[27] The recording opens with a grand choral opening, with the soprano rising stepwise and reaching the top of a crescendo at the moment that Husky sings the first note of the melody. They then alternate textless syllables and phrases from Husky's vocals for the opening verse. These are not static parts, but ones that require the inner voices to move independently of the others. All the more fascinating is the Anita Kerr Singers' role in building a climax in this recording. Like the Orbison recording, the emotional peak of Husky's "A Falling Star" does not come until the end, when the hook is repeated, cementing it in the listeners' memories. Here, the Anita Kerr Singers expand the range to the widest point heard in the recording, with soaring soprano melodies that seem to launch the performance into the same cosmic space as the beloved to whom Husky is singing. In this instance, the sopranos emulate the sound of violins played in third or fourth position, shrieking along with a dramatic intensity that is further conveyed through the intense bowing and vibrato that are needed to make those notes speak at the volumes that the arrangement requires.

The Anita Kerr Singers, therefore, could create dramatic intensity while also saving the producers from hiring additional musicians for a session.

The strength of the Anita Kerr Singers' arrangements can be attributed to Kerr herself, who brought a rather extensive musical training to her work in Nashville. In an interview with journalist Michael Streissguth, Kerr, who came to Nashville from Memphis in 1948, recalled that she came to session work through a familiar pathway—WSM:

> Jack Stapp at WSM heard about me and the vocal group [I formed in Nashville]; so then he called me and asked me to talk with him. So I went to WSM and he hired me to direct this eight-voice choir which was on a regional network there. It was called *Sunday Down South* with Snooky Lanson. So I started writing and conducting and singing with this eight-voice choir and then the A&R man from Decca Records, Paul Cohen, was in and out of WSM all the time because that was really the beginning of all the recording in Nashville. . . . So, Paul would come by and he heard the group and he wanted a choir on a religious song that Red Foley was doing. He asked me if I would write the arrangement and the choir sing with Red on it. That was the beginning. He was really the one who gave us the name the Anita Kerr Singers.[28]

Kerr's on-the-job experience as an arranger and the skill of her singers led to regular work for the group, particularly with Owen Bradley. As she told Streissguth, "[I]f I was hired to write the arrangement and they say, 'Bring your singers,' they know if I wrote it, the singers could read it."[29] She went on to suggest that her ability to write out more complex arrangements led her group to work with certain kinds of artists, noting that "I think the things we did were closer to pop because we could read [music] whereas the Jordanaires—most of their sessions were faked."[30] Additionally, her ability to read and write music and to communicate with musicians who did also put her in a unique position to serve in something of a directorial or production role. She recalled, for instance, making some rather significant suggestions about the ways that the string players approached timing that led to an important change in the ways that the string quartet worked:

> We had tried strings from the symphony orchestra and they just didn't play right on the beat. . . . I knew that Brenton [Banks] besides being a violinist was a good pianist. I knew he really played the piano with a beat. I said, "What they really need is someone in charge to tell them to play with them that they can follow and to tell them when they are ahead of the beat or behind the beat." In those days, those violinists weren't raised on hearing rhythm as much as the younger violinists now are. All they played really was symphony music. . . .
>
> When they did play the arrangement, they weren't right on the beat. Brenton, as leader of the strings, the concertmaster, they had to do what he said. He played beautifully, but even though he played beautifully, the second reason we really wanted him to be the leader was because they needed help in the rhythm department.[31]

In this position, then, Kerr could serve in a significant production role, guiding other musicians and hiring her own singers in the process. As such, she was able to put her own creative stamp on both the vocals and the rest of the arrangement, a stamp that, while audible, has been given relatively little public credit.[32]

The Jordanaires relied on written arrangements much less frequently than the Anita Kerr Singers did, instead relying almost entirely on "faked" arrangements that were created on the spot. As a consequence of their accelerated creation, they were often much less complex than written arrangements. Complexity often requires forethought, and written notation can serve as a mnemonic device to help guide singers through that complexity during the session. Although the Jordanaires did occasionally use shape notes from the gospel songbook tradition to denote specific melodic lines and chord voicings, they more often than not used the Nashville Number System to lay out the harmonic progression and scale degree numbers to set the initial voicing of the first chord they were to sing. Consequently, the Jordanaires were able to produce consistent and, for the most part, supportive but not invasive backing vocals for the artists they accompanied.

Listening to the Jordanaires' work over their more than twenty years of intense studio work, one hears a remarkable consistency in their approach to creating these arrangements, even as substitute members came and went over the years. To begin, the Jordanaires frequently used fairly compact chord voicings that were aided by the group's all-male composition. The bass voice in the group—normally Ray Walker—typically sang the root of the chord, leading him to jump across the range of a major sixth, while the other singers in the group would typically move in stepwise motion. For the most part, these harmonies would be sounded in long rhythmic durations, unfolding as half notes and whole notes in common time. With these chord voicings and voice-leading practices, the Jordanaires would also commonly play with vocal effects that closely approximated the sounds of rhythm and blues horn sections, changing "oohs" into "aahs" to brighten their timbre. As such, they were able to add to the overall textural density of a recording, lending volume and intensity to the singer's performance. Occasionally, the Jordanaires would also echo key words, such as the song's hook, or double the lead singer's lyrics to emphasize a particular line.

A particularly interesting example of the Jordanaire's work can be heard in Elvis Presley's 1957 recording of "(Let Me Be Your) Teddy Bear"—a cut recorded not in Nashville but at Hollywood's Radio Recorders.[33] Here, the Jordanaires take the boogie woogie feel that the pianist Dudley Brooks provides as their cue, creating a syncopated counterpoint to Presley's hiccupping vocal performance, singing a riff that could have been pulled from a Joe Turner or Louis Jordan record. They also provide an answer to the last line of each verse; when Presley sings the first half of the line "Oh let me be / your teddy bear," the Jordanaires answer, "Oh let him be." In this case, they function as a coercive force, amplifying Presley's desire to be used as a potential lover's plaything. Notably, in the song's bridge, the Jordanaires darken the timbre of their voices and replace their earlier "bop-a-dah-dah" with an "oo-wah" that evokes the sound of trumpets and trombones played with a plunger mute. As such, the Jordanaires here are able to channel the sounds of rhythm and blues to amplify the work of early rock and roll artists. Unlike horn players, who were often used to add excitement to a recording, their vocal flexibility could also be deployed on a ballad that might be cut on the same session.

A more solemn Jordanaires sound can be heard in "Can't Help Falling in Love with You," which Presley recorded for the 1961 film *Blue Hawaii*.[34] Here, the Jordanaires use their stepwise voice-leading and rhythmically slow chorale style to create a sense of solemnity and sacredness that frames the speaker's supplication to the object of his desire. Surrounded by an arpeggiated piano part that evokes the Bach-Gounod *Ave Maria* and a glockenspiel that recalls the sounds of church bells, the Jordanaires here make this love sound like something ordained by a divine power. So powerful is this sensation of holiness and supernatural power that the slightly out-of-tune lap steel guitar—which is meant to evoke the Hawaiian vistas depicted in the film—almost drops completely out of earshot. Instead, listeners are drawn into a special moment that we are led to believe will have great significance to everyone involved. (In the film, the song is featured as Elvis presents a music box to his girlfriend's grandmother, who is seated in front of an audience gathered together to celebrate her birthday.)

Backing vocalists were commonly heard on Nashville Sound–era recordings, but guitarists were ubiquitous. Nashville's music industry was built around the performance of string band music, and the guitar—in both its Spanish and Hawaiian forms—was central to that development. Singers learned to accompany themselves with simple "cowboy" chords in the first position, along with bass runs that connected the chords. The guitar was, in those cases, a melodic instrument, a harmonic instrument, and a rhythmic instrument. And the steel guitar—whether in the form of the Dobro, the electric lap steel, or, later, the electric pedal steel—provided valuable countermelodies that accentuated the vocal line. Not surprisingly, then, Nashville's A Team was loaded with guitar players, so much so that, when John Sebastian wrote his paean to the city, "Nashville Cats," he remarked that "there's thirteen hundred and fifty-two guitar pickers in Nashville."[35] Rather than providing detailed biographies of each of the many guitarists who worked in Nashville, this section seeks to explore the roles that these musicians played in the studio. As such, we will be considering the various lead and rhythm guitar styles that they brought to their work, interspersing elements of their biographies into the discussion.

As the postwar Nashville recording industry began to boom, any number of guitarists could have made their marks as session musicians. For the most part, rhythm guitar parts in much country music were not terribly complicated, requiring fluency in first-position open chords (often referred to as "cowboy chords" because of their ubiquity in the genre) and relatively little working knowledge of the fretboard. Barre chords— commonly heard in the work of jazz musicians, including western swing musicians—were mostly unheard of in honky-tonk and bluegrass music, and guitarists were not expected to play in the "flat keys," as sharp-inflected keys are easier to play in the guitar's standard tuning (EADGBE). As such, a rhythm guitarist could accompany a singer using a fairly restricted harmonic vocabulary, relying instead on their right-hand technique to create a steady rhythmic framework for the lead instruments and vocals to ride upon. When tethered to a singer as part of a road show, then, a rhythm guitarist could work steadily without needing to develop a wide-ranging technique. But, even in the early days of the Nashville recording industry, session musicians were not called upon to accompany country music alone, nor was country music a monolithic musical genre. Instead, country music was a wide-ranging genre that required rhythm guitarists to be competent not only as strummers of cowboy chords but as musicians with a wide harmonic vocabulary and an ability to play up and down the neck. It should not be surprising, then, that very few guitarists who passed through the Nashville studio scene during the height of the Nashville Sound era actually specialized in rhythm playing. Rather, session guitarists were expected, for the most part, to be capable as both lead and rhythm guitarists, and they often switched roles within a single recording session, let alone across an entire day of sessions or an entire recording career.

It was not uncommon for Nashville Sound–era sessions to hire as many as three different guitarists for a single recording session. During the heyday of the tic-tac bass, one of those guitarists would play it, while another would play rhythm and the third would cover the lead. As the tic-tac bass fell out of favor in the mid-1960s, two distinct rhythm guitar parts accompanied the lead, often with one rhythm player emphasizing a higher frequency range than the other. And, when two rhythm guitarists were not called for on a particular track, one of the guitarists might be called upon to play mandolin, banjo, or another stringed instrument to add some timbral diversity to the recording. As such, the primary expectation for any guitarist was to be flexible and broadly competent on a wide variety of instruments. Ray Edenton, for instance, told interviewer Morris Levy that it was imperative that he "be able to adapt quickly. . . . That's what separated studio musicians from a lot of road musicians."[36] Additionally, because they knew that a variety of guitars and other instruments might be needed at any given time, guitarists frequently bought instruments and amplifiers that they left at the various studios, helping to save on setup time and the hassle of transporting them from place to place.[37]

The best rhythm guitarists tend to go unnoticed, as they blend unobtrusively into the rhythm section. Yet they were often hired for session work because they brought a unique approach to their playing that helped the overall recording stand out in the vast popular music marketplace. Such was the case with rhythm guitarist Jack Shook, who was one of the leading guitarists in Nashville in the decade after World War II. A native of Decatur, Illinois, Shook came to session work after extensive journeyman work as a pop musician (at one point accompanying Kate Smith in her network radio broadcasts) and as a country musician working with the Missouri Mountaineers on the *Grand Ole Opry*. Country music historians Charles Wolfe and John Rumble have suggested that Shook offered a "distinctive [approach to] rhythm playing—enhanced by a left-handed style in which he struck his guitar strings from treble to bass," an approach that they credit with "giv[ing] a commercial edge to recordings by Hank Williams ('Lost Highway') and numerous others."[38] Not surprisingly, the recordings that he played on often have a stronger treble sound that made them stand out from others. But, as Harold Bradley noted, this distinctive technique also had a significant drawback: he struggled to make headway as a lead guitarist because guitar manufacturers often built electric guitars for right-handed players only. As a consequence, it was nearly impossible to flip the guitars over without losing access to some of the higher frets and, in some cases, being able to balance the instrument on his leg. Not surprisingly, then, as demand for guitarists with diverse abilities came to dominate the Nashville recording scene, Shook struggled to develop a lead style and his recording career declined.[39] After two decades as a recording guitarist, he continued playing for live programs on WSM and other shows from the early 1960s until 1982.[40]

Ray Edenton, too, made significant inroads as a rhythm guitarist thanks to a distinctive approach to the instrument. A native of Virginia, Edenton worked on the *Old Dominion Barn Dance* in Richmond, Virginia, and the *Grand Ole Opry* before hitting the road with such rising Nashville stars as Marty Robbins and Webb Pierce.[41] Although Edenton played lead on a few sessions, he played rhythm almost exclusively. As he told interviewer David Simons, "When I came to town in '52 and heard guys like Thumbs Carllile, Hank Garland and Chet [Atkins], I just stopped right there and let it be known that I was available to play good rhythm, if anyone wanted to hire me."[42] In a world in which nearly anyone could play rhythm guitar successfully, Edenton developed a sophisticated approach to the instrument that helped him stand out from the crowd: "Now I was a little bit more uptown than a lot of the rhythm players. Hell, most of them couldn't play six-string chords on the guitar. Because all you had to do when I first started playing sessions was put your strings down real low and just made a 'chk chk.' I made a good 'chk'. I made a pretty one."[43] This sound substituted well for drums, which were not always acceptable on country recordings, but, as he noted, Atkins grew tired of the sound as more and more sessions included drums: "Chet got me to raising my strings because he hated that damn sound. He says, "Hell, you sound like a drum. I don't want two drums." So he'd make me raise my strings up, play with a little tone. He really got me started playing with a tone because I'd never played with a tone except for open strings like a bluegrass band."[44] The resulting sound, when combined with the tic-tac and an electric lead guitar, allowed for the creation of a complex guitar part that emphasized the entire frequency spectrum and that articulated the downbeats and the upbeats (in coordination with the drums and bass), while also allowing for a counter-melody to the vocals or fills between lines.

As is often the case in popular music production, tastes and attitudes changed, and old familiar sounds became quickly dated as they saturated radio airplay, jukeboxes, and records, and Edenton found himself needing to develop new techniques that would help him continue to make meaningful contributions to sessions and to work steadily.[45] His major innovation was to substitute a banjo string for the acoustic guitar's third string, the G string.[46] This substitution made the G string sound an octave higher than standard tuning, giving the guitar a shimmering sound and opening its voicing. This "high-third" tuning also emulated the sound of a twelve-string guitar, an instrument that was becoming increasingly popular during the late 1950s as a consequence of the popular folk music revival.[47] His earliest successes with this new tuning came in his work with the Everly Brothers.[48] As Edenton told Rich Kienzle, the high-third tuning allowed him to add to the already strong rhythm guitar parts that Don Everly brought to the studio:

> I started using the one high G on a flat-top [acoustic] guitar. Don Everly played flat-top, and he tuned his to a[n open] G chord. A lot of old folksingers and black singers used that tuning. Don got a real wide sound with that, so I was looking for something to go in the middle of that sound. That's why I started using the high third in there. I learned to play a lot of those rhythm licks with him for a stronger sound.[49]

This "stronger sound" was undoubtedly caused by the sheer number of octaves that were present when the two guitars were combined. The open G tuning used by Don Everly—from low to high, DGDGBD—already included one octave between Gs, and the high-third string added another octave when both guitars were played in an open tuning.[50] Additionally, Everly's tuning encompassed two octaves of Ds. Octaves being the strongest interval and fifths and fourths (the interval between G and D and its inversion, respectively) coming in a close second and third in the overtone series, the combination of these two guitar parts then created a strong and powerful sound of parallel octaves, fifths, and fourths that helped to give the Everly Brothers' recordings a particular strength on transistor radios, which were notoriously tinny as a consequence of their construction. This sound helped to propel the Everly Brothers to stardom, and Edenton became their go-to rhythm guitarist from his first session with them in 1957 until they began making most of their records in Los Angeles in 1963.[51]

Eventually, Edenton extended his restringing of the guitar to include the first, second, and fourth strings, as well, after hearing guitarist Grady Martin do it.[52] The resulting instrument was essentially a twelve-string guitar, which gives the opportunity to extend the sound of the guitar up an octave without needing to capo it at the twelfth fret; capoing at the twelfth fret can make a flat-top acoustic guitar like the Martin D-18 and the Fender that Edenton owned sound much less resonant than if it were fretted near the headstock.[53] As he told Kienzle, this new sound was best when "used . . . in conjunction with another guitar to give a wide tonal spread on the rhythm sound—a lot of highs, both on the high end and the low end. So actually, your high string would be one octave—sometimes more—above your standard [tuned] guitar."[54] This sound can be heard on a variety of major hit recordings from the mid- to late 1960s, particularly those of Connie Smith, George Hamilton IV, and Lynn Anderson, among many others.[55]

Although he was not very active as a lead guitarist, Edenton did find that the high-third tuning afforded him some opportunities to share the lead duties with his colleagues. George Hamilton IV, for instance, called on Edenton to play "flat-top lead," as he recalled to me:

I developed a thing where I'd played, I'd guess you called it tenths, one on the low harmony and the lead up top. And then when I went to the high string, I used one high string and one low string in the harmonies. Like "When This Day Ends" is one I remember. [Hums] And we called it tenths. I don't know what it really is musically. But wide harmony, and he'd want me to play that.[56]

He explained to Kienzle that this technique of playing harmonies in tenths—or thirds with an extra octave added between them—also led to some interesting duets with steel guitarist Pete Drake on those sessions. He noted that his first session with Hamilton "was about the time . . . Pete Drake first came up here. Pete and I did all kinds of records, playing two parts, tenths . . . , and using the high third."[57]

Edenton seems to have chosen to work primarily as a rhythm guitarist. A versatile rhythm guitarist, he was certainly able to play in a wide variety of styles, but it may also become clear that his gender may have helped him continue to work in an environment that was full of potential competition. Edenton was a popular fellow in his community, often fishing with his colleagues during their spare time and, by the 1970s, even traveling to Atlanta with colleague Charlie McCoy to take in hockey games on a regular basis.[58] Film footage captured during a recording session for Leon Russell's 1973 album *Hank Wilson's Back* reveals Edenton to be an affable character, smiling, laughing, and enthusiastically participating in the joy of making music together at Bradley's Barn in Mt. Juliet, Tennessee.[59] And during our conversation, he laughed easily and proved to be a genuinely fun person to talk with. As such, Edenton may very well reflect one of the major archetypes of southern masculinity, a fun-loving, hard-living person who blurs the lines between work and play. As such, he likely fit in well personally with the musicians who were working in the session scene, and his musical consistency and great personality made up for any shortcomings that his lead work may have had. This is not to suggest, by any means, that Edenton did not deserve the work that was sent his way, or to indicate that the music that he played was subpar. But it does raise interesting questions about the agency that individual musicians may have been afforded as a consequence of their gender in a largely male-dominated creative space.

If the number of guitarists who specialized in rhythm guitar was relatively low, the number of guitarists who played both lead and rhythm guitar on Nashville Sound–era recording sessions was quite high. Since guitar duties were often split from one song to another during an individual recording session, it is often quite difficult to ascertain the origin of many iconic lead guitar lines from discographical records and studio logs alone. Rather, we must rely on the memories of firsthand witnesses; not surprisingly, given the sheer number of sessions these musicians played on, many of these memories have faded, except in the case of iconic hits or recordings that had a particularly memorable creative challenge. Often, lead guitar parts were awarded to the bandleader for a particular session, particularly in the case of Grady Martin, who recorded lead guitar lines on thousands of tracks over the course of his career. But just as commonly, the guitarist who created the most interesting hooks, fills, and solos during rehearsal was given the chance to shine on a particular take. But this space to shine was still relatively limited, as the time restrictions on commercial recordings—three minutes or less to accommodate radio airplay—often limited solos to half-choruses, making each note played even more significant than if the guitarists were granted a longer space to demonstrate their abilities. Although lead guitarists were not afforded much time to demonstrate their virtuosity, close listening that is correlated to oral histories and discographical information reveals that many of the lead guitarists had found ways to use their distinctive skills to create identifiable stylistic approaches to lead guitar work. Over time, other guitarists learned to emulate these styles, a skill that was especially useful if the guitarist who had innovated a particular approach was not hired for a session that demanded that approach, but the soundmark of the innovator was clearly present in the work of the emulator.[60]

In the minds of many country music fans—and music fans, more generally, for that matter—Chet Atkins represents the epitome of country guitar playing, and his presence as one of the leading producers and record executives in Nashville for more than five decades has helped to cement his legacy as one of the city's most significant musical figures. Like many of his contemporaries, Atkins developed his skills through extensive radio and road work, including a notable four-year stint at radio station WNOX in Knoxville, Tennessee, where he immersed himself in the station's extensive library of recordings by top guitarists in jazz, pop, and classical music; another at WLW in Cincinnati, where he teamed up with country-jazz duo Homer Haynes and Jethro Burns; and stints on

WSM's *Grand Ole Opry* (with Red Foley), WRVA in Richmond, Virginia, and KWTO in Springfield, Missouri.[61] An accomplished fiddler as well as a guitarist, Atkins's path was a circuitous one, the product of music industry machinations, promises met and unfulfilled, and family demands.[62] In fact, it was his return to WNOX in 1948 that brought him one of the greatest opportunities of his early career: the chance to work with Mother Maybelle and the Carter Sisters.[63] After producing his first sessions for Steve Sholes at RCA Victor, Atkins moved permanently to Nashville in 1950, where he quickly became one of the leading guitar players in the city, and by 1957, he was chosen to be the primary producer in RCA Victor's new Nashville facility, where he worked until his partial retirement in 1973.[64]

From the very outset of his career, Atkins brought a unique approach to playing the electric guitar that helped him stand out from his colleagues. Numerous reports indicate that Atkins was almost obsessive about his practice regimen, often even playing the guitar in the control room during the sessions that he was producing (but not playing on).[65] He was also exceptionally eclectic in his musical influences and his willingness to learn the nuances of a particular style and to incorporate them into his own playing; as Rich Kienzle has noted: "[Atkins] endlessly sought new inspirations and influences, whether they involved flamenco guitar music, jazz albums by guitarist and onetime country player Johnny Smith, or records by pianists Erroll Garner and Ralph Sutton." Kienzle also notes the strong influence of such musicians as jazz musicians George Barnes and Django Reinhardt, as well as blues musicians T-Bone Walker, John Lee Hooker, and Lonnie Johnson, among others.[66] But Atkins is perhaps best known for his work as a finger-picker, largely eschewing the flat plectrum used by many string band guitarists in favor of the extended dexterity that could come from using each of the digits on the right hand to pluck the strings. Atkins adapted the strong thumb-picking style developed by such guitarists as Mose Rager, Ike Everly, and, most famously, Merle Travis—each of whom had roots in and around Muhlenberg County, Kentucky—by using more digital independence to play even flashier parts. The Muhlenberg County sound—known as "Travis picking" everywhere except Nashville, where it is widely known as "Chet picking"—features a strong bass note played by the thumb and alternating between the lower strings on the guitar and a clear melody played on its higher strings.[67] As such, guitarists could accompany themselves without needing additional instrumentation as support, and the strong thumb strokes helped to give a certain drive to the performance that was widely appreciated in Nashville and beyond.[68]

Atkins is perhaps the most widely known guitarist, thanks in large part to his successful solo recording career, which extended well past his retirement from RCA Victor. But his contributions as a guitarist on Nashville recording sessions were much less significant than his production work. Instead, two lead guitarists covered most of that work from the mid-1950s until the 1970s: Hank Garland and Grady Martin. Both were skilled single-string soloists who were capable of playing blazing lead lines up and down the neck and driving electric riffs that could push a rock and roll recording to new heights.

Hank Garland was, like Atkins, reared on the road, taking his first road gig as a member of Paul Howard and His Georgia Cotton Pickers when he was fifteen years old and making his *Opry* debut with the group a short time after joining.[69] Strongly influenced by such guitarists as Maybelle Carter, Arthur Smith, Billy Byrd, Django Reinhardt, and Charlie Christian, Garland began playing sessions by the time he was seventeen years old, likely first working with Cowboy Copas during his early sessions for King Records in Cincinnati, who kept him working for three years.[70] Bassist Bob Moore told Kienzle that Garland, like Atkins, was dedicated to his practice, recalling that, when he lived with Garland in the late 1940s, "I used to get up every morning to go do a radio show at 5:30 with Lester Flatt and Earl Scruggs. When my alarm would go off, Hank would get up and be practicing even before I finished my breakfast. I'd go do the show and another at noon, then I'd come home. There was Hank, still listening to Django Reinhardt."[71] He also recalled:

> Hank used to sit around and show me how he was developing the muscle in his right thumb. He'd take a pick and hold it in all these different positions between the forefinger and thumb and just work

it as fast as he could without a guitar. He'd sit around and do that to develop strength, and that's one of the things that helped him because none of the other guitarists could get around with a pick like he could. It seemed like everything he did was just so easy. It looked like he wasn't doing anything. With his left hand[,] he'd do all these finger exercises from one end of the guitar to the other, and he would play on the low *E* string as high as he could and learn any jazz run. He would sit and play it from one fret to the next, learning it in every position.[72]

This dedication to practice was likely vital to his success as a session musician, because the work that he was doing there required him to play not only in a variety of keys (to accommodate the needs of the singer), but to create interesting countermelodies, fills, and riffs that would support a song with relatively little time to plan ahead. As such, a fluency not only in fretboard geography but also in lick creation and melodic formation would have stood him in good stead. But daily practice without real-world opportunities to put the individual elements from that practice together does not always yield great results. Fortunately, Garland also maintained a regular presence in the local Nashville jazz scene, holding court at the Carousel Club with Bob Moore, Brenton Banks, and Buddy Harman, among others, including a teenaged vibraphonist from Louisville, Kentucky: future National Endowment for the Arts Jazz Master Gary Burton.[73] As a consequence, Garland brought not only technical facility, a responsive ear, and a deep understanding of melodic construction to his solos to his work, but a working sense of song structure and a variety of ways to apply his technical innovations.

Garland's session work began in earnest by 1949, when he left the road to begin working extensively on Decca accounts supervised by Paul Cohen and Owen Bradley. By the mid-1950s, he had played guitar on many of the more sophisticated country-jazz and western swing recordings made in Nashville, and by the time Owen Bradley and Chet Atkins began to seek new, more sophisticated accompaniments for the country-pop records that they were hoping to make in the second half of the decade,

Garland's sophisticated lead work fit the bill.[74] Not surprisingly, then, he provided the lead guitar work for most of Patsy Cline's Decca recordings, as well as those of RCA Victor's Eddy Arnold and others. But, like all session guitarists, he was also called to play on straight-ahead country sessions as well as rockabilly and rock and roll recordings, which were increasingly being made in Nashville studios as the major labels began to make inroads in those markets and smaller labels sought the quality sound that a professional Nashville studio and session band could offer.[75] Unfortunately, Garland was not afforded the opportunity to develop many new approaches to lead guitar playing in Nashville studios because his career ended abruptly following a devastating 1961 automobile accident.[76] So, whereas longer-tenured guitarists could change their approach to the instrument as musical tastes and attitudes changed, Garland's output is relatively homogeneous by comparison. As such, it provides a relatively convenient repertory for us to use to understand his particular approach to playing lead on country and pop recordings in the late 1950s.

If Garland's musicianship on a comparatively limited number of recordings is widely revered for its sophistication, his colleague Grady Martin's extensive recorded output over a more than four-decade career is noteworthy for its diversity. A skilled electric guitarist, Martin was a master craftsman of exciting guitar riffs that helped to electrify the rockabilly and nascent rock and roll scene of the mid- to late 1950s, including most notably the blazing lead work on the Johnny Burnette Trio's "The Train Kept a-Rollin'."[77] A skilled jazz guitarist in his own right, Martin was also a highly sought-after lead guitarist for the country-pop recordings that helped to build the notion of the Nashville Sound in the late 1950s and early 1960s, revealing a remarkably sensitive touch that stands in stark contrast to his work with rockabilly and rock and roll artists. Unlike Garland, who seldom bent the strings to create "blue notes" or to give the guitar a vocal character, Martin's work is frequently marked by a tendency to bend the strings, creating not only a vocal character but adding a "raw" character to the work. And in 1959, he brought the nylon-stringed classical guitar to Nashville's attention through his work on Marty Robbins's *Gunfighter Ballads* album, which found him playing, as Charlie McCoy recalled, "a borrowed guitar."[78] His extensive improvisations on "El Paso" from that album stand as one of the most highly respected pieces of session work among the Nashville studio musicians of that era, an achievement that is particularly noteworthy considering that the accompaniment was improvised for nearly five minutes without repeating significant ideas or clamming notes and that the musicians only needed two takes to create it.[79]

One factor that united Nashville's lead guitarists was their shared admiration for jazz guitarists such as Charlie Christian, Django Reinhardt, and Barney Kessel, among many others. Steve Waksman has noted, though, that the guitarists of the Nashville A Team did not embrace all forms of jazz, but instead demonstrated a "taste for melody [that] led to a preference for a style of improvisation that owed more to swing styles of the 1930s than to the harmonically complex and even dissonant forms of jazz that had taken shape since the 1940s."[80] Listening carefully to the recordings that emanated from Nashville studios during the late 1950s, one finds confirmation of this focus on melodic improvisation. As Waksman notes, guitarists seldom ventured into the realm of chordal extensions and harmonic substitutions heard in modern jazz of the 1950s, nor do we hear them exploring freer improvisational practices as one might hear on contemporary albums such as Ornette Coleman's *The Shape of Jazz to Come* (1959), among others. In fact, Waksman points to several interviews and memoirs in which guitarists such as Atkins publicly disavowed modern jazz practices in favor of preserving the integrity of "the melody."[81]

Although Waksman does not extend this argument to specific musical examples, he does seem to imply that this attitude can be heard in the arranging and performance practices of the Nashville Sound era. However, there are a number of indications—both musical and rhetorical—that indicate that the approach to melody that Waksman discerns in these guitarists' attitudes toward jazz shaped their approaches to playing lead on country recordings. Nashville Sound–era session musicians frequently talk about their role in serving both the recording artist and the song itself, making sure that their contributions do not cover up the vocal melody. Charlie McCoy, for instance, recalled a lesson that Martin taught him during his first years as a session musician in the early 1960s:

We were doing a session at Owen Bradley's studio. During the first take of one of the songs, I started feeling my oats, playing nearly every lick I knew. I looked over at Grady and saw him shooting me a dirty look. When they played the tape back, I walked over to Grady to ask him if something was wrong.

"You're playing too much," he said. "Listen to the words. If you can't hear and understand every word, you're playing too much." This was the best advice that anyone ever gave me about studio playing. For the rest of my career, I let this be my guide: Less is more. Take a listen to some of Grady's playing, and you'll hear a perfect illustration of this concept.[82]

Taking McCoy's advice, it can be particularly instructive to listen to the solos and fills that guitarists such as Martin and Garland contributed to the recordings they made and to note the clear and frequent presence of the melody in their work. For instance, Garland, in his introduction to Patsy Cline's recording of "I Fall to Pieces," can be heard echoing the song's primary melodic and lyrical hook, much as a church pianist might use the last line of a hymn to help the congregation find their pitch and to recall the hymn's most iconic passage. Similarly, Martin's guitar work on Marty Robbins's "El Paso," while distinctive in many ways, essentially riffs off the song's opening motive—"Out in the West Texas town of El Paso"—while adding flourishes that give it a distinctive "south of the border" flavor.

If the first generation of lead guitarists to make a career in Nashville were largely inspired by jazz guitarists who prized melody, the second generation of lead guitarists who made a career in the city's studios were inspired by a different genre with strong African American roots: rhythm and blues (as well as rockabilly and rock and roll). An influx during the mid-1960s of guitarists born in the 1940s revealed the seminal role of the music that these guitarists heard on overnight rhythm and blues stations, such as Nashville's WLAC, and on the rock and pop hit parades of the 1950s. Although they were adept melodists in their own right, they were just as comfortable leaning on blues evocations and electronic effects to pull additional emotion out of a vocal performance.

Guitarist Jerry Kennedy, for instance, came to Nashville from Shreveport, Louisiana, in March 1961, following a stint on the *Louisiana Hayride*, a barn dance program that freely blended rock and country acts and that served as a vital stage in the upward mobility of many artists who thrived during the 1950s and 1960s.[83] As a teenager, he also worked with a number of leading honky-tonk singers in the Shreveport circuit, playing and singing on the road and in the studio with Webb Pierce, Slim Whitman, and Johnny Horton.[84] A talented six-string picker and dobroist, Kennedy found regular studio work in Nashville shortly after his arrival in the city, working primarily for Shelby Singleton, who was the A&R man at Mercury, as both a producer and a guitarist.[85] After the Dutch company Philips purchased Mercury Records in 1961, Kennedy was constantly in demand, both as a producer and a session musician, because the label needed to keep product moving out not only on Mercury, but on its subsidiary label, Smash, as well.[86] He told interviewer Morris Levy, for instance, that, in the wake of Philips's purchase of Mercury, Music Row studios began adding a 1 a.m. session just to accommodate the increased demand; as such, there was also more work for session musicians and more room for musicians like himself to find work. As he told interviewer Jennifer Ember Pierce, the long hours eventually caught up to him during a session:

One time I fell asleep during the session. I was playing what we call "the chink," which is played on the 2 and 4 beat and I was not accustomed to doing that. Ray Edenton was the guy who always got stuck with "the chink" beat. You had to really be right on it too, because Buddy Harman was the drummer and Buddy's like a human metronome. The "chink" beat is playing rhythm on an electric guitar. I can remember it was a Claude Gray session and I was feeling so "beat up" and so tired, and I was playing 1 "chink," 3 "chink," 1 "chink," and, at one point, I woke up immediately after I missed playing one of those "chinks." I can't remember whether it was Bob Moore on bass, or Buddy Harman on drums, who was just grinning at me. They knew what I did, but they were the only ones who knew. I'm sure it would have been discovered later on in the control room, but I stopped momentarily, because I knew I'd missed it and I couldn't let it go that way. I just dozed right off. It was pretty crazy; [*sic*] but I got it right.[87]

Kennedy found that, with his background in rock and roll and country, he was frequently sought after to provide accompaniment for more rock-oriented sessions, telling Levy that "[i]f somebody wanted a rock kind of thing, they called me. Not that Grady couldn't do it. He did very well. Hank [Garland] could do it. He did it very well. But I was rawer. . . . Everybody stuck with what they did, and they did it well."[88] This approach can be heard on a wide variety of recordings, including most notably Jeannie C. Riley's 1968 recording of "Harper Valley PTA," which finds Kennedy playing blues-influenced dobro licks behind Riley's no-nonsense and somewhat sassy telling of the time her "mama socked it to the Harper Valley PTA."

Reggie Young, too, came to Nashville with an interest in both country and rhythm and blues music. As he told Pierce, he was profoundly influenced by the music he heard on Memphis radio station WHBQ and Nashville stations WLAC and WSM.[89] These stations—shaped by the market forces of a segregated US South that insisted that musics be distributed to radio listeners according to the racial identities of the musicians who made them—unintentionally challenged the segregated status quo as they traveled through the air and came unfiltered through the speakers of young people's radios.[90] As such, the budding guitarist found himself with regular access to a variety of rhythm and blues and country musicians, and, as he told Pierce, he even used the radio as a surrogate guitar instructor:

Another mid-1950s radio show that I liked was a show called *Two Guitars*. It was broadcast live from WSM/Nashville, and featured Chet Atkins, Jerry Byrd playing steel, and the rhythm guitar player was Ray Edenton. It aired in the afternoon, and if I ran home from school, I would just make it in time to hear the program, that is if weather conditions were favorable. I would sit there with the guitar in hand and try to learn some new licks from the master himself, Chet Atkins.[91]

Young, too, hit the road, albeit on a much wider scale than Kennedy did, playing first with a band that joined a number of rock and roll and rockabilly acts in a package show, and later with Johnny Horton, whom he accompanied on the *Louisiana Hayride* program.[92] After returning to Memphis in 1958, he worked with Bill Black, best known as the drummer in Elvis Presley's original group, until around 1964—a stint interrupted only by two years of military service in Ethiopia.[93]

By the mid-1960s, Young was working regularly as a session musician in Memphis and Muscle Shoals, the other two corners of what Charles Hughes has described as the "country-soul triangle."[94] As Roben Jones has documented in her detailed history of Memphis's American Studios, Young played a pivotal role in a number of key soul recordings, including sessions with Aretha Franklin and many others.[95] His work at American Studios also included some sessions with Elvis Presley, who had recorded in both Nashville and Memphis over the course of his extensive career (including many of his film soundtracks during the 1960s); the American Studios rhythm section—which included Young—formed the backing band for some of Presley's work during his comeback efforts in the late 1960s.[96] In building his reputation as a session musician, Young had encountered many of the leading younger session musicians in the "country-soul triangle," including several musicians from Muscle Shoals, Alabama, that would later come to Nashville. It was through that network that Young found his way to Nashville, as well; he told Pierce:

I was just passing through town [Nashville] on my way back to Memphis from Atlanta, and stopped into Nashville to see a friend of mine, David Briggs, who along with Norbert Putnam owned Quadraphonic Studios. David asked me if I would like to stay a while and do some record dates. I said "yes." And, [sic] I've been here ever since.

The only image I had had in my mind of the Nashville music scene was what I had seen on television in Memphis. I thought everyone in the music business in Nashville dressed like cowboys and wore their hair in crew cuts. Boy, was I ever mistaken.[97]

Young happened to come to town at a pivotal time in the Nashville recording scene's history, a time that increasingly found younger, rock-oriented artists flocking to the city in an effort to connect to the countercultural scene's rural-oriented rhetoric, imagery, and sounds.[98] He quickly became a highly sought-after guitarist among that community, especially as one of his last Memphis recordings hit the pop charts; as he told Pierce:

One of the last records I played on prior to leaving Memphis was Danny O'Keefe's "Good Time Charlie's Got the Blues," and that record had already charted and was getting airplay before I moved to Nashville. I got a lot of work because Nashville producers hired me to play the same kind of style I had played on that Top 10 record. Specifically, my style, on O'Keefe's record, was to use a volume pedal, and squeeze out notes to simulate the sounds of a steel guitar.[99]

Yet, despite being sought after for his specific approach to playing electric lead guitar, he also found that the Nashville recording scene required guitarists to emulate the sounds of others, as well:

Grady Martin was the top session guitar player in Nashville at that time. Grady is one of the best country players for playing single note lines there ever was. He always played exactly the right choice of notes the song called for. No one had more taste than Grady.

I was playing on a session shortly after I had moved to Nashville and the producer said to me, "Could you play this with a Grady Martin 'feel'?"

I said, "Why don't you get Grady to play that, he can do it a lot better than I can."

I wasn't being sarcastic, [sic] I was just being honest. I couldn't imagine why anyone would hire me to play like Grady Martin. It didn't make any sense to me when they could have gotten the real thing.[100]

Of course, the producer's rationale—apparently unstated in this exchange—was one that guided nearly every activity in the Nashville recording scene: an instrumentalist may be hired because of the specific skills that they bring to the session, but they must be able to emulate a variety of other sounds and styles in order to serve the song. Young learned this lesson, it seems, because his career as a leading Nashville session musician—one of the first musicians to be able to charge "double scale," or twice the agreed-upon union rate for a session—lasted well into the 1980s.[101]

Nashville guitarists needed to differentiate themselves from one another to stand out from a large crowd of competitors, but Nashville's session pianists needed to argue simply for the instrument's inclusion in country recordings. The piano was not a key instrument in country bands prior to the Nashville Sound era, but it became one in many Nashville Sound–era productions, regardless of the particular style of music that was being recorded, thanks to Floyd Cramer and Hargus "Pig" Robbins. Although pianists had been largely absent from much country music prior to the mid-1950s—with the notable exception of western swing, a country subgenre with deep musical ties to ragtime and jazz—the piano came to play a central role in filling the spaces between lines of lyrics, providing obligato melodies that accentuated the vocal melody, and contributing to the overall rhythmic feel of a track.[102] The piano came to be such a significant instrument in Nashville sessions that it is rather difficult to locate sessions for which a pianist was not hired. It's particularly striking that two pianists are commonly cited as regular members of the Nashville A Team, suggesting that their presence was not merely a novelty, but was in fact central to the overall work that the A Team did.

For a pianist working in Nashville, the demand to be stylistically fluent was as great as that placed on guitarists. In fact, these two instruments did the most work to signify the style that a recording artist and producer were attempting to invoke. African American rhythm and blues musicians, and the subsequent explosion of white rockabilly and early rock and roll artists, placed a high premium on a strong rhythmic pulse. Widely popularized in country music by King Records artist Moon Mullican in the late 1940s and early 1950s, pianists frequently played chords in straight eighth notes with accents on the backbeat, occasionally breaking into virtuosic pyrotechnics for fills between lines of lyric.[103] Sacred numbers, on the other hand, called for greater solemnity, often requiring the skills of a good church pianist who could provide chordal accompaniment without getting in the way of the spiritual message. For more upbeat sacred songs, the pianist might be expected to play in the style of a southern gospel pianist, using techniques drawn from stride and ragtime, while, at other times, the pianist might be called upon to move to the organ, an instrument that, despite having the same keyboard layout, requires a distinct keyboard technique (sliding the fingers from key to key rather than striking each one individually to obtain a legato effect).[104] And at still other times, the instrument was relegated to a rhythmic function, accentuating and contributing to the rhythm section of acoustic guitar, bass (often a combination of acoustic upright bass and an electric bass guitar), and drums.

Floyd Cramer was perhaps the most publicly visible member of the Nashville A Team, in large part because he maintained a thriving solo recording career that generated product that was put in front of the record-buying public well into the 1990s through mail-order compilations.[105] Born in Samti, Louisiana, and raised in Huttig, Arkansas, Cramer grew up with a piano in his home and was, as journalist Rich Kienzle noted, "largely self-taught."[106] At the age of eighteen, Cramer returned to Louisiana, where he played on Shreveport's *Louisiana Hayride* and made some of his first recordings, accompanying *Hayride* artists and cutting his own solo sides for the Abbott Records label.[107] In 1955, Cramer moved to Nashville, where he began recording with such former *Hayride* artists as Jim Reeves and Elvis Presley.[108] Through this work, Cramer secured even more regular session work, keeping him gainfully employed making music with an even wider range of musicians than he could have encountered at the *Hayride*. As journalist Alan Shelton noted in a 1981 retrospective of the Nashville Sound era, Cramer's work was everywhere: "[B]y 1960 it was estimated that Cramer's style was being featured on a quarter of all the American hit recordings, including those by Elvis Presley and Pat Boone."[109]

Cramer developed a trademark piano style that came to be known as the "slip-note" style. The style, which makes use of a quick non-chord grace note before landing on the chord tone, helped to make the piano sound like the stringed instruments that were more commonly found in country music. As Cramer told *Country Music Telegram* in 1978, "You hit one note and slide almost simultaneously to another. . . . It is a sort of near-miss on the keyboard. You don't hit the note you intend to strike right off, but you 'recover' instantly and then hit it. The result is a lonesome sound."[110] As Kienzle observes, Cramer "later compared [the 'slip-note' style] to Mother Maybelle Carter's signature guitar style."[111] In an interview recorded prior to a recording session in the mid-1960s, Carter herself noted that Cramer had credited her autoharp style—particularly the way that she switched between chord bars—as an influence on the "slip-note" style.[112] Yet, as Kienzle has noted, the style was more directly derived from a piano part played by songwriter Don Robertson in a demonstration recording of "Please Help Me, I'm Falling," a song that Cramer would later record with Hank Locklin. Struck by "the . . . pedal-steel-like phrasing" that Robertson brought to the piano part, Atkins instructed Cramer "to learn the part overnight" to prepare for Locklin's session to cut the song.[113] The Cramer "slip-note" style—one of several that he deployed in his session work— might be heard as favoring appoggiaturas that emphasize the third and fifth of a particular chord by sounding the second or sixth, respectively, as well as a closed chord voicing that places the fifth of the chord in the soprano voice.[114]

Perhaps no greater example of the "slip-note" style at work can be found than Cramer's 1960 solo recording, "Last Date." "Last Date" is built around these principles: grace notes approaching chord tones from below (the second) or from above (the sixth) ornamenting a fairly uninteresting melody that spans the easily singable range of a major tenth. Cramer uses the greater flexibility and strength of his thumb, index, and middle fingers to articulate the melody and to land forcefully on the grace notes, while his pinky and ring fingers—notoriously weaker and less flexible—play a drone on the root of the chord. Also characteristic of Cramer's style is a tendency to locate the melody in the same range as a skilled soprano can sing, implicitly reinforcing country music's vocal-centric tendencies. The drone, which is located in a comparatively higher register than the vocal melody, creates a sort of delicate and sometimes shimmering sound that can have the effect of making the recording sound more delicate.

The delicate and tender nature of Cramer's style also lends itself well to the creation of alternative narratives around the work. Although the song has become closely associated with nostalgia for teenaged romance, there is nothing in the instrumental itself to indicate that "Last Date" has anything to do with love. But, by 1961, new lyrics had been written for the song by Skeeter Davis and Boudleaux Bryant in which the speaker becomes aware that her romantic relationship was coming to an end over a rather meaningless tiff and the partner's interest in another person. Skeeter Davis's 1961 recording of "Last Date (With You)" features Cramer's opening slip-note lick—in the same key as his original—but the slip-note approach is adapted to create a particularly emotional harmony vocal. Davis's vocal melody sits comfortably in her power register, while the harmony vocals are in a range that adds a degree of tension and urgency to the performance. Cramer's piano, which plays an accompanimental role in this recording, then serves to add a sense of sentimentality and melancholy that accentuates the underlying emotion of the lyrics. "Last Date" was also revamped a second time, this time in 1972 by Conway Twitty, who called it "(Lost Her Love) On Our Last Date." In this case, the slip-note style is completely absent, as Twitty's recording does not use a piano. Instead, Cramer's signature licks are translated for the pedal steel guitar, returning the slip-note style to one of its possible sonic sources.

Some of Cramer's most iconic session work also makes use of the techniques heard in "Last Date," particularly the use of register to make room for the vocal performance. Cramer's contributions to Jim Reeves's 1959 recording of "He'll Have to Go," for instance, finds Cramer plays a relatively simple accompaniment that is more noteworthy for its persistent eighth note undulations than for anything distinctive. Cramer does not use the slip-note style here, but instead uses his characteristic voicing to emphasize the root of each chord, which he plays in root position (with the root at the top of the voicing). Joined by a particularly resonant vibraphone and the soprano voices of Anita Kerr and Dottie Dillard, Cramer's piano voicings leave a wide berth for Reeve's resonant baritone vocals and carefully frame one side of an intimate telephone conversation between the speaker and a cheating partner.[115] But Cramer's piano, combined with the other accompanying instruments in the same register, also emphasize the speaker's delusion, as he wants to pretend that nothing is wrong with his relationship. These almost too-quiet sparkling highs seem to convey a desire for domestic stability and tranquility that is no longer possible for the speaker and his cheating lover. Through these devices, eavesdropping listeners become even more keenly aware of the speaker's delusions.

Cramer's slip-note style is often heard as a musical hook that draws listeners into a particular recording throughout his time as a leading member of the Nashville A Team. Beginning with Locklin's "Please Help Me, I'm Falling," Cramer frequently used the slip-note technique to harmonize the melody of the song's hook at the song's outset, as well as in short instrumental interludes between sections of the song. So popular was Cramer's slip-note style that arrangers even used the slip-note sound as inspiration for their string arrangements, as we can hear in the string arrangement for Patsy Cline's take on "Faded Love" (1963).

But Cramer was a much more versatile pianist than his association with the slip-note style would indicate. One area that stands out quite prominently in Cramer's session work is his contribution to rock and roll and rockabilly sessions, sessions for which his slip-note approach would have been too country and sentimental. Cramer was a regular member of the band that backed Elvis Presley during his Nashville sessions for RCA Victor until the recording of the *Harum Scarum* soundtrack in 1965, which found Elvis using a new band as a consequence of scheduling difficulties.[116] Here, Cramer can be heard using both his left and his right hands—his left hand is notably absent from much slip-note playing—to provide a strong rhythmic drive to the recordings. He also continues to make extensive use of the octave between C5 and C6 for decorative playing and rhythmically busy solos. But just as common is a strong chordal comping that one can hear in the octave from C4 to C5, loading the recording's midrange alongside the buzzing acoustic rhythm guitars and somewhat distorted electric lead guitars and adding a sense of urgency and excitement to the overall performance. The combination of these two styles can be heard quite prominently in Presley's 1957 recording of "Jailhouse Rock," where the registral density and rhythmic energy were particularly valuable.

Cramer can also be heard emulating the style of rhythm and blues pianists in many recordings. In these cases, Cramer does not play a rhythmic role, but instead creates a constant barrage of fills that ride atop the lyrics and fill the gaps between lines. One way that he drew from the rockabilly vocabulary was to add triplet figures in the octave from C5 to C6. This technique can be heard quite clearly in Marvin Rainwater's 1957 recording of "Whole Lotta Woman."[117] In Jimmy Newman's "Carry On," recorded for Dot Records in 1958, Cramer offers a full imitation of Jerry Lee Lewis, including shimmering rolled chords, a bustling shuffle rhythm, and a hearty dose of glissandi.[118] This approach can also be heard in his work with "the Female Elvis," Janis Martin, whose 1956 RCA Victor recording of "Drugstore Rock 'n' Roll" provides a slightly more restricted version.[119]

Floyd Cramer's session work began to dwindle significantly in the mid-1960s for a variety of reasons, not the least of which was his effort to continue building his solo career. Solo careers were notoriously difficult for session musicians to maintain, in large part because the constant demands of the studio during the week limited travel for gigs to weekends. As a consequence of that time limitation, musicians were also prevented from traveling long distances, particularly in the days before air travel became widely available. This created the space for other pianists to fill his session responsibilities, but those pianists were expected to emulate Cramer's style in order to get ahead, as session pianist and arranger Bill Pursell recalled to interviewer Terry Klefstad. Other session musicians told him: "'Well, you're going to have to study Floyd Cramer. You're going to have to see what he's doing in sessions.' So I would look at Floyd Cramer and find he couldn't play an even C major scale, yet he's doing all these sessions. . . .

[T]he first session with Homer and Jethro that I got, I thought, 'Well, they want to see what I can do.' So I was all over the piano, playing everything and so forth. It wasn't what they wanted, and after the session, Jethro looked at me and said, 'Well, it's good to see you again, Bill,' and then I knew I had flunked because it was a very curt, polite way of saying, 'Well, that's not quite what we wanted.' And so I learned to do the Floyd thing, or whatever it has to be."[120]

Whereas Cramer was widely celebrated for his particular stylistic vocabulary, pianist Hargus "Pig" Robbins gained a reputation as one of the city's most versatile pianists. Robbins was the beneficiary of the music program at the Tennessee School for the Blind, where he took his first piano lessons as a primary school student.[121] Music was one of the principal areas of instruction at many schools for the blind throughout the segregated US South. Such internationally recognized musicians as the Blind Boys of Alabama and Doc Watson developed their musical skills in such schools, which saw entertainment as one of the relatively few job opportunities that was available to visually disabled men.[122] Although Braille notation was available, the musical pedagogy at these institutions necessarily relied on aural/oral instruction, encouraging students to use their ears to pick out tunes and harmonies.[123] (That this came from the sense that people with visual disabilities were able to compensate for that perceived shortcoming through an improved sense of hearing is probably worth noting as an underlying, if not unproblematic, assumption.)[124] For the vocal groups that emerged from African American schools for the blind in Mississippi and Alabama, the "trainer" system that they used to teach everyone to sing could be applied easily to the pedagogy of the blind.[125] But standard piano pedagogy would have required a radical overhaul given its strong reliance on written notation and its emphasis on the Western classical canon.[126] Robbins told interview Douglas B. Green that his musical interests—and his aural skills—quickly outgrew the classical focus of that pedagogical tradition:

Classical! That was their whole bit. . . . They frown upon trying to pick up country tunes or pop tunes or boogie woogie or rock and roll or whatever. But if you've got some ability, you're not just going to stick with the classical stuff. I started figuring out anything I could hear on the radio. The early stuff, I guess, was hillbilly, because that's what I'd heard all my life, and then I kind of got into dixieland [*sic*], and then rock and roll came along.[127]

Robbins's interests in rock and roll also led him to pick up the saxophone, which he played onstage when "the piano wasn't in good enough shape to really compete with the loud guitars and drums. . . ."[128]

Such broad musical interests undoubtedly helped him as he began to seek professional opportunities as a session musician, much as it had helped many other musicians in the Nashville A Team. Unfortunately for Robbins, though, the piano duties at most sessions were already covered, initially leaving him with demo sessions.[129] But when Cramer scored a hit with "Last Date," he serviced fewer accounts, leaving room for Robbins, who had learned Cramer's slip-note approach. As he told Green: "Floyd Cramer had come out with 'Last Date' and then kind of retired from the recording scene after that . . . [,] and when he quit, I was really just about the only one around who could play in that pedal style that was so popular, and that didn't hurt me any."[130] Robbins also pointed to the expansion of the Nashville studio scene as another factor that made space for him to work more regularly, noting that "the business was really growing, and that kind of made room for another band, because one or two bands had it more or less sewed up before. It was an exciting time for me. I couldn't wait to get up out of bed in the morning to get at it."[131]

Although Robbins could emulate the Cramer style, Green notes that Robbins "developed his own distinct style at the keyboard by featuring the melody in the left hand played against the chords in the right. Robbins calls this his 'Maybelle Carter' technique, because it echoes the famous guitar style pioneers in the 1920s by playing the melody on her bass strings and strumming the treble for rhythm."[132] It is particularly interesting that both Cramer and Robbins credited Carter as the source of their piano style, but that both of them developed their own interpretation of that style in their respective work. Cramer's style seems to have focused primarily on

Carter's tendency to use hammer-ons (playing an open string and then striking the string on a fret) and pull-offs (playing a stopped string and pulling the finger away to let the open string ring), as revealed by his tendency to use approach the third of a chord from beneath (much as a guitarist might move from an open A string to a fretted B in a G major chord) and the sixth from above (much as a guitarist might play a fretted E on the D string before releasing the string in a G major chord). These hammer-ons and pull-offs are quite commonly heard in the broad string band tradition, particularly on the guitar and banjo, so Cramer's efforts represent a rather broad interpretation of that approach.[133] Robbins, on the other hand, reveals a more nuanced take on the Carter style, acknowledging that Carter played the melodies on the guitar's bass strings, and working diligently to emulate that approach. Robbins's take on this can be heard quite clearly in his contributions to Charley Pride's "Kiss an Angel Good Morning" (1971), which also offers a variation on bluegrass guitarist Lester Flatt's famous "G run."

Elements of this approach can be heard clearly in Robbins's contributions to Charlie Rich's iconic Epic recording of "Behind Closed Doors."[134] The recording begins with a brief piano introduction that emulates the Cramer slip-note style; this lick is also heard as a transition following the first chorus. But as Rich's vocals enter, Robbins begins to emphasize the lower register of the piano, offering a commentary on Rich's lyrics through a series of filigreed chordal figurations and licks that trail off into the bass register. This is precisely the kind of figuration that a particularly skilled bluegrass flatpicker might add to their accompaniment, adding a degree of rhythmic interest beyond simply strumming a chord. Interestingly, the rhythm guitar player here does not offer a similar accompaniment, in large part because too much filigree would have created unnecessary clutter in the arrangement and would have potentially led to unnecessary mixing challenges. Instead, the uncredited rhythm guitarist strums straight eighth notes, emphasizing the upstroke to help propel the performance forward.

Another striking element of Robbins's contributions to Rich's "Behind Closed Doors" is the sense of rhythmic propulsion that Robbins gives to the performance. In his 1977 interview with Douglas Green, Robbins observed that rhythm was a big part of what he liked to contribute to a recording:

> What I like on records is a lot of full rhythm. . . . To me, that means a lot of octaves in the right hand. It just fills up a record and gives it a lot of midrange. Now, on the pedals, I just use a very light sustain, if any, and occasionally the soft pedal if the producer wants it super soft and muted, but I do this very sparingly. I think a lot of piano players make the mistake of using too much sustain, because to me it all runs together and becomes messy sounding. It just doesn't sound good on record.[135]

Robbins's disdain for the sustain pedal can be heard clearly in "Behind Closed Doors"; any sustain that is heard is, for the most part, the result of Robbins depressing the key and not releasing it, allowing the note to decay without extra assistance. Additionally, it should be noted that Robbins uses a particularly percussive attack, leading the front edge of the note and almost anticipating the beat at times. This is particularly clear in his articulation of bass notes during the song's chorus. Signaled by a snare drum, the band kicks in at full volume, with the electric bass, tic-tac guitar, and Robbins's left hand locking together (with minor variations) to the other two bass parts. This kind of emphasis on rhythm—and particularly the bass—can be heard in a number of Billy Sherrill productions, including Tammy Wynette's 1967 Epic debut, "I Don't Wanna Play House," and her landmark 1968 single, "Stand by Your Man" (where Robbins is practically pounding the left hand throughout the song's iconic chorus); George Jones's "The Grand Tour" (1974) (which also showcases Robbins playing an absolutely heartbreaking introduction that turns into the echo of the heartbroken speaker's voice in an empty house); and the great Wynette-Jones duets.[136]

Unlike Floyd Cramer, whose work might be heard as an effort to embellish the lyrics with some sort of musical embroidery, Robbins offered a broader musical commentary on the lyrics, often interweaving an iconic lick between the lyrics in a manner that accentuates the psychological drama of a particular song or that effectively sets the stage for the song's plot. The Wynette-Jones duet recording of Bobby Braddock's composition "Golden Ring" uses a pawnshop wedding band to tell the story of a romance that bloomed quickly and faded just as fast. This ring, which was "just a cold metallic thing," seems to be doomed to a constant cycle of love and loss, living a perverse version of its matrimonial symbolism. The primary musical instruments heard in this arrangement are the acoustic guitar, which is played in an exceptionally busy flatpicking style, and Robbins's contribution—possibly made at the suggestion of producer Billy Sherrill, who guitarist Chip Young recalled "usually had a piano lick or something that he wanted [to hear]"—stands out in only one significant place.[137] In the second verse, when the couple stands before a minister to take their vows, the lyric remarks that "an old upright piano plays that old familiar tune," and Robbins intones the incipit of Wagner's wedding march from Act III of *Lohengrin*. With this simple reference, Robbins draws the listener into the song's narrative and then quickly fades away, calling forth the traces of so many weddings. Considering that this is a heartbreak song, one may very well argue that this brief quotation helps to universalize the song by calling forth the memory of the audience's own matrimonial hopes and dreams and leaving them unfulfilled through its incompleteness. Its brevity may also be read as foreshadowing of the impeding cataclysmic end to the protagonists' marriage, coming in the next verse when, "in a small, two-room apartment," the couple "fights their final round."

Similarly, Robbins's Carter-style hammer-ons in Charley Pride's "Wonder Could I Live There Anymore" (1970)—a session that he told Green was "his most representative piano work"—also works to invoke a sense of memory and nostalgia.[138] The song, penned by Bill Rice, reflects upon the speaker's simple upbringing, where everyone is busy working hard, struggling to pay the bills, and yet managing to love one another, and ponders whether it would be possible to return to the simple ways of his childhood. Speaking to the broader upward mobility of so many country music fans in the 1960s, the speaker notes that "it's nice to think about it, maybe even visit," but that it would be impossible to return there after living in the middle class. Robbins's piano plays a key role throughout the recording, answering each of Pride's lines about life in the country with a series of rustic-sounding Carter-style licks that emulate the sounds of banjos and guitars on the front porch. But, strikingly, as the speaker indicates his lack of interest in moving back home, Robbins's hammer-ons and bass runs are subsumed by a string orchestra, which offers a polite, middle-class sheen on those reflections. It seems that, although the memories of rural life are strong, those memories can be sublimated for the sake of middle-class politeness. When Pride's race is considered in this equation, the narrative becomes all the more profound. As an African American musician from Mississippi, he was undoubtedly aware of the complex ways that race and class performance intersected for upwardly mobile southern blacks who were still restricted by the de jure and de facto results of Jim Crow.[139]

Instruments that take a leading role undoubtedly stand out in a recording, and the stylistic idiosyncrasies that these musicians developed seem to have been useful tools in helping them obtain and maintain careers in the studio. But it might seem less likely that rhythm section musicians would have a similar need, particularly given the Nashville Sound's general avoidance of intense rhythm section sounds. Yet the rhythm section was responsible for holding the tempo, adding some rhythmic interest, controlling the overall dynamic shape of the performance, and grounding the harmonic progression of the song, making their presence essential and their specific skills invaluable to the creation of a memorable recording.

Although pianists and drummers were sometimes optional additions to Nashville Sound–era recording sessions, one would be hard-pressed to find a recording session where that was not at least one, if not as two, bass players working. The only instrument that shares that degree of prominence is, unsurprisingly, the guitar. As a consequence, several bass players were able to maintain regular work schedules and steady incomes working the sessions along Music Row and, as the recording scene expanded in the late 1960s and early 1970s, around Nashville. The rise of the Nashville recording industry also paralleled significant developments in the bass itself.[140] Since the advent of country recording in the 1920s, the double bass—also known as the acoustic bass, upright bass, or, in some settings, the "doghouse bass"—was the standard bass instrument to be captured on wax. But the double bass was far from an ideal recording instrument for a number of reasons. It is a quiet instrument, making it rather difficult for many microphones to pick up, particularly in the prewar years and the decade immediately following World War II, when most sessions were recorded around only one or two microphones. In those sessions, the priority was to capture the vocals, so bass players would not be able to position themselves close to the microphone; in fact, the instrument's acoustic outputs—the F holes on the instrument's top—were located far below the microphone and out of reach of its polar pattern. The acoustic bass's beautiful tone could also be smothered by louder string band instruments, such as the guitar, banjo, and fiddle, and electrified instruments such as the lap steel and the electric lead guitar dominated the audio field. As such, the acoustic bass was simply difficult to hear.

Added to these acoustic challenges was the fact that many bass players picked up the instrument simply because it was the only instrument that was available for them to play in a band. Since it is tuned to the same pitches as the lowest four strings on a guitar (only an octave lower), it was rather easy for many musicians to move from the guitar to the acoustic bass, especially if a song was to be sung in a guitar-friendly key, such as E, A, D, or G (as many were). Unfortunately, the relatively low barrier of entry on the acoustic bass meant that many musicians were able to develop passable skills on the instrument without developing proper technique. As such, many country bassists were unable to draw the best tone from the instrument, further exacerbating the audibility problems that they were experiencing.[141] To draw tone from an acoustic bass, one must possess precise and nuanced left- and right-hand technique. But since the bass would often be felt more than heard on a recording, tone was often sacrificed in favor of strong rhythm.

By the end of the 1950s, the acoustic bass became much more audible than it had been during the first decade of recording in Nashville, thanks in large part to improvements in the capabilities of the recording studios themselves. With the opening of the Quonset Hut in 1955 and

RCA's permanent studios in 1956, the recording consoles themselves were expanded to allow for the placement of additional microphones around the studio.[142] As a consequence, it became increasingly possible to dedicate a microphone to the acoustic bass, therefore creating an opportunity to capture its sound directly and to weave it into the overall mix of the recording. As such, the tone of the acoustic bass became a key part of many iconic recordings from the 1950s and 1960s. It was through these developments that dedicated bass players became all the rage in Nashville, and bassists who could produce a beautiful tone were particularly at an advantage in that move.

Bassist Bob Moore is widely accepted as one of the most significant figures in pulling the bass out of the margins of Nashville country music. A native of Nashville, Moore came to the session scene with a wide variety of musical experiences, particularly in country and "society" music, what many jazz scholars have described as "sweet" jazz.[143] He became interested in music, in part, as a consequence of his work as a shoeshine boy, which brought him backstage at the *Opry*. While still in junior high school, he played in a country band with several of his classmates and even recorded a single with Bob Jennings. By high school, he was touring Oklahoma with Jamup & Honey, a blackface comedic duo that worked on the *Grand Ole Opry*; he was a member of Paul Howard and His Arkansas Cotton Pickers, a western swing band that had been associated with the *Opry*; and he was performing with such leading country acts as Little Jimmy Dickens, Flatt & Scruggs, and Eddy Arnold. By 1950, Moore was working in both Nashville, where he was recording radio transcriptions with Marty Robbins, and in Springfield, Missouri, where former *Opry* star Red Foley was working on the *Ozark Jubilee*; there he was joined by former Dickens bandmate and future Nashville session guitarist Grady Martin.[144] As Michael McCall has noted, Moore and Martin would "back Foley on weekends and then rush back to Nashville to perform with Robbins on Monday and Tuesday, heading back to Springfield on Wednesday."[145] Through his session work in Nashville and his connections to Foley, Moore began to meet some of the leaders of the Nashville recording scene and was soon playing bass not only on Decca sessions, but RCA Victor

and Columbia sessions, as well. From those early successes, he went on to
be one of the most recorded bassists in the history of popular music in the
United States, maintaining an active career well into the 1970s.[146]

Moore was an important bassist not only for his contributions to the
recording scene, but also for his work in removing the bass from its traditional string band role as the instrument that the band's comedian would
play. As he told Rich Kienzle in an interview for *No Depression*, "In those
days, a bass player was a comedian in the band. I was something new;
I was a player, not a comedian."[147] A significant reason for that is that he
took his instrument seriously, not the comedy; other bass players had
sought out comedy as their primary line of work, and the bass was a tool
to get them on stage. As such, the bass was simply not a serious instrument. But Moore worked diligently to learn his instrument and to develop
technique, thanks in part to the support of other journeyman musicians
in Howard's band who encouraged him to practice scales.[148] Scale practice
undoubtedly helped Moore to develop fluency in a variety of keys and
taught him how to connect various chords to one another. Furthermore,
if Moore focused on playing scales up and down the bass's neck, he could
develop a more stable, rounded sound throughout the entire range of the
instrument, an ability that is particularly prized by jazz and classical musicians, but that could also be of use to a recording bassist. Finally, Moore's
scale practice likely helped him to develop a more nuanced understanding of intonation, a musical characteristic that is particularly challenging
to develop on a fretless stringed instrument such as the acoustic bass and
that is absolutely essential as bassists work to provide a stable and in-tune
foundation for the rest of the ensemble. In other words, if the bass player
cannot play in tune, it is terribly difficult for the other musicians in the
group to play in tune, as well.

Moore's practice regimen seems to have yielded remarkable results, as
identified by both Moore and the musicians he worked most closely with.
As Harold Bradley told interviewer Morris Levy in 1996, Moore "played
with good intonation, and he played with a nice tone. And instead of
playing way up high on the fingerboard of the bass, like Ernie [Newton]
did—which gives you a big round sound—Bob played back down near the

bridge, which gave you a distinct sound [Bradley snaps] when he pulled it. So it probably recorded better. People take note of that when they sit in the studio every day."[149] In a 2011 interview with *Bass Player* magazine, Moore noted that aspiring recording bassists should focus on the fundamentals of tone, intonation, and fluency in a variety of keys and positions, arguing that "even if you're not a schooled player, [you should] learn the correct positions on your bass. And most important, learn how to pull the string the right way. That's the most essential thing of all."[150] When combined with improvements in microphone technology, then, Moore was able to create a bass sound that was both clear and in tune, while also demonstrating an ability to play bass lines with more melodic interest than many other bassists in Nashville at the time.[151]

Moore's contributions can be heard on thousands of recordings to have emerged from the Nashville studio scene during the entire Nashville Sound era, as his career spanned from the scene's earliest days to the end of the 1970s. As such, we have a large body of material to listen to as we try to get a sense of Moore's approach to tone, harmony, and timing. Listening to his work on Conway Twitty's "It's Only Make Believe" (1970), for instance, Moore can be heard anticipating the beat and using his distinctive approach to pulling the string near the instrument's bridge to put a sharp attack on each note.[152] As a consequence, his bass tone presents a slight punch just ahead of the beat, which pushes the performance forward. But, despite the sharp attack, the tone of the bass note is not degraded; in fact, we can hear a very clear tone that rings for nearly an entire beat before Moore mutes the string. The resulting tone sets a firm harmonic foundation that allows Twitty to gauge his intonation and that works well with the piano, an instrument that would quickly reveal any intonation problems.

Bob Moore's bass tone was also frequently doubled by an electric bass, most commonly played by guitarist Harold Bradley. Heard prominently in the recordings of Patsy Cline, among many others, the "tic-tac bass" that Bradley developed accentuated the acoustic bass without completely overtaking it. As Bradley told interviewer John Rumble:

The acoustic bass didn't record evenly. Some of the notes would drop out, and so, naturally, it would drop out on the radio, and that note would come out on the radio as a kind of a bass. So it reinforced whatever the bass was doing.[153]

He went on to explain that the doubling between the electric and acoustic bass was not always an exact doubling, but could instead be understood as a complementary practice in which the two bassists worked together to fill in all the parts, as he noted in discussing his work on Cline's iconic 1961 recording of "Crazy":

He [bassist Bob Moore] was only playing [beats] one and three. But I was able to play the in-between notes, [hums], stuff like that. With the click in that, it wasn't overwhelming. If you played that on the bass, the sound was like shooting off a cannon in the low end because it's so powerful and dominating, so I could keep the record interesting even when there were no fills, by playing a little connecting-up stuff. Also, I could give him [Owen] a note that would reproduce on the radio.[154]

This click, it should be noted, was the result not simply of the instrument, but of the necessary use of a flatpick to produce those sounds; it is nearly impossible to play the bass with the fingers when one is also using the heel of the palm to mute the strings.

The origins of the tic-tac bass sound can be traced to a particularly ineffective and cheaply made Danelectro six-string bass guitar that Harold Bradley purchased at a local Nashville music store.[155] As he recalled, the instrument was so poorly built that it was nearly impossible to keep in tune, and the techniques that Bradley developed to minimize these limitations led to the creation of its distinctive sound. As he recounted:

[T]he tic-tac bass guitar was a different animal [than the upright acoustic bass], because it was like a $90 piece of junk. Didn't have a rod in the neck. And now the necks on both of mine are bowed. And the scale is weird. It won't tune to anything. You have to tune up to whatever key you're playing in. You have tuned in the key of F, and you play, that's fine, but then if you go along to B-flat or something else like C, you have to tweak the tuning again. But the main thing that I did was, I don't know why I did it, but I put my hand over the bridge and muted the strings. And it helped the intonation. You didn't notice any intonation difference between what I was playing and the bass, acoustic bass.[156]

As pianist "Pig" Robbins began to double the bass notes, as well, it became even more imperative that Bradley work on the tic-tac's intonation, as it would become immediately clear that the instrument was out of tune when joined by still more instruments playing the same lines.[157]

The process of filling in these parts was often a collaborative one, especially at first, as Moore and Bradley were learning how to complement one another. At times, Moore made suggestions about the shape of the bass line and how the two of them could double it effectively, as Bradley recounted to me:

Bob was a great bass player. He and I worked out a lot of the bass lines. But he had some ideas on how the bass should do if you're changing keys, and you're playing G D G D and before you go to C, he wants you to play two Gs . . . , because it's weaker when you play G D G D G D and you go from D to the C. So I thank him for that. . . . [N]ow I think most kind of everybody does that.[158]

One particularly striking example of this kind of playing can be heard in Brenda Lee's recording of "I'm Sorry" (1960), recorded at the Quonset Hut under Owen Bradley's production guidance.[159] Here, Bob Moore plays a rather plodding bass line that emphasizes the first and third beats of each measure and that stays fairly close to the root and fifth scale degree of each chord; he offers very few stepwise lead-ins to other chords or new sections of the form. (This could be exacerbated by the song's harmonic hook, which features an oscillation between the tonic and the leading-tone chords.) Pianist Floyd Cramer and rhythm guitarists Hank Garland and Grady Martin accentuate a steady triplet pattern to add to the rhythmic interest, while the Anita Kerr Singers provide a soft pad and a string quartet responds to Lee's vocals, playing variations on the "I'm Sorry" motive. But the performance may have begun to drag if not for Harold Bradley's contribution on the tic-tac bass. Here, he plays a sort of loping figure that arpeggiates the chords and strikes all four beats of each measure. Additionally, he accentuates the song's compound meter by anticipating beats one and three by one eighth note. As a consequence, the tempo remains consistent (a real challenge at such a slow tempo), the primary subdivision of the beat is confirmed, and the bass register is filled out. And, in a recording that has no drums at all, the combination of tic-tac bass and steady downstrokes on the rhythm guitar helps to provide a solid rhythmic underpinning to the performance.

The sound of the tic-tac bass was particularly prominent in Owen Bradley's Decca sessions, but he was far from the only producer to explore novel ways to record the bass during the late 1950s and early 1960s. Tic-tac became the Nashville method, but it's worth noting that nearly every popular music record producer of the era struggled to get bass sounds that they liked and that would translate well over jukeboxes and AM car and transistor radios.[160] Phil Spector, in his efforts to develop what he described as a "wall of sound" in his work with Ronettes, the Shangri-Las, and others, often employed multiple bass players on a single session, achieving much the same effect that Owen Bradley did with only two bassists.[161] In Detroit, session bassist James Jamerson experimented with a direct injection technique to improve the sound of his electric bass, resulting in a sound that many other bassists have emulated using other technologies.[162] In England, engineer Geoff Emerick worked closely with Beatle Paul McCartney to develop bass sounds that approximated those of McCartney's favorite Motown records using the technologies that were available in the United Kingdom during the late 1960s and early 1970s.[163] Ultimately, what all of these engineers and musicians were attempting to do was to overcome the noise and frequency response limitations of contemporary recording and playback equipment in order to produce sounds that were both audible and musically pleasing, particularly in cars and on transistor radios and jukeboxes. But each of them had different ideas of what made the music interesting. In Nashville, production tended to emphasize space, and we can hear an effort to build an uncluttered sound through the use of the tic-tac. Interestingly, Harold Bradley pointed out that, as recording techniques were developed to capture the sound of the bass drum, the tic-tac was replaced in many sessions; it was not maintained because its primary purpose—the "click"—could be found in another, more suitable instrument.[164]

As the electric bass began to gain acceptance in popular music circles during the mid-1950s, it came to replace the acoustic bass on more and more sessions, leading to new opportunities for bassists who specialized in the instrument. Two bassists in particular came to fill that niche: Henry Strzelecki and Norbert Putnam. Both of these musicians were a generation younger than the session musicians who built Music Row, and they brought new musical sensibilities into the studio, including prior experiences with the rock and roll and rhythm and blues sounds that had been popularized during the 1950s. As a consequence, they were—like other session musicians who began to come to the city in the mid-1960s—responsible for changing the sounds of country music in some fundamental ways by the close of the 1960s and the early 1970s. Yet, at the same time, they were still expected to perform in all of the major country styles, as well.

Birmingham, Alabama, native Henry Strzelecki came to the electric bass through country and southern gospel music. He grew up in a musical family, "playing and singing on ukuleles and pianos and whatever there was at the house," as he told interviewer John Rumble. In his teens, his father lent him the money to buy his first bass, and it wasn't long before he was playing with the Louvin Brothers on Birmingham radio station WVOK and gigging with a variety of local country acts. By his junior year of high school, he had dropped out of school to take a job as a trumpeter with a band led by saxophonist Gene Hendrickson, a former member of the Tommy and Jimmy Dorsey bands. The band's pianist taught Strzelecki to read musical notation in an effort to help him develop his skills and maintain steady employment as a musician. After a year or so on the road, he returned to Birmingham, where he formed the Four Flickers, a Top 40–oriented group that performed daily on a WAPI-TV program hosted by Country Boy Eddie. The group was a "professional group" that wore matching uniforms—"the glittery, shiny stuff, you know, tuxedo type, because we played nightclubs, supper clubs, did a little TV, and like I said, we played anywhere they'd let us" along a "southern circuit" that included Birmingham, Atlanta, Biloxi, and Shreveport. Realizing that they needed to perform some of their own material if they were going to garner attention, the Four Flickers recorded Strzelecki's composition "Long Tall Texan" for Lee Records in Memphis. Inspired by a chance sighting of country singer Tex Ritter at a Birmingham drive-in, it promulgated the Four Flickers to regional fame as their recording hit the charts in Birmingham and other cities, allowing the group to raise its fees "from $100 a week to about $2,500 for the group a week." Later, he played with a group called the Four Counts, which recorded with an all-star crew of New Orleans musicians including Huey "Piano" Smith and Mac Rebennack (aka Dr. John).[165]

In his travels around the southern music scene, young Strzelecki also had a rare opportunity to perform on a major-label recording in Nashville. At age seventeen, he accompanied rock and roll singer Baker Knight to Nashville to record a session for Decca at the Quonset Hut, playing bass alongside such Nashville A Team all-stars as Grady Martin, Hank Garland, and Farris Coursey. As he told Rumble, bassist Bob Moore even came by the session to check Strzelecki out: "They had Bob Moore, who's one of my best friends today and has been for years and years . . . , sit in the wings, actually up in the echo chamber, waiting to see whether I was going to be able to play or not, because they'd never heard me. And Owen [Bradley] was a stickler. Oh boy, he was a stickler, always has been and still is today, about having his music played right and sound right, and that's the reason he's always been great, because he cares about it. Well, of course, I was scared to death, and we played for four hours, and when we finished, the only person that said anything to me at all was Hank Garland. Me, being the kid, the true kid that I really was, they didn't know whether I could play or not, so after the first couple of songs, I think they sent Bob home, but I never did know Bob was up there. . . . So anyway, I finished the session myself, and it came out on Decca."[166]

By the time that Henry Strzelecki came to Nashville on a permanent basis, then, he had developed a wide-ranging musical background as both a bassist—playing an acoustic upright bass—and trumpeter. He had performed in a variety of live venues, from supper clubs and fraternity parties to radio and television broadcasts and had recorded in several different studios with bands of his own making and with professional studio musicians. He could play and sing mainstream popular music, country music, and rock and roll. And he had even written a song that had earned some regional chart success. A reading musician who could also function in an oral/aural environment, Strzelecki was well-rounded, but essentially an outsider to the Nashville scene. When he and his wife, Ruth, moved there in November or December 1960, he hoped that his one session at Decca had left an impression with guitarist Hank Garland, the only musician who stuck around to talk with him afterward.[167] When he got to town, he reached out to Garland, who not only remembered Strzelecki, but also opened the door for him to get started, offering him a gig at the Carousel Club, a jazz club in the Printer's Alley section of downtown Nashville. There, he played bass weeknights in a duo with pianist Bill Pursell and as a member of a quartet with Pursell, Garland, and drummer Buddy Harman on Friday nights.[168] By 1961, Garland was inviting Strzelecki to join him on recording sessions, first for an independent label artist named Gene Kennedy and then for RCA Victor recording artist Eddy Arnold, one of the label's strongest-selling artists.[169] From that point forward, his date-book would be full of session work for years to come: "That December, I got here on the 4th, and he'd hired me for about, I think, fourteen sessions that month plus the jobs I was doing at Carousel."[170]

Garland was generous to Strzelecki by offering him regular work in the studio, but it is unlikely that he would have been able to survive as a bassist in a crowded field had it not been for the exponential growth of the city's recording scene in the early 1960s and his own musical versatility. As he told Rumble, "they needed more bass players here at the time [I moved to Nashville] than they did guitar players, so I went back to bass" after a lifetime playing the guitar.[171] Recording at first as an acoustic bassist, Strzelecki found himself filling in wherever possible.[172] Much as other musicians have reported of their own experiences, Strzelecki was taken under the wing of some of the more experienced session musicians working along Music Row and was given the opportunity to further hone his musical skills. In particular, Harold Bradley and Grady Martin played a prominent role in this development, much as Bob Moore had helped Bradley expand his skill set:

> Back in the sixties . . . , the director of the session would tell you, "Put something in there." Even the bass, even me. Or, "Why don't you play with me on this, play the same notes I'm playing." Harold Bradley would do that a lot. "Play with me on this, and then you do whatever else it is you normally do the rest of the song." That's the way they taught you, really, what to play on the sessions when you were the new kid on the block coming in. They knew I knew the right proper notes to play for the chords and stuff, because they had heard me play enough to know that I did know. But making a record, they would ask you to play certain things. And if it was feasible and possible to do on the upright bass, which is what I did most of my sessions on in the early sixties, then I would try to copy what they wanted me to play. Then a lot of times I would throw in my own licks, and they would . . . play along with me.[173]

Thus, as more musicians came to town in search of session work and as demand grew for their labor, the sessions themselves became vital sites of professional training that allowed for the continued growth of the recording scene. Needless to say, this took a great deal of generosity on the part of the older musicians in the city and a deep awareness of the need to continue cultivating the session scene. As a consequence, the scene could expand while experiencing relatively minimal growing pains, because the growth seems to have unfolded—for the most part—in a spirit of cooperation and mutual appreciation, much as one might expect in a trade union with a strong apprenticeship program.

By the late 1960s, Strzelecki augmented his acoustic bass work with the assistance of a Fender Jazz Bass that he obtained in either 1965 or 1966.[174] Unlike the Danelectro bass that Bradley had used to develop the tic-tac sound, the Fender Jazz Bass was a high-end instrument that had much better intonation and electronic circuitry, which allowed it to be a more consistent instrument both in the studio and in live performances.[175] As he noted, the Fender bass gave him a sound with "more definition" than an acoustic bass could.[176] Experimenting with a variety of different amplifiers, he decided that Fender amplifiers worked best for his sound, and he was constantly "trying different strings, different pickups" to get a sound that he was pleased with and that could provide a solid tone to compete with the other instruments in an arrangement.[177] In particular, he was listening for a "clean" sound, or a sound that was "less muddy," particularly in the lower registers of the instrument.[178]

Strzelecki was often hired to work with some of the more progressive artists to record in Nashville in the second half of the 1960s, including such musician-favorites as Willie Nelson and Jerry Reed. Strzelecki's electric bass work is noteworthy not for its technical brilliance, as flashy runs were simply not appropriate for much of the material that he was working on. But what is significant is his ability to lock in with the bass drum—which was becoming louder and louder by 1968 and 1969—and drive a performance forward. Working closely with drummers Jerry Carrigan and Kenny Buttrey on many of these sessions, Strzelecki often played a syncopated figure with the bass drum pedal that helped to add an element of funkiness to many RCA productions.

Such is the case in Reed's recording of the Jimmy Martin bluegrass classic "Freeborn Man," which was recorded during a July 8, 1968, session for RCA Victor.[179] Recorded with a full horn section and with clear eyes toward a pop crossover hit, Reed's take on "Freeborn Man" showcases his distinctive guitar style, which expanded the Chet Atkins finger-picked style by emphasizing a strong syncopated downstroke with the thumb and that offered sharp and timbrally bright off-beats on the guitar's higher strings. As well, Reed's vocals are laid back and use a great deal of rubato, almost floating on top of a metrically steady accompaniment.

Strzelecki and Buttrey emphasize the inherent syncopation of Reed's guitar by playing sharply on beat one, the upbeat of beat two, and beat four, creating a punchy, funky foundation for the recording. Strzlecki also mutes the strings to keep things from ringing together, helping to sharpen the attacks of each note. As a consequence, much like the tic-tac bass of Harold Bradley, Strzlecki's electric bass, when combined with the bass drum of the drum set, provided a "click" that could cut through on car and portable transistor radios.[180] As Strzelecki noted in a June 1990 interview with John Rumble, the electric bass addressed a major challenge of recording the bass:

> [I]t got to be so much more dependable [than the acoustic bass], the electric bass did, and it was easier to get on the tape. Back then the bass and the bass drum would cancel each other out a lot, so when the bass drum would cancel out the upright bass, well, I'd go to the electric bass a lot of times for that reason. Again, it was according to what key we were in, who was playing drums, and if you could get it on the record or not. . . . A lot of times I would do sessions with Buddy Harman, and Buddy's bass drum would just cancel me out. A lot of times they wouldn't let Buddy play bass drum on early records because he canceled the bass out with his bass drum.[181]

With these improvements to the bass, though, Strzelecki was able to add both tone and punch to the bass part.

Another bassist who was quite prominent in the Nashville scene during the second half of the 1960s and early 1970s was Norbert Putnam. Like Strzelecki, Putnam was an Alabama native who had come of age playing in rock and pop bands for white social events in high schools, outdoor concerts, and along the southern fraternity circuit.[182] Inspired by the slap bass techniques deployed by Elvis Presley collaborator Bill Black, Putnam's first band, the Rhythm Rockers, capitalized on the popularity of the sounds emerging from Sun Records.[183] By 1958, Putnam and Briggs had joined forces with then-fifteen-year-old drummer Jerry Carrigan, to begin playing rhythm and blues in the Alabama college circuit with a

group called the Mark V. In the process of changing his focus from rockabilly to rhythm and blues, Putnam switched from a Kay upright bass (the
same instrument that Strzelecki played) to a Fender Precision Bass, which
would give him a bigger live sound and would ultimately allow him to be
more flexible in his construction of musical lines.[184] The Mark V quickly
rose to regional fame thanks to their travels to colleges and universities
in the area, and they soon drew the attention of music publisher Tom
Stafford, whose SPAR Music was looking for a group to record demonstration records in exchange for "free passes to the movies and all the codeine
cough syrup we could stomach."[185] Through this work, Putnam and the
rest of the Mark V had the opportunity to work with a number of African
American and white singers and songwriters, including Arthur Alexander,
Dan Penn, Donnie Fritts, and Spooner Oldham.[186] Soon, producer Rick
Hall opened FAME Recording Studios in Muscle Shoals, Alabama, in an
effort to produce recordings for the rhythm and blues marketplace, and
Putnam and the Mark V quickly became involved in the sessions booked
there.[187] As historian Charles Hughes has noted, Putnam and his fellow
musicians in the Muscle Shoals scene built their careers by accompanying African American rhythm and blues (and, later, soul) musicians and,
through that work, gained a degree of credibility not only as technically
capable musicians, but as musicians who could channel a sort of essentialized blackness through their playing. As the white musicians behind the
sound of many black recording artists, that is, Putnam and his colleagues
could claim deep roots in African American musical culture while also
capitalizing on its cachet as white musicians who had more freedom to
move around in the marketplace.[188] And, as later outgrowths of the southern soul scene—especially southern rock—demonstrate, musicianship is
always tied up with a masculinity that channels mythologies of African
American sexual prowess.[189]

Putnam's experiences in Muscle Shoals and, later, on the road with
rhythm and blues and soul musicians in the early 1960s helped him to
build a network of colleagues and mentors in the southern music industry,
ranging from RCA Victor producer Felton Jarvis to Atlanta-based producer and music publisher Bill Lowery.[190] He was beginning to consider

new opportunities, in part because the wages that he was capable of
drawing in Muscle Shoals were minimal, and Nashville, with its seemingly endless supply of session work, its deep pool of recording artists,
and its guaranteed union wage, began to seem all the more desirable.[191]
But, although Nashville seemed like a paradise for a young and hungry
musician in search of better opportunities, it wasn't altogether clear that
he would be able to make it there, and producer Rick Hall took advantage
of that doubt in order to try to convince Putnam to stay in the Shoals.
Putnam recalled:

> When Rick Hall heard about our impending move, he called to ask
> if I could come over, said he needed to talk to me. So a few hours
> later I walked into his office and sat down, hoping it was going to
> be a short meeting. Rick began by saying, "Briggs and Carrigan are
> gonna do great, but I'm concerned that you may have a tougher time
> of it. Have you listened carefully to Bobby Moore's bass on all those
> great records? Do you really think anyone would hire you in place
> of him?"
>
> Well, I had to admit there was no way to compare my skills to the
> great Bob Moore, especially on the acoustic bass. Rick then went on
> to say, "Putt, you'll never make it up there. You'll be running back
> home with your tail between your legs before two months are out."[192]

Hall then offered Putnam a guaranteed weekly salary of one hundred
dollars and the opportunity to serve as the rhythm section's bandleader,
which, despite being a tempting offer, he rejected in favor of maintaining
the unity of the "Muscle Shoals Rhythm Section," a move that proved to
be particularly wise in light of the group's reception. With the assistance of
Jerry Bradley (Owen Bradley's son), Putnam and his colleagues were able
to find an apartment, and they moved there in early 1965.[193]

Upon arriving in Nashville and joining the Nashville Musicians Union,
Putnam and his colleagues began working with greater regularity, doing
demo sessions. As Putnam recalled:

After only a few short months, we were picking up stacks [of checks] every week. Yes, life was good. We were in the good graces of the union and we were working tons of demo sessions for [Bob] Beckham, Jerry Bradley and Fred Rose. The demos were later played for most of the top Nashville producers, and inquiries were forthcoming. Producers would ask who's that bass player, who's the drummer? Soon the demo work was bringing calls for master sessions.[194]

Because demonstration recordings were not supposed to be distributed for public consumption, musicians were paid at a lower rate than they were for master sessions.[195] The move to master sessions was a significant one financially, then. But like other session musicians before and after him, Putnam's move to master sessions also led to new directions for the sounds emerging from the city's studios. Putnam noted, for instance, that he worked a session with arranger Bill Justis early in his time in Nashville, despite the fact that Justis was an established arranger who "simply had no reason to seek out new players."[196] But because Justis liked the bass line that he had heard on the demonstration recording, he sought out Putnam to play the master session.[197] Rather than hiring a musician to emulate the sound of Putnam's playing, then, Justis thought it wisest to hire the musician who played it in the first place. But, as Putnam noted, Justis was taking quite a risk in hiring him, given the sheer number of demo sessions that Putnam was playing and the short memory that often comes from such work; in fact, Putnam had trouble remembering the part until producer Fred Foster played the demo for him. As Putnam recalled:

Was this some wild, crazy part I had played off the top of my head on one of Bob Beckham's wild-and-wooly demo sessions? One of those ludicrous parts, overplayed to try to gain notice? Obviously, my plan had backfired and now I had been found out. Resigned to my fate, all life gone, I just sat there staring at all those indecipherable bass notes [on the bass part that Justis had written with the hope of transcribing Putnam's earlier bass line], as old pro Bill astutely shouted out to the control room, "Hey Fred, play a few bars of the demo for the kid, I must have taken it down wrong!"

A few seconds later the giant "voice of the theatre" loud speakers came to life in a thundering roar, and the demo track started to play. And *YES! I REMEMBERED!*[198]

From that session, Justis called Putnam regularly for sessions, including most notably with artist Bobby Goldsboro.[199]

Unlike most of the other musicians whose entry to the Nashville session scene has been documented here, Putnam's arrival marked not only a shift in personnel but a shift in aesthetics. Much as Rich Hall had prognosticated, there was little demand for Putnam on many "straight country" sessions, as musicians such as Bob Moore, Junior Husky, and Henry Strzelecki had locked that work up, for the most part. But the presence of musicians with rock, rhythm and blues, and soul backgrounds in Nashville helped to push the city into new expressive territories, particularly those that very directly riffed on African American modes of expression.[200] Through the second half of the 1960s, Nashville became an increasingly diverse recording environment, at least musically, thanks in large part to the work of such musicians as Bob Dylan, Linda Ronstadt, and Ringo Starr in the city.[201] These changes are often overblown to the point of overlooking the significant work that Nashville session musicians did with pop artists and other artists seeking crossover opportunities in the first half of the 1960s, but they are still worth noting, not for their uniqueness, but for their role in pushing country in new directions. That is, earlier pop crossover work in Nashville studios often found national artists coming to Nashville to get a countrified pop treatment, but the work of the Muscle Shoals Rhythm Section actually pushed country music in new directions at the same time that it was offering a "rootsier" sound for national recording artists. It is also worth noting that Putnam and the Muscle Shoals Rhythm Section were more than capable of playing country sessions, as they did—both as a unit and as individual session musicians—for Owen Bradley and Chet Atkins.[202]

One of the best examples of this sort of transformation is Tony Joe White's "Polk Salad Annie," which he recorded for Monument Records in 1968.[203] For the most part, the recording is built around a pulsing vamp over a pedal point E, played by Putnam. Unlike a straight country recording, which would have found a bassist playing an alternating root-fifth passage on beats one and three of each bar (perhaps with a walk-up or walk-down to connect chords or sections of the form), Putnam offers a soul-inspired bass line that is built around a straight eighth-note pulse, which drummer Jerry Carrigan locks into with the high-hat and bass drum. The vamp allows White to open the recording with a spoken introduction as one might hear on a Lightnin' Hopkins record, channeling a rural blues sound in both the vocals and in the accompaniment. As White moves toward a singing voice in the first verse, Putnam moves away from the pedal point and toward a line that uses the root, fifth, and octave of the chord (spaced closely on the fingerboard of the electric bass) to emphasize the song's blues modality and skipping rhythmically across three strings, adding a syncopated bounce as he moved. And in the song's chorus, which is indicated by a move to the subdominant chord, Putnam begins to fill in the space between chord tones with more passing notes, thereby increasing the sense of momentum in the groove by filling the pitch space. As a consequence of these subtle moves, Putnam is able to channel a southern soul sound for a white recording artist, eventually propelling White to chart success that was difficult for African American performers to obtain.[204]

Some of Putnam's most significant session work—both in terms of its profile and the longevity of his relationship with the artist—was with Elvis Presley, a figure whose presence in Nashville was long and storied.[205] The 1970 album *That's the Way It Is* prominently features Putnam's bass work in a number of settings, from the rather sedate (but still grooving) take on Paul Simon's "Bridge over Troubled Water" to the up-tempo "Stranger in the Crowd." What is particularly striking in all of Putnam's work on this album, though, is his ability to use the bass as both an instrument to stabilize harmonies and tempi and as an instrument of melodic interest. Nashville bassists, for the most part, focused almost exclusively on the bass's fundamental roles, but Putnam worked hard to free the instrument from that role and to turn it into something that could both support and expand the performance. Listening to Putnam's take on "Stranger in the Crowd" alongside some of the Motown hits played by bassist James Jamerson (of the legendary studio band, the Funk Brothers) reveals remarkable similarities. For instance, both Putnam and Jamerson tend to place a strong emphasis on beat one of each bar, offering an anchor for the tempo and the meter that complements the drummer's work. In "Stranger in the Crowd," for instance, the drummer—Carrigan—plays a sixteenth-note pattern on the high-hat cymbal and snare that offers a steady subdivision of the beat and, in emphasizing the upbeats of each beat, also contributes to the groove. With the help of a steady groove in the drums, then, Putnam is free to use the remainder of the measure to create interesting walk-ups between chords, using a skipping syncopated rhythm that is supported by the drummer's upbeats and a syncopated bass drum. Putnam's melodies are not anything intricate, and they don't show flashes of brilliant technique that require him to move up and down the fretboard with great fluency. But, using relatively closed hand positions, he is able to move freely within the space between the root and the fifth, creating new contours and countermelodies.[206] And, in "Stranger in the Crowd," particularly, it is worth noting that the bass is the *primary* melodic instrument. The guitars on the session are offering punctuating chord stabs, functioning as rhythm instruments, and the strings are holding notes across multiple measures. As such, Putnam's bass and Presley's vocals might be heard as countermelody and melody, respectively.

The bass underwent one of the most dramatic transformations of any instrument in Nashville during the twenty years or so that the Nashville recording industry was establishing itself as a dominant force. In a country music landscape that was somewhat dismissive of drums, the bass—along with the rhythm guitar—took on an almost exclusively rhythmic role in the first decade or more of the Nashville Sound era, holding down the tempo and the harmonies and sticking primarily to the root and fifth of the scale, with only occasional scalar passages to link chords and formal sections. But, with the advent of both the electric bass (first in the form of the tic-tac

and later in the adoption of the Fender bass) and better microphone techniques to record the drums, bassists could augment the instrument's role
as a particular song dictated. But we should not interpret these developments as technologically determinant; that is, just because there were new
instruments and techniques around, musicians did not have to make use of
them.[207] In fact, there is plenty of evidence to show that musicians selected
their instruments to suit each individual song that they were recording,
often at the discretion of the producer. As such, Putnam and Strzelecki
maintained their acoustic bass chops and contributed to many sessions as
acoustic bassists alongside their work on the electric bass. And some bassists, such as Bob Moore, largely chose to ignore the electric instruments
altogether in favor of maintaining their excellent acoustic bass sound.[208]
As a consequence, we must remember that these musicians were agents in
their own work who were hired not only because of their availability to fill a
recording session slot (much like a temporary worker might fill a shift on a
factory floor), but also because they brought something unique to the work.

Unlike the bass, which can be found in recorded country music in the
genre's first decade, drums have an exceptionally complicated history
within the genre. Although one can certainly find examples of musicians
who used drums on their recordings and in live performances in the pre–
World War II era, the overwhelming majority of those artists were pur-
veyors of western swing music, a style of music that blended elements of
traditional American fiddling with the sounds of hot jazz and classic blues.
These musicians, as Jean Boyd has pointed out in her extensive oral history project with multiple generations of western swing musicians, often
saw themselves not as country musicians but, first, as jazz musicians. They
were also very interested in dancing, as many of the most lucrative gigs
came from playing large ballrooms and dancehalls in Texas, Oklahoma,
and California.[209] In those cavernous spaces—and in an age before high-
quality public address systems—the drums were essential tools in providing a steady beat that would guide the dancers in their movements around
the dance floor.[210] But, looking broadly at musics that were fell under the
broad "hillbilly"—and later "country and western"— rubric, drums are

virtually absent from recordings from the early 1920s through the mid-1950s. In fact, one famous story indicates that Nashville's august *Grand Ole Opry* was so disapproving of drums that, when western swing pioneer Bob Wills played the program in 1944, stage managers tried to require him to hide the drummer behind the curtain rather than having him onstage.[211]

This bias against drums on the *Grand Ole Opry* continued well into the Nashville Sound era and had ripple effects on the sounds of country music, more generally. Guitarist Ray Edenton, for instance, recalled for me a story in which long-time Roy Acuff sideman Bashful Brother Oswald (Beecher Kirby) explained to him that, since drums had not been a part of the early *Opry*, a drumless *Opry* was been a tradition that he thought was worth maintaining.[212] As a consequence of these restrictions on the *Opry*, musicians had to learn to make accommodations. Lightnin' Chance, for instance, played the bass with a drum head attached to its upper left quadrant, and he developed a style of playing that allowed him to "stir the soup" with a drum brush while also playing notes on the bass's strings. Joe Zinkan was sought after for his slap bass technique because it could provide the rhythmic drive that a small drum set might.[213] And rhythm guitar players throughout the country music industry learned to play "sock rhythm," a technique that has antecedents in the jazz guitar work of Count Basie guitarist Freddie Green and that requires the guitarist to mute the strings with the palm of the hand and to play with a percussive downstroke.

From a recording perspective, too, the drums posed a number of problems. In the early days of the Nashville recording industry, a drum set could simply overpower the other instruments on the session and, even more importantly, could drown out the vocals altogether. Since vocals were the most important part of most recordings, the drums were simply unusable. As a consequence, many musicians developed alternative instrumentation to provide that rhythmic support, including using body percussion or playing on suitcases and cardboard boxes.[214] And even as microphones improved and the engineers in Nashville studios learned new techniques to record the drums, the limitations of monophonic mixing and mastering for long-playing records still made the drums a potential liability in a recording. So it should not be surprising that Nashville had comparatively few drummers working in its studios during the Nashville Sound era in relation to both the number of drummers working in popular music recording more broadly and the number of guitarists and bassists who were working around town. In fact, a survey of the discographical records from the Nashville Sound era reveal major contributions by only two drummers: Murray "Buddy" Harman and Jerry Carrigan.

A Nashville native, Buddy Harman was not the first drummer to work sessions in Nashville; Farris Coursey had been the drummer on many of the earliest sessions in the city, including landmark sessions for Red Foley.[215] But Harman, whose biography is detailed at length in Chapter 2, was, by far, the longest-tenured drummer in the city's recording studios, and, as a consequence of his long career and his rather intense dedication to his work, he stands as one of the most-recorded drummers not only in Nashville, but in the US popular music community, more generally.[216] In a genre that tended to dismiss the drums as unnecessary, Harman carved out a space for himself in the Nashville recording community by being a versatile drummer who was willing to play a supportive role without standing out in an obtrusive manner. By the end of the 1950s, Harman was working a steady session schedule, sometimes working "as many as twenty-six sessions a week. . . . But I was young enough to handle it. . . . I was doing three or four a day for years."[217] In fact, he was so busy that he needed to invest in additional drum sets. "For a while," he recalled, "I kept a set of drums in every studio I got to working so much, I just didn't have time to carry a set and tear them down and carry them to the next studio and set them up."[218] Most of this work was, as he described it, "straight-ahead country," but as recording technologies and tastes changed, he was granted more freedom to play with sticks (moving from two brushes to one brush and one stick and finally to two sticks) and to use the bass drum more forcefully. Of course, like all session musicians, Harman was not stuck in a single rut; rather, he noted that he had to respond to the demands of different producers and recording artists. And perhaps more importantly, he learned how to create a complementary drum sound for each song through a process of subtraction: "I don't try to play everything I know on every song."[219]

Occasionally, Harman was given the opportunity to contribute something more interesting to a recording. With pop artists such as Roy Orbison and the Everly Brothers, both regulars in the Nashville studios, Harman created rhythmic hooks that helped to propel the recording to the top of the charts, as one can hear in the throbbing and insistent snare blasts of Orbison's "Oh, Pretty Woman" and the Latin-tinged rhythms of the Everly's "Cathy's Clown." Moreover, when Elvis Presley came to town, Harman sometimes found himself recording alongside longtime Presley drummer D. J. Fontana, which required that Harman find a way to support Fontana's work without stepping on it. To achieve that, he observed, he learned to play the "same rhythm, but different fills."[220] In these situations, session time had to be devoted to working out the specifics of the arrangement and experimenting with different grooves. Consequently, these challenges often reduced the overall productivity of the session, but, as Harman noted, the opportunity to try something even more creative than normal was typically quite rewarding.[221]

Because he was working as many as twenty-six sessions a week, the body of Harman's recorded work is extensive and diverse. Because he was defining the role of the drums in recorded country music, Harman's work is absolutely foundational to the country genre as a whole, but, at the same time, one has to listen very carefully to pick up on the subtleties of his approach to the instrument. A flexible drummer who was as capable playing jazz and Latin music as country, Harman's style is perhaps best understood as one of understated simplicity.[222] Because drums did not record terribly well in the early days of his recording career—he recalls that they "missed a lot of tom tom fills because there was only one overhead mic" in those earliest sessions—his contributions are often felt, more than they are heard.[223] In fact, that is one of the most important things that Harman highlighted when he thought back to his days with the Nashville A Team—consistent tempi: "We had a good studio band. . . . Everybody seemed to feel what we were doing and had the concept of what was happening. . . .

Everybody had a good time feel. We didn't have hardly any rushing or dragging problems with this particular band."[224]

Thanks to Harman's efforts to popularize the drums more widely in country music and in Nashville recording sessions, more generally, there was more work for drummers in the city by the mid-1960s. Jerry Carrigan, a member of the Muscle Shoals Rhythm Section with Norbert Putnam, came to Nashville in 1965 along with his bandmates and helped to expand the drummer's role in the genre and to lead a new push for heavier drum sounds. Carrigan told interviewer Morris Levy that he and his Muscle Shoals colleagues were often hired because they "offered . . . a little bit different style of playing country music [than the Nashville A Team]. . . . We had a bit of trouble with some of the grooves of it. . . . [P]eople would hire us because they knew we were going to take a different approach to the music. . . ."[225] He later told interviewer Allen Smith that the older session musicians "didn't like that [my] shuffle at all. But they said shuffle and I played shuffle! Dotted eighths and sixteenths. What they wanted was triplets with the middle gone. Lazy shuffle I call it. Nice shuffle. Country shuffle. When I finally figured out how to play it I learned how to play it pretty well. I liked to play it."[226] In a 2009 interview with Bill Lloyd, Carrigan explained that he would occasionally visit other people's sessions so he could learn how to play the shuffle in the style that Buddy Harman played it.[227]

One can discern the sources of these difficulties by comparing and contrasting the differences in the sounds of Muscle Shoals soul and Nashville country around the year 1965. If soul music put a strong emphasis on beat one and used extensive subdivisions of the beat to create a sense of groove, country music—with its predominant eighth-note pulse and strong emphasis on both beats one and three of the bar—offered less to build a groove on. And since country music of 1965 tended to favor a considerably spare arrangement, a busier groove would have necessarily drawn attention away from the vocals and, perhaps even more importantly, the lyrics that those vocals conveyed. Carrigan's challenges were likely exacerbated by the fact that he claims to have "never listened to country" prior to moving to Nashville, focusing instead on rhythm and blues music.[228]

Carrigan claimed that the members of Nashville's A Team were not entirely hospitable to him when he moved to the city, noting to interviewer Allen Smith: "[T]here was a long little initiation there. There were some strange things going on. I'd come back from lunch break and there'd be notes on my drums. 'Go Home.' 'We don't need you.' 'Go back to Muscle Shoals.' Just all this stuff. Little notes laid on my drums."[229] But, despite these jabs, Carrigan survived in Nashville because he found particularly strong support from the city's original session musicians and leading producers: Owen Bradley and Chet Atkins. Bradley, for instance, noticed that the established session musicians were sabotaging Carrigan's efforts in the studio during the session that produced Warner Mack's 1965 hit record "The Bridge Washed Out" and decided to put a stop to it:

> I was the only new one in there. It was me and Grady Martin and Bob Moore and Ray Edenton and Floyd Cramer. And Owen finally said, "Now listen, that drummer is Jerry Carrigan. He's a friend of mine. I hired him cause [*sic*] I like the way he plays and he's playing what I want him to play. I suggest y'all play with him or I'll ask you all to leave and he and I will finish the session." That's exactly what he said. And I never will forget it. He just took up for me. Owen was a wonderful man. . . . The problems began to go away after that because word had spread that Owen had said that.[230]

But Carrigan's career as a studio musician really took off as a consequence of Atkins's enthusiasm, which led to his near domination of sessions at RCA Victor through the early 1970s.[231] Atkins was particularly excited by Carrigan's drumming style not for its flashiness, but for its technique. Carrigan recalled that Atkins

> liked the fact that I played the music with a little different feel and also, I didn't play really hard and loud. He liked that. He used to tell people, "Listen to his bass drum. He's got the softest sound in his bass drum." But I just didn't think there was any need to stomp around on drums and beat around.[232]

Considering country music's long-standing concern about conveying bass sounds and creating a sense of "punch" in their recordings, it may be a bit surprising that Atkins was drawn to the subtlety of Carrigan's bass drum. But, with improved microphone placement, the bass drum was becoming more and more audible in Nashville recordings during the late 1960s, and a soft bass drum also allowed for a more subtle use of ghost strokes—quiet strokes of the drum that precede a louder one—to quietly increase the intensity of the groove.

This technique can be heard quite clearly throughout Carrigan's work. The title track of Connie Smith's 1966 album *Born to Sing*, for instance, offers a great example. In this Bob Ferguson–produced recording, Carrigan offers an example of the "country shuffle," in which he offers a slightly lighter anacrusis to beats one and three of the measure. As a consequence, the bass drum— which is combined here with a muted electric bass—provides a punch on the downbeats and a lilt on the offbeats. When combined with relatively light skipping triplet strokes on the high-hat and a fairly crisp stroke on the snare drum on beat two, Carrigan is able to lock in with Ray Edenton and Jimmy Lance's rhythm guitar parts to create a seamless pulse of triplet eighth notes that supports Smith's lilting vocals. In Sammi Smith's 1972 recording of "Where Grass Won't Grow" (released on Mega LP *Something Old, Something New, Something Blue*), we can hear Carrigan offering a similar kind of groove in the bass drum.[233] Here, the bass drum becomes increasingly busy as the performance moves through a series of stepwise modulations upward, starting with an eighth note pickup to beat one in the second verse, adding a pickup to beat three in the third verse, and concluding with a pickup to every beat by the recording's conclusion. These eighth note pickups are only slightly softer than the strokes on the beat, but they are not as strong as the important downbeats. As such, they help to propel the drama of the song, which is fairly down-tempo and could easily drag down to nothing.

Carrigan's final significant contributions as a session drummer came near the end of the 1970s, during which time he made use of the entire drum set, including especially the tom toms and a louder snare drum. The sound, which he first used on Charlie Rich's "Behind Closed Doors" in 1973, came to dominate country recordings during the mid- to late

1970s, particularly sessions produced by Billy Sherrill. As Carrigan told Bill Lloyd in 2009, he tuned his Ludwig snare drum so that it would be particularly resonant.[234] As was often the case in Nashville, as recording technologies became more advanced, drum sounds could improve. By the mid-1970s, Nashville studios were beginning to expand to eight-track and sixteen-track consoles, which allowed for many more microphone inputs, including several for the drums—placed both close to the drums and overhead.[235] Additionally, mastering engineers had developed better techniques for capturing resonant sounds (particularly bass sounds) in the grooves of a long-playing record, making it possible to reproduce the sounds that the drummer and bassist were creating in the studio.[236] As such, Carrigan was able to use those technological advantages to his musical advantage, creating more dynamic accompaniments that helped, ultimately, to accentuate the drama of the performances captured on them.

Although the drums were not terribly important to country music recordings in the first years of the Nashville Sound era, they were absolutely essential parts of nearly every recording by its close. As a consequence, more drummers were able to find steady work in the city, much as had been the case for other instrumentalists as well. But perhaps even more important is the fact that the drums came to be not just a time-keeping device, but a way to help increase the overall dynamic range of a particular recording. The entrance and exit of drums, the complexity or simplicity of the groove, and the overall timbre of the instruments themselves helped to convey a sense of the song's emotional tenor and to accentuate the narrative arc of a particular song.

Nashville was teeming with session musicians by the mid-1970s, with at least three distinct generations of musicians often working together periodically while also servicing dramatically different accounts. As the music industry continued to boom through the end of the 1970s, these session musicians could find regular work by maintaining both a vast stylistic vocabulary and by providing distinctive sounds and personality traits to a session. This chapter has barely scratched the surface in terms of documenting the many musicians who were active in the Nashville recording scene, but the individuals presented here demonstrate the importance of musical diversity, innovation, and collaboration to their work.

Just as noteworthy as the musicians who were active for two or more decades are those musicians who played on only a few sessions. Although it should be noted that many of the most successful musicians either came to Nashville as a band already (as was the case with the Muscle Shoals crowd) or acted as if they were one, it is just as noteworthy to point out that the musicians who were able to build long careers as session musicians were willing to find ways to fit in and blend with the practices that were already in place when they arrived. Although the session musicians I have encountered are generally unwilling to talk in negative terms about their former colleagues or the artists with whom they worked, one can easily imagine that, in a community that values—and indeed thrives on—collaboration, musicians who were unwilling to "play along" would not be called for additional session work.[237] Moreover, musicians who were excellent technical musicians but who were unable to play unobtrusively might also have found Nashville session work to be constricting and may have been overlooked when producers, contractors, and bandleaders were calling musicians for sessions.

Although session work may not have been suitable for everyone, there was ample opportunity for musicians to find gainful employment in other supportive roles. Musicians could play on demonstration sessions, supporting the work of songwriters and music publishers, and could even maintain a regular working schedule while doing such work. They could travel on the road with leading recording artists, supporting them by providing some showmanship and recreating elements of their most popular commercial recordings. They could record with the hundreds of aspiring country recording artists who traveled to Nashville to create audition tapes and to record albums that could be sold at local and regional venues. So, even if they weren't working on major-label productions, session musicians could find regular work—often at union scale.

As the preceding examples have demonstrated, the best Nashville session musicians were far from interchangeable cogs in an expansive music industry machine. Rather, they brought specialized skills, interesting ideas, and a desire to collaborate with one another. And, just as the recording artists they worked with often developed specific musical brands to help them stand out in a crowded musical marketplace, so, too, did session musicians distinguish themselves in subtle ways, making their work indispensable to a particular session.

Afterword

By the mid-1970s, Nashville was undisputedly the leader in country music record production, and it had ascended to a level of not only national, but international prominence in the music industry. Even as upstart country music scenes like the Austin progressive country scene that emerged during the early 1970s tried to assert their own unique brand, Nashville was undoubtedly the place that musicians needed to visit if they wanted to sign songwriting contracts, reach national radio audiences, and produce high-quality recordings that could allow them to compete in the increasingly crowded popular music marketplace.[1] Similarly, as musicians associated with the "Outlaw country" movement that emerged from within the Nashville music scene in the mid-1970s declared their independence from the strict Nashville studio system, they still frequently made use of Nashville session musicians and continued to release their albums on the major labels that had helped to establish Music Row in the first place.[2] And as country music reached newfound levels of popularity in the late 1970s and early 1980s (a phenomenon perhaps best represented

Nashville Cats. Travis D. Stimeling, © Oxford University Press (2020). Oxford University Press.
DOI: 10.1093/oso/9780197502815.001.0001

by the success of the John Travolta and Debra Winger film *Urban Cowboy*), Nashville's music industry seemed to be in no danger of slowing down.[3]

But, at the same time that country music was garnering national attention again, its sounds were changing in fairly dramatic ways. Increasingly, the recordings that drew the attention of radio listeners and record buyers were those that channeled some elements of contemporary rock music, including especially the sounds of southern rock. As such, the musical talents and abilities of the session musicians who had helped to build the studio scene were less useful to record production than they had been in previous years, and a new wave of session musicians came to Nashville to fill that particular niche. Moreover, as bands such as Alabama came to dominate radio airplay in the late 1970s and early 1980s, many session musicians found themselves displaced by bands that recorded as a unit. And, perhaps even more importantly, country artists who had flourished during the 1960s and 1970s were themselves marginalized by shifts in public taste, radio programming, and record label marketing, leaving those session musicians, arrangers, and producers who had been active in developing the sounds of those artists with fewer sessions to keep themselves busy.[4]

At the same time, the mid-1970s marked a major turning point in the lives of many of the session musicians who had been on the scene since the beginning of the Nashville Sound era. Musicians who, like Harold Bradley, had been involved in the scene since the late 1940s were nearing retirement age, marking two or more decades as contributors to an increasingly frenetic studio scene. Such a lifestyle took a toll on personal relationships, as well as the physical and mental well-being of some musicians, and the shifting tastes of the country music industry provided some musicians with an opportunity to step away from their work.[5] As members of the Nashville Musicians Association, these session musicians had been contributing to a pension fund for their entire recording careers, funding that allowed them to slow their pace or stop working altogether. As such, many of the musicians who were active in the 1950s, 1960s, and early 1970s began to curtail their schedules or to stop playing altogether. By the 1980s, many of the session musicians involved with the A Team had retired, some putting their instruments back in their cases never to be heard again.[6] Still other participants in the Nashville session scene of the postwar decades used the changing country music landscape as an opportunity to diversify their career portfolios and develop new audiences. Chet Atkins, for instance, began to transition away from production by the early 1970s, allowing him to focus more attention on his recording and performing career.[7] Charlie McCoy—arguably one of the most versatile musicians in the Nashville A Team—offset his declining studio schedule with regular work as the music director of the syndicated television program *Hee Haw*, as well as frequent tours to Europe, where he was a featured soloist and a frequent collaborator with European country artists, many of whom were deeply invested in the older styles of country music that McCoy had contributed to.[8]

Despite the changes to the country music landscape in the late 1970s and 1980s, session work has remained available for many of the Nashville A Team musicians well into the present day. Mainstream artists who channel the sounds of classic country recordings from the A Team's heyday have frequently hired such musicians as Pig Robbins, Harold Bradley, and Charlie McCoy to play on their projects, and numerous lesser-known artists have also called upon their talents. Much as these musicians had been selected by Nashville Sound–era recording artists as a way to solidify their musical brand, so, too, have more contemporary recording artists hired the A Team musicians to capture those iconic sounds of past hits. As a consequence, some of these musicians can still be found at sessions, even as they approach their eighth decade, playing along with musicians decades younger and serving as elder statesmen in a musical community that is both intensely aware of its history and constantly looking toward the future.[9]

As is the case in most music scenes—whether small or large, local or translocal—the Nashville Sound–era recording scene was created by a group of people with competing objectives, contradictory aesthetics, and varying degrees of commitment to the scene.[10] Despite the extensive archive of oral histories, trade and popular press publications, and recordings that document the work of these musicians and producers, it remains very difficult to capture the full extent of the day-to-day discussions, debates, and collaborations in a study such as this. However, as this study has demonstrated, Nashville's recording thrived on a diversity of opinions, musical abilities, and approaches to collaboration. Although music scenes have certainly been destroyed by conflict, creative, interpersonal, and ideological friction might also help to sustain complex and long-lasting music scenes. Scenes invariably thrive on a certain degree of assent to common values (musical or otherwise), but too much agreement among scene participants can also lead to stagnation, which can be as destructive as divisions. As such, we might see debate, disagreement, and reconciliation as a tool to create a more diverse musical ecosystem within which still more musicians can thrive. Such was certainly the case as new waves of musicians came to Nashville to find work in the studio scene. Although musicians from Muscle Shoals and Memphis undoubtedly represented a threat to the continued financial and creative security of some long-standing participants in the Music Row scene, they also brought new creative ideas that helped to attract new recording artists to the city and to diversify the sounds of country music—an important component of country radio's long-term success.

At the same time, as several scholars have observed, it is impossible to separate the political conditions outside of the recording studio from those within it.[11] Nashville's Music Row thrived during the height of the post–World War II Civil Rights movement, and, with notable exceptions, was itself a segregated music scene. As a consequence, the musicians working in Nashville's recording studios during the 1950s and 1960s had little interaction with African American musicians working in the city, who themselves maintained a thriving musical community.[12] By the late 1960s, some country recording artists publicly vowed their support for segregationist presidential candidate George Wallace (then governor of Alabama), and some of the musicians profiled in this study continued to accompany those artists on recordings. Similarly, as the Vietnam War raged on, many country recording artists came out as ardent hawks, even cutting recordings with pro-war messages.[13] In their recollections and oral testimonies, Nashville session musicians seldom discuss politics, and it would be easy to see their silence on political issues as an act of complicity. But session musicians, engineers, and even producers must often put aside their own political ideologies in order to continue working in many professional settings. Financial pressures, then, often trump political ones. As a consequence, it might be more productive to see the comparative political silence of these session musicians within the context of a variety of competing pressures that made it difficult to discuss such things.

Related to these political issues is the general absence of women in the narratives surrounding record production in Nashville, as well as in other music industry cities around the United States. This study has attempted to demonstrate the key role that women played within the tracking rooms of Music Row, focusing particularly on the key contributions of such musicians as Anita Kerr and Velma Smith. But just as important—and beyond the scope of this study—were the contributions of women working along Music Row in other significant capacities. Diane Pecknold's work, for instance, has demonstrated the significant role that women such as BMI's Frances Preston and the Country Music Association's Jo Walker-Meador played in shaping the country music industry of the 1960s and 1970s, and Paula Bishop's dissertation on the Everly Brothers has pointed to the key role that songwriter Felice Bryant played in the development of the group's iconic sound.[14] But, as my conversations with Pat McCoy and Rose Drake indicated, the network of female clerical workers on Music Row was, in many ways, the lubrication that kept the gears of the Music Row machine running. As such, this work begs for an even deeper investigation into the lives of the women who worked on Music Row, a need that becomes all the more urgent with each passing day.[15]

It is also worth noting that the session musicians who flourished during the heyday of the Nashville A Team were far from the only musicians who were working in such a capacity, and, perhaps even more importantly, they were working within the context of a deeply connected and highly competitive national music industry. House bands at Motown and Stax, as well as Los Angeles's Wrecking Crew and the Muscle Shoal Rhythm Section, were working under very similar circumstances, in many cases, and they were deeply aware of the work that each group was doing. As

Albin Zak has noted, the postwar record industry was built around novelty, and musicians in one recording scene often emulated the sounds of those in another in order to gain a competitive edge.[16] Musicians in Los Angeles, Detroit, and Memphis emulated the sounds that the Nashville A Team pioneered in their efforts to channel country sounds on their own sessions, just as the A Team pulled from mainstream pop and soul music in their efforts to reach a broad audience.[17] Furthermore, Nashville musicians sometimes trained with session musicians in other scenes (as was the case with drummers Buddy Harman and Hal Blaine) and collaborated in the studio (as was the case with singer Millie Kirkham and the Jordanaires), giving them firsthand opportunities to learn from one another. As a consequence, it is essential that we consider the recording scenes of the postwar decades as simultaneously in competition and cooperation with one another.

Finally, this study points to the value of extended exploration of recorded music as a vital primary document that offers insights into a variety of issues. As a physical object, a recording can tell us a great deal about how an artist is marketed to an audience, how the creative process is documented, and how a particular label sees its place within the commercial music marketplace. And as an aesthetic object, we can hear traces of numerous creative decisions made in collaboration and partnership with others and begin to understand the many factors that contributed to the recording's creation and reception. As a gateway to those creative decisions, recordings also allow us to expand our understanding even further by considering the attitudes, beliefs, and practices of those people, which, by extension, permits the formation of a deep contextual understanding of the recording. This study, therefore, contributes to the broader "musicology of recording" by using recordings primarily as a tool to listen *in* to the factors relating to this music's creation, rather than listening *out* for its reception. Yet, at the same time, both perspectives are of vital importance to our understandings of popular music's significance, and only when they are put in dialogue with one another can we begin to grasp the remarkable power that this music has.

INTRODUCTION

1. Harold Bradley, resume and biographical statement, typescript, in author's possession.
2. For a seminal discussion of the role that popular music has played in public commercial spaces, consult Jonathan Sterne, "Sounds like the Mall of America: Programmed Music and the Architectonics of Commercial Space," *Ethnomusicology* 41, no. 1 (January 1997): 22–50.
3. Charles K. Wolfe, *A Good-Natured Riot: The Birth of the Grand Ole Opry* (Nashville: Country Music Foundation Press and Vanderbilt University Press, 1999), 261–265.
4. Despite the prominence of session musicians in the production of US popular music in the 1950s, musicologist Albin Zak has observed of the 1950s and early 1960s that the market also demonstrated an interest in "no-fi" music performed and recorded by apparent amateurs (Albin J. Zak, III, "No-Fi: Crafting a Language of Recorded Music in 1950s Pop," in *The Art of Record Production: An Introductory Reader for a New Academic Field*, eds. Simon Frith and Simon Zagorski-Thomas [Farnham, UK: Ashgate, 2012], 43–56).
5. Albin J. Zak, III, *I Don't Sound Like Nobody: Remaking Music in 1950s America* (Ann Arbor: University of Michigan Press, 2010).
6. This is not an exclusively US-based phenomenon. In fact, a number of recent studies have demonstrated the important role that session musicians have played in the production of recorded music for the past several decades. See, for instance, Louise Meintjes, *Sound of Africa!: Making Music Zulu in a South African Studio* (Durham, NC: Duke University Press, 2003), 44, 83; Greg Booth, *Behind the Curtain: Making Music in Mumbai's Film Studios* (New York: Oxford University Press, 2008); Eliot Bates, *Digital Tradition: Arrangement and Labor in Istanbul's Recording Studio Culture* (New York: Oxford University Press, 2016), 127–138; Kiranmayi Indraganti, *Her Majestic Voice: South Indian Female Playback Singers and Stardom, 1945–1955* (New Delhi: Oxford University Press, 2016).

7. Charles Portis, "That New Sound from Nashville," *Saturday Evening Post* (February 12, 1966): 34.

8. "Country Music: The Nashville Sound," *Time* (November 27, 1964): 79.

9. John Grissim, *Country Music: White Man's Blues* (New York: Coronet, 1970), 21–26; Paul Hemphill, *The Nashville Sound: Bright Lights and Country Music* (New York: Simon & Schuster, 1970; paperback ed., New York: Ballantine Books, 1975), 34–37; Preston Collins and Jim Dennett, dirs., *Music City, U.S.A.* (Gemini Pictures, 1966); Jay J. Sheridan, dir., *Nashville Rebel* (American International, 1966); Leif Rise, dir., *Road to Nashville* (Crown International Pictures, 1967); Robert Elfstrom and David Hoffman, dirs., *The Nashville Sound* (The Nashville Co., 1970); Robert Altman, dir., *Nashville* (Paramount, 1975).

10. Isabel Campelo, "'That Extra Thing': The Role of Session Musicians in the Recording Industry," *Journal on the Art of Record Production* 10 (July 2015), http://arpjournal. com/that-extra-thing-the-role-of-session-musicians-in-the-recording-industry/ (accessed January 25, 2018).

11. Several excellent overviews of the production challenges in the recording industry's first decades are available. Among them are David Morton, *Off the Record: The Technology and Culture of Sound Recording in America* (New Brunswick, NJ: Rutgers University Press, 2000), 17–23; David L. Morton, Jr., *Sound Recording: The Life Story of a Technology* (Baltimore, MD: Johns Hopkins University Press, 2004), 26, 57–60, 64–67; Robert Philip, *Performing Music in the Age of Recording* (New Haven, CT: Yale University Press, 2004), 26–42; Andre Millard, *America on Record: A History of Recorded Sound*, 2nd ed. (Cambridge: Cambridge University Press, 2005), 285–295; Susan Schmidt Horning, *Chasing Sound: Technology, Culture, and the Art of Studio Recording from Edison to the LP* (Baltimore, MD: Johns Hopkins University Press, 2013), 13–22, 45–49. Several firsthand accounts of recording in the phonograph era have been anthologized in Timothy D. Taylor, Mark Katz, and Tony Grajeda, eds., *Music, Sound, and Technology in America: A Documentary History of Early Phonograph, Cinema, and Radio* (Durham, NC: Duke University Press, 2012), 84–94.

12. James Alan Williams, "Phantom Power: Recording Studio History, Practice, and Mythology," Ph.D. dissertation, Brown University, 2006, 40–46.

13. Philip, *Performing Music in the Age of Recording*, 47–49; Charles Kronengold, "Accidents, Hooks, and Theory," *Popular Music* 24, no. 3 (October 2005): 381–397; Mark Katz, *Capturing Sound: How Technology Has Changed Music*, rev. ed. (Berkeley: University of California Press, 2010), 29–41. Katz notes that it is the "repeatability" of recordings that has led to a greater awareness of mistakes and observes that this awareness has exerted impacts on both recording practice and live musical practice.

14. Meintjes, *Sound of Africa!*, 90–93; Bates, *Digital Tradition*, 123–148.

15. For a broad overview of the economic factors involved in postwar record production, consult Gerben Bakker, "Adopting the Rights-Based Model: Music Multinationals and Local Music Industries since 1945," *Popular Music History* 6, no. 3 (2011): 307–343.

16. For more background on this transition from live radio performances to disc jockey shows, consult, among others, Robert George White, Jr., "Martin Block and WNEW: The Rise of the Recorded Music Radio Format, 1934–1954," Ph.D. dissertation, Bowling Green State University, 1981; Gilbert A. Williams, "The Black Disc Jockey as a Cultural Hero," *Popular Music and Society* 10, no. 3 (1986): 79–90; Russell Sanjek and David Sanjek, *American Popular Music Business in the 20th Century* (New York: Oxford University Press, 1991), 83–84, 88–90, 140–141; James P. Kraft, *Stage to Studio: Musicians and the Sound Revolution, 1890–1950* (Baltimore, MD: Johns Hopkins University Press, 1996), 136–192 Ben Fong-Torres, *The Hits Just Keep on Coming: The History of Top 40 Radio* (San Francisco: Backbeat Books, 2001), 15–46; Tim Anderson, "'Buried under the Fecundity of His Own Creations': Reconsidering the Recording Bands of the American Federation of Musicians, 1942–1944 and 1948," *American Music* 22, no. 2 (Summer 2004): 231–269; Zak, *I Don't Sound like Nobody*, 9–42; Eric Weisbard, "Country Radio: The Dialectic of Format and Genre," in *The Oxford Handbook of Country Music*, ed. Travis D. Stimeling (New York: Oxford University Press, 2017), 233–237.

17. Bakker, "Adopting the Rights-Based Model," 311. On jukeboxes, consult Sanjek and Sanjek, *American Popular Music Business in the 20th Century*, 52–56, 116–117, 170–173; William Howland Kenney, *Recorded Music in American Life: The Phonograph and Popular Memory, 1890–1945* (New York: Oxford University Press, 1999), 166–167; Millard, *America on Record*, 168–170.

18. Zak, *I Don't Sound Like Nobody*, 5–8. I borrow the notion that sounds could be "worn out" from the composer John Cage, who suggests that the "intellectualization" of sound can make us think that a sound's expressive power has been exhausted. In his 1959 "Lecture on Nothing," he remarked, "I begin to hear the old sounds—the ones I had thought worn out, worn out by intellectualization—I begin to hear the old sounds as though they are not worn out. Obviously, they are not worn out. They are just as audible as the new sounds. Thinking had worn them out. And if one stops thinking about them, suddenly they are fresh and new" (John Cage, "Lecture on Nothing," in *Silence: Lectures and Writing* [Middletown, CT: Wesleyan University Press, 1961], 117).

19. For more background on hooks in popular songs and recordings, consult Gary Burns, "A Typology of 'Hooks' in Popular Records," *Popular Music* 6, no. 1 (January 1987): 1–20; Jocelyn Neal, "The Metric Makings of a Country Hit," in *Reading Country Music*, ed. Cecilia Tichi (Durham, NC: Duke University Press, 1998), 322–337; Peter Mercer-Taylor, "Two-and-a-Half Centuries in the Life of a Hook," *Popular Music and Society* 23, no. 2 (Summer 1999): 1–15; Don Traut, "'Simply Irresistible': Recurring Accent Patterns as Hooks in Mainstream 1980s Music," *Popular Music* 24, no. 1 (January 2005): 57–77; Kronengold, "Accidents, Hooks, and Theory"; Jocelyn R. Neal, "Analysis and Performance across the Canon: 'When Recollection Is All We've Got': Analytical Exploration of 'Catchy' Songs," *College Music Symposium* 47 (2007): 12–22; John Seabrook, *The Song Machine: Inside the Hit Factory* (New York: W. W. Norton, 2015), 200–204.

20. Morris Levy, "Nashville Sound-Era Studio Musicians," in *Country Music Annual 2000*, eds. Charles K. Wolfe and James E. Akenson (Lexington: University Press of Kentucky, 2000), 23.

21. Harold Bradley, interview with Morris Levy, February 22 or 23, 1996, Morris Levy Interviews (ARC-0487), Box 1, Folder 2, Rock and Roll Hall of Fame Library and Archives, Cleveland, OH.

22. Of course, musical authorship and ownership are problematic concepts that have been widely theorized. Although a rehearsal of those debates would be far beyond the scope of the present study, it is worth noting that several scholars have attempted to connect these questions to issues of musical labor. See, for instance, Christina Baade, Susan Fast, and Line Grenier, "Musicians as Workers: Sites of Struggle and Resistance," *MUSICultures* 41, no. 1 (2014): 1–2; John Williamson, "Cooperation and Conflict: The British Musicians' Union, Musical Labour and Copyright in the UK," *MUSICultures* 41, no. 1 (2014): 73–92; Matt Stahl, "Public, Private, Popular: Pop Performers, Liberalism and the Limits of Rights," *MUSICultures* 41, no. 1 (2014): 94–114.

23. Richard A. Peterson, *Creating Country Music: Fabricating Authenticity* (Chicago: University of Chicago Press, 1997), 185–201; Joli Jensen, *The Nashville Sound: Authenticity, Commercialization, and Country Music* (Nashville: Vanderbilt University Press, 1998); Jeffrey J. Lange, *Smile When You Call Me a Hillbilly: Country Music's Struggle for Respectability* (Athens: University of Georgia Press, 2004), 159–254; Craig Havighurst, *Air Castle of the South: WSM and the Making of Music City* (Urbana: University of Illinois Press, 2007), 138–223; and Diane Pecknold, *The Selling Sound: The Rise of the Country Music Industry* (Durham, NC: Duke University Press, 2007).

    For more background on Nashville's educational and religious life, consult, among others, William H. McRaven, *Nashville: Athens of the South* (Nashville: Tennessee Book, 1949); Christine Kreyling, Wesley Paine, Charles W. Waterfield, Jr., and Susan Ford Wiltshire, *Nashville: Athens of the South* (Nashville: Vanderbilt University Press, 1996); and Mary Ellen Pethel, *Athens of the New South: College Life and the Making of Modern Nashville* (Knoxville: University of Tennessee Press, 2017).

24. John W. Rumble, "DJ Convention," in *The Encyclopedia of Country Music*, 2nd ed., eds. Paul Kingsbury, Michael McCall, and John Rumble (New York: Oxford University Press, 2012), 141; Pecknold, *The Selling Sound*, 133–167.

25. Pecknold, *The Selling Sound*, 200–235.

26. Pecknold, *The Selling Sound*, 133–167; Kim Simpson, "Country Radio's Growing Pains in the Music Trades, 1967–1977," *American Music* 27, no. 4 (Winter 2009): 500–514; Weisbard, "Country Radio," 234–235.

27. See, for instance, David Simons, *Studio Stories: How the Great New York Records Were Made* (San Francisco: Backbeat Books, 2004); Roben Jones, *Memphis Boys: The Story of American Studios* (Jackson: University Press of Mississippi, 2011); Kent Hartman, *The Wrecking Crew: The Inside Story of Rock and Roll's Best-Kept Secret* (New York: Thomas Dunn Books, 2012); Carla Jean Whitley, *Muscle Shoals Sound Studio: How the Swampers Changed American Music* (Charleston, SC: The History Press, 2016); Andrew Flory, *I Hear a Symphony: Motown and Crossover*

R&B (Ann Arbor: University of Michigan Press, 2017). Additionally, several documentary films have recently considered the place of session musicians in the creation of US popular music, including Paul Justman, dir., *Standing in the Shadows of Motown* (Artisan Entertainment, 2002); Danny Tedesco, dir., *The Wrecking Crew!* (Magnolia Pictures, 2008/2015); Morgan Neville, dir., *20 Feet from Stardom* (Tremolo Productions/Gil Friesen Productions, 2013); and Greg Camalier, dir., *Muscle Shoals* (Magnolia Pictures, 2014).

28. Jay Orr, ed., *Dylan, Cash, and the Nashville Cats: A New Music City* (Nashville: Country Music Foundation, 2015); Ray Walker, "Patsy Cline and Owen Bradley," in *Patsy Cline: Crazy for Loving You*, eds. Mick Buck and John W. Rumble (Nashville: Country Music Foundation, 2012), 48–51, 54–56, 60–61; Jay Orr, ed., *Home of 1,000 Hits: Historic RCA Studio B, Nashville* (Nashville: Country Music Foundation, 2016).

29. Diane Pecknold, "The Country Music Association, the Country Music Foundation, and Country Music's History," in *The Oxford Handbook of Country Music*, ed. Travis D. Stimeling (New York: Oxford University Press, 2017), 55–84.

30. At the time of this writing, only seven members of the Nashville A Team have been inducted into the Country Music Hall of Fame (Country Music Hall of Fame and Museum, "Inductees List," https://countrymusichalloffame.org/index.php/Inductees [last accessed January 27, 2018]).

31. The current induction policies have been in place since 2009. For more information, consult Sarah Skates, "New Procedures for Election to the Country Music Hall of Fame," *Music Row* (February 25, 2009), https://musicrow.com/2009/02/new-procedures-for-election-to-the-country-music-hall-of-fame/ (last accessed January 27, 2018).

32. Calvin Gilbert, "Unsung Heroes Honored at Musicians Hall of Fame Induction," *CMT News* (November 27, 2007), http://www.cmt.com/news/1575159/unsung-heroes-honored-at-musicians-hall-of-fame-induction/ (last accessed January 28, 2018).

33. My examination of several hundred LP sleeves held in Middle Tennessee State University's Center for Popular Music and the University of North Carolina at Chapel Hill's Southern Folklife Collection revealed that, with rare exceptions, most session musicians received absolutely no credit in sleeve notes. Notable exceptions, however, include the primary backing vocal groups and arrangers, both of which commonly received special attention.

Nashville was not, however, the only recording center where this was the case. Instead, as a production hub in a much larger, multisite production network, Nashville-created product was published using the standards of the broader popular music industry. Only in jazz and classical music—which were considered to be prestige formats for most labels—did musicians receive extensive attention in the packaging during the decades under consideration here.

34. Hartman, *The Wrecking Crew*, 97–102. Interestingly, the Wrecking Crew's place in the production of early recordings by the Byrds continues to be ignored, as evidenced by Tim Holmes, "US and Them: American Rock's Reconquista," *Popular Music and Society* 30, no. 3 (July 2007): 343–353.

35. This model has been widely critiqued in Jason Toynbee, *Making Popular Music: Musicians, Creativity, and Institutions* (London: Arnold, 2000), 34–67; Roy Shuker, *Popular Music: The Key Concepts*, 4th ed. (New York: Routledge, 2017), 22–24; Yrjö Heinonen, "The Creative Process of the Beatles Revisited: A Multilevel Analysis of the Interaction between Individual and Collaborative Creativity," *Popular Music History* 9, no. 1 (2014): 32–47;

36. Alex DiBlasi, "In Defense of the Monkees," *American Music Review* 41, no. 2 (Spring 2012), http://www.hisam.org/ (last accessed January 29, 2018).

These notions of authenticity have been described as "rockism" by journalists and scholars alike. For useful background, consult, among others: Robert Christgau, "Rockism Faces the World," *The Village Voice* 35 (January 2, 1990): 67; Kalefa Senneh, "The Rap Against Rockism," *New York Times* (October 31, 2004), http://www.nytimes.com/2004/10/31/arts/music/31sann.html (accessed November 9, 2012); Douglas Wolk, "Thinking about Rockism," *Seattle Weekly* (May 4, 2005), http://www.seattleweekly.com/2005-05-04/music/thinking-about-rockism.php/ (accessed November 9, 2012); Michael J. Kramer, "Rocktimism?: Pop Music Writing in the Age of Rock Criticism," *Journal of Popular Music Studies* 24, no. 4 (December 2012): 590–592; Miles Parks Grier, "Said the Hooker to the Thief: 'Some Way Out' of Rockism," *Journal of Popular Music Studies* 25, no. 1 (March 2013): 31–55.

Several scholars have explored the impacts of rockist notions of authenticity on women's musical expression, revealing some of their more obvious consequences. See, among others: Sara Cohen, "Men Making a Scene: Rock Music and the Production of Gender," in *Sexing the Groove: Popular Music and Gender*, ed. Sheila Whiteley (London and New York: Routledge, 1997), 17–18; Norma Coates, "(R)evolution Now? Rock Music and the Political Potential of Gender," in *Sexing the Groove: Popular Music and Gender*, ed. Sheila Whiteley (London and New York: Routledge, 1997), 52; Travis D. Stimeling, "Taylor Swift's 'Pitch Problem' and the Place of Adolescent Girls in Country Music," in *Country Boys and Redneck Women: New Essays in Gender and Country Music*, eds. Diane Pecknold and Kristine McCusker (Jackson: University Press of Mississippi, 2016), 84–101.

37. Rich Kienzle, "Floyd Cramer, 1933–1997," *Country Music* (March–April 1998): 54; Charlie McCoy with Travis D. Stimeling, *Fifty Cents and a Box Top: The Creative Life of Nashville Session Musician Charlie McCoy* (Morgantown: West Virginia University Press, 2017), 87–108; Joe Nick Patoski, *Willie Nelson: An Epic Life* (New York: Little, Brown, 2008), 357–362.

38. Simon Zagorski-Thomas, *The Musicology of Record Production* (Cambridge: Cambridge University Press, 2014), 28–29.

39. Among other examples, consider Brian Harker, *Louis Armstrong's Hot Five and Hot Seven Recordings* (New York: Oxford University Press, 2011); Catherine Tackley, *Benny Goodman's Famous 1938 Carnegie Hall Jazz Concert* (New York: Oxford University Press, 2012); Peter Elsdon, *Keith Jarrett's The Koln Concert* (New York: Oxford University Press, 2012).

40. Albin J. Zak, III, *The Poetics of Rock: Cutting Tracks, Making Records* (Berkeley: University of California Press, 2001); Jay Hodgson, *Understanding Records: A Field Guide to Recording Practice* (New York: Continuum, 2010); Allan F.

Moore, *Song Means: Analysing and Interpreting Recorded Popular Song* (Farnham, UK: Ashgate, 2012).

41. Allan F. Moore and Ruth Dockwray, "The Establishment of the Virtual Performance Space in Rock," *Twentieth-Century Music* 5, no. 2 (September 2008): 219–241; Allan F. Moore, Patricia Smith, and Ruth Dockwray, "A Hermeneutics of Spatialization for Recorded Song," *Twentieth-Century Music* 6, no. 1 (March 2009): 83–114; Ruth Dockwray and Allan F. Moore, "Configuring the Sound-Box, 1965–1972," *Popular Music* 29, no. 2 (May 2010): 181–197. For one country-oriented study that makes use of these methods, consult Travis D. Stimeling, "Narrative, Vocal Staging and Masculinity in the 'Outlaw' Country Music of Waylon Jennings," *Popular Music* 32, no. 3 (2013): 343–358.

42. Don Michael Randel, "The Canons in the Musicological Toolbox," in *Disciplining Music: Musicology and Its Canons*, eds. Katherine Bergeron and Philip V. Bohlman (Chicago: University of Chicago Press, 1992), 10–22.

43. Mark Katz, *Capturing Sound: How Technology Has Changed Music*, revised ed. (Berkeley: University of California Press, 2010), 2.

44. Katz, *Capturing Sound*, 94–108.

45. Robert Philip, *Performing Music in the Age of Recording* (New Haven, CT: Yale University Press, 2004); Nicholas Cook, "Methods for Analysing Recordings," in *The Cambridge Companion to Recorded Music*, eds. Nicholas Cook, Eric Clarke, Daniel Leech-Wilkinson, and John Rink (Cambridge: Cambridge University Press, 2009), 221–245; Daniel Leech-Wilkinson, "Recordings and Histories of Performance Style," in *The Cambridge Companion to Recorded Music*, eds. Nicholas Cook, Eric Clarke, Daniel Leech-Wilkinson, and John Rink (Cambridge: Cambridge University Press, 2009), 246–262; idem, *The Changing Sound of Music: Approaches to Studying Recorded Musical Performance* (London: CHARM, 2009); Colin Lawson, "Recreating History: A Clarinettist's Retrospective," in *The Cambridge Companion to Recorded Music*, eds. Nicholas Cook, Eric Clarke, Daniel Leech-Wilkinson, and John Rink (Cambridge: Cambridge University Press, 2009), 263–266.

46. Among more recent attempts to make sense of collaborative creativity and authorship in music, consult: Simon P. Keefe, "'Die Ochsen am Berge': Fran Xaver Süssmayr and the Orchestration of Mozart's Requiem, K. 626," *Journal of the American Musicological Society* 61, no. 1 (Spring 2008): 1–65; Robert D. Levin, Richard Maunder, Duncan Druce, David Black, Christoph Wolff, and Simon P. Keefe, "Finishing Mozart's Requiem: On 'Die Ochsen am Berge': Franz Xaver Süssmayr and the Orchestration of Mozart's Requiem, K. 626," *Journal of the American Musicological Society* 61, no. 3 (Fall 2008): 583–608; Pedro Rebelo, "Dramaturgy in the Network," *Contemporary Music Review* 28, nos. 4–5 (August–October 2009): 387–393; Valerie Pearson, "Authorship and Improvisation: Musical Lost Property," *Contemporary Music Review* 29, no. 4 (August 2010): 367–378; Nathan Platte, "Music for *Spellbound* (1945): A Contested Collaboration," *Journal of Musicology* 28, no. 4 (Fall 2011): 418–463; Katharina Clausius, "Historical Mirroring, Mirroring History: An Aesthetics of Collaboration in *Pulcinella*," *Journal of Musicology* 30, no. 2 (Spring 2013): 215–251;

47. Virgil Moorefield, *The Producer as Composer: Shaping the Sounds of Popular Music* (Cambridge, MA: MIT Press, 2005), xiii.

48. Meintjes, *Sound of Africa!*, 9, 146–216; Louise Meintjes, "The Politics of the Recording Studio: A Case Study from South Africa," in *The Cambridge Companion to Recorded Music*, eds. Nicholas Cook, Eric Clarke, Daniel Leech-Wilkinson, and John Rink (Cambridge: Cambridge University Press, 2009), 84–97; Bates, *Digital Tradition*, 45–117.

49. Thomas Porcello, "'Tails Out': Social Phenomenology and the Ethnographic Representation of Technology in Music-Making," *Ethnomusicology* 42, no. 3 (Autumn 1998): 500.

   Scholars have also shown interest in the ways that particular communities come together to define production standards, recording technologies, and playback methods. See, among others: Paul Théberge, *Any Sound You Can Imagine: Making Music/Consuming Technology* (Hanover, NH: Wesleyan University Press, 1997); Jonathan Sterne, *mp3: The Meaning of a Format* (Durham, NC: Duke University Press, 2012), esp. 128–183; Susan Schmidt Horning, *Chasing Sound: Technology, Culture, and the Art of Studio Recording from Edison to the LP* (Baltimore, MD: Johns Hopkins University Press, 2013); Thomas Porcello, "Music Mediated as Live in Austin: Sound, Technology, and Recording Practice," in *Wired for Sound: Engineering and Technologies in Sonic Cultures*, eds. Paul D. Greene and Thomas Porcello (Middletown, CT: Wesleyan University Press, 2005), 103–117.

50. Kenney, *Recorded Music in American Life*, 182.

51. Among many, consider Kenney, *Recorded Music in American Life*; Karl Hagstrom Miller, *Segregating Sound: Inventing Folk and Pop Music in the Age of Jim Crow* (Durham, NC: Duke University Press, 2010).

52. On record collecting, consult, among others: Will Straw, "Sizing Up Record Collections: Gender and Connoisseurship in Rock Music Culture," in *Sexing the Groove: Popular Music and Gender*, ed. Sheila Whiteley (New York: Routledge, 1997), 3–16; Simon Reynolds, "Lost in Music: Obsessive Record Collecting," in *This Is Pop: In Search of the Elusive at Experience Music Project*, ed. Eric Weisbard (Cambridge, MA: Harvard University Press, 2004), 289–307; Roy Shuker, "Beyond the 'High Fidelity' Stereotype: Defining the (Contemporary) Record Collector," *Popular Music* 23, no. 3 (October 2004): 311–330; idem, *Wax Trash and Vinyl Treasures: Record Collecting as a Social Practice* (Farnham, UK: Ashgate, 2016); John Dougan, "Objects of Desire: Canon Formation and Blues Record Collecting," *Journal of Popular Music Studies* 18, no. 1 (2006): 40–65.

   On bootlegging, consult Mark Neumann and Timothy A. Simpson, "Smuggled Sound: Bootleg Recording and the Pursuit of Popular Memory," *Symbolic Interaction* 20, no. 4 (February 1997): 319–341; Lee Marshall, "For and Against the Record Industry: An Introduction to Bootleg Collectors and Tape Traders," *Popular Music* 22, no. 1 (January 2003): 57–72; Alex Cummings, "Collectors, Bootleggers, and the Value of Jazz, 1930–1952," in *Sound in the Age of Mechanical Reproduction*, eds. David Suisman and Susan Strasser (Philadelphia: University of Pennsylvania Press, 2010), 95–114; Rebekah Farrugia and Nancy Gobatto, "Shopping for Legs and Boots: Tori Amos's *Original Bootlegs*, Fandom, and Subcultural Capital,"

Popular Music and Society 33, no. 3 (July 2010): 357–375; Gary Warren Melton, "An Examination of the Bootleg Record Industry and Its Impact upon Popular Music Consumption," *Journal of Popular Music Studies* 26, nos. 2–3 (June 2014): 399–408.

On audio archives and memory, consult, among others: Erika Brady, *A Spiral Way: How the Phonograph Changed Ethnography* (Jackson: University Press of Mississippi, 1999), 118–126; Samuel Kahunde, "Repatriating Archival Sound Recordings to Revive Traditions: The Role of the Klaus Wachsmann Recordings in the Revival of the Royal Music of Bunyoro-Kitara, Uganda," *Ethnomusicology Forum* 21, no. 2 (August 2012): 197–219; Martha Sprigge, "Tape Work and Memory Work in Post-War Germany," *Twentieth-Century Music* 14, no. 1 (February 2017): 49–63.

53. Joseph G. Schloss, *Making Beats: The Art of Sample-Based Hip-Hop* (Middletown, CT: Wesleyan University Press, 2004).

54. Mark Katz, *Groove Music: The Art and Culture of the Hip-Hop DJ* (New York: Oxford University Press, 2012).

55. Among the more relevant sound studies work for this study are Lily E. Hirsch, "Weaponizing Classical Music: Crime Prevention and Symbolic Power in the Age of Repetition," *Journal of Popular Music Studies* 19, no. 4 (2007): 342–358; Trevor Pinch and Karin Bijsterveld, "New Keys to the World of Sound," in *The Oxford Handbook of Sound* Studies, eds. Trevor Pinch and Karin Bijsterveld (New York: Oxford University Press, 2011), 3–35; Karin Bijsterveld, Eefje Cleophas, Stefan Krebs, and Gijs Mom, *Sound and Safe: A History of Listening Behind the Wheel* (New York: Oxford University Press, 2013).

56. Travis D. Stimeling, "Situating Country Music Studies," in *The Oxford Handbook of Country Music*, ed. Travis D. Stimeling (New York: Oxford University Press, 2017), 1–12.

57. Aaron A. Fox, "White Trash Alchemies of the Abject Sublime: Country as 'Bad' Music," in *Bad Music: The Music We Love to Hate*, eds. Christopher J. Washburne and Maiken Derno (New York: Routledge, 2004), 39–61.

58. See, among others, Barbara Ching, *Wrong's What I Do Best: Hard Country Music and Contemporary Culture* (New York: Oxford University Press, 2001); Aaron A. Fox, *Real Country: Music and Language in Working-Class Culture* (Durham, NC: Duke University Press, 2004); Nadine Hubbs, *Rednecks, Queers, and Country Music* (Berkeley: University of California Press, 2014).

59. Peterson, *Creating Country Music*; Patrick Huber, *Linthead Stomp: The Creation of Country Music in the Piedmont South* (Chapel Hill: University of North Carolina Press, 2008); *idem*, "The 'Southernness' of Country Music," in *The Oxford Handbook of Country Music*, ed. Travis D. Stimeling (New York: Oxford University Press, 2017), 31–53; Miller, *Segregating Sound*, 187–214.

60. Jean A. Boyd, *The Jazz of the Southwest: An Oral History of Western Swing* (Austin: University of Texas Press, 1998); *idem*, *"We're the Light Crust Doughboys from Burrus Mill": An Oral History* (Austin: University of Texas Press, 2003); *idem, Dance All Night: Those Other Southwestern Swing Bands, Past and Present* (Lubbock: Texas Tech University Press, 2012); Rich Kienzle, *Southwest Shuffle: Pioneers of Honky-Tonk, Western Swing, and Country Jazz* (New York: Routledge, 2003).

61. See, for instance, Eric Weisbard, *Top 40 Democracy: The Rival Mainstreams of American Music* (Chicago: University of Chicago Press, 2014), 152–153, 233.

62. Jensen, *The Nashville Sound*, esp. 38–61; Pecknold, *The Selling Sound*.

63. Henry Kingsbury, *Music, Talent, and Performance: A Conservatory Cultural System* (Philadelphia: Temple University Press, 2001).

64. Harold Bradley, interview with John W. Rumble, May 14, 1991, Country Music Foundation Oral History Collection, OHC 35.

65. Mark Christopher Samples, "A Package Deal: Branding, Technology, and Advertising in Music of the 20th and 21st Centuries," Ph.D. dissertation, University of Oregon, 2012.

66. Pecknold, *The Selling Sound*, 133–167; Kim Simpson, "Country Radio's Growing Pains in the Music Trades, 1967–1977," *American Music* 27, no. 4 (Winter 2009): 500–514; Weisbard, "Country Radio," 234–235.

CHAPTER 1

1. Mary Ellen Pethel, *Athens of the New South: College Life and the Making of Modern Nashville* (Knoxville: University of Tennessee Press, 2017); Charles K. Wolfe, *A Good-Natured Riot: The Birth of the Grand Ole Opry* (Nashville: Country Music Foundation Press and Vanderbilt University Press, 1999); William Allen Poe, "Nashville, Tennessee," in *The Encyclopedia of Religion in the South*, 2nd ed., eds. Samuel S. Hill and Charles H. Lippy (Macon: Mercer University Press, 2005), 538–539.

2. Here, I think it is worthwhile to consider that the overt racialization of musical genres in the 1920s might be productively heard not only as an example of implicit and explicit bias, but also, following Charles Hiroshi Garrett, as a response to the complexities of race and representation. As Garrett notes, "We may be attracted to music that attempts to produce a sense of multicultural equality or upset by music that serves to encode racial prejudice, but rarely does there exist music so unambiguous and one-dimensional. One the contrary, individual pieces of music, at times whole genres, hold our attention precisely because their efforts to grapple with musical and cultural tensions do not, sometimes cannot, produce clear-cut solutions" (Charles Hiroshi Garrett, *Struggling to Define a Nation: American Music and the Twentieth Century* [Berkeley: University of California Press, 2008], 44).

3. Russell Sanjek and David Sanjek, *American Popular Music and Its Business in the 20th Century* (New York: Oxford University Press, 1991), 20.

   This phenomenon, and its racial implications, has been widely documented. Consult, among others: Archie Green, "Hillbilly Music: Source and Symbol," *Journal of American Folklore* 78, no. 309 (July–September 1965): 204–228; Richard A. Peterson, *Creating Country Music: Fabricating Authenticity* (Chicago: University of Chicago Press, 1997), 12–51, 55–94; William Howland Kenney, *Recorded Music in American Life: The Phonograph and Popular Memory, 1890–1945* (New York: Oxford University Press, 1999), 135–157; Anthony Harkins, *Hillbilly: A Cultural History of an American Icon* (New York: Oxford University Press, 2004), 71–102; J. Lester Feder, " 'Song of the South': Country Music, Race, Region, and the Politics of Culture, 1920–1974," Ph.D. dissertation, University of California at Los

Angeles, 2006, 45–143; Karl Hagstrom Miller, *Segregating Sound: Inventing Folk and Pop Music in the Age of Jim Crow* (Durham, NC: Duke University Press, 2010), 187–214; Angela Denise Hammond, "Color Me Country: Commercial Country Music and Whiteness," Ph.D. dissertation, University of Kentucky, 2011, 21–62; Edward P. Comentale, *Sweet Air: Modernism, Regionalism, and American Popular Song* (Urbana: University of Illinois Press, 2013), 72–116; Patrick Huber, "Black Hillbillies: African American Musicians on Old-Time Records, 1924–1932," in *Hidden in the Mix: The African American Presence in Country Music*, ed. Diane Pecknold (Durham, NC: Duke University Press, 2013), 19–81; Patrick Huber, "The New York Sound: Citybilly Recording Artists and the Creation of Hillbilly Music, 1924–1932," *Journal of American Folklore* 127, no. 504 Spring 2014): 140–158; Erich Nunn, *Sounding the Color Line: Music and Race in the Southern Imagination* (Athens: University of Georgia Press, 2015), 16–105; Charles L. Hughes, "Country Music and the Recording Industry," in *The Oxford Handbook of Country Music*, ed. Travis D. Stimeling (New York: Oxford University Press, 2017), 207–209; Patrick Huber, "The 'Southernness' of Country Music," in *The Oxford Handbook of Country Music*, ed. Travis D. Stimeling (New York: Oxford University Press, 2017), 39; Brian Ward and Patrick Huber, *A&R Pioneers: Architects of American Roots Music on Record* (Nashville: Vanderbilt University Press, 2018), 45–157.

4. As Richard K. Spottswood's remarkable multivolume discography demonstrates, the recording industry's interest in ethnic music performed by people in the United States was quite extensive. For more information, consult Richard K. Spottswood, *Ethnic Music on Records: A Discography of Ethnic Recordings Produced in the United States, 1893–1942*, 7 vols. (Urbana: University of Illinois Press, 1990). See also Bill C. Malone and David Stricklin, *Southern Music/American Music*, rev. and expanded ed. (Lexington: University Press of Kentucky, 2003), 58–70; Andre Millard, *America on Record: A History of Recorded Sound*, 2nd ed. (Cambridge: Cambridge University Press, 2005), 88–91.

5. For more information on recording in the 1920s, consult, among others, David L. Morton, Jr., *Sound Recording: The Life Story of a Technology* (Westport, CT: Greenwood Press, 2004; paperback ed., Baltimore, MD: Johns Hopkins University Press, 2006), 55–68; Susan Schmidt Horning, *Chasing Sound: Technology, Culture, and the Art of Studio Recording from Edison to the LP* (Baltimore, MD: Johns Hopkins University Press, 2013), 11–55; Don Law, Jr., qtd. in Michael Jarrett, *Producing Country: The Inside Story of the Great Recordings* (Middletown, CT: Wesleyan University Press, 2014), 20–21; Ward and Huber, *A&R Pioneers*, 159–198.

6. Among the early artists to make the long train trips to New York, New Jersey, and Indiana was Ernest Stoneman, who made significant contributions as a recording artist prior to his extensive recording work in the Bristol sessions. See Ivan L. Tribe, *The Stonemans An Appalachian Family and the Music that Shaped Their Lives* (Urbana: University of Illinois Press, 1993), 36–56.

7. Tony Russell, "Country Music on Location: 'Field Recording' before Bristol," *Popular Music* 26, no. 1 (January 2007): 26. For more on these sessions and their consequences, consult Wayne W. Daniel, *Pickin' on Peachtree: A History*

of Country Music in Atlanta (Urbana: University of Illinois Press, 1990), 67–86; Charles K. Wolfe, "The Bristol Syndrome: Field Recordings of Early Country Music," in *Country Music Annual 2002*, eds. Charles K. Wolfe and James E. Akenson (Lexington: University Press of Kentucky, 2002), 202–221; Patrick Huber, *Linthead Stomp: The Creation of Country Music in the Piedmont* South (Chapel Hill: University of North Carolina Press, 2008), 43–102; Barry Mazor, *Ralph Peer and the Making of Popular Roots Music* (Chicago: Chicago Review Press, 2015), 31–120; David Brackett, *Categorizing Sound: Genre and Twentieth-Century Popular Music* (Berkeley: University of California Press, 2016), 113–118; Ward and Huber, *A&R Pioneers*, 33–34.

8. Russell, "Country Music on Location," 26–27. See also Ward and Huber, *A&R Pioneers*, 159–198.

9. Nolan Porterfield, *Jimmie Rodgers: The Life and Times of America's Blue Yodeler* (Urbana: University of Illinois Press, 1979), 84–103; Mark Zwonitzer with Charles Hirshberg, *Will You Miss Me When I'm Gone?: The Carter Family and Their Legacy in American Music* (New York: Simon & Schuster, 2004), 81–96; Charles K. Wolfe and Ted Olsen, eds. *The Bristol Sessions: Writings about the Big Bang of Country Music* (Jefferson, NC: McFarland, 2005); Beth Harrington, *The Winding Stream: An Oral History of the Carter and Cash Family* (Georgetown, MA: PFP, 2014), 21–31; Mazor, *Ralph Peer and the Making of Popular Roots Music*, 91–120.

10. Charles K. Wolfe, *Tennessee Strings: The Story of Country Music in Tennessee* (Knoxville: University of Tennessee Press, 1977), 43–44.

11. Horning, *Chasing Sound*, 11–31; Ward and Huber, *A&R Pioneers*, 159–198.

12. Horning, *Chasing Sound*, 13–55.

13. Ward and Huber, *A&R Pioneers*, 189–191.

14. Tony Russell, *Country Music Records: A Discography, 1921–1942* (New York: Oxford University Press, 2004).

15. Daniel, *Pickin' on Peachtree*, 67–108. See also Gavin James Campbell, *Music and the Making of a New South* (Chapel Hill: University of North Carolina Press, 2004), 100–142; Huber, *Linthead Stomp*, 43–102.

16. Pamela Grundy, "'We Always Tried to Be Good People': Respectability, Crazy Water Crystals, and Hillbilly Music on the Air, 1933–1935," *Journal of American History* 81, no. 4 (March 1995): 1591–1620; David B. Pruett, "Music City, U.S.A.: Charlotte, North Carolina," paper presented to the Society for American Music, Tempe, AZ, March 2003; idem, "Commercial Country as Process: WBT, Charlotte, and the Creation of a Country Music Center," paper presented to the International Country Music Conference, Belmont University, May 2003; Huber, *Linthead Stomp*, 39–41, 249–252; Dick Spottswood, *Banjo on the Mountain: Wade Mainer's First Hundred Years* (Jackson: University Press of Mississippi, 2010).

17. Lisa Krissoff Boehm, "Chicago as Forgotten Country Music Mecca," in *The Hayloft Gang: The Story of the* National Barn Dance (Urbana: University of Illinois Press, 2008), 101–118; Paul L. Tyler, "The Rise of Rural Rhythm," in *The Hayloft Gang: The Story of the National Barn Dance* (Urbana: University of Illinois Press, 2008), 19–71. For more background on the Chicago scene, consult Michael Ann Williams, *Staging Tradition: John Lair and Sarah Gertrude Knott* (Urbana: University of

Illinois Press, 2006), 39–61; the remaining essays in Chad Berry, ed., *The Hayloft Gang: The Story of the National Barn Dance* (Urbana: University of Illinois Press, 2008); Kristine M. McCusker, *Lonesome Cowgirls and Honky-Tonk Angels: The Women of Barn Dance Radio* (Urbana: University of Illinois Press, 2008).

18. Sanjek and Sanjek, *American Popular Music Business in the 20th Century*, 47–78; Malone and Stricklin, *Southern Music/American Music*, 71–74; Millard, *America on Record*, 136–139, 170–175, 178.

19. Sanjek and Sanjek note that, by 1932, "recorded music now was heard frequently over the approximately 600 independent radio stations. Many of them featured live performers and electrical transcriptions. Live talent was paid as little as a few dollars. Electrical transcriptions cost between $40 and $150 a week. As a consequence, broadcasts began to buy records at list price, or get them free in return for publicity." They go on to note that efforts to stamp out the broadcast of commercial recordings in 1933 were largely unsuccessful because "property rights ended once a record was sold, a legal opinion vigorously opposed by manufacturers and many leading artists" (*American Popular Music Business in the 20th Century*, 48–49).

20. Richard A. Peterson, *Creating Country Music: Fabricating Authenticity* (Chicago: University of Chicago Press, 1997), 118–136. Oral histories and memoirs of early country music artists are filled with references to this practice. Among others, consult Kristine M. McCusker, "Rose Lee Maphis and Working on Barn Dance Radio, 1930–1960," in *The Women of Country Music: A Reader*, eds. Charles K. Wolfe and James E. Akenson (Lexington: University Press of Kentucky, 2003), 63–64.

21. For more background on advertising on hillbilly programs, consult Ivan M. Tribe, "The Economics of Hillbilly Radio: A Preliminary Investigation of the 'P.I.' System in the Depression Decade and Afterward," *JEMF Quarterly* 20 (Fall–Winter 1984): 76–83; Grundy, "'We Always Tried to Be Good People'"; Alexander Russo, "Passing Pappy's Biscuits: Dynamics of Uneven Modernization in Regional Radio Voices," in *Music and the Broadcast Experience: Performance, Production, and Audiences*, eds. Christina Baade and James A. Deaville (New York: Oxford University Press, 2016), 173–190.

22. For more background on the development of recording technologies in the radio industry, consult Morton, *Off the Record*, 50–54.

23. Pamela Fox, *Natural Acts: Gender, Race, and Rusticity in Country Music* (Ann Arbor: University of Michigan Press, 2009), 17–62.

24. Barn dances have received a great deal of attention in recent years, both in scholarship and local histories. For more background on these programs, consult, among others: Pete Stamper, *It All Happened in Renfro Valley* (Lexington: University Press of Kentucky, 1999); Williams, *Staging Tradition*; Berry, ed., *The Hayloft Gang*; McCusker, *Lonesome Cowgirls and Honky-Tonk Angels*; Stephanie Vander Wel, "'I Am a Honky Tonk Girl': Country Music, Gender, and Migration," Ph.D. dissertation, University of California at Los Angeles, 2008, 28–81.

25. Wolfe, *A Good-Natured Riot*, 8–10.

26. Wolfe notes, for instance, that "a typical show in October [1927] 'received over 200 messages from 32 states' (*Tennesseean*, October 24, 1927), though newspapers

commented that the appeal of the show 'seems a mystery to a number of people' (*Tennesseean*, September 18, 1927)" (Wolfe, *A Good-Natured Riot*, 21).

27. Wolfe, *A Good-Natured Riot*, 5–6; Craig Havighurst, *Air Castle of the South: WSM and the Making of Music City* (Urbana: University of Illinois Press, 2007), 11–12.

28. Wolfe, *A Good-Natured Riot*, 5.

29. Havighurst notes, for instance, that corporate leaders at National Life were aware of this potential when they built the station, observing that "National Life officials predicted that under the right conditions, its station could reach Canada, Mexico, Cuba, and (inaccurately, it turned out) Europe" (Havighurst, *Air Castle of the South*, 12).

30. Wolfe, *A Good-Natured Riot*, 21–22.

31. Havighurst, *Air Castle of the South*, 73.

32. Wolfe, *A Good-Natured Riot*, 166–178.

33. Havighurst, *Air Castle of the South*, 72.

34. Wolfe, *A Good-Natured Riot*, 24. For a broader discussion of the impacts of barn dances and schoolhouse bookings, consult Jeffrey J. Lange, *Smile When You Call Me a Hillbilly: Country Music's Struggle for Respectability, 1939–1954* (Athens: University of Georgia Press, 2004), 19–66.

35. Lange, *Smile When You Call Me a Hillbilly*, 70.

36. Wolfe, *A Good-Natured Riot*, 253–265; Charles K. Wolfe, *Classic Country: Legends of Country Music* (New York: Routledge, 2001), 19; McCusker, *Lonesome Cowgirls and Honky-Tonk Angels*, 103–123.

37. Lange, *Smile When You Call Me a Hillbilly*, 67–86. For more background on the Armed Forces Radio Network, consult Morton, *Sound Recording*, 103–106.

38. Doug Bradley and Craig Werner, *We Gotta Get Out of This Place: The Soundtrack of the Vietnam War* (Amherst: University of Massachusetts Press, 2015), 57–60, 170, 207.

39. Peter LaChapelle, *Proud to Be an Okie: Cultural Politics, Country Music, and Migration to Southern California* (Berkeley: University of California Press, 2007), 76–110.

40. Wolfe, *Tennessee Strings*, 75–76.

41. LaChapelle, *Proud to Be an Okie*, 159–179; Vander Wel, "'I Am a Honky-Tonk Girl,'" esp. chs. 3 and 4.; McCusker, *Lonesome Cowgirls and Honky-Tonk Angels*, 124–152.

42. Lange, *Smile When You Call Me a Hillbilly*. This "struggle for respectability" comes from Lange's subtitle.

43. Lange, *Smile When You Call Me a Hillbilly*, 71–72.

44. Ward and Huber, *A&R Pioneers*, 135.

45. ASCAP was founded in 1914. More details on its establishment and efforts to begin collecting royalties can be found in Sanjek and Sanjek, *American Popular Music Business in the 20th Century*, 16–20.

46. Lange, *Smile When You Call Me a Hillbilly*, 72.

47. Patrick Huber, "The New York Sound, 145.

48. Rumble, "Fred Rose and the Development of the Nashville Music Industry, 1942-1954," 29–30.

49. Among many others, consult Steven P. Dandaneau, *A Town Abandoned: Flint, Michigan, Confronts Deindustrialization* (Albany: State University of New York Press, 1996); Jefferson Cowie, *Capital Moves: RCA's Seventy-Year Quest for Cheap Labor* (Ithaca, NY: Cornell University Press, 1999; paperback ed., New York: New Press, 2001); Sean Safford, *Why the Garden Club Couldn't Save Youngstown: The Transformation of the Rust Belt* (Cambridge, MA: Harvard University Press, 2009); Chad Broughton, *Boom, Bust, Exodus: The Rust Belt, the Maquilas, and a Tale of Two Cities* (New York: Oxford University Press, 2015).

50. This history has been thoroughly documented in a wide range of sources. Consult, among others: Charles Hamm, *Yesterdays: Popular Song in America* (New York: W. W. Norton, 1979), 109–140, 253–325; David A. Jasen, *Tin Pan Alley: The Composers, the Songs, the Performers, and Their Times—The Golden Age of American Popular Music from 1886 to 1956* (New York: D. I. Fine, 1988); Robert W. Snyder, *The Voice of the City: Vaudeville and Popular Culture in New York* (New York: Oxford University Press, 1989); Sanjek and Sanjek, *American Popular Music Business in the 20th Century*, 3–32; Dale Cockrell, *Demons of Disorder: Early Blackface Minstrels and Their World* (Cambridge: Cambridge University Press, 1997); Gillian M. Rodger, *Champagne Charlie and Pretty Jemima: Variety Theater in the Nineteenth Century* (Urbana: University of Illinois Press, 2010), 149–157.

51. For more background on Southern Peer Music, consult Mazor, *Ralph Peer and the Making of Popular Roots Music*, 121–222.

52. Rumble, "Fred Rose and the Development of the Nashville Music Industry, 1942–1954," 1.

53. Rumble, "Fred Rose and the Development of the Nashville Music Industry, 1942–1954," 2–3.

54. Wolfe, *A Good-Natured Riot*, 253–265; Wolfe, *Classic Country*, 19; Huber, *Linthead Stomp*, 259–261.

55. John W. Rumble, "Fred Rose," in *The Encyclopedia of Country Music*, 2nd ed., eds. Paul Kingsbury, Michael McCall, and John W. Rumble (New York: Oxford University Press, 2012), 439.

56. Rumble, "Fred Rose and the Development of the Nashville Music Industry, 1942–1954," 6–18, 46–47, 52–61.

57. Rumble, "Fred Rose and the Development of the Nashville Music Industry, 1942–1954," 24–27. See also 36–40, 61–64 for a more detailed musical analysis of some of Rose's compositions from the 1930s.

58. Rumble, "Fred Rose and the Development of the Nashville Music Industry," 116; Michael Kosser, *How Nashville Became Music City, U.S.A.: Fifty Years of Music Row* (Milwaukee: Hal Leonard, 2006), 22–24; Diane Pecknold, *The Selling Sound: The Rise of the Country Music Industry* (Durham, NC: Duke University Press, 2007), 57–58.

Huber writes about Acuff's settlement with Dorsey Dixon for "I Didn't Hear Anybody Pray" (also known as "Wreck on the Highway") in *Linthead Stomp*, 259–261.

59. For more discussion of the Music Row neighborhood's development, consult Hill, *Country Comes to Town*, 47–55.

60. Kosser, *How Nashville Became Music City, U.S.A.*, 28–29; Bar Biszick-Lockwood, *Restless Giant: The Life and Times of Jean Aberbach and Hill and Range Songs* (Urbana: University of Illinois Press, 2010). Kosser also notes that other music businesses were located along Franklin Road and at the Cumberland Lodge Building (29).

61. Sanjek and Sanjek, *American Popular Music Business in the 20th Century*, 63–65. For more background on Peer's operations, consult Barry Mazor, *Ralph Peer and the Making of Popular Roots Music* (Chicago: Chicago Review Press, 2015), esp. chs. 4–5. On the Aberbachs, consult Biszick-Lockwood, *Restless Giant*, chs. 6–9.

62. Rumble, "Fred Rose and the Development of the Nashville Music Industry, 1942–1954," 148–149.

63. Mary A. Bufwack and Robert K. Oermann, *Finding Her Voice: Women in Country Music, 1800–2000* (Nashville: Vanderbilt University Press and Country Music Foundation Press, 2003), 331–332.

64. Cary Ginell, "The Grand Ole Opry," in liner notes to *Red Foley: Old Shep, The Red Foley Recordings, 1933–1950* (Bear Family BCD 16759 FL, 2006), 56; Cary Ginell, Dave Sax, and Richard Weize, "The Discography, 1933–1950," in liner notes to *Red Foley: Old Shep, The Red Foley Recordings, 1933–1950* (Bear Family BCD 16759 FL, 2006), 82.

65. Neil V. Rosenberg and Charles K. Wolfe, *The Music of Bill Monroe* (Urbana: University of Illinois Press, 2007), 37–75.

66. John W. Rumble, "Brown Radio Productions," *The Encyclopedia of Country Music*, 2nd ed., eds. Paul Kingsbury, Michael McCall, and John W. Rumble (New York: Oxford University Press, 2012), 55

67. Michael D. Freda, comp., *Eddy Arnold Discography, 1944–1996* (Westport, CT: Greenwood Press, 1997), 1–25; Michael Streissguth, *Eddy Arnold: Pioneer of the Nashville Sound* (New York: Schirmer Books 1997), 60–62, 72–73; Martin Hawkins, *A Shot in the Dark: Making Records in Nashville, 1945–1955* (Nashville: Vanderbilt University Press and Country Music Foundation Press, 2006), 15–16.

68. Millard, *America on Record*, 185.

69. Sanjek and Sanjek, *American Popular Music Business in the 20th Century*, 51, 61, 79–81; Tim Anderson, "'Buried under the Fecundity of His Own Creations': Reconsidering the Recording Bands of the American Federation of Musicians, 1942–1944 and 1948," *American Music* 22, no. 2 (Summer 2004): 231–269. Sanjek and Sanjek note that "in the first year of their strike, union musicians lost four million dollars, while the record makers prospered" (Sanjek and Sanjek, *American Popular Music Business in the 20th Century*, 80). Additionally, as jazz historian Scott DeVeaux has observed, many jazz critics and historians have suggested that the strike led to gaps in the documentation of musical styles, a claim that DeVeaux believes has been overblown (Scott DeVeaux, *The Birth of Bebop: A Social and Musical History* [Berkeley: University of California Press, 1997], 295–299).

70. Sanjek and Sanjek, *American Popular Music Business in the 20th Century*, 80.

71. Sanjek and Sanjek note, for instance, that, by the end of 1943, "Victor began to run out of materials and seriously considered meeting with Petrillo" (Sanjek and Sanjek, *American Popular Music Business in the 20th Century*, 80–81).

72. For more background on the jukebox industry, consult John Broven, *Record Makers and Breakers: Voices of the Independent Rock 'n' Roll Pioneers* (Urbana: University of Illinois Press, 2009), 16–19. Radio distribution of these independents has been widely covered, as well, but two of the more pertinent sources for the present study are Louis Cantor, *Dewey and Elvis: The Life and Times of a Rock 'n' Roll Deejay* (Urbana: University of Illinois Press, 2005); Broven, *Record Makers and Breakers*, 93–115.

73. Broven, *Record Makers and Breakers*, 15.

74. One need only look at some of the books focusing on independent record labels of this era to note the stylistic diversity that these independent labels captured. In addition to Broven's *Record Makers and Breakers*, consult, among many others: Colin Escott with Martin Hawkins, *Good Rockin' Tonight: Sun Records and the Birth of Rock 'n' Roll*, paperback ed. (New York: St. Martin's Griffin, 1992); Nadine Cohodas, *Spinning Blues into Gold: The Chess Brothers and the Legendary Chess Records* (New York: St. Martin's Press, 2000); Tony Olmsted, *Folkways Records: Moses Asch and His Encyclopedia of Sound* (New York: Routledge, 2003); John Hartley Fox, *King of the Queen City: The Story of King Records* (Urbana: University of Illinois Press, 2009); Nathan D. Gibson with Don Pierce, *The Starday Story: The House That Country Music Built* (Jackson: University of Mississippi Press, 2011); Robert Greenfield, *The Last Sultan: The Life and Times of Ahmet Ertegun* (New York: Simon & Schuster, 2011).

75. Fox, *King of the Queen City*, 3.

76. King Records historian John Hartley Fox notes that the station's signal even had international reach, recounting that "Jethro Burns remembered one time asking for letters on-air and receiving fan mail from Australia, Hong Kong, and China" (Fox, *King of the Queen City*, 15).

77. Fox, *King of the Queen City*, 12–21; Rich Kienzle, *Southwest Shuffle: Pioneers of Honky-Tonk, Western Swing, and Country Jazz* (New York: Routledge, 2003), 35–47.

78. Fox, *King of the Queen City*, 17–19.

79. Clifford R. Murphy, *Yankee Twang: Country and Western Music in New England* (Urbana: University of Illinois Press, 2014), 60–62. Hawkshaw Hawkins, for instance, recorded sixteen sides for King in August and September 1946 (Michel Ruppli, comp., *The King Labels: A Discography*, vol. 1 [Westport, CT: Greenwood Press, 1985], 9).

80. Fox, *King of the Queen City*, 53–54; Rick Bird, "Herzog Is Hallowed Ground," *CityBeat* (Cincinnati, OH), November 16, 2009, https://www.citybeat.com/music/music-feature/article/13015806/herzog-is-hallowed-ground (last accessed March 25, 2018).

81. Earl Herzog, qtd. in Fox, *King of the Queen City*, 53.

82. Pee Wee King, qtd. in Wade Hall, *Hell-Bent for Music: The Life of Pee Wee King* (Lexington: University Press of Kentucky, 1996), 171. It is worth noting that this direct-to-audience market continues to be an important part of the country music economy, allowing artists to continue to provide new material to audiences that would otherwise not be reached by the marketing and distribution networks of the mainstream country music industry.

83. Peterson, *Creating Country Music*, 125–127.

84. Jim Bulleit, qtd. in Hawkins, *A Shot in the Dark*, 27.

85. Hawkins, *A Shot in the Dark*, 28–29.

86. Hawkins, *A Shot in the Dark*, 31.

87. Hawkins, *A Shot in the Dark*, 33.

88. For more background on Bullet's output, consult Hawkins, *A Shot in the Dark*, 39–70.

89. Hawkins, *A Shot in the Dark*, 71.

90. Hawkins notes, for instance, that Stokes "acted for many of the small record labels . . . and brokered lease deals and buy-outs well into the 1950s" (*A Shot in the Dark*, 73).

91. Hawkins, *A Shot in the Dark*, 80.

92. As Hawkins has indicated, Cheker and World Records seem to have focused principally on hillbilly music, while the Select and World catalogues were more pop-oriented (Hawkins, *A Shot in the Dark*, 71–86).

93. The postwar rhythm and blues scene in Nashville was documented as part of the Country Music Hall of Fame and Museum's *Night Train to Nashville: Music City Rhythm & Blues* exhibit, which ran from March 27, 2004, through December 31, 2005. For more information, consult https://countrymusichalloffame.org/exhibits/exhibitdetail/night-train-to-nashville-music-city-rhythm-blues#.WrpGqNMbPOQ (last accessed March 27, 2018). Most notable in this area, alongside Bullet (literally next door), was Tennessee Records. For more background, consult Hawkins, *A Shot in the Dark*, 115–139.

94. Russell, *Country Music Records*, 16.

95. Ward and Huber, *A&R Pioneers*, 289–290.

96. Mike Taylor, "Hank Williams Sessions," *Hank Williams—A Comprehensive Discography*, http://www.hankwilliamsdiscography.com/HankWilliams/HWSession.php (last accessed July 24, 2018).

97. Horning, *Chasing Sound*, 57.

98. Horning, *Chasing Sound*, 56.

99. Hawkins, *A Shot in the Dark*, 141.

100. Hawkins, *A Shot in the Dark*, 141. Magnetic tape was a higher fidelity medium that also permitted technicians to edit recordings with a razor blade. Direct injection allowed for electrified instruments to be plugged directly into the recording console, which eliminates room noise and amplifier noise. And overdubbing allows musicians to add sounds to the recording one at a time, creating musical sounds (like singing with oneself) that are not possible in a live environment.

101. Hawkins, *A Shot in the Dark*, 71.

102. Hawkins, *A Shot in the Dark*, 71. Hawkins also notes that "the *Tennesseean* carried photographs of Likens recording Buck Buchanon's hillbilly group in his living room and experimenting with the acoustics in his bathroom" (Hawkins, *A Shot in the Dark*, 76–78).

103. Havighurst, 145–146; John W. Rumble, "The Emergence of Nashville as a Recording Center: Logbooks from the Castle Studio, 1952–1953," *Journal of Country Music*

7, no. 3 (December 1978): 34n2; Scott Faragher, *Nashville in Vintage Postcards* (Charleston, SC: Arcadia, 1999), 30.

104. Aaron Shelton, qtd. in Havighurst, *Air Castle of the South*, 151.

105. Rumble, "The Emergence of Nashville as a Recording Center," 23. Havighurst details these improvements in some detail: "In spare hours, they cleaned the paneling and painted the walls. They placed sound baffles around the room, installed a U-shaped vocal booth, and assembled their own monitors for studio playback, designed after the large Altec-Lansing horn speakers used in movie houses. WSM, then upgrading equipment, sold the team a Steinway studio grand piano, a Hammond organ with a revolving speaker cabinet, and a small celesta. The Castle crew poured nearly all of their first-year earnings back into the studio . . ." (Havighurst, *Air Castle of the South*, 151).

106. For more background on the transition from shellac to vinyl in the record manufacturing process, consult Richard Osborne, *Vinyl: A History of the Analogue Record* (Burlington, VT: Ashgate, 2012), 67–86.

107. Rumble, "The Emergence of Nashville as a Recording Center," 22.

108. Rumble, "The Emergence of Nashville as a Recording Center," 23; Havighurst, *Air Castle of the South*, 151.

109. Aaron Shelton recalled, for instance, that "after spending the entire day at RCA studios [in Chicago], I was convinced that we were doing a better job in some respects" (Aaron Shelton, qtd. in Havighurst, *Air Castle of the South*, 174).

110. Rumble, "The Emergence of Nashville as a Recording Center," 27–28; Havighurst, *Air Castle of the South*, 151.

111. Rumble, "The Emergence of Nashville as a Recording Center," 24–27, 30–34.

112. Havighurst, *Air Castle of the South*, 174.

113. Charles K. Wolfe, *In Close Harmony: The Story of the Louvin Brothers* (Jackson: University Press of Mississippi, 1996), 38–39.

114. Charlie Louvin, qtd. in Wolfe, *In Close Harmony*, 40–41. Wolfe also notes that the Louvins also cut their first sides for Capitol Records at Castle (Wolfe, *In Close Harmony*, 52).

115. Ronnie Pugh, *Ernest Tubb: The Texas Troubadour* (Durham, NC: Duke University Press, 1996), 129–130.

116. Havighurst, *Air Castle of the South*, 203.

117. Rumble, "The Emergence of Nashville as a Recording Center," 24.

118. Havighurst, *Air Castle of the South*, 145. For more background on the musical aesthetics of radio broadcasting, consult Shawn VanCour, *Making Radio: Early Radio Production and the Rise of Modern Sound Culture* (New York: Oxford University Press, 2018), 69–96.

119. Kosser, *How Nashville Became Music City, U.S.A.*, 168–170

120. Harold Bradley identified this group as the core in an interview with Morris Levy (Harold Bradley, interview with Morris Levy, February 22 or 23, 1996, Morris Levy Interviews, Box 1, Folder 2, Rock and Roll Hall of Fame Archives). Zinkan's early career was recounted to me by Nashville bassist Kent Blanton (telephone interview with author, September 8, 2014).

121. Havighurst indicates that the crackdown on the Castle project was the result of WSM station manager Jack DeWitt's distrust of WSM Artist Service Bureau head Jim Denny and frustration that the music publishing company that Denny co-owned with Webb Pierce, Cedarwood Music, was profiting from *Opry* artists (Havighurst, *Air Castle of the South*, 190–191).

122. Havighurst, *Air Castle of the South*, 191–192. A photograph of the Tulane's demolition is held in the Nashville Public Library's Digital Collections and is available at http://digital.library.nashville.org/cdm/ref/collection/nr/id/6274 (last accessed March 29, 2018). For more information on the redevelopment of Nashville's downtown, consult Jeremy Hill, "'Country Music Is Wherever the Soul of a Country Music Fan Is': Opryland U.S.A. and the Importance of Home in Country Music," *Southern Cultures* 17, no. 4 (2001): 95–96.

123. Havighurst, *Air Castle of the South*, 191–192

124. Ward and Huber, *A&R Pioneers*, 289; Pecknold, *The Selling Sound*, 91.

125. Jeremy Hill has traced the efforts to develop this neighborhood in *Country Comes to Town: The Music Industry and the Transformation of Nashville* (Amherst: University of Massachusetts Press, 2016), 31–76.

126. Glen Snoddy, interview with John W. Rumble, Nashville, TN, August 15, 1983, Country Music Foundation Oral History Project, Country Music Hall of Fame and Museum, OHC274-LC.

127. Columbia purchased the Bradley facilities in 1962 (Snoddy, interview with John W. Rumble, August 15, 1983; Ward and Huber, *A&R Pioneers*, 290).

128. Bill Ivey, "The Bottom Line: Business Practices That Shaped Country Music," in *Country: The Music and the Musicians from the Beginnings to the '90s*, rev. and updated ed., eds. Paul Kingsbury, Alan Axelrod, and Susan Costello (New York: Abbeville, 1994), 291–295; Ward and Huber, *A&R Pioneers*, 293.

129. Terry Lindvall and Andrew Quicke, *Celluloid Sermons: The Emergence of the Christian Film Industry, 1930–1986* (New York: New York University Press, 2011), 66–78.

130. Hawkins, *A Shot in the Dark*, 230–231; John W. Rumble, *Home of 1,000 Hits: Historic RCA Studio B, Nashville* (Nashville: Country Music Foundation Press, 2016), 18.

131. Peter Guralnick, *Last Train to Memphis: The Rise of Elvis Presley* (New York: Back Bay Books, 1995), 224–234.

132. Charles K. Wolfe, *Classic Country: Legends of Country Music* (New York: Routledge, 2001), 211. For more background on the RCA Victor studio, consult Rumble, *Home of 1,000 Hits; idem*, "Behind the Board with Bill Porter, Part One," *Journal of Country Music* 18, no. 1 (1996): 27–40; *idem*, "Behind the Board with Bill Porter, Part Two," *Journal of Country Music* 18, no. 2 (1996): 20–30; *idem*, "Behind the Board with Bill Porter, Part Three," *Journal of Country Music* 19, no. 1 (1997): 24–31.

133. For more background on Monument's Nashville operation, consult Larry Crane and Kyle Lehning with Bergen White, "Fred Foster: Monuments of Sound," *Tape Op* 118 (March–April 2017): 38–48.

134. Tracey E. W. Laird, *Louisiana Hayride: Radio and Roots Music along the Red River* (New York: Oxford University Press, 2004); Clifford Murphy, *Yankee Twang: Country and Western Music in New England* (Urbana: University of Illinois

Press, 2014); Ivan M. Tribe, *Mountaineer Jamboree: Country Music in West Virginia* (Lexington: University Press of Kentucky, 1984), 43–72, 169–182.

135. See, for instance, Bar Biszick-Lockwood, *Restless Giant: The Life and Times of Jean Aberbach and Hill and Range Songs* (Urbana: University of Illinois Press, 2010), 171–228.

136. John W. Rumble, "Fred Rose and the Development of the Nashville Music Industry, 1942–1954," Ph.D. dissertation, Vanderbilt University, 1980, 274.

137. One such label was Starday Records, which had deep connections with the Texas honky-tonk scene, as well. For more background, consult Nathan D. Gibson with Don Pierce, *The Starday Story: The House That Country Music Built* (Jackson: University Press of Mississippi, 2011); Andy Bradley and Roger Wood, *House of Hits: The Story of Houston's Gold Star/Sugarhill Recording Studios* (Austin: University of Texas Press, 2010), 41–60.

138. On crossover marketing in country music, consult Joli Jensen, *The Nashville Sound: Authenticity, Commercialization, and Country Music* (Nashville: Country Music Foundation Press and Vanderbilt University Press, 1998); Keith Negus, *Music Genres and Corporate Cultures* (New York: Routledge, 1999), 105–106; Fabian Holt, *Genre in Popular Music* (Chicago: University of Chicago Press, 2007), 63–79; Pecknold, *The Selling Sound*; Jocelyn R. Neal, "'Nothing but a Little Ole Pop Song': Patsy Cline's Music Style and the Evolution of Genre in the 1950s," in *Sweet Dreams: The World of Patsy Cline*, ed. Warren Hofstra (Urbana: University of Illinois Press, 2013), 128–153.

139. Even a cursory exploration of the Castle logs, for instance, reveals this phenomenon (Rumble, "The Emergence of Nashville as a Recording Center").

140. Harold Bradley told interviewer Morris Levy that Cooper, Owen Bradley, and Atkins worked throughout their careers to ensure the strength of the union by consistently lobbying for the musicians themselves, and he suggested that the sense of "solidarity" in the Nashville local, as well as the guarantee that they would be paid for their work, helped to draw musicians from other cities there (Harold Bradley, interview with Morris Levy, February 22 or 23, 1996, Morris Levy Interviews, Box 1, Folder 2, Rock and Roll Hall of Fame Archives).

141. Bradley noted that this schedule was established after the Bradleys opened their studio on Sixteenth Avenue South (Harold Bradley, interview with Morris Levy, November 19, 1997, Morris Levy Interviews, Box 1, Folder 3, Rock and Roll Hall of Fame Archives).

142. Charlie McCoy with Travis D. Stimeling, *Fifty Cents and a Box Top: The Creative Life of Nashville Session Musician Charlie McCoy* (Morgantown: West Virginia University Press, 2017), 72.

143. Arranger Bergen White, for instance, wrote lead sheets in his early days in the Nashville scene (Bergen White, telephone interview with author, September 5, 2014).

144. Note, for instance, the publication of Willie Nelson's demonstration recordings in *Crazy: The Demo Sessions* (Sugar Hill SHCD 1073, 2003).

145. Bradley notes that Cooper was the "first president to step up and demand a demo scale" (Bradley, interview with Morris Levy, February 22 or 23, 1996). Alice

M. Gant, in her 1972 study of the Nashville music industry, noted that "the rates for demos are even lower than those for jingles: for two hours or less, each [musician] received $24.00 plus $10.00 for each additional hour, with the leader or contractor receiving double" (Alice M. Gant, "The Musicians in Nashville," *Journal of Country Music* 3, no. 2 [Summer 1972]: 29).

146. Hill, *Country Comes to Town*, 31–76.

147. Rose Drake, interview with author, May 29, 2017, Murfreesboro, TN.

148. Tom T. Hall, *The Storyteller's Nashville: A Gritty and Glorious Life in Country Music*, rev. and expanded ed. (Nashville: Spring House Press, 2016), 101–104.

149. "Historic RCA Studio B," https://www.reddstewart.com/historic-rca-studio-b (last accessed July 23, 2018).

150. Among others, Jensen, *The Nashville Sound*, 38–61; Holt, *Genre in Popular Music*, 67–72; Pecknold, *The Selling Sound*, 85–94.

151. This subject has been taken up most notably in scholarship that focuses on the positioning of the white working class vis-à-vis country music. See, for instance, Barbara Ching, *Wrong's What I Do Best: Hard Country Music and Contemporary Culture* (New York: Oxford University Press, 2001), 8–25; Aaron A. Fox, *Real Country: Music and Language in Working-Class Culture* (Durham, NC: Duke University Press, 2004), 20–46; Nadine Hubbs, *Rednecks, Queers, and Country Music* (Ann Arbor: University of Michigan Pres, 2014), 23–50.

152. Jensen, *The Nashville Sound*, 21–37; Lange, *Smile When You Call Me a Hillbilly*, 198–201; Pecknold, *The Selling Sound*, 95–103.

153. For an extensive survey of the history around "easy listening," consult Tim J. Anderson, *Making Easy Listening: Material Culture and Postwar American Recording* (Minneapolis: University of Minnesota Press, 2006).

154. This narrative is strong in the literature on the Nashville Sound era, as well as in the local folklore. At the present time, however, there appears to be scant data to confirm these assertions.

155. Lange, *Smile When You Call Me a Hillbilly*, 198–220.

156. Charles Portis, "That New Sound from Nashville," *Saturday Evening Post* 239, no. 4 (February 12, 1966): 31; Joe Wilson, *Lucky Joe's Namesake: The Extraordinary Life and Observations of Joe Wilson*, ed. Fred Bartenstein (Knoxville: University of Tennessee Press, 2017), 17.

157. Gibson with Pierce, *The Starday Story*.

158. The notion of an "authenticity crisis" is most extensively discussed in Philip Auslander, "Seeing Is Believing: Live Performance and the Discourse of Authenticity in Rock Music," *Literature and Psychology* 44, no. 4 (1998): 1–26.

159. Richard A. Peterson, "The Dialectic of Hard-Core and Soft-Shell Country Music," in *Reading Country Music: Steel Guitars, Opry Stars, and Honky-Tonk Bars*, ed. Cecelia Tichi (Durham, NC: Duke University Press, 1998): 234–255.

160. Jensen, *The Nashville Sound*, 118–135.

161. These debates become especially clear in Bill Ivey, "Commercialization and Tradition in the Nashville Sound," in *Folk Music and Modern Sound*, eds. William Ferris and Mary L. Hart (Jackson: University Press of Mississippi, 1982), 129–138; Fox, *Real Country*; Pecknold, *The Selling Sound*; 168–199; Pamela Fox and Barbara

Ching, eds., *Old Roots, New Routes: The Cultural Politics of Alt.Country* (Ann Arbor: University of Michigan Press, 2008).

162. Jensen positioned the "uptown" sounds of the Nashville Sound with the "down-home" sounds of string band sounds (*The Nashville Sound*, 21–37).

163. Pecknold, *The Selling Sound*, 105–110, 220; Hill, *Country Music Comes to Town*, 31–55. See also: Paul Ackerman, "C.&W. Field Lauds BMI for Promotion of Rural Music," *Billboard* (November 17, 1956): 16, 20; "Clement in Tennessee Waltz with Country Music Support," *Billboard* (August 11, 1962): 20.

164. Pecknold, *The Selling Sound; idem*, "The Country Music Association, the Country Music Foundation, and Country Music's History," in *The Oxford Handbook of Country Music*, ed. Travis D. Stimeling (New York: Oxford University Press, 2017), 55–84.

CHAPTER 2

1. The Lovin' Spoonful, *Hums of the Lovin' Spoonful* (Kama Sutra KL-8054, 1966).
2. The Del McCoury Band, *The Family* (Ceili Music 2001, 1999).
3. Morris S. Levy, "Nashville Sound-Era Studio Musicians," in *Country Music Annual 2000*, eds. Charles K. Wolfe and James E. Akenson (Lexington: University Press of Kentucky, 2000), 23.
4. See also Joli Jensen, *The Nashville Sound: Authenticity, Commercialization, and Country Music* (Nashville: Country Music Foundation Press and Vanderbilt University Press, 1998), 123–124.
5. Henry Kingsbury, *Music, Talent, and Performance* (Philadelphia: Temple University Press, 1988), 59–84.
6. Travis D. Stimeling, "'To Be Polished More than Extended': Musicianship, Masculinity, and the Critical Reception of Southern Rock," *Journal of Popular Music Studies* 26, no. 1 (March 2014): 121–136.
7. Music educator Lucy Green, in her study *How Popular Musicians Learn*, observes that notation plays an interesting role in popular music production: "In popular music, notation includes conventional staff notation, guitar tablature, drum notation[,] and chord symbols, all of which are often referred to as 'charts.' Although . . . notation in one form or another plays a role in learning for many popular musicians in the early stages, it is always heavily mixed in with aural practices, and used as a supplement rather than a major learning resource. After the early stages, published scores are used only by some function bands and session musicians, some of whom may have sight-reading abilities. Unpublished notation is used in a variety of circumstances, such as when a musical director or bandleader may hand out their own pre-written charts, or may 'scribble' something down and pass it to the musician during the session itself. In the latter case, the notation has the status of a mere instruction and is liable to be thrown away as soon as the instruction is internalized by the musician. Notation is also used as a memory-jogger whereby musicians may prepare themselves for a session after having worked with a demo or other recording, or may write down ideas and instructions for themselves during a session. In all these latter cases, notation does not have the function of preserving or passing on the music for, as already seen, these practices

occur primarily through aural means which pay attention to musical aspects that are not readily notatable" (Lucy Green, *How Popular Musicians Learn: A Way Ahead for Music Education* [Aldershot, UK: Ashgate, 2001], 38).

8. On barn dance authenticity, consult, among others, Richard A. Peterson, *Creating Country Music: Fabricating Authenticity* (Chicago: University of Chicago Press, 1997), 97–117; Hugh Barker and Yuval Taylor, *Faking It: The Quest for Authenticity in Popular Music* (New York: W. W. Norton, 2007), 57–58; Kristine M. McCusker, *Lonesome Cowgirls and Honky-Tonk Angels: The Women of Barn Dance Radio* (Urbana: University of Illinois Press, 2008), 70; Pamela Fox, *Natural Acts: Gender, Race, and Rusticity in Country Music* (Ann Arbor: University of Michigan Press, 2009), 17–62.

9. There is extensive literature on the place of guitars, banjos, and mandolins in nineteenth-century domestic culture. See, for instance, Karen Linn, *That Half-Barbaric Twang: The Banjo in American Popular Culture* (Urbana: University of Illinois Press, 1991); Jeffrey J. Noonan, *The Guitar in America: Victorian Era to Jazz Age* (Jackson: University Press of Mississippi, 2008); *idem*, *The Guitar in American Banjo, Mandolin, and Guitar Periodicals, 1882–1933* (Middleton, WI: Music Library Association, 2009), *idem*, "Highbrow, Lowbrow and Middlebrow: An Introduction to America's Progressive Era Mandolin Orchestra," *Musique, images, instruments: Revue française d'organologie et d'iconographie musicale* 12 (2010): 170–189; April and Lance Ledbetter, comp., *Never a Pal like Mother: Vintage Songs and Photographs of the One Who's Always True* (Atlanta: Dust-to-Digital, 2011); Nicholas Pyall, "Guitar Stringing in Late Nineteenth-Century North America; The Emergence of Steel," *Journal of the American Musical Instrument Society* 40 (2014): 29–74; Walter Carter, *The Mandolin in America: The Full Story from Orchestras to Bluegrass to the Modern Revival* (Milwaukee: Backbeat Books, 2017), 8–35.

10. Stimeling, "'To Be Polished More than Extended.'"

11. Buddy Spicher, qtd. in Jim Christian, "Buddy Spicher: Master of Double Stops," *Fiddler Magazine* 5, no. 3 (Fall 1998): 20, non-punctuation interpolations in original. Spicher began working with Snow in 1957 (Buddy Spicher, interview with author, Nashville, TN, July 29, 2014).

    For more background on Chubby Wise's stint with Snow, consult Randy Noles, *Orange Blossom Boys: The Untold Story of Ervin T. Rouse, Chubby Wise, and the World's Most Famous Fiddle Tune* (Anaheim Hills, CA: CENTERSTREAM, 2002), 131–150.

    For more on Vaden and his work with Snow, consult Charles Wolfe, liner notes to *Hank Snow: The Singing Ranger—I'm Movin' On* (Bear Family BCD 15426, 1988), 3–4.

12. Suzi Burgher Payne, interview with author, February 3, 2015.

13. Charles K. Wolfe, *Kentucky Country: Folk and Country Music of Kentucky* (Lexington: University Press of Kentucky, 1982), 19–43.

14. Payne, interview with author, February 3, 2015.

15. Payne, interview with author, February 3, 2015.

16. Payne, interview with author, February 3, 2015; Brian Mansfield, "Pioneering Nashville Guitarist Velma Smith Dies," *USA Today* (August 1, 2014), https://www. usatoday.com/story/life/music/2014/08/01/velma-smith-nashville-guitarist-dies/ 13454861/ (accessed September 14, 2017). Mileage estimated using Google Maps.

17. Richard D. Smith, *Can't You Hear Me Calling: The Life of Bill Monroe, Father of Bluegrass* (Boston: Little, Brown, 2000), 3–46; Neil V. Rosenberg and Charles K. Wolfe, *The Music of Bill Monroe* (Urbana: University of Illinois Press, 2007), 1–36.

18. Payne recounted that the Williams Sisters "were also invited to participate in a talent show in another community called Elkton, Kentucky. . . . Elkton is in the next county over in Todd Country, and it was there that Bill Monroe . . . heard them and became quite interested in their talent and invited Mildred and Velma to audition for an appearance on the *Grand Ole Opry*. They went by the Williams Sisters at that time" (Payne, interview with author, February 3, 2015).

19. Payne, interview with author, February 3, 2015; Elizabeth Roe Schlappi, *Roy Acuff, the Smoky Mountain Boy*, 2nd ed. (Gretna, LA: Pelican, 1997), 96.

20. Payne, interview with author, February 3, 2015; Schlappi, *Roy Acuff,* 96–97.

21. Schlappi, *Roy Acuff,* 93. Payne noted that the two were actually married to each other twice, indicating that Velma Smith had told her that "they were both just too young" the first time (Payne, interview with author, February 3, 2015).

22. Payne, interview with author, February 3, 2015.

23. Bill Ivey, "Chet Atkins," in *Stars of Country Music*, eds. Bill C. Malone and Judith McCulloh (Urbana: University of Illinois Press, 1975; paperback ed., New York: Da Capo Press, 1991), 276–277; Steve Waksman, *Instruments of Desire: The Electric Guitar and the Shaping of Musical Experience* (Cambridge, MA: Harvard University Press, 1999), 83; Rich Kienzle, "Chet Atkins, Guitarist: The Sound, the Style, the Influence," in *Chet Atkins: Certified Guitar Player*, ed. John W. Rumble (Nashville: Country Music Foundation Press, 2011), 32–33.

24. Rich Kienzle, "Grady Martin," in *The Encyclopedia of Country Music*, 2nd ed., eds. Paul Kingsbury, Michael McCall, and John W. Rumble (New York: Oxford University Press, 2012), 312–313.

25. Rich Kienzle, "Hank Garland: Legendary Country-Jazz Artist," *Guitar Player* (January 1981): 76–86; *idem*, "Hank Garland," in *The Encyclopedia of Country Music*, 2nd ed., eds. Paul Kingsbury, Michael McCall, and John W. Rumble (New York: Oxford University Press, 2012), 183.

26. Ray and Polly Edenton, interview with author, August 3, 2014. See also Rich Kienzle, "Ray Edenton: Nashville Studio Rhythm Specialist," *Guitar Player* (May 1981): 76.

27. Kienzle, "Ray Edenton," 76.

28. Kienzle, "Ray Edenton," 77.

29. David Simons, "Ray Edenton's 'A-Team' Memories," *The Journal* 203 (June–July 2000): 11; Ray and Polly Edenton, interview with author, August 3, 2014.

30. Kienzle, "Ray Edenton," 77.

31. Ray and Polly Edenton, interview with author, August 3, 2014.

32. Lynn Abbott and Doug Seroff, *Ragged but Right: Black Traveling Shows, "Coon Songs," and the Dark Pathway to Blues and Jazz* (Jackson: University Press of Mississippi,

2007); Gillian M. Rodger, *Champagne Charlie and Pretty Jemima: Variety Theater in the Nineteenth Century* (Urbana: University of Illinois Press, 2010); Lynn Abbott and Doug Seroff, *The Original Blues: The Emergence of the Blues in African American Vaudeville* (Jackson: University Press of Mississippi, 2017); Nicholas Gebhardt, *Vaudeville Melodies: Popular Musicians and Mass Entertainment in American Culture, 1870–1929* (Chicago: University of Chicago Press, 2017); Rob King, *Hokum!: The Early Sound Slapstick Short and Depression-Era Mass Culture* (Berkeley: University of California Press, 2017).

33. Schlappi, *Roy Acuff*, 84.

34. Kent Blanton, interview with author, September 8, 2014. Footage of Zinkan's slap bass style can be found in several television performances from the 1960s, which are archived on Blanton's YouTube channel (https://www.youtube.com/channel/UC6-8f7r19PwVVm1UjdaGWZQ [last accessed April 2, 2018]).

35. Ernie Newton, interview with Douglas Green, September 24, 1974, Country Music Foundation Oral History Project OH136-LC, Country Music Foundation Library, transcript, p. 1.

36. As Newton remembered: "[W]hen I was, oh, about eight years old, I guess, my grandmother came up. She'd come up every summer and stay with her daughter, who was my aunt. She brought me up a trumpet one time, and this is when they first came out—'Margie,' and when 'Margie' first came out, I'd heard it. So I didn't know a thing about this trumpet or anything like that. It was a coronet [*sic*] is what it was. She brought it up there, and I got that thing and I got to blowing. Then I learned to play 'Margie' and a couple other tunes. But 'Margie' was the big thing.

    "I'd get out there at night, and I'd play 'Margie' on the coronet [*sic*]. Then the people all around the countryside, you know, they was a half a mile away, maybe a mile away, but they could hear it, and then they'd all applaud. . . . Then I'd play again. Then if they didn't applaud, I figured they had enough of it, so I wouldn't play it anymore. . . . That was my audience. That was one of my first real audiences that I ever had" (Newton, interview with Douglas Green, September 24, 1974, transcript, p. 3).

37. Newton, interview with Douglas Green, September 24, 1974, transcript, pp. 2, 4.

38. Newton, interview with Douglas Green, September 24, 1974, transcript, pp. 5–6.

39. Newton, interview with Douglas Green, September 24, 1974, transcript, pp. 7–8.

40. Newton, interview with Douglas Green, September 24, 1974, transcript, p. 8.

41. Newton, interview with Douglas Green, September 24, 1974, transcript, pp. 8–9. For more background on Alexander Pantages and the Pantages circuit, consult Taso G. Lagos, "Hollywood Mogul: Alexander Pantages and the Anti-Immigrant Narratives of William Randolph Hearst's *Los Angeles Examiner*," *Journal of Modern Greek Studies* 30, no. 1 (May 2012): 50–54.

42. Robert L. Stone, *Sacred Steel: Inside an African American Steel Guitar Tradition* (Urbana: University of Illinois Press, 2010), 53–62; John Troutman, *Kika Kila: How the Hawaiian Steel Guitar Changed the Sound of Modern Music* (Chapel Hill: University of North Carolina Press, 2016), 74–152.

43. Newton, interview with Douglas Green, September 24, 1974, transcript, pp. 9–10, interpolations in original.

44. As he recalled to Green: "When the Depression hit, these loggers would come out of the North, out of Canada, [and] come down there. They'd come down there with a lot of money, maybe two of them. What they'd do, they'd gamble up there, and then the two or three that made the big win, the rest of the guys stayed in Canada, and they'd come down and they'd stay down there for a month and just party and blow the money, you know.

"So I got hep to this. I was working with a trio. One was a trumpet player, and then an accordion player and myself [on guitar]. . . .

"So we'd work in what we called the Red Hill Country Club. There was another one up there . . . Lolita's Country Club. Of course, we knew everybody working there, and they wanted us to come over. We worked with a cup at the end of—hung on the end of my guitar. The accordion player, he had a cup hung on his accordion. The trumpet player had a cup hung on his belt. We'd stroll through the crowd, and if they wanted you to play a tune, they'd take a dollar or two dollars, I forget, and put it in the cup.

"When these loggers would come down there, we always knew when they were coming. We got word when they were coming down, because they'd come loaded with money. I'd do these things like 'Waiting for Ships That Never Come In,' and I used to do this recitation, you know. The recitation starts as, 'Life was just a game of stud poker and you get a hand in the pot,' and all that stuff. And I'd cry, see. I can work myself into a pitch where I can just absolutely cry. Tears roll down my eyes. What I'd do, I'd sit on the floor like a—I worked into an act. I'd sit on the floor and I'd sing it barefooted. I'd put a big old cowboy hat on my head, big old black hat, and sit there just like an orphan, lost child, you know, and I'd cry and sing this thing. Listen, they'd throw money at me like it was just going out of style!" (Newton, interview with Douglas Green, September 24, 1974, transcript, pp. 11–12, interpolations in original).

45. Tony Russell, *Country Music Records: A Discography, 1921–1942* (New York: Oxford University Press, 2004), 774.

46. Newton, interview with Douglas Green, September 24, 1974, transcript, pp. 13–14. Cowboy music historian Douglas Green notes that the Arizona Wranglers appeared in the October 1935 film *Stormy* (Universal), but this was long after Newton left the group (Douglas B. Green, *Singing in the Saddle: The History of the Singing Cowboy* [Nashville: Country Music Foundation Press and Vanderbilt University Press, 2002], 200).

47. Newton, interview with Douglas Green, September 24, 1974, transcript, p. 14.

48. Newton, interview with Douglas Green, September 24, 1974, transcript, p. 14, interpolations in original.

49. Newton, interview with Douglas Green, September 24, 1974, transcript, pp. 15–16, interpolations in original. For more general background on the *National Barn Dance*, consult George C. Biggar, "The WLS National Barn Dance Story: The Early Years," in *Exploring Roots Music: Twenty Years of the JEMF Quarterly*, ed. Nolan Porterfield (Lanham, MD: Scarecrow Press, 2004), 34–44.

50. Chad Berry, *Southern Migrants, Northern Exiles* (Urbana: University of Illinois Press, 2000), 31–59; James N. Gregory, *The Southern Diaspora: How the Great*

Migrations of Black and White Southerners Transformed America (Chapel Hill: University of North Carolina Press, 2005), 43–80; Wilson J. Warren, *Tied to the Great Packing Machine: The Midwest and Meatpacking* (Iowa City: University of Iowa Press, 2007), 49–72; Paul L. Tyler, "The Rise of Rural Rhythm," in *The Hayloft Gang: The Story of the National Barn Dance*, ed. Chad Berry (Urbana: University of Illinois Press, 2008), 19–71.

51. Green, *Singing in the Saddle*, 20–93.

52. For more background on Les Paul's early career, consult Robb Lawrence, *The Early Years of the Les Paul Legacy, 1915–1963* (Milwaukee: Hal Leonard, 2008), 1–48.

53. Newton, interview with Douglas Green, September 24, 1974, transcript, pp. 16–17. For more background on Waring, consult Virginia Waring, *Fred Waring and the Pennsylvanians* (Urbana: University of Illinois Press, 1997). See also Ivey, "Chet Atkins," 275.

    Paul recounted that it was during this stint with Waring that he began to experiment with the electric guitar in a public setting: "I really believe that the first person to use the electric pickup, to exploit it, was when I was with Fred Waring in the latter part of '36, '37—in there. Between there and 1941 was the real exploitation of the electric Spanish guitar, where they can hear it three or five nights a week, or whatever nights I played a solo with Fred Waring.

    "In fact, when I started, we gave the listening audiences a choice. We played one show with the straight [acoustic] guitar and one show with the electric guitar, and the mail poured in . . ." (Les Paul, qtd. in Lawrence, *The Early Years of the Les Paul Legacy*, 11).

54. Newton, interview with Douglas Green, September 24, 1974, transcript, p. 17, interpolations added.

55. Newton, interview with Douglas Green, September 24, 1974, transcript, pp. 17–18, interpolations in original.

56. Newton, interview with Douglas Green, September 24, 1974, transcript, p. 18. For more background on the Goodman Quartet, consult Ross Firestone, *Swing, Swing, Swing: The Life and Times of Benny Goodman* (New York: W. W. Norton, 1993), 181–184; Catherine Tackley, *Benny Goodman's Famous 1938 Carnegie Hall Jazz Concert* (New York: Oxford University Press, 2012), 19–27.

57. Lissa Fleming May, "Early Musical Development of Selected African American Jazz Musicians in Indianapolis in the 1930s and 1940s," *Journal of Historical Research in Music Education* 27, no. 1 (October 2005): 21–32; Katherine Walker, "Cut, Carved, and Served: Competitive Jamming in the 1930s and 1940s," *Jazz Perspectives* 4, no. 2 (August 2010): 183–208; Dana Gooley, "The Outside of 'Sitting In': Jazz Jam Sessions and the Politics of Participation," *Performance Research* 16, no. 3 (September 2011): 43–48; Christina Baade, "Airing Authenticity: The BBC Jam Sessions from New York, 1938/39," *Journal of the Society for American Music* 6, no. 3 (August 2012): 271–314.

58. Newton recalled, "It was just Teddy Wilson and Lionel Hampton and [Benny] Goodman and [Gene] Krupa. Then I got to know Wilson. We played with Wilson, and Lionel Hampton, he's a great friend. I know Krupa vaguely. I know these, because we went to Harlem and jammed, nights. Every night, play somewhere, we

used to. Every night. That's where we got to know [people] like Roy Eldridge and all those, Chu Berry and all those, and we got to play with them.

"We went up there to live up there and learn what they were doing. When we first went up there, we'd sit there, just watch, just amazed. We couldn't believe what they were laying. Little backwards bends. There'd be a little trio in there. There'd be a bass player and playing so much bass, they'd scare me. I wouldn't never think of a bass player inside of a—so finally, we just eased into it, you know, and then we worked ourselves to the front" (Newton, interview with Douglas Green, September 24, 1974, transcript, p. 20).

He also added: "Les and I, we played. We'd go in there. I mean, some of the greatest things in my life in playing, like we'd be playing there and there'd be Teddy Wilson on piano, Chu Berry on horn, and Roy Eldridge on trumpet. It'd be a closed session. It would be Les Paul, myself, and a kid by the name of 'Guts' on drums.

"The drummer and I would turn around and we'd face one another, and we'd play right into the wall. We'd [sic] didn't pay no attention to nobody else, and there's no such thing as a bass player taking a solo. I mean the bass player and the drummer were there to keep that rhythm going. And that's what we done. Boy, they'd play, and I mean, they'd start off, and lord, we'd go from there. Wilson is one of the greatest piano players that I've ever played with. Roy played great trumpet. Chu Berry played great sax.

They'd battle all night long, you know. Of course, these guys didn't battle. Nobody'd dare step off on the stand against them. . . . We'd go up there and we'd go on the session like that and nobody—they'd get their horn out, you know, and get like they're going—and somebody would grab them by the shoulder and say, "Don't get on that stand. Don't get up there. If you do, we'll throw you out of the place." They wouldn't let them. But, of course, they let Les and I up there. We was [sic] well known around there, and they heard us all the time.

"We'd moved in, but there was [sic] a lot of bass players that I've sit there and I'd be playing bass, like well-known bands, and they'd sit there. I'd say, "Get up there and play bass."

"They'd say, 'Man, you sit there. You sit there. You're doing all right; you're doing all right . . .'" (Newton, interview with Douglas Green, September 24, 1974, transcript, pp. 21–22, interpolations added).

59. Newton, interview with Douglas Green, September 24, 1974, transcript, pp. 22–23. The transcript says "Slim Seward," but Newton notes that the bassist was known for a song called "Play, Fiddle, Play." Slim Stewart recorded that song with his trio for Savoy Records on January 30, 1945 ("Savoy Records Discography:1945," *JazzDisco. org*, https://www.jazzdisco.org/savoy-records/discography-1945/ [accessed April 4, 2018]).

60. Newton, interview with Douglas Green, September 24, 1974, transcript, p. 23.

61. Newton, interview with Douglas Green, September 24, 1974, transcript, pp. 23–24.

62. Newton, interview with Douglas Green, September 24, 1974, transcript, p. 24. The exact date of this move is unclear from the oral testimony, but it likely happened after April 1946, when Foley became the host of the *Opry*'s Prince Albert Segment

(Cary Ginell, liner notes to *Red Foley: Old Shep—The Red Foley Recordings, 1933–1950* [Bear Family BCD 16759 FL, 2006], 56).

63. Newton, interview with Douglas Green, September 24, 1974, transcript, p. 23.

64. Newton, interview with Douglas Green, September 24, 1974, transcript, p. 24.

65. Newton, interview with Douglas Green, September 24, 1974, transcript, p. 25, interpolations in original.

66. Robert Cantwell, *When We Were Good: The Folk Revival* (Cambridge, MA: Harvard University Press, 1996), 22–26. A number of examples may be found in Loyal Jones, *Country Music Humorists and Comedians* (Urbana: University of Illinois Press, 2008).

67. Newton, interview with Douglas Green, September 24, 1974, transcript, p. 24, interpolation added.

68. Newton, interview with Douglas Green, September 24, 1974, transcript, pp. 25–26, interpolations in original. These memories are corroborated by the discographical work of Neil Rosenberg and Charles Wolfe, who document that Newton played on Monroe's Decca sessions on March 17, 1951, April 23–24, 1951, July 1, 1951, July 18–19, 1952, July 26, 1952, November 28, 1953, January 7–8, 1954, January 14, 1954, June 26, 1954, September 4, 1954, and December 31, 1954, as well as the Gannaway film shorts that were produced at Vanderbilt University over the course of several years between 1954 and 1956 (Rosenberg and Wolfe, *The Music of Bill Monroe*, 103–105, 107–112).

69. Newton, interview with Douglas Green, September 24, 1974, transcript, pp. 26–27, most interpolations in original.

70. Murphy Hicks Henry, *Pretty Good for a Girl: Women in Bluegrass* (Urbana: University of Illinois Press, 2013), 46–53; Rosenberg and Wolfe, *The Music of Bill Monroe*, 113.

71. Galen E. Leitzel, "The History and Development of the American Public School Concert Band (1920–1941) and Its Influence on Concert Band Repertoire," DMA dissertation, Shenandoah Conservatory, 2006, 37–69; Sandra Wieland Howe, *Women Music Educators in the United States: A History* (Lanham, MD: Scarecrow Press, 2014), 107–238; Jill M. Sullivan and Amy E. Spears, "All-Female School Bands: Separate Spheres and Gender Equality," in *Women's Bands in America: Performing Music and Gender*, ed. Jill M. Sullivan (Lanham, MD: Rowman & Littlefield, 2017), 95–125.

72. Among many others, consult Charles L. Pierce, "A History of Music and Music Education of the Seventh-Day Adventist Church," DMA dissertation, Catholic University of America, 1976; *Church Music in Baptist History* (Nashville: Historical Commission of the Southern Baptist Convention; Southern Baptist Historical Society, 1984); Hugh T. McElrath, "Turning Points in the Story of Baptist Church Music," *Baptist History and Heritage* 19, no. 1 (January 1984): 13–15; Wesley L. Forbis, "The Sunday School Board and Baptist Church Music," *Baptist History and Heritage* 19, no. 1 (January 1984): 18–20; Harry L. Eskew, "Southern Baptist Contributions to Hymnody," *Baptist History and Heritage* 19, no. 1 (January 1984): 29–31; William J. Reynolds, "The Graded Choir Movement among Southern Baptists," *Baptist History and Heritage* 19, no. 1 (January 1984): 55–62; Paul McCommon, "Trends in Southern Baptist Church Music since 1915," *Baptist*

History and Heritage 21, no. 3 (July 1986): 50–56; Susan Kitts Messer, "The Southern Baptist Children's Choir Curricula from 1941 through 1985 and Influences of Major Music Education Trends upon the Curricula," Ph.D. dissertation, Louisiana State University, 1988, 16–52; Jeannette Fresne, "History of the Stamps Baxter Singing Schools," *Journal of Historical Research in Music Education* 30, no. 1 (October 2008): 21–38; Kevin Donald Kehrberg, " 'I'll Fly Away': The Music and Career of Albert E. Brumley," Ph.D. dissertation, University of Kentucky, 2010; Stephen Shearon and Mary Nichols, *I'll Keep on Singing: The Southern Gospel Convention Tradition*, DVD, Murfreesboro: Middle Tennessee State University, 2010; Kristine M. McCusker, "Funeral Music and the Transformation of Southern Culture, 1935–1945," *American Music* 30, no. 4 (Winter 2012): 426–452.

73. Women's roles as piano teachers in the home have been largely overlooked by scholars. However, some sources point to the important role that women played in the development of piano pedagogy and in the consumption of piano music. See, for early twentieth-century examples: Bonny H. Miller, "A Mirror of Ages Past: The Publication of Music in Domestic Periodicals," *Notes* (Second Series) 50, no. 3 (March 1994): 883–901; Debra Brubaker Burns, Anita Jackson, and Connie Arrau Sturm, "Unsung Heroines: Contributions of Selected Early Twentieth-Century Women to American Piano Pedagogy," *American Music Teacher* 52, no. 3 (December 2002–January 2003): 24–28.

74. Jill M. Sullivan, "Women Music Teachers as Military Band Directors during World War II," *Journal of Historical Research in Music Education* 39, no. 1 (October 2017): 78–105.

75. Diane Pecknold and Kristine M. McCusker, "Introduction," in *Country Boys and Redneck Women: New Essays in Gender and Country Music*, eds. Diane Pecknold and Kristine M. McCusker (Jackson: University Press of Mississippi, 2016), *xvii*n20.

76. These attitudes have persisted well into the present day, as music educator Lucy Green has shown in her research in the United Kingdom. See: Lucy Green, "Exposing the Gendered Discourse of Music Education," *Feminism & Psychology* 12, no. 2 (2002): 137–144.

77. The case of New England composer Charles Ives is particularly instructive here. Consult, among others: Stuart Feder, *Charles Ives, "My Father's Song": A Psychoanalytic Biography* (New Haven, CT: Yale University Press, 1992), 118–127; Timothy A. Johnson, *Baseball and the Music of Charles Ives: A Proving Ground* (Lanham, MD: Scarecrow Press, 2004).

78. Martha Dennis Burns, "A Gallery of Teachers and Students: The Female Piano Teacher in Antebellum America," in *Piano Roles: A New History of the Piano*, ed. James Parakilas (New Haven, CT: Yale University Press, 2002), 134–140.

79. Charlie McCoy with Travis D. Stimeling, *Fifty Cents and a Box Top: The Creative Life of Nashville Session Musician Charlie McCoy* (Morgantown: West Virginia University Press, 2017), 30–31.

80. Terry Klefstad, *Crooked River City: The Musical Life of Nashville's William Pursell* (Jackson: University Press of Mississippi, 2018), 78–79.

81. Chas Williams, *The Nashville Number System*, 7th ed. (n.p.: Chas Williams, 2005), 1.

82. John Bealle, *Public Worship, Private Faith: Sacred Harp and American Folksong* (Athens: University of Georgia Press, 1997); Kay Norton, *Baptist Offspring, Southern Midwife: Jesse Mercer's* Cluster of Spiritual Songs *(1810)—A Study in American Hymnody* (Warren, MI: Harmonie Park, 2002); James R. Goff, Jr., *Close Harmony: A History of Southern Gospel* (Chapel Hill: University of North Carolina Press, 2002), 14–32; Buell E. Cobb, Jr., *The Sacred Harp: A Tradition and Its Music* (Athens: University of Georgia Press, 2004); David Warren Steel with Richard H. Hulan, *The Makers of the Sacred Harp* (Urbana: University of Illinois Press, 2010); Stephen Shearon, Harry Eskew, James C. Downey, and Robert Darden, "Gospel Music 2. Southern Gospel Music," in *Grove Music Online*, https://doi-org.www. libproxy.wvu.edu/10.1093/gmo/9781561592630.article.A2224388 (last accessed April 11, 2018).

    For more background on the history of the Western notational system commonly used today, consult Geoffrey Chew and Richard Rastall, "Notation III.4.ii. Notes: Shapes, Colours, Abbreviations," in *Grove Music Online*, https://doi.org/ 10.1093/gmo/9781561592630.article.20114 (last accessed April 10, 2018).

83. Nicholas Temperley, "The Old Way of Singing: Its Origins and Development," *Journal of the American Musicological Society* 34, no. 3 (Autumn 1981): 511– 544; Indian Bottom Association, *Old Regular Baptists: Lined-Out Hymnody from Southeastern Kentucky* (Smithsonian Folkways SFW40106, 1997); *Songs of the Old Regular Baptists: Lined-Out Hymnody from Southeastern Kentucky*, Vol. 2 (Smithsonian Folkways SFW50001, 2003); Howard Dorgan, *The Old Regular Baptists of Central Appalachia: Brothers and Sisters in Hope* (Knoxville: University of Tennessee Press, 2001), 59–63.

84. Carol Ann Pemberton, "Lowell Mason: His Life and Work," Ph.D. dissertation, University of Minnesota, 1971; Michael Broyles, "Lowell Mason on European Church Music and Transatlantic Cultural Identification: A Reconsideration," *Journal of the American Musicological Society* 38, no. 2 (Summer 1985): 316–348; Martha Dennis Burns, "The Power of Music Enhanced by the Word: Lowell Mason and the Transformation of Sacred Singing in Lyman Beecher's New England," *Annual Proceedings of the Dublin Seminar for New England Folklife* 21 (1998): 139– 150; David W. Music, "Tunes by Lowell Mason and Thomas Hastings in Southern United States Shape-Note Tune Books of the Early Nineteenth Century," *Journal of Musicological Research* 26 (2007): 325–352; Todd R. Jones, "The Relationship between Lowell Mason and the Boston Handel and Haydn Society, 1815–1827," Ph.D. dissertation, University of Kentucky, 2017.

85. T. H. Breen, "The Great Wagon Road," *Southern Cultures* 3, no. 1 (1997): 22–57; John Alexander Williams, *Appalachia: A History* (Chapel Hill: University of North Carolina Press, 2002), 48–49; Fiona Ritchie and Doug Orr, *Wayfaring Strangers: The Musical Voyage from Scotland and Ulster to Appalachia* (Chapel Hill: University of North Carolina Press, 2014), 158–166.

86. Harry Eskew, "William Walker's 'Southern Harmony': Its Basic Editions," *Latin American Music Review/Revista de Música Latinoamericana* 7, no. 2 (Autumn– Winter 1986): 137–148; *idem*, "Southern Harmony and Its Era," *The Hymn: A Journal of Congregational Song* 41, no. 4 (October 1990): 28–34; Glenn Wilcox,

"Introduction," in William Walker, *The Southern Harmony and Musical Companion*, facsimile edition, ed. Glenn C. Wilcox (Lexington: University Press of Kentucky, 1993), *iii–xiii*.

87. A particularly useful discussion of these traditions can be found in Kiri Miller, *Traveling Home: Sacred Harp Singing and American Pluralism* (Urbana: University of Illinois Press, 2008). See also Goff, *Close Harmony*, 37–38.

    On the spread of the *Sacred Harp*, consult Steele and Hulan, *The Makers of the Sacred Harp*, 3–19.

88. Goff, *Close Harmony*, 35–44.

89. Goff, *Close Harmony*, 44–51; Stephen Shearon, "Kieffer, Aldine," in *Encyclopedia of American Gospel Music*, ed. W. K. McNeil (New York: Routledge, 2005), 215–217.

90. Goff, *Close Harmony*, 53–54.

91. Goff, *Close Harmony*, 62–123.

92. Goff, *Close Harmony*, 123–166.

93. Goff, *Close Harmony*, 209–213.

94. Lynn Abbott and Doug Seroff, *To Do This, You Must Know How: Music Pedagogy in the Black Gospel Tradition* (Jackson: University Press of Mississippi, 2013), 113–196.

95. Abbot and Seroff, *To Do This, You Must Know How*, 11–112. Chapters 2–4 highlight Birmingham, Chicago, and New Orleans, respectively.

96. Abbot and Seroff, *To Do This, You Must Know How*, 149–151.

97. Goff, *Close Harmony*, 210.

98. Charles Wolfe, "Jordanaires," in *The Encyclopedia of Country Music*, 2nd ed., eds. Paul Kingsbury, Michael McCall, and John W. Rumble (New York: Oxford University Press, 2012), 254; Gayle F. Wald, *Shout, Sister, Shout!: The Untold Story of Rock-and-Roll Trailblazer Sister Rosetta Tharpe* (Boston: Beacon Press, 2007), 102–104.

99. Gordon Stoker, interview with Douglas B. Green, November 22, 1974, Country Music Foundation and Library, OH-179, transcript, p. 2.

100. Stoker, interview with Douglas B. Green, November 22, 1974, transcript, p. 2. Stoked recalled, "I used to go and play piano for them when I was a little bitty boy."

101. Neil Matthews, Jr., *The Nashville Numbering System: An Aid to Playing by Ear*, 2nd ed. (Milwaukee: Hal Leonard, 1984), 4. For more background on the Oak Ridge Quartet and the Oak Ridge Boys, consult Goff, *Close Harmony*, 174–177.

102. For historical background on these phenomena, consult Paula Lockheart, "A History of Early Microphone Singing, 1925–1939: American Mainstream Popular Singing at the Advent of Electronic Microphone Amplification," *Popular Music and Society* 26, no. 3 (2003): 367–386; Allison McCracken, *Real Men Don't Sing: Crooning in American Culture* (Durham, NC: Duke University Press, 2015), 74–125. Additionally, documentary evidence of these changing practices can be found in Floyd Gibbons, "How to Train a Singing Voice for Broadcasting: The Art of Crooning," in *Music, Sound, and Technology in America: A Documentary History of Early Phonograph, Cinema, and Radio*, eds. Timothy D. Taylor, Mark Katz, and Tony Grajeda (Durham, NC: Duke University Press, 2012), 316.

103. Stoker, interview with Douglas B. Green, November 22, 1974, transcript, p. 3.

104. Gordon Stoker, interview with Morris Levy, February 8, 1996, Morris Levy Interviews, ARC-0487, Box 1, Folder 6, Rock and Roll Hall of Fame Library and Archives.

105. Stoker, interview with Douglas B. Green, November 22, 1974, transcript, p. 4.

106. For but one example from a leading school of music, consult Mary H. Wennerstrom, "The Undergraduate Core Music Curriculum at Indiana University," *Journal of Music Theory Pedagogy* 3, no. 1 (Spring 1989): 153–158.

107. Ray Walker, interview with John Rumble, July 1, 1991, Country Music Foundation Library, OHC-310.

108. The Jordanaires, "Dig a Little Deeper," https://www.youtube.com/watch?v=YKKM9aIFLt4 (last accessed April 11, 2018). For more background on the popular postwar African American gospel quartets, consult Robert M. Marovich, *A City Called Heaven: Chicago and the Birth of Gospel Music* (Urbana: University of Illinois Press, 2015), 204–228.

109. The Jordanaires, "Workin' on a Building," https://www.youtube.com/watch?v=tADJ7vLv4hk (last accessed September 21, 2017).

110. Stoker, interview with Morris Levy, February 8, 1996.

111. Charlie McCoy, interview with author, July 30, 2014, Nashville, Tennessee; Charlie McCoy with Travis D. Stimeling, *Fifty Cents and a Box Top: The Creative Life of Nashville Session Musician Charlie McCoy* (Morgantown: West Virginia University Press, 2017), 58.

112. Stoker, interview with Morris Levy, February 8, 1996. On McCoy's efforts to transmit the Nashville Number System, consult McCoy with Stimeling, *Fifty Cents and a Box Top*, 58–59, 171.

113. Bergen White, telephone interview with author, September 5, 2014.

114. Neil Matthews, Jr., "A Fool Such as I," Country Music Foundation Library, 4.Z.015.5; Elvis Presley, "(Now and Then There's) A Fool Such as I" b/w "I Need You," RCA Victor 47-7506 (1959); Ron Barry, *The Elvis Presley American Discography* (Phillipsburg, NJ: Spectator Service, Maxigraphics, 1976), 25.

115. Neil Matthews, Jr., "It's Now or Never," Country Music Foundation Library, 4.Z.015.3.; Elvis Presley, "It's Now or Never" b/w "A Mess of Blues," RCA Victor 447-0628 (1960); Barry, *The Elvis Presley American Discography*, 44.

116. Bergen White, telephone interview with author, September 5, 2014.

117. Ray Stevens, telephone interview with author, December 17, 2014; Ray Stevens with C. W. "Buddy" Kalb, *Ray Stevens' Nashville* (Tallahassee: Father & Son, 2014), 30–68.

118. Babcock noted that his formal music education also paid dividends as a singer and as a leader of the Nashville Edition, a vocal group that came to dominate the session scene in the late 1960s and 1970s. He told interviewer Morris Levy: "When we first started with the Edition, the Jordanaires had a system that Neil Matthews had devised, and it's called the 'number system.' It wasn't brand new because the number system is used in classical music. Matter of fact, I studied it in college. They use Roman numerals. And every chord has a designation. . . . But Neil sort of adapted that to country music, and he used shape notes for the Jordanaires. So they had a system where they could really go through it fast. When we first started out, we

were just doing it by the lyrics, trying to remember, and we were a little slow. We did a session for a man one time over at Columbia, and it took us a long time. He left. He said, 'Well, kids, practice up. . . .' That meant we weren't making any more for him." He went on to note that he developed his own variation on the Nashville Number System that used Roman numerals and individual voice parts written out with Arabic numerals to denote the scale degree that each singer should sing (Joe Babcock, interview with Morris Levy, March 15, 1996, Morris Levy Interviews, Box 1, Folder 1, ARC-0487, Rock and Roll Hall of Fame Archives and Library).

119. Charlie McCoy, interview with author, July 30, 2014.
120. Charlie McCoy, interview with author, July 30, 2014. For more detail, consult McCoy with Stimeling, *Fifty Cents and a Box Top*, 16–17.
121. McCoy, interview with author, July 30, 2014. See also McCoy with Stimeling, *Fifty Cents and a Box Top*, 27–30; Joan Cook, "Renée Longy, Pianist, Music Theoritician, Bernstein's Teacher," *New York Times* (May 22, 1979), https://www.nytimes.com/1979/05/22/archives/renee-longy-pianist-music-theoretician-bernsteins-teacher.html (last accessed April 2, 2019).
122. For more background on the Nashville Number System, consult Neil Matthews, Jr., *The Nashville Numbering System: An Aid to Playing by Ear* (Milwaukee: Hal Leonard, 1984); Williams, *The Nashville Number System*.
123. McCoy, interview with author, July 30, 2014.
124. Buddy Harman, interview with Morris Levy, January 19, 1996, Morris Levy Interviews, Box 1, Folder 7, Rock and Roll Hall of Fame Archives and Library, Cleveland, Ohio.
125. Harman, interview with Morris Levy, January 19, 1996.
126. Harman, interview with Morris Levy, January 19, 1996; Harold Bradley, interview with Morris Levy, February 22, 1996, Morris Levy Interviews, Box 1, Folder 2, ARC-0487, Rock and Roll Hall of Fame Library and Archives.
127. Billy Amendola, "An Interview with Hal Blaine," *Modern Drummer* (July 2005), https://www.moderndrummer.com/2005/07/hal-blaine-2/ (accessed September 21, 2017).
128. Amendola, "An Interview with Hal Blaine"; "Buddy Harman: The Original Country Drummer," *Modern Drummer* (January 2011), https://www.moderndrummer.com/2011/01/buddy-harman/ (accessed September 21, 2017).
129. For more background on Mullican, consult Rich Kienzle, *Southwest Shuffle: Pioneers of Honky-Tonk, Western Swing, and Country Jazz* (New York: Routledge, 2003), 114; Jon Hartley Fox, *King of the Queen City: The Story of King Records* (Urbana: University of Illinois Press, 2009), 74–78. Various reports indicate that this session may have occurred in 1951 or 1952, but the most credible source suggests that it was the September 26, 1952, King Records session held at Castle (Dick Grant et al., "Moon Mullican," *Prague Frank's Country Music Discographies* (posted May 3, 2016) http://countrydiscoghraphy2.blogspot.com/2016/05/moon-mullican.html (last accessed April 12, 2018).
130. Harman, interview with Morris Levy, January 19, 1996; Bradley, interview with Morris Levy, February 22, 1996.

131. Ray Edenton recounted: "I worked a lot of sessions, especially with Chet. And you wasn't allowed to put drums on a record back then on a country record.

"TS: Why is that?

"RE: Oh a bunch of old farts that didn't know no different. Said, 'We ain't having no damn drums.' I can hear Oswald now with Acuff saying that. 'Take them dang'— he wouldn't cuss. He said, 'Take them dang drums out of here.' Made him mad if you put drums on his, on the Opry even. So that's the [reason]. I played Chet, Chet was more uptown than most of them. Way above his time. I did a lot of sessions for him. And sometimes he'd give me a pasteboard box with a drum brush. And I'd just play that. [makes drum brush sound] Boudleaux Bryant had the funniest thing. Boudleaux was a character, you know who he was?

"TS: Yeah.

"RE: He was writing a lot of songs and getting started, and he and Felice. He did ... people did a lot of his records, his songs, you know? And this was about the time the Everlys struck with all his songs, one right after the other. We played on all of them. And Boudleaux come to the session with a bag of marbles. It was funny. We'd laugh. Put them on his lap and che-che-che-che. Couldn't play on drums.

"TS: But you could play a bag of marbles.

"RE: Played a bag of marbles. " (Ray Edenton, interview with author, Nashville, TN, August 3, 2014).

132. Harman, interview with Morris Levy, January 19, 1996.

133. Bradley, interview with Morris Levy, February 22, 1996.

134. Harman, interview with Morris Levy, January 19, 1996.

135. Harman, interview with Morris Levy, January 19, 1996.

136. Joli Jensen, *The Nashville Sound: Authenticity, Commercialization, and Country Music* (Nashville: The Country Music Foundation Press and Vanderbilt University Press, 1998), 5.

137. Jensen, *The Nashville Sound*, 23–37; Barbara Ching, *Wrong's What I Do Best: Hard Country Music and Contemporary Culture* (New York: Oxford University Press, 2001); Fox, *Real Country*; Diane Pecknold, *The Selling Sound: The Rise of the Country Music Industry* (Durham, NC: Duke University Press, 2007), 49–51.

138. Lawrence W. Levine, *Highbrow/Lowbrow: The Emergence of Cultural Hierarchy in America* (Cambridge, MA: Harvard University Press, 1988), 83–168; Ralph P. Locke, "Music Lovers, Patrons, and the 'Sacralization' of Culture in America," *19th-Century Music* 17, no. 2 (Autumn 1993): 149–173; Christina Bashford, *The Pursuit of High Culture: John Ella and Chamber Music in Victorian England* (Woodbridge, UK: Boydell Press, 2007); Joseph Horowitz, *Classical Music in America: A History of Its Rise and Fall* (New York: W. W. Norton, 2005), 250–253.

139. For more insights into Nashville's efforts to establish itself as a cultural leader in the South, consult Henry McRaven, *Nashville: "Athens of the South"* (Chapel Hill, TN: Scheer & Jervis, 1949); Christine Kreyling, Wesley Paine, Charles W. Waterfield, Jr., and Susan Ford Wiltshire, *Classical Nashville: Athens of the South* (Nashville: Vanderbilt University Press, 1996).

140. *Who's Who in American Music: Classical*, first edition (New York: R. R. Bowker, 1983), 244–245; Peter Cooper, "Sheldon Kurland—Violinist, String Arranger—Dies at 81," *Nashville [Tenn.] Tennessean* (February 6, 2010), http://blogs.tennessean.com/tunein/2010/01/06/sheldon-kurland-violinist-string-arranger-dies-at-81/.

For more background on Peabody College, consult "The Peabody Semicentennial," *Peabody Journal of Education* 2, no. 5 (March 1925): 278–281; Vanderbilt University Peabody College of Education and Human Development, "History," http://peabody.vanderbilt.edu/about/explore/history.php (accessed September 18, 2015).

141. Box 146, Folder 2, Louis T. Nicholas Papers, Vanderbilt University Special Collections MSS 314.

142. Box 145, Folder 10, Louis T. Nicholas Papers, Vanderbilt University Special Collections MSS 314.

143. Cooper, "Sheldon Kurland."

144. *Who's Who in American Music: Classical*, 245; Cooper, "Sheldon Kurland"; "On the Passing of Shelly Kurland, Peter's Father," *Film Nashville*, posted January 9, 2010, https://filmnashville.org/on-the-passing-of-shelly-kurland-peters-fathe/.

145. Cooper, "Sheldon Kurland."

146. "Shelly Kurland," *New York Times* (January 9, 2010), http://www.legacy.com/obituaries/nytimes/obituary.aspx?pid=138323526; Musicians Hall of Fame, "Shelly Kurland," http://www.musicianshalloffame.com/virtual-tours/shelly-kurland/ (accessed September 25, 2015). Kurland also published the humorous book *An Adult Guide to the Orchestra* (Nashville: Darkhorse Books, 2002).

147. Nashville Symphony Orchestra, "About: Mission & History," https://www.nashvillesymphony.org/about/history (accessed September 25, 2015); Nashville Symphony Orchestra, "NSO Concerts—1955–1970 (in author's possession).

148. "Lillian Vann Hunt," *Nashville [Tenn.] Tennessean* (May 10, 2009).

149. Program for Peabody Women's Club Guest Musical Tea, May 6, 1955, Louis T. Nicholas Papers, Vanderbilt University Special Collections, MSS 314.

150. "Lillian Vann Hunt," *Nashville [Tenn.] Tennesseean*; Program for Peabody Women's Club Musical Tea, April 18, 1947, Box 145, Folder 1, Louis T. Nicholas Papers, Vanderbilt University Special Collections MSS 314; Program for Peabody Women's Club Guest Musical Tea, May 6, 1955, Louis T. Nicholas Papers, Vanderbilt University Special Collections, MSS 314; Program for Sigma Alpha Iota Recital, May 25, 1958, Box 145, Folder 18, Louis T. Nicholas Papers, Vanderbilt University; Recital program, George Peabody College for Teachers, February 26, 1956, Box 148, Folder 1, Louis T. Nicholas Papers, Vanderbilt University Special Collections, MSS 314; Recital program, George Peabody College for Teachers, February 17, 1957, Box 148, Folder 1, Louis T. Nicholas Papers, Vanderbilt University Special Collections, MSS 314; Recital program, George Peabody College for Teachers, October 19, 1958, Box 148, Folder 1, Louis T. Nicholas Papers, Vanderbilt University Special Collections, MSS 314; Recital program, George Peabody College for Teachers, February 22, 1959, Box 148, Folder 1, Louis T. Nicholas Papers, Vanderbilt University Special Collections, MSS 314; Recital program, George Peabody College for Teachers, March 22, 1959, Box 148, Folder 1, Louis

T. Nicholas Papers, Vanderbilt University Special Collections, MSS 314; Recital program, George Peabody College for Teachers, November 15, 1959, Box 148, Folder 1, Louis T. Nicholas Papers, Vanderbilt University Special Collections, MSS 314; Recital program, George Peabody College for Teachers, November 13, 1960, Box 148, Folder 1, Louis T. Nicholas Papers, Vanderbilt University Special Collections, MSS 314.

151. Nashville Symphony Orchestra, "NSO Orchestra Rosters—1955–1970" (in author's possession).

152. Byron Bach, undated typescript, personal collection of Carole Ann Bach (copy in author's possession).

153. Nashville Symphony Orchestra, concert programs for October 26–27, 1959 and March 7–8, 1960.

154. Byron Bach, undated typescript. As his daughter Carole Ann Bach noted, "he worked during the day at the chemical company. I think most of the rehearsals took place during the evening, and all of the sessions took place in the evening. Or almost all of them. . . . I mean, some of them went well into . . . one or two or three in the morning" (Carole Ann Bach, interview with author, August 29, 2014).

155. Cathy Bach Guenther, interview with author, September 26, 2014.

156. Byron Bach personal ledgers, 1972–1975, personal collection of Cathy Bach Guenther (copies in author's possession).

157. Rhodes College, *The Lynx* (Memphis, 1952), 25.

158. *Manning's Ithaca Directory 1957* (Schenectady: H. A. Manning, 1957), 405; *Polk's Nashville Suburban Director* (n.p.: R. L. Polk, 1958), 965.

159. Austin-Peay State University Office of Public Relations and Marketing, "Jazz Event to Honor Local Music Legend Solie Fott," https://www.apsu.edu/archived-news/2014/06/jazz-event-honor-local-music-legend-solie-fott.php (posted June 4, 2014; last accessed August 20, 2018); Austin-Peay State University, *Farewell & Hail* (1973), 161.

160. Tennessee State University became a land-grant institution in 1958 (Tennessee State University, "About TSU: An HBCU Legacy," http://www.tnstate.edu/about_tsu/history2.aspx> [last accessed March 30, 2019]).

161. P. J. Broume and Clay Tucker, *The Other Music City: The Dance Bands and Jazz Musicians[,] 1920 to 1970* (Nashville: American Press Printing, 1990), chapter 4 (no page numbers).

162. W. O. Smith, *Sideman: The Long Gig of W. O. Smith: A Memoir* (Nashville: Rutledge Hill Press, 1991), 206–207.

163. W. O. Smith, *Sideman*, 207.

164. Broume and Tucker, *The Other Music City*, chapter 4 (no page numbers).

165. Beegie Adair, qtd. in Broume and Tucker, *The Other Music City*, chapter 4 (no page numbers).

166. Marc Myers, "Interview: Gary Burton (Part 1)," http://www.jazzwax.com/2010/07/interview-gary-burton-part-1.html (posted July 26, 2010). This group recorded an album for RCA Victor, *After the Riot at Newport* (RCA Victor LPM-2302), later that year.

167. Anita Kerr, qtd. in Michael Streissguth, *Voices of the Country: Interviews with Classic Country Performers* (New York: Routledge, 2004), 64.

168. Douglas Gomery, *Patsy Cline: The Making of an Icon* (Bloomington: Trafford, 2011), 208.

169. Leo Jackson, qtd. in Larry Jordan, *Jim Reeves: His Untold Story* (n.p., Page Turner Books, 2011), 301.

170. Anita Kerr, qtd. in Larry Jordan, *Jim Reeves: His Untold Story* (n.p., Page Turner Books, 2011), 301. See also Kerr, qtd. in Streissguth, *Voices of the Country*, 64.

171. Streissguth, *Voices of the Country*, 42–52.

172. Smith, *Sideman*, 214, 233; Leonard Morton and Fletcher Moon, interview with author, May 18, 2015.

173. Charles L. Hughes, *Country Soul: Making Music and Making Race in the American South* (Chapel Hill: University of North Carolina Press, 2015).

174. Diane Pecknold, "Negotiating Gender, Race, and Class in Post-Civil Rights Country Music: How Linda Martell and Jeannie C. Riley Stormed the Plantation," in *Country Boys and Redneck Women: New Essays in Gender and Country Music*, eds. Diane Pecknold and Kristine M. McCusker (Jackson: University Press of Mississippi, 2016), 150–151.

175. Leonard Morton and Fletcher Moon, interview with author, May 18, 2015.

176. For more information on the racial politics of Nashville Sound–era Nashville, consult Hugh Davis Graham, "Desegregation in Nashville: The Dynamics of Compliance," *Tennessee Historical Quarterly* 25, no. 2 (Summer 1966): 135–154; Sonya Ramsey, "'We Will Be Ready Whenever They Are': African American Teachers' Responses to the *Brown* Decision and Public School Integration in Nashville, Tennessee, 1954–1956," *Journal of African American History* 90, no. 1–2 (Winter 2005): 29–51; Linda T. Wynn, "The Dawning of a New Day: The Nashville Sit-Ins, February 13–May 10, 1960," *Tennessee Historical Quarterly* 50, no. 1 (Spring 1991): 42–54; Scott Frizzell, "Not Just a Matter of Black and White: The Nashville Riot of 1967," *Tennessee Historical Quarterly* 70, no. 1 (Spring 2011): 26–51.

177. The Nashville Symphony Orchestra's personnel rosters for the period 1955 to 1970 do not list Banks as a performer, but do note W. O. Smith's membership beginning in 1963 (Nashville Symphony Orchestra, "NSO Orchestra Rosters—1955–1970" [in author's possession]).

178. Nashville Symphony Orchestra, "NSO Concerts, 1955–1970" (in author's possession).

179. Buddy Spicher, interview with author, July 29, 2014.

180. Bergen White, interview with author, September 5, 2014.

181. For more background on the Nashville Number System, consult Neil Matthews, Jr., *The Nashville Numbering System: An Aid to Playing by Ear* (Milwaukee: Hal Leonard, 1984); Williams, *The Nashville Number System*.

182. Bergen White, interview with author, September 5, 2014.

183. Carole Ann Bach, interview with author, August 29, 2014.

184. Carole Ann Bach, interview with author, August 29, 2014.

185. Cathy Bach Guenther, interview with author, September 26, 2014.

186. Rick Bragg, *Jerry Lee Lewis: His Own Story* (New York: HarperCollins, 2014), 19–105.

187. Cathy Bach Guenther, for instance, has recalled that her father was particularly fond of George Beverly Shea and that Brenda Lee later recalled that Bach "was just precious" (Cathy Bach Guenter, interview with author, September 26, 2014).

188. Stevens with Calb, *Ray Stevens' Nashville*, 86.

189. "Roy Orbison session, RCA Studio B, c. August 8, 1960," Country Music Hall of Fame and Museum, Nashville, TN, D.1988.1.2027 Negative, Photographic. This session generated six takes, two of which were released: "Today's Teardrops" b/w "Blue Angel," Monument MO 425 (Richard Weize, "Discography," in liner notes to *Orbison* [Bear Family BCD 16423 GL, 2001], 72).

190. Bergen White, telephone interview with author, September 5, 2014.

191. Bergen White, telephone interview with author, September 5, 2014; Cathy (Bach) Guenther, telephone interview with author, September 26, 2014.

192. Louise Meintjes, "The Politics of the Recording Studio: A Case Study from South Africa," in *The Cambridge Companion to Recorded Music*, eds. Nicholas Cook, Eric Clarke, Daniel Leech-Wilkinson, and John Rink (Cambridge: Cambridge University Press, 2009), 86. Meintjes offers a more in-depth discussion of the issues arising from her fieldwork in "Reaching 'Overseas': South African Engineers, Technology, and Tradition," in *Wired for Sound: Engineering and Technologies in Sonic Cultures*, eds. Paul D. Greene and Thomas Porcello (Middletown, CT: Wesleyan University Press, 2004), 23–46. See also Beverly Diamond, "Media as Social Action: Native American Musicians in the Recording Studio," in *Wired for Sound: Engineers and Technologies in Sonic Cultures*, eds. Paul D. Greene and Thomas Porcello (Middletown, CT: Wesleyan University Press, 2004), 129.

193. Bruno Nettl, *Heartland Excursions: Ethnomusicological Reflections on Schools of Music* (Urbana: University of Illinois Press, 1995), 34–35

194. Morris Levy, "Nashville Sound-Era Studio Musicians," in *Country Music Annual 2000*, eds. Charles K. Wolfe and James E. Akenson (Lexington: University Press of Kentucky, 2000), 22–29.

195. The foreignness of recording to an orchestral musician's life is perhaps best summarized by conductor Michael Haas, who reminds other conductors that "the rules for recording are simple: the producer needs *one* take of the musical material right in all of the fundamentals. Another cosmetically good take is useful in case the first take reveals something unnoticed at the time of recording. These can be nasty little bugs like tape or disc faults, a mistake that is not noticed until the calmer environment of post-production, a watch peeping or the buzz of a building's generator that shows up only when inter-splicing. Beyond needing two 'clean' takes, basic orchestral balance should also be right. It is difficult to take down heavy brass or percussion afterwards. Other balance points can usually be accommodated if necessary" (Michael Haas, "Studio Conducting," in *The Cambridge Companion to Conducting*, ed. José Antonio Bowen [Cambridge: Cambridge University Press, 2003], 34).

196. For more background on the history of music appreciation in US education, consult Rebecca Bennett, "Debating Music 'Appreciation' outside the American Classroom, 1930–1950," *Journal of Historical Research in Music Education* 33,

no. 2 (April 2012): 128–151; Robert J. Ball, "Joseph Machlis and the Enjoyment of Music: A Biographical Appreciation of a Great Teacher," *Musical Quarterly* 95 (2013): 613–643.

197. Carole Ann Bach, telephone interview with author, August 29, 2014; Cathy (Bach) Guenther, telephone interview with author, September 26, 2014.

198. Louise Meintjes, "The Politics of the Recording Studio: A Case Study from South Africa," in *The Cambridge Companion to Recorded Music*, eds. Nicholas Cook, Eric Clarke, Daniel Leech-Wilkinson, and John Rink (Cambridge: Cambridge University Press, 2009), 86.

CHAPTER 3

1. Joli Jensen, *The Nashville Sound: Authenticity, Commercialization, and Country Music* (Nashville: Country Music Foundation Press/Vanderbilt University Press, 1998), 120–128; Bill Ivey, "The Bottom Line: Business Practices That Shaped Country Music," in *Country: The Music and the Musicians, from the Beginnings to the '90s* (Nashville: Country Music Foundation Press; New York: Abbeville Press, 1994), 296.

2. Jensen, *The Nashville Sound*, 38–61; Fabian Holt, *Genre in Popular Music* (Chicago: University of Chicago Press, 2007), 66–72.

3. See, among others: Richard A. Peterson, *Creating Country Music: Fabricating Authenticity* (Chicago: University of Chicago Press, 1997), 139–144; Rich Kienzle, *Southwest Shuffle: Pioneers of Honky-Tonk, Western Swing, and Country Jazz* (New York: Routledge, 2003).

4. Bill C. Malone and Jocelyn R. Neal, *Country Music, U.S.A.*, 3rd rev. ed. (Austin: University of Texas Press, 2010), 246. This text appears in editions published before Neal was brought on as a co-author.

5. Joe Allison, interview with John Rumble, May 27, 1994, Country Music Foundation Oral History Collection, OHC6.

6. Karl Hagstrom Miller, *Segregating Sound: Inventing Folk and Pop Music in the Age of Jim Crow* (Durham, NC: Duke University Press, 2010); Patrick Huber, "Black Hillbillies: African American Musicians on Old-Time Records, 1924–1932," in *Hidden in the Mix: The African American Presence in Country Music*, ed. Diane Pecknold (Durham, NC: Duke University Press, 2013), 19–81; Erich Nunn, *Sounding the Color Line: Music and Race in the Southern Imagination* (Athens: University of Georgia Press, 2015), 45–77.

7. Simon Frith, "Pop Music," in *The Cambridge Companion to Pop and Rock*, eds. Simon Frith, Will Straw, and John Street (Cambridge: Cambridge University Press, 2001), 95. Folklorist Joe Wilson, who worked in Nashville in the late 1950s, offers one of the most visceral reactions to the Nashville Sound's crossover efforts: "There was a determination in the industry to make music that would be palatable to a huge percentage of the population. In order to do that, you added 'doo-wah' choruses a la the Jordanaires—who were in tremendous use at the time—and the string section of the Nashville Symphony. You cut off all the sharp edges. You 'packaged' it.

    Country music stopped being a rural music form. Above all, they wanted to get rid of those crude-sounding banjos and other acoustic instruments. They wanted to get rid of songs about mama dying and other emotional material that just scared the hell out of those middle[-]class, plastic-eared people they wanted to sell to. . . .

I have to say that, as a business decision, I can't quarrel with what they did. It worked; country music's share of the market grew tremendously during that period. . . . No one ever asked whether the music was good. No one ever asked it if was beautiful" (Joe Wilson, *Lucky Joe's Namesake: The Extraordinary Life and Observations of Joe Wilson*, ed. Fred Bartenstein [Knoxville: University of Tennessee Press, 2017], 17).

8. Eric Weisbard, *Top 40 Democracy: The Rival Mainstreams of American Music* (Chicago: University of Chicago Press, 2014), 4.

9. Kevin J. H. Dettmar, *Is Rock Dead?* (New York: Routledge, 2006), 58–59; David Brackett, *Interpreting Popular Music* (Cambridge: Cambridge University Press, 1995; paperback ed., Berkeley: University of California Press, 2000), 89–91.

10. David Brackett, *Categorizing Sound: Genre and Twentieth-Century Popular Music* (Berkeley: University of California Press, 2016), 281–283.

11. B. Lee Cooper, "Promoting Social Change through Audio Repetition: Black Musicians as Creators and Revivalists, 1953–1978," *Tracking: Popular Music Studies* 2, no. 1 (Winter 1989): 2–46; Brackett, *Interpreting Popular Music*, 34–74.

12. Diane Pecknold, "Making Country Modern: The Legacy of Modern Sounds in Country and Western Music," in *Hidden in the Mix: The African American Presence in Country Music* (Durham, NC: Duke University Press, 2013), 88–90.

13. Michael Coyle, "Hijacked Hits and Antic Authenticity: Cover Songs, Race, and Postwar Marketing," in *Rock over the Edge: Transformations in Popular Music Culture*, eds. Roger Beebe, Denise Fulbrook, and Ben Saunders (Durham, NC: Duke University Press, 2002), 133–158; Ian Inglis, "Embassy Records: Covering the Market, Marketing the Cover," *Popular Music and Society* 28, no. 2 (May 2005): 163–170; B. Lee Cooper, "Charting Cultural Change, 1953–57: Song Assimilation through Cover Recording," in *Play It Again: Cover Songs in Popular Music*, ed. George Plasketes (Aldershot, UK: Ashgate, 2010; reprint ed., New York: Routledge, 2016), 43–76; Don Cusic, "In Defense of Cover Songs: Commerce and Credibility," in *Play It Again: Cover Songs in Popular Music*, ed. George Plasketes (Aldershot, UK: Ashgate, 2010; reprint ed., New York: Routledge, 2016), 223–229.

14. Among others, consult Simon Frith, *Sound Effects: Youth, Leisure, and the Politics of Rock 'n' Roll* (New York: Pantheon Books, 1981), 39–57; Allan F. Moore, "Authenticity as Authentication," *Popular Music* 21, no. 2 (May 2002): 209–223; Richard Middleton, *Voicing the Popular: On the Subjects of Popular Music* (New York: Routledge, 2006), 199–246; Hugh Barker and Yuval Taylor, *Faking It: The Quest for Authenticity in Popular Music* (New York: W. W. Norton, 2007); Hans Weisethaunet and Ulf Lindberg, "Authenticity Revisited: The Rock Critic and the Changing Real," *Popular Music and Society* 33, no. 4 (October 2010): 465–485.

15. Diane Pecknold, *The Selling Sound: The Rise of the Country Music Industry* (Durham, NC: Duke University Press, 2007). See also: Jensen, *The Nashville Sound*; Fabian Holt, *Genre in Popular Music* (Chicago: University of Chicago Press, 2007), 73–76; Bill C. Malone, "Patsy Cline and the Transformation of the Working-Class South," in *Sweet Dreams: The World of Patsy Cline*, ed. Warren R. Hofstra

(Urbana: University of Illinois Press, 2013), 17–21; Jocelyn R. Neal, "'Nothing but a Little Old Pop Song': Patsy Cline's Music Style and the Evolution of Genre in the 1950s," in *Sweet Dreams: The World of Patsy Cline*, ed. Warren R. Hofstra (Urbana: University of Illinois Press, 2013), 128–153; Nathan D. Gibson, "What's International about International Country Music?: Country Music and National Identity around the World," in *The Oxford Handbook of Country Music*, ed. Travis D. Stimeling (New York: Oxford University Press, 2017), 502–504.

16. Bill Ivey, "Commercialization and Tradition in the Nashville Sound," in *Folk Music and Modern Sound*, eds. William Ferris and Mary L. Hart (Jackson: University Press of Mississippi, 1982), 134–135.

17. Ivey, "Commercialization and Tradition in the Nashville Sound," 135.

18. Harold Bradley, interview with John W. Rumble, May 14, 1991, Country Music Foundation Oral History Collection, OHC 35.

19. Buddy Spicher, interview with author, Nashville, TN, July 29, 2014.

20. Charlie McCoy, interview with author, Nashville, TN, July 30, 2014.

21. Jensen, *The Nashville Sound*, 130, discusses the impact of these demands on songwriting.

22. Jensen, *The Nashville Sound*, 121. This phenomenon is discussed in relation to the entire popular music industry in Albin J. Zak, III, *I Don't Sound like Nobody: Remaking Music in 1950s America* (Ann Arbor: University of Michigan Press, 2010); Mark Christopher Samples, "A Package Deal: Branding, Technology, and Advertising in Music of the 20th and 21st Centuries," Ph.D. dissertation, University of Oregon, 2012, 10.

23. Jensen, *The Nashville Sound*, 105.

24. Ivey noted, for instance, that "the approach to recording in this period allowed musicians great latitude in determining what specific lines would be played by which instruments at which particular moment in a performance" (Ivey, "Commercialization and Tradition in the Nashville Sound," 136).

25. Jeffrey J. Lange, *Smile When You Call Me a Hillbilly: Country Music's Struggle for Respectability, 1939–1954* (Athens: University of Georgia Press, 2004), 71. Lange notes, for instance that this process was influenced by "southern migrants in the North . . . [who congregated] in 'hillbilly taverns' located near defense plants [and] looked to jukeboxes to hear the songs that local radio stations virtually ignored. Not surprisingly, 50 percent of all Detroit locations equipped with a jukebox in 1944 reported the inclusion of country music selections on their machines; in St. Louis, the number rose to 70 percent."

26. Lange, *Smile When You Call Me a Hillbilly*, 162.

27. For more on this phenomenon, consult Wes Smith, *The Pied Pipers of Rock 'n' Roll: Radio Deejays of the '50s and '60s* (Marietta, GA: Longstreet, 1989); Gilbert Williams, "The Black Disc Jockey as a Cultural Hero," *Popular Music and Society* 10, no. 3 (1986): 79–90; Ben Fong-Torres, *The Hits Just Keep on Coming: The History of Top 40 Radio* (San Francisco: Backbeat Books, 2001); Louis Cantor, *Dewey and Elvis: The Life and Times of a Rock 'n' Roll Deejay* (Urbana: University of Illinois Press, 2005).

28. See, among others: Russell Sanjek and David Sanjek, *American Popular Music Business in the 20th Century* (New York: Oxford University Press, 1991), 173–174; Trent Hill, "The Enemy Within: Censorship in Rock Music in the 1950s," *South Atlantic Quarterly* 90, no. 4 (Fall 1991): 675–707; Kerry Segrave, *Payola in the Music Industry: A History, 1880–1991* (Jefferson, NC: McFarland, 1994), 100–119; Michael T. Bertrand, *Race, Rock, and Elvis* (Urbana: University of Illinois Press, 2000), 138–157, 160–188; Glenn C. Altschuler, *All Shook Up: How Rock 'n' Roll Changed America* (New York: Oxford University Press, 2003), 134–160.

29. Fong-Torres, *The Hits Just Keep on Coming*, 81–83.

30. Weisbard, *Top 40 Democracy*, 2.

31. Weisbard, *Top 40 Democracy*, 9.

32. Ron Rodman, "Road Formats in the United States: A (Hyper)Fragmentation of the Imagination," in *Music and the Broadcast Experience: Performance, Production, and Audiences*, eds. Christina L. Baade and James Deaville (New York: Oxford University Press, 2016), 235.

33. Fong-Torres, *The Hits Just Keep on Coming*, 37–39; Weisbard, *Top 40 Democracy*, 4–6; Richard W. Fatherley and David T. MacFarland, *The Birth of Top 40 Radio: The Storz Stations' Revolution of the 1950s and 1960s* (Jefferson, NC: McFarland, 2014).

34. Jocelyn R. Neal, "The Metric Makings of a Country Hit," in *Reading Country Music: Steel Guitars, Opry Stars, and Honky-Tonk Bars*, ed. Cecilia Tichi (Durham, NC: Duke University Press, 1998), 322–337; Travis Stimeling, "Taylor Swift's 'Pitch Problem' and the Place of Adolescent Girls in Country Music," in *Country Boys and Redneck Women: New Essays in Gender and Country Music*, eds. Diane Pecknold and Kristine M. McCusker (Jackson: University Press of Mississippi, 2016), 91–93.

35. Rodman, "Radio Formats in the United States," 239.

36. Harold Bradley, interview with John Rumble, May 14, 1991, Country Music Foundation Library, OHC-35. Bradley confirmed this in an interview with me in August 2014, noting that the tic-tac "gave you a click, and it also gave you a note, and on a transistor radio, that note became important to my brother. He wanted that bass all the time" (Harold Bradley, interview with author, August 1, 2014).

37. Bradley, interview with John Rumble, May 14, 1991, transcript, p. 17, interpolations in original. This click, it should be noted, was the result not simply of the instrument, but of the necessary use of a flatpick to produce those sounds; it is nearly impossible to play the bass with the fingers when one is also using the heel of the palm to mute the strings.

38. Billy Sherrill, qtd. in March Myers, *Anatomy of a Song: The Oral History of 45 Iconic Hits That Changed Rock, R&B and Pop* (New York: Grove Press, 2016), 130. Recent scholarship by Karin Bijsterveld et al. has shown that drivers began to develop new relationships with their car radios during the 1950s and 1960s, both in the United States and Europe, observing that, "whereas early car radio was sold as a companion to the lonely driver, in the 1960s it came to be defined as a sonic assistant helping drivers to cope with their lack of solitude on the road: to musically control their temper in situations of traffic jams and badly behaving fellow drivers. The listening driver was thus encapsulated in new ways: not only mentally detached from the sound of the engine, but also guided by the mood-improving sound of his car radio

equipment" (Karin Bijsterveld, Eefje Cleophas, Stefan Krebs, and Gijs Mom, *Sound and Safe: A History of Listening Behind the Wheel* [New York: Oxford University Press, 2014], 73, emphasis in original). Format radio undoubtedly played a role in helping people to maintain their mood.

39. Spicher, interview with author, Nashville, TN, July 29, 2014. Sanders played on ten sessions with Shepard between April 1954 and December 1956; these sessions were held at the Capitol Records studios in Hollywood. When Shepard began recording in Nashville in May 1958, she dropped the fiddle altogether (Chris Skinker, Richard Weize, and Laurence J. Zwisohn, "Jean Shepard: The Discography, 1952–1964," in liner notes to *Jean Shepard: The Melody Ranch Girl* [Bear Family BCD 15905-EI, 1996], 28–34.

40. Charlie McCoy with Travis D. Stimeling, *Fifty Cents and a Box Top: The Creative Life of Nashville Session Musician Charlie McCoy* (Morgantown: West Virginia University Press, 2017), 80.

41. Don Roy and Richard Weize, "Marty Robbins: Western Discography," in liner notes to *Marty Robbins: Under Western Skies* (Bear Family BCD 15646 DI, 1995), 40; "Billy Walker: Part 1," *PragueFrank's Country Music Discographies*, http://country-discoghraphy2.blogspot.com/2014/02/billy-walker-part-1.html (posted February 18, 2014; last accessed May 7, 2018).

   Country broadcasting personality Ralph Emery noted that the similarity between the two songs raised some concerns, recalling a show that he and Walker were performing on: "Billy had recorded several successful country songs, including 'Cross the Brazos at Waco,' a cowboy tune that the public thought sounded amazingly like 'El Paso,' a Marty Robbins song. It was the trumpets and harmony patterns that Marty used ['El Paso' does not have any trumpets, but Robbins's 1976 single 'El Paso City' does].

   "Billy was defensive about the misconception. The band knew it, and broke into 'El Paso' one night as Billy walked on stage.

   "That miffed Billy, who finished his set . . ." (Ralph Emery with Tom Carter, *Memories: The Autobiography of Ralph Emery* [New York: Macmillan, 1991], 244–245).

42. These timecards are available on microfilm at the Country Music Foundation Library, Country Music Hall of Fame and Museum, Nashville, TN. Pat McCoy, who worked at the Nashville Federation of Musicians during this time, confirmed that the union disposed of the old timecards after seven years (Pat McCoy, interview with author, May 28, 2017, Nashville, TN).

43. Robert Altman, dir., *Nashville* (Paramount, 1975).

44. Tracey E. W. Laird, *Louisiana Hayride: Radio & Roots Music along the Red River* (New York: Oxford University Press, 2005), 11–15; Colin Escott, liner notes to *Jim Reeves: Welcome to My World* (Bear Family BCD 15656 PI, 1994), 7–12.

45. Joel Whitburn, *Top Country Singles, 1944 to 2001* (Menomonee Falls, WI: Record Research, 2002), 287–288.

46. Are den Dulk, Kurt Rokitta, and Richard Weize, "Jim Reeves: The Discography," in *Jim Reeves: Welcome to My World* (Bear Family BCD 15656 PI, 1994), 82–84; Charles Wolfe, "Jim Beck," in *The Encyclopedia of Country Music*, 2nd ed., eds. Paul

Kingsbury, Michael McCall, and John W. Rumble (New York: Oxford University Press, 2012), 29.

47. Escott, notes to *Jim Reeves: Welcome to My World*, 7.

48. den Dulk et al., "Jim Reeves: The Discography," 84.

49. den Dulk et al., "Jim Reeves: The Discography," 90–91.

50. den Dulk et al., "Jim Reeves: The Discography," 90.

51. Escott suggests that Reeves had made a move toward a more pop-oriented sound as early as April 1956, noting that, "[i]n early April [1956] he returned to Nashville to play the 'Opry' and rehearse for a session. The lead cut was *My Lips Are Sealed*. It came from the New York song mill, giving an early indication of Jim's intention to change his sound. The song was ideally suited to his new style, and the addition of the chorus showed that the intention was to try for the pop market—not the rock 'n' roll market. The song went on to become his biggest record since *Yonder Comes a Sucker*, a year earlier" (Colin Escott, liner notes to *Jim Reeves: Welcome to My World*, 33).

52. On Reeves's changing vocal style, consult Jocelyn R. Neal, "The Twang Factor in Country Music," in *The Relentless Pursuit of Tone: Timbre in Popular Music*, eds. Robert Fink, Melinda Latour, and Zachary Wallmark (New York: Oxford University Press, 2018), 56.

53. den Dulk et al., "Jim Reeves: The Discography," 91; Joel Whitburn, *Top Country Singles, 1944 to 2011*, 5th ed. (Menomonee Falls, WI: Record Research, 2002), 288.

54. Whitburn, *Top Country Singles*, 161.

55. Whitburn, *Top Country Singles*, 161, 288.

56. Whitburn, *Top Country Singles*, 71.

57. Escott notes, for instance, that "[i]n early April [1956] he [Reeves] returned to Nashville to play the 'Opry' and rehearse for a session" (Escott, liner notes to *Jim Reeves: Welcome to My World*, 33). See also: Michael Jarrett, *Producing Country Music: The Inside Story of the Great Recordings* (Middleport, CT: Wesleyan University Press, 2014), 64.

58. Chet Atkins, interview with Dave Bussey, qtd. in Colin Escott, liner notes to *Jim Reeves: Welcome to My World*, 41.

59. See, for instance, liner notes to *Jim Reeves: Welcome to My World*, 92, 95.

60. Chet Atkins, qtd. in Escott, liner notes to *Jim Reeves: Welcome to My World*, 41–42.

61. Tommy Hill, qtd. in Escott, liner notes to *Jim Reeves: Welcome to My World*, 42.

62. RCA Victor LSP 1950, 37/47-7855, LSP 2487, and 47/61-7643, respectively.

63. Anita Kerr, qtd. in Michael Streissguth, *Voices of the Country: Interviews with Classic Country Performers* (New York: Routledge, 2004), 60.

64. Video footage of Reeves working at RCA Studio B on February 26, 1963, as well as numerous session photographs printed in the liner notes to *Jim Reeves: Welcome to My World*, support this assertion. See: "Jim Reeves . . . Recording "Blue Canadian Rockies" in Studio (Live Video from 1963-HQ)" https://www.youtube.com/watch?v=1ejFPPXQoGc (posted November 7, 2013, last accessed May 1, 2018); Liner notes to *Jim Reeves: Welcome to My World* (Bear Family 15656 PI, 1994), 98–99, 101–103.

65. Kerr, qtd. in Michael Streissguth, *Voices of the Country*, 59.

66. Royce Morgan, interview with John Rumble, March 29, 1997, Country Music Foundation Oral History OHC183, Country Music Foundation Library and Archives.

67. den Dulk et al., "Jim Reeves: A Discography," 94.

68. Suzi Burgher Payne, telephone interview with author, February 3, 2015.

69. den Dulk et al., "Jim Reeves: A Discography," 91–97.

70. Streissguth, *Voices of the Country*, 60–61.

71. Whitburn, *Top Country Singles*, 288.

72. Malcolm Macfarland and Ken Crossland, *Perry Como: A Biography and Complete Career Record* (Jefferson, NC: McFarland Press, 2009), 127–129, 183. Como's visits were covered regularly in the Nashville press. See, for instance: "Como Cuts Record Despite Cold," *Nashville Tennessean* (February 10, 1965); Kathy Sawyer, "Perry Como Sings Praise of Good Old Nashville," *Nashville Tennesseean* (August 22, 1967).

    It is also worth noting that, according to the sleeve notes to the album *The Scene Changes*, Como used a very different band from the Reeves sound: "Then, backing Perry instrumentally, there was a group of instrumentalists whose names are truly a vital part of the Nashville scene. In fact, these boys help make the Nashville sound the 'Nashville Sound!' They are: guitarists Grady Martin, Ray Edenton, Hal [*sic*] Bradley and Jim Wilkerson; pianist Floyd Cramer; sax specialist Boots Randolph; drummer Buddy Harman (he added an extra fillip via tambourine); Bob Moore of the rhythmic bass; Charlie McCoy, harmonica man; and steel guitarist Pete Drake, trumpet trombonist Cam Mullins, and saxophonist Dutch McMillin" (Red O'Donnell, sleeve notes to Perry Como with the Anita Kerr Quartet, *The Scene Changes* [RCA Victor LSP-3396, 1965]).

73. Russ Wapensky and Richard Weize, "Young Love: Sonny James, The Capitol (1950s), NBC, RCA Victor and Dot Discography," in *Sonny James: Young Love* (Bear Family BCD 16373, 2007), 46.

74. Whitburn, *Top Country Singles*, 167.

75. Wapensky and Weize, "Young Love: Sonny James, The Capitol (1950s), NBC, RCA Victor and Dot Discography," 44–57.

76. Wapensky and Weize, "Young Love: Sonny James, The Capitol (1950s), NBC, RCA Victor and Dot Discography," 45–46, 54–56.

77. Wapensky and Weize, "Young Love: Sonny James, The Capitol (1950s), NBC, RCA Victor and Dot Discography," 47, 54; "Sonny James: Sonny," https://www.discogs.com/Sonny-Sonny/release/5709696 (last accessed May 6, 2018). It is also worth noting that Atkins and James had been roommates in their early career (Dave Samuelson, liner notes to *Sonny James: Young Love* [Bear Family BCD 16373, 2007)], 11).

78. Ken Nelson noted in his memoir that, as the A&R man for Capitol, he took a hands-on approach to production: "My responsibilities were to find new artists and negotiate their contracts. If they didn't write their own songs or bring me suitable ones, I would find songs for them. I approved all songs to be recorded. If the artist didn't have his own orchestra, I would hire the background musicians. I would set the time, book the studio, and designate the recording engineer. In the recording

booth[,] I would sit next to the engineer and between us we would make sure the balances of the orchestra and voice or voices were correct.

"At the beginning of each recording[,] I would open the microphone and give a master number. We would re-do the record until both the artist and I were satisfied with the performance, although I had the final say. I had to make out a session report, which included the master and take numbers, the song title, the composers and publisher of the songs, sign the musician's contract, and turn it in for payment. The next day[,] I would be sent acetates of the session. If I felt the equalization, the highs or lows, was not right, I'd get with the engineer and correct them. When the master was finalized[,] I would set a release date and get with the promotion department. With albums, I would assemble them, six tracks on each side, meet with the art department, approve the album cover, and many times I would write the liner notes" (Ken Nelson, *My First 90 Years Plus 3* [Pittsburgh; Dorrance, 2007], 99–100).

See also Samuelson, liner notes to *Sonny James: Young Love*, 28–29.

79. Samuelson notes that James joined the *Opry* in October 1962 and requested a meeting with Nelson shortly thereafter (Samuelson, liner notes to *Sonny James: Young Love*, 29–30).

80. Whitburn, *Top Country Singles*, 167. This record would stand until the mid-1980s, when the group Alabama placed twenty-one consecutive number ones on the charts (Whitburn, *Top Country Singles*, 4).

81. Whitburn, *Top Country Singles*, 167.

82. Whitburn, *Top Country Singles*, 167.

83. "The Southern Gentlemen," https://www.sonnyjames.com/hof/photo-galleries/the-southern-gentlemen/ (last accessed May 7, 2018); Gary Robble, interview with author, Nashville, Tennessee, May 23, 2017.

84. Robble, interview with author, May 23, 2017.

85. Robble, interview with author, May 23, 2017.

86. Robble noted, "I don't remember how we got into it [vocal backgrounds]—I think maybe Dwayne had been here the first year, and he had become friends with the Jordanaires, especially with Ray" (Robble, interview with author, May 23, 2017).

87. Robble, interview with author, May 23, 2017.

88. Robble recalled: "Well, the guy that owned the car lot where Lin worked, we'd go down there and sing at it. . . . [O]ne day, he just said, 'Well, I've got a friend, and I think he ought to hear you sing.' And so he set up a Saturday morning appointment at 9:30 in the Melrose section of town at an apartment, and we all went over there. . . . And so we went up—I was the spokesman for the group—and we went up and knocked on the door, and this bald-headed man answers the door, and I said, 'I'm Gary Robble, and we're the Parsons Quartet.' He said, 'Well, I'm Archie Campbell. Come on in!' We didn't know who he was, didn't know anything. And he talked to us for a while and [he said], 'Well, sing for me!' So I pulled out a pitch pipe. . . . And so we sang. . . . [W]e're doing these Negro spirituals and 'This Old House' and 'Swing Down, Sweet Chariot' and 'Dry Bones' and all the other stuff. I mean, we had a big repertoire song-wise. We could have sung to him two days, maybe one day. And when it all ended, he finally said, 'Well, you boys are good. . . .'

[H]e said, 'You guys are good enough to be in the *Grand Ole Opry*,' and two weeks later we replaced the Jordanaires as the *Grand Ole Opry* quartet. It was just that simple. Had our own slot. Got to do the Coke commercials" (Robble, interview with author, May 23, 2017).

89. During our interview, Robble demonstrated a remarkable fluency in musical vocabulary and a keen ear for the subtle differences between the sounds of different vocal groups. For example, he remarked that "we did strange key changes and just figured out a way to do it. We'd work and work and work and go, 'Ah, we got it!' and he'd just, 'Whew, how'd you do that?' Yeah, and it was just ear. We just heard stuff. Where the Jordanaires used a lot of sixths, Neil Matthews especially, punchin' the sixth. We didn't go to sixths, but we sure used a lot of sevenths. . . . It wasn't barbershop but it [was] real tight, different than the Jordanaires. . . . [The] Jordanaires kind of featured Gordon [Stoker]. You heard a lot of Gordon. Lin, our first tenor, just had a really blending voice, and the voice that carried our quartet, it just happened to be me. We were built around the lead singer, so they'd take their harmonies and build them around me" (Robble, interview with author, May 23, 2017).

90. Robble, interview with author, May 23, 2017.

91. Robble, interview with author, May 23, 2017.

92. Robble, interview with author, May 23, 2017.

93. Robble, interview with author, May 23, 2017.

94. As Robble recounted, "[I]n . . . my hometown, they played Tab Hunter's 'Young Love'" (Robble, interview with author, May 23, 2017).

95. Robble, interview with author, May 23, 2017. Robble noted that those restrictions were "in his contract."

96. Robble noted, for instance, that Nelson had given James free rein to select his repertoire, among other things. He hypothesized that Nelson had "so steered Sonny the wrong direction in the fifties that . . . he left him alone" (Robble, interview with author, May 23, 2017).

97. "James Holds Trio," *Billboard* 76, no. 36 (September 5, 1964): 16.

98. "The Boys in the Band," *Billboard* 81, no. 42 (October 18, 1969): A42.

99. Robble, interview with author, May 23, 2017.

100. "Sonny James," *PragueFrank's Country Music Discographies*, http://countrydiscography.blogspot.com/2011/04/sonny-james.html (posted April 27, 2011; last accessed May 7, 2018); "Sonny James—*Till the Last Leaf Shall Fall*," https://www.discogs.com/Sonny-James-Till-The-Last-Leaf-Shall-Fall/release/9581806 (last accessed May 7, 2018). Robble indicated that those sessions marked "the only time Ken Nelson was on our sessions. . . . And I know why. . . . It was to [tell] Sonny, 'Let's see if these boys can cut it. I'm not going to let you get them on your sessions and ruin them'" (Robble, interview with author, May 23, 2017).

101. Robble, interview with author, May 23, 2017. These assertions about attribution are based on a survey of several hundred album sleeves held in the Southern Folklife Collection, University of North Carolina at Chapel Hill.

102. Robble, interview with author, May 23, 2017.

103. "Sonny James," *PragueFrank's Country Music Discographies*, http://countrydis-cography.blogspot.com/2011/04/sonny-james.html (posted April 27, 2011; last accessed May 7, 2018).

104. Robble, interview with author, May 23, 2017.

105. "Sonny James," https://countrymusichalloffame.org/Inductees/InducteeDetail/sonny-james (last accessed May 7, 2018).

106. Capitol released the album *Southern Gentleman* (Capitol T-779) in 1957 ("Sonny James—*Southern Gentleman*," https://www.discogs.com/Sonny-James-Southern-Gentleman/master/862183 [last accessed May 7, 2018]).

107. Richard Weize, "Connie Smith: The Discography," in *Connie Smith: Born to Sing* (Bear Family BCD 16368 DI, 2001), 38.

108. Ferguson produced all but one session and one overdub session for Smith in the decade between 1964 and 1974 (Weize, "Connie Smith: The Discography," in *Connie Smith: Born to Sing*, 37–44; idem, "Connie Smith: The Discography," in *Connie Smith: Just for What I Am* (Bear Family BCD 16814 EK, 2012), 58–67). On chart placement, consult Whitburn, *Top Country Singles*, 324–325.

109. Mary A. Bufwack and Robert K. Oermann, *Finding Her Voice: Women in Country Music, 1800–2000* (Nashville: Country Music Foundation Press and Vanderbilt University Press, 2003), 292–293.

110. Connie Smith, qtd. in Colin Escott, liner notes to *Connie Smith: Born to Sing* (Bear Family BCD16368 DI, 2001), 10.

111. Whitburn, *Top Country Singles*, 324.

112. This work is traced in *Bill Anderson: The First Ten Years, 1956–1966* (Bear Family BCD 17150 DK, 2011).

113. Weize, "Connie Smith: The Discography," in *Connie Smith: Born to Sing*, 37–44; idem, "Connie Smith: The Discography," in *Connie Smith: Just for What I Am*, 58–59.

114. Jensen observes that "a good, successful country song . . . has a strategic differ-ence designed to catch the ear of the A&R man, the disc jockey, and the listener" (Jensen, *The Nashville Sound*, 130). I would suggest that this extends beyond the song to recordings, as well.

115. Ray Edenton, interview with author, Gallatin, TN, August 3, 2014.

116. Whitburn, *Top Country Singles*, 324.

117. "I Can't Remember" was recorded on March 17, 1965 (Weize, "Connie Smith: The Discography," in *Connie Smith: Born to Sing*, 39).

118. "Nobody but a Fool (Would Love You)" was recorded on October 14, 1965 (Weize, "Connie Smith: The Discography," in *Connie Smith: Born to Sing*, 39).

119. "If I Talk to Him" was recorded on August 5, 1965 (Weize, "Connie Smith: The Discography," in *Connie Smith: Born to Sing*, 39).

120. "Ain't Had No Lovin'" was recorded on April 7, 1966, and "I'll Come Runnin'" was recorded on August 25, 1966 (Weize, "Connie Smith: The Discography," in *Connie Smith: Born to Sing*, 40–41).

121. "The Hurtin's All Over" was recorded on August 25, 1966, "Cincinnati, Ohio" was recorded on October 28, 1966, and "Run Away Little Tears" was recorded on February 27, 1968 (Weize, "Connie Smith: The Discography," in *Connie Smith: Born*

to Sing, 42–43; Weize, "Connie Smith: The Discography," in *Connie Smith: Just for What I Am*, 58).

122. Kris Kristofferson, for instance, told Nelson biographer Joe Nick Patoski that "Willie was the hero of the soulful set—the people who were in the business because they loved the soul of country music" (Joe Nick Patoski, *Willie Nelson: An Epic Life* [New York: Little, Brown, 2008], 210).

123. Nelson's first session for RCA Victor was November 12, 1964 (Richard Weize, "Willie Nelson: The Discography," in *Willie Nelson: Nashville Was the Roughest* [Bear Family BCD 15831 HK, 2003], 49). Chart data drawn from Whitburn, *Top Country Singles*, 244. For a broad overview of Nelson's life and work during this period, consult Patoski, *Willie Nelson*, 145–212.

124. Willie Nelson, in a 1976 *Rolling Stone* interview with journalist Ed Ward, noted, for instance, that "I couldn't' get anybody on the executive end of [RCA] interested in promoting me as an artist. . . . They might have been hoping that one of my records might accidentally do something on its own without their having to spend a lot of money promoting it" (Ed Ward, "Willie Nelson: Breakthrough of a Lone-Star Legend," *Rolling Stone* 204 [January 15, 1976]: 18).

Admittedly, in my own earlier writings on Nelson, I have fallen victim to this tempting critical trap (Travis D. Stimeling, "'Phases and Stages, Circles and Cycles': Willie Nelson and the Concept Album," *Popular Music* 30, no. 3 [October 2011]: 391).

125. Weize, "Willie Nelson: The Discography," 49–51, 58.

126. Weize, "Willie Nelson: The Discography," 51.

127. Weize, "Willie Nelson: The Discography," 50.

128. Pecknold, *The Selling Sound*, 200–235.

129. Ivey, "Commercialization and Tradition in the Nashville Sound," 135; Pecknold, *The Selling Sound*, 133–167.

130. Jensen, *The Nashville Sound*, 21.

CHAPTER 4

1. See, for instance, Bill Ivey, who suggested that "a recording system in which the instrumentalists rarely read standard notation and a system in which arrangers were relegated to the pedestrian task of arranging strings and horns for overdub sessions allowed the creative impulses of studio musicians to escape with some regularity" ("Commercialization and Tradition in the Nashville Sound," in *Folk Music and Modern Sound*, eds. William Ferris and Mary T. Hart [Jackson: University Press of Mississippi, 1982], 136).

2. This history is traced in great detail in Diane Pecknold, *The Selling Sound: The Rise of the Country Music Industry* (Durham, NC: Duke University Press, 2007).

3. Andrew Flory, *I Hear a Symphony: Motown and Crossover R&B* (Ann Arbor: University of Michigan Press, 2017).

4. See, for instance, Antoine Hennion's classic study "The Production of Success: An Anti-Musicology of the Pop Song," *Popular Music* 3 (1983): 159–193.

5. Here, I am deeply influenced by Archie Green's conception of "laborlore," which he defines as forms of expressive culture including "a robust picket line chant; a

tool chest lid lined with faded dues slips; a secret hand clasp in a dim entry way; an echo of John Lewis's or Eugene Debs's oratory; a visit to a weathered stone marker at Homestead or Ludlow" (Archie Green, "Laborlore," in *Torching the Fink Books and Other Essays on Vernacular Culture* (Chapel Hill: University of North Carolina Press, 2001), 47. For a more recent example, consult Chad Broughton, *Boom, Bust, Exodus: The Rust Belt, the Maquilas, and a Tale of Two Cities* (New York: Oxford University Press, 2015), 11–17.

6. See, for instance, Tim Sterner Miller's treatment of the technological developments and innovations in the steel guitar community in "This Machine Plays Country Music: Invention, Innovation, and the Pedal Steel Guitar," in *The Oxford Handbook of Country Music*, ed. Travis D. Stimeling (New York: Oxford University Press, 2017), 177–204.

7. The Country Music Hall of Fame and Museum, for instance, regularly hosts a "Nashville Cats" series in which session musicians, producers, and songwriters are interviewed for a public audience; their colleagues are frequently in the audience for these events.

8. Rare examples can be found in the recording of Patsy Cline's "Crazy" (1961), for which Owen Bradley dedicated a three-hour session to the vocals, and Bob Dylan's *Blonde on Blonde* (1966), which found the band doing more than a dozen takes on some songs (Mick Buck and John W. Rumble, eds., *Patsy Cline: Crazy for Loving You* [Nashville: Country Music Foundation Press, 2012], 56; personal notes on session recordings for *Blonde on Blonde*, Bob Dylan Archives, New York, May 24, 2016).

9. A great example of this can be found in Alan B. Krueger and Alexandre Mas, "Strikes, Scabs, and Tread Separations: Labor Strife and the Production of Defective Bridgestone/Firestone Tires," National Bureau of Economic Research, NBER Working Paper Series, Working Paper 9524, http://www.nber.org/papers/w9524 (posted February 2003; last accessed July 2, 2018).

10. Gordon Stoker, interview with Douglas B. Green, November 22, 1974, Country Music Foundation Oral History Project, OH 179.

11. Folklorist Joe Wilson, for instance, has suggested that these efforts to reach the middle class were ultimately detrimental to the musical tradition, arguing that "there was a determination in the industry to make music that would be palatable to a huge percentage of the population. In order to do that, you added 'doowah' choruses a la the Jordanaires—who were in tremendous use at that time—and the string section of the Nashville Symphony. You cut off all the sharp edges. You 'packaged it.'

"Country music stopped being a rural music form. Above all, they wanted to get rid of songs about mama dying and other emotional material that just scared the hell out of those middle class, plastic-eared people they wanted to sell to. But I happened to like those sharp edges that were being rounded off" (Joe Wilson, *Lucky Joe's Namesake: The Extraordinary Life and Observations of Joe Wilson*, ed. Fred Bartenstein [Knoxville: University of Tennessee Press, 2017], 17).

12. Richard A. Peterson, "The Dialectic of Hard-Core and Soft-Shell Country Music," in *Reading Country Music: Steel Guitars, Opry Stars, and Honky-Tonk Bars*, ed.

Cecelia Tichi (Durham, NC: Duke University Press, 1998), 234–255; Travis D. Stimeling, "Taylor Swift's 'Pitch Problem' and the Place of Adolescent Girls in Country Music," in *Country Boys and Redneck Women: New Essays in Gender and Country Music* (Jackson: University Press of Mississippi, 2016), 84–101.

13. Susan McClary, *Feminine Endings: Music, Gender, and Sexuality* (Minneapolis: University of Minnesota Press, 1991), 80–111.

14. I borrow the terms "uptown" and "downhome" from Joli Jensen, *The Nashville Sound: Authenticity, Commercialization, and Country Music* (Nashville: Country Music Foundation Press and Vanderbilt University Press, 1998), 21–37.

15. Price's recordings from the mid-1950s commonly feature the harmony vocals of guitarist Clifton Howard "Van Howard" Vandevender (Rich Kienzle, liner notes for *Ray Price and the Cherokee Cowboys* [Bear Family BCD 15843 JK, 1995], 18; Richard Weize and Rich Kienzle, "Ray Price: The Bullet & Columbia Discography (1950–1966), in *Ray Price and the Cherokee Cowboys* [Bear Family BCD 15843 JK, 1995], 64, 66–67).

16. Steve Eng, "Anita Kerr/Anita Kerr Singers," in *The Encyclopedia of Country Music*, 2nd ed., eds. Paul Kingsbury, Michael McCall, and John W. Rumble (New York: Oxford University Press, 2012), 262–263. These groups included the Marijohn Singers (led by songwriter and publisher Marijohn Wilkins and featuring arranger Bergen White from time to time) and the Nashville Edition (founded by Joe Babcock), which reached millions of American households through its contributions to the syndicated television show *Hee Haw*. Among others, consult Joe Babcock, interview with Morris Levy, March 15, 1996, Morris Levy Interviews, ARC-0487, Box 1, Folder 5, Rock and Roll Hall of Fame Archives; Bergen White, telephone interview with author, September 5, 2014.

17. Available discographical information does not indicate who the backing vocalists on this session were (Richard Weize, Michel Ruppli, Phil Watson, Praguefrank, Kirk McMillan, Steve Hathaway, Vaclav Zpatecka, and Tore Brennoden, "Stonewall Jackson," Praguefrank's Country Music Discographies, http://countrydiscoghraphy2.blogspot.com/2015/08/stonewall-jackson.html [posted August 1, 2015; last accessed June 27, 2018]).

18. For more background on the function of hooks, consult Gary Burns, "A Typology of 'Hooks' in Popular Records," *Popular Music* 6, no. 1 (January 1987): 1–20; Peter Mercer-Taylor, "Two-and-a-Half Centuries in the Life of a Hook," *Popular Music and Society* 23, no. 2 (Summer 1999): 1–15.

19. The session was held on April 5, 1961 (Richard Weize, "The Discography: 1961–1966," in *Don Gibson: The Singer, The Songwriter: 1961–1966* [Bear Family BCD 15664 DI, 1991], 18).

20. Jocelyn R. Neal, "The Metric Makings of a Country Hit," in *Reading Country Music: Steel Guitars, Opry Stars, and Honky-Tonk Bars*, ed. Cecelia Tichi (Durham, NC: Duke University Press, 1998), 322–337.

21. Notable exceptions include Connie Smith, who was paired with the Anita Kerr Singers for her early sessions with Decca, and Dottie West, whose RCA work often includes them, as well.

22. Jada Watson, "Toward a Data-Driven Analysis of Gender Representation in *Billboard* Country Songs Chart, 1985–Present," paper presented at the International Country Music Conference, Nashville, TN, June 2017; *idem*, "'Girl on the Billboard': Changing *Billboard* Methodologies and Ecological Diversity in Hot Country Songs," paper presented at International Association for the Study of Popular Music—US Branch, Nashville, TN, March 2018; *idem*, "Changing *Billboard* Methodologies and Ecological Diversity in Hot Country Songs," paper presented at International Country Music Conference, Belmont University, June 2018.

23. Johnny Wright, interview with Charles Wolfe, July 15, 1987, WOLFE-01074, Side 2, Charles K. Wolfe Audio Collection, Center for Popular Music, Middle Tennessee State University, Murfreesboro, TN. See also Stephanie Vander Wel, "'I Am a Honky-Tonk Girl': Country Music, Gender, and Migration, Ph.D. dissertation, University of California at Los Angeles, 2008, 215–220. And for a broader discussion of voice and vocality in country music, consult, among others, Richard Leppert and George Lipsitz, "'Everybody's Lonesome for Somebody': Age, the Body, and Experience in the Music of Hank Williams," *Popular Music* 9, no. 3 (October 1990): 259–274; David Brackett, *Interpreting Popular Music* (Cambridge: Cambridge University Press, 1995; reprint ed., Berkeley: University of California Press, 2000), 75–107; Robynn J. Stilwell, "Vocal Decorum: Voice, Body, and Knowledge in the Prodigious Singer, Brenda Lee," in *She's So Fine: Reflections of Whiteness, Femininity, Adolescence, and Class in 1960s Music*, ed. Laurie Stras (Burlington, VT: Ashgate, 2010), 57–88; Travis D. Stimeling, "Taylor Swift's 'Pitch Problem' and the Place of Adolescent Girls in Country Music," in *Country Boys and Redneck Women: New Essays in Gender and Country Music*, eds. Diane Pecknold and Kristine McCusker (Jackson: University Press of Mississippi, 2016), 84–101; Stephanie Vander Wel, "The Singing Voice in Country Music," in *The Oxford Handbook of Country Music*, ed. Travis D. Stimeling (New York: Oxford University Press, 2017), 157–175.

24. Michael Streissguth, *Voices of the Country: Interviews with Classic Country Performers* (New York: Routledge, 2004), 58. Cline biographer Douglas Gomery suggests, though, that Bradley may have chosen to use the Jordanaires because they "had helped Elvis make hits; perhaps, Bradley reasoned, they could do the same for Patsy Cline" (Douglas Gomery, *Patsy Cline: The Making of an Icon* [Bloomington: Trafford, 2011], 177).

25. Interestingly, no backing vocalists are credited in the discographical record (Richard Weize, "Discography," in *Orbison* [Bear Family BC 16423 GL, 2001], 76).

26. For more background on the influence of Latin American musical styles on the US popular music styles of the 1950s, consult John Storm Roberts, *The Latin Tinge: The Impact of Latin American Music on the United States*, 2nd ed. (New York: Oxford University Press, 1999), 127–159.

27. This session was held on May 21, 1957 (Michel Ruppli, Praguefrank, Larry Davis, Henk Scholts, Chris Huskey, Michal Gololobov, Kittra Moore, Thieu Van De Vorst, Bernd Siegemund, Phil Watson, Rog Peyton, "Ferlin Husky, Part 1," Praguefranks Country Music Discographies, http://countrydiscoghraphy2.blogspot.com/2016/03/ferlin-husky-part-1.html [posted March 23, 2016; last accessed June 26, 2018]).

28. Anita Kerr, qtd. in Michael Streissguth, *Voices of the Country: Interviews with Classic Country Performers* (New York: Routledge, 2004), 56–57.

29. Kerr, qtd. in Streissguth, *Voices of the Country*, 57–58.

30. Kerr, qtd. in Streissguth, *Voices of the Country*, 58.

31. Kerr, qtd. in Streissguth, *Voices of the Country*, 64.

32. Steve Eng, for instance, notes that the lack of credits may have led to Kerr's decision to leave Nashville (Eng, "Anita Kerr/Anita Kerr Singers," 262–263.

33. Ernst Mikael Jørgensen and Erik Rasmussen, "Sessionography," in liner notes for *Elvis: The King of Rock 'n' Roll—The Complete 50's Masters* (RCA 07863 66050-2, 1992), n.p.

34. The session was held on March 23, 1961, and featured a mixture of Nashville and Los Angeles session musicians (Praguefrank, Bill Daniels, and Kurt Rokitta, "Elvis Presley, Part 1," Praguefrank's Country Music Discographies, http://countrydiscoghraphy2.blogspot.com/2016/05/elvis-presley-part-1.html [posted May 29, 2016; last accessed June 27, 2018]).

35. The Lovin' Spoonful, "Nashville Cats" (Kama Sutra 219, 1966).

36. Ray Edenton, interview with Morris Levy, February 8, 1996, Morris Levy Interviews, ARC-0487, Box 1, Folder 5, Rock and Roll Hall of Fame Archives.

37. Jerry Kennedy, interview with Morris Levy, January 16, 1996, Morris Levy Interviews, ARC-0487, Box 2, Folder 1, Rock and Roll Hall of Fame Archives; Harold Bradley, interview with Morris Levy, February 22 or 23, 1996, Morris Levy Interviews, Box 1, Folder 2, Rock and Roll Hall of Fame Archives; Harold Bradley, interview with author, August 1, 2014.

38. Charles Wolfe and John W. Rumble, "Jack Shook," in *The Encyclopedia of Country Music*, 2nd ed., eds. Paul Kingsbury, Michael McCall, and John W. Rumble (New York: Oxford University Press, 2012), 461. For more information on Shook's work with Williams, consult Bob Pinson's discography, published as an appendix to Colin Escott, *Hank Williams: The Biography* (New York: Back Bay Books, 2004), 332–336, 344–347.

39. Bradley, interview with Morris Levy, Febraury 22 or 23, 1996.

40. Wolfe and Rumble, "Jack Shook."

41. Rich Kienzle, "Ray Edenton: Nashville Studio Rhythm Specialist," *Guitar Player* (May 1981): 76–77; David Simons, "Ray Edenton's 'A-Team' Memories," *The Country Music Journal* no. 55 (June–July 2000): 11.

42. Simons, "Ray Edenton's 'A-Team' Memories," 11.

43. Ray and Polly Edenton, interview with author, August 3, 2014.

44. Ray and Polly Edenton, interview with author, August 3, 2014.

45. For more on this phenomenon, consult Albin J. Zak III, *I Don't Sound like Nobody: Remaking Music in 1950s America* (Ann Arbor: University of Michigan Press, 2010).

46. Rich Kienzle notes that this tuning had been used by "western swing bandleader Hank Penny . . . in the late '30s, but it had largely been forgotten" (Kienzle, "Ray Edenton," 77). In our conversation, Edenton noted that "I might've stole it from somebody else. Hell, I don't know. We stole from everybody" (Ray and Polly Edenton, interview with author, August 3, 2014).

47. See, for example, Richard Johnston and Dick Boak, *Martin Guitars: A Technical Reference* (Milwaukee: Hal Leonard, 2009), 110–113.

48. Simons, "Ray Edenton's 'A-Team' Memories," 11.

49. Kienzle, "Ray Edenton," 77.

50. Paula Jean Bishop, "The Roots and Influences of the Everly Brothers," Ph.D. dissertation, Boston University, 2011, 154–156; Dale Turner, "Hole Notes with Dale Turner: The Signature Open-G-Tuned Rhythm Style of Don Everly," *Guitar World* (April 21, 2014), https://www.guitarworld.com/uncategorized/hole-notes-dale-turner-signature-open-g-tuned-rhythm-style-don-everly (last accessed November 28, 2017).

51. Simons, "Ray Edenton's 'A-Team' Memories," 12; Richard Weize, "The Everly Brothers Columbia & Cadence Discography," in liner notes to *Classic Everly Brothers* (Bear Family BCD 15618 CI, 1992), 35–37; Andrew Sandoval, Russ Wapensky, and Richard Weize, "The Everly Brothers, 1960–1965 Warner Bros. Discography," in liner notes to *The Everly Brothers: The Price of Fame* (Bear Family BCD 16511 GL, 2005), 134–140.

52. Kienzle, "Ray Edenton," 78; Simons, "Ray Edenton's 'A-Team' Memories," 12.

53. Edenton's manufacturer and setup preferences can be found in Kienzle, "Ray Edenton," 78. His Fender acoustic is currently housed in the Musicians Hall of Fame in Nashville.

54. Kienzle, "Ray Edenton, 78 (interpolation in original).

55. Of Lynn Anderson's "Rose Garden," Edenton told Simons: "Remember the song 'I Never Promised You a Rose Garden?' Remember that intro? Glenn Sutton, who was married to Lynn Anderson, was producing her session. I was there playing rhythm that day, and Glenn comes over to me and says, 'Can you give me an Everly Brothers intro for this song?' So I'm trying to come up with something that will please him, but I know it's got to be something fast—because that's what an Everly riff would be like. So I just pulled off that opening lick on the guitar—putting it in that 'blue beat'—and they just copied it for fiddle. And there it was. So I owe that one to Don Everly" (Simons, "Ray Edenton's 'A-Team' Memories," 12). Guitarist Chip Young, though, claimed that he was the one who presented the distinctive upstroke rhythm to the band during that session (Chip Young, interview with Morris Levy, December 18, 1997, Morris Levy Interviews, ARC-0487, Box 3, Folder 2, Rock and Roll Hall of Fame Library and Archives).

 Edenton's work with Smith is discussed in detail in Chapter 3. His contributions to Hamilton IV's recordings are documented in Richard Weize, "George Hamilton IV: The Canadian Discography," liner notes for *George Hamilton IV: My North Country Home* (Bear Family BCD 17146 CH, 2011), 44–50.

56. Ray and Polly Edenton, interview with author, August 3, 2014.

57. Kienzle, "Ray Edenton," 77.

58. Charlie McCoy with Travis D. Stimeling, *Fifty Cents and a Box Top: The Creative Life of Nashville Session Musician Charlie McCoy* (Morgantown: West Virginia University Press, 2017), 159–161.

59. This footage can be found in Les Blank, dir., *A Poem Is a Naked Person* (Les Blank Films, 1974; released 2015).

60. I take the term "soundmark" from the field of acoustic ecology: "A term derived from 'landmark' used in soundscape studies to refer to a community sound which is unique, or possesses qualities which make it specially regarded or noticed by the people in that community" (Barry Truax, ed., *Handbook for Acoustic Ecology*, 2nd ed. [Burnaby, BC: Cambridge Street, 1999], https://www.sfu.ca/sonic-studio/handbook/Soundmark.html [last accessed June 27, 2018]).

61. Charles K. Wolfe, *Kentucky Country: Folk and Country Music of Kentucky* (Lexington: University Press of Kentucky, 1982), 130–132; Michael Cochran, "American Icon: The Musical Journey of Chet Atkins," in *Chet Atkins: Certified Guitar Player* (Nashville: Country Music Foundation Press, 2011), 13–17.

62. Cochran, "American Icon," 17–20.

63. Cochran, "American Icon," 20.

64. Cochran, "American Icon," 20–23

65. Ray Edenton, qtd. in John W. Rumble, "Chet Atkins: Producer, RCA's Man in Nashville," in *Chet Atkins: Certified Guitar Player*, ed. John W. Rumble (Nashville: Country Music Foundation Press, 2011), 81.

66. Rich Kienzle, "Chet Atkins, Guitarist: The Sound, the Style, the Influence," in *Chet Atkins: Certified Guitar Player*, ed. John W. Rumble (Nashville: Country Music Foundation, 2011), 32–33.

67. For more background on Muhlenberg County thumb-picking, consult Dylan Schorer, Jim Ohlschmidt, and Thom Bresh, "Travis Style: The Life and Legacy of Thumbpicking King Merle Travis," *Acoustic Guitar* 9 (December 1998): 52–63; "A Thumb Pickers Family Tree: Seminal Sources for Muhlenberg County, Kentucky Guitar Style from Shultz and Jones to Atkins," *Journal of Country Music* 22, no. 1 (2001): 25; Erika Brady, "Contested Origins: Arnold Schultz and the Music of Western Kentucky," in *Hidden in the Mix: The African American Presence in Country Music*, ed. Diane Pecknold (Durham, NC: Duke University Press, 2013), 100–118.

68. Kienzle, "Chet Atkins, Guitarist," 32, 34; Steve Waksman, *Instruments of Desire: The Electric Guitar and the Shaping of Musical Experience* (Cambridge: Harvard University Press, 1999), 88–94.

69. Rich Kienzle, "Hank Garland: Legendary Country Jazz Artist," *Guitar Player* (January 1981), 77.

70. Kienzle, "Hank Garland," 77; Bradley, interview with author, August 1, 2014.

71. Bob Moore, qtd. in Kienzle, "Hank Garland," 77.

72. Bob Moore, qtd. in Kienzle, "Hank Garland," 78.

73. Burton joined Garland, Atkins, Boots Randolph, Brenton Bolden Banks (on piano), Bob Moore, and Buddy Harman on the RCA Victor album *After the Riot at Newport* (RCA LPM-2302, 1960). He also contributed to Hank Garland's album *Jazz Winds from a New Direction* (Columbia CL1572/CS8372, 1961) and was signed by Atkins to a contract with RCA Victor. For more background, consult Rich Kienzle's liner notes to the Bear Family reissue (BCD 15447, 1999); *idem*, "For Gary Burton, It Started in Nashville. Really," *Community Voices*, http://communityvoices.post-gazette.com/arts-entertainment-living/get-rhythm/item/

37465-for-gary-burton-it-started-in-nashville-really (posted October 3, 2013; last accessed June 28, 2018).

74. Kienzle, "Hank Garland," 78, 80.

75. Kienzle notes, though, that Garland was not as comfortable with these styles as he was with country and jazz (Kienzle, "Hank Garland," 80).

76. Kienzle, "Hank Garland," 76.

77. "The Train Kept a-Rollin'" was recorded in Nashville on July 2, 1956 (Richard Weize, Praguefrank, Bill Daniels, Tony Watson, Dik De Heer, and Stuart Colman, "Johnny Burnette," *Praguefrank's Country Music Discographies*, http://country-discography.blogspot.com/2009/09/johnny-burnette.html [posted September 29, 2009; last accessed June 28, 2018]).

78. Charlie McCoy makes this observation in David Barrett, "Charlie McCoy Interview Snippet for BluesHarmonica.com with David Barrett," https://www.youtube.com/watch?v=UPaZenhUhGE (posted August 30, 2013; last accessed June 28, 2018).

79. Charlie McCoy noted that, when he was called upon to play on Bob Dylan's "Desolation Row," he "was playing a very poor imitation of Grady Martin's classical guitar sound. Grady inspired every guitarist who ever heard him, and, like everyone else, I did my best to play like him. The notes could be copied, but Grady's impeccable taste was all his own" (McCoy with Stimeling, *Fifty Cents and a Box Top*, 81). See also Diane Diekman, *Twentieth Century Drifter: The Life of Marty Robbins* (Urbana: University of Illinois Press, 2012), 68.

80. Waksman, *Instruments of Desire*, 85.

81. Waksman, *Instruments of Desire*, 85–86.

82. McCoy with Stimeling, *Fifty Cents and a Box Top*, 54–55.

83. Jerry Kennedy, interview with Morris Levy, January 16, 1996, Morris Levy Interviews, ARC-0487, Box 2, Folder 1, Rock and Roll Hall of Fame Library and Archives.

84. Jerry Kennedy, qtd. in Jennifer Ember Pierce, *Playin' Around: The Lives and Careers of Famous Session Musicians* (Lanham, MD: Scarecrow Press, 1998), 88. For more background on the *Louisiana Hayride*, consult Tracey E. W. Laird, *The Louisiana Hayride: Radio and Roots Music along the Red River* (New York: Oxford University Press, 2014).

85. Pierce, *Playin' Around*, 89; Kennedy, interview with Morris Levy, January 16, 1996.

86. Kennedy, interview with Morris Levy, January 16, 1996. For more background on Sam Phillips, Philips Electronics, and Mercury Records, consult Michael Kosser, *How Nashville Became Music City, U.S.A.* (Milwaukee: Hal Leonard, 2006), 58–65; Peter Guralnick, *Sam Phillips: The Man Who Invented Rock 'n' Roll* (New York: Little, Brown, 2015), 465–477.

87. Kennedy, qtd. in Pierce, *Playin' Along*, 92.

88. Kennedy, interview with Morris Levy, January 16, 1996.

89. Pierce, *Playin' Along*, 62–63.

90. Michael Bertrand, *Race, Rock, and Elvis* (Urbana: University of Illinois Press, 2000); Charles Hughes, *Country Soul: Making Music and Making Race in the American South* (Chapel Hill: University of North Carolina Press, 2015), 16–18.

91. Reggie Young, qtd. in Pierce, *Playin' Along*, 63.

92. Pierce, *Playin' Along*, 63–64.

93. Pierce, *Playin' Along*, 65–67.

94. Hughes, *Country Soul*, 2.

95. Roben Jones, *Memphis Boys: The Story of American Studios* (Jackson: University Press of Mississippi, 2010).

96. Young, qtd. in Pierce, *Playin' Along*, 68–69.

97. Young, qtd. in Pierce, *Playin' Along*, 71.

98. For more background on this phenomenon, consult Jay Orr, ed., *Dylan, Cash, and the Nashville Cats: A New Music City* (Nashville: Country Music Foundation Press, 2015).

99. Young, qtd. in Pierce, *Playin' Along*, 71–72.

100. Young, qtd. in Pierce, *Playin' Along*, 72–73.

101. Young told Pierce that he began charging double scale in January 1979 with the full support of his guitarist colleagues (Young, qtd. in Pierce, *Playin' Along*, 73).

102. For more background on western swing and its many varieties, consult, among others: Rich Kienzle, *Southwest Shuffle: Pioneers of Honky-Tonk, Western Swing, and Country Jazz* (New York: Routledge, 2003), esp. 3–79; Jean A. Boyd, *The Jazz of the Southwest: An Oral History of Western Swing* (Austin: University of Texas Press, 1998); *idem, Dance All Night: Those Other Southwestern Swing Bands, Past and Present* (Lubbock: Texas Tech University Press, 2012).

103. For more background on Mullican, consult Kienzle, *Southwest Shuffle*, 114; Jon Hartley Fox, *King of the Queen City: The Story of King Records* (Urbana: University of Illinois Press, 2009), 74–78; Ryan Brasseaux, *Cajun Breakdown: The Emergence of an American Made Music* (New York: Oxford University Press, 2009), 166–169; David Sanjek, "What's Syd Got to Do with It?: King Records, Henry Glover, and the Complex Achievement of Crossover," in *Hidden in the Mix: The African American Presence in Country Music*, ed. Diane Pecknold (Durham, NC: Duke University Press, 2013), 306–338.

104. Scott Healy, "Hammond B-3 Basics for Pianists," *Keyboard* (April 27, 2010), https://www.keyboardmag.com/lessons/hammond-b-3-basics-for-pianists (last accessed June 28, 2018).

105. A television ad for one of these collections can be found at https://www.youtube.com/watch?v=pdU77wy_f-M (posted December 17, 2011; last accessed June 28, 2018).

106. Rich Kienzle, "Floyd Cramer, 1933–1997," *Country Music* (March–April 1998): 54.

107. Kienzle, "Floyd Cramer," 54; Colin Escott, notes to *Jim Reeves: Welcome to My World* (Bear Family BCD 15656 PI), 7. For broader context, consult Laird, *Louisiana Hayride*, 103–115.

108. Kienzle, "Floyd Cramer," 54.

109. Shelton, Alan. "Chet Atkins and the Nashville Sound," *Country Music World* no. 10 (August 5–18, 1981): 27.

110. "Top Billing Signs Floyd Cramer," *Country Music Telegram* (July 1978): 3.

111. Kienzle, "Floyd Cramer," 54.

112. Maybelle Carter interview, unknown date, WOLFE-00961, Side 1, Charles K. Wolfe Audio Collection, Center for Popular Music, Middle Tennessee State University, Murfreesboro, TN.

113. Kienzle, "Floyd Cramer," 54. See also Chet Atkins, qtd. in Michael Jarrett, *Producing Country: The Inside Story of the Great Recordings* (Middletown, CT: Wesleyan University Press, 2014), 67; John W. Rumble, "Chet Atkins: Producer—RCA's Man in Nashville," in *Chet Atkins: Certified Guitar Player*, ed. John W. Rumble (Nashville: Country Music Foundation Press, 2011), 80.

114. Keyboardist Tom Brislin, offering a lesson on the Cramer style, observes three principal manners in which Cramer deployed the "slip note" approach. He argues that "the basics of the Floyd Cramer style are simple. On a major triad, start with the root, the second, and the fifth, and slip up from the second to the third . . . , as opposed to slipping up from the minor third. . . . When playing the fifth of a major triad with the root above it, slip up to the sixth. . . . With both licks you can slip right back down, too . . . " (Tom Brislin, "The Floyd Cramer Style," *Keyboard* [September 2008]: 37).

   Robert L. Doerschuk also notes that the Cramer style consists of more than the slip note, but is also tied intimately to particular chord voicings: "Just as trees from tiny acorns grow, so does the improvisational language of country piano evolve from the Floyd Lick. By placing a pair of consecutive notes below a single stationary note, this figure suggests an approach to harmony based on the droning effect cultivated by fiddlers and banjo players long before us uppity keyboard types were allowed to sink our hands into the country stewpot. . . .

   "In the traditional Western diatonic scale, drones generally settle onto the octave or the 5th, and tend to work better in major keys. A major third, when played against an accompanimental drone on the 5th note of the scale, can stir emotions that range from mournful to intimate and homey, much as a minor 3rd can in a blues context. Consider the moan of a 'lonesome' train whistle; depending on what neighborhood your imagination inhabits, you're probably hearing it as either a minor 3rd above a root (blues) or an open 5th above a major 3rd with no root (country)" (Robert L. Doerschuk, "Beyond Floyd: The Harmonic Convergence," *Keyboard* [March 1993]: 118).

115. Arie den Dulk, Kurt Rokitta, and Richard Weize, "Jim Reeves: The Discography," in liner notes for *Jim Reeves: Welcome to My World* (Bear Family BCD 15656 PI, 1994), 96. On the use of "implied conversation" in country songwriting, consult Jocelyn R. Neal, "Narrative Paradigms, Musical Signifiers, and Form as Function in Country Music," *Music Theory Spectrum* 29 (2007): 46, 46n19.

116. McCoy with Stimeling, *Fifty Cents and a Box Top*, 71–73.

117. This session was held in December 1957, but no specific date is available in the discographical records (Richard Weize, "Marvin Rainwater: The Discography," in liner notes for *Marvin Rainwater: Classic Recordings* [Bear Family BCD 15600 DI, 2007], n.p.).

118. This session was held on January 6, 1958 (Michel Ruppli, Richard Weize, Mario Manciotti, Praguefrank, Pierre Monnery, Dave Sax, Bernd Siegmund, Carl LaFong, Thieu Van De Vorst, Bill Daniels, and Wade Falcon, "Jimmy Newman,"

Praguefrank's Country Music Discographies, http://countrydiscoghraphy2. blogspot.com/2015/11/jimmy-newman.html [posted November 30, 2015, last accessed June 29, 2018]).

119. Praguefrank, Richard Weize, Mario Manciotti, and Kittra Moore, "Janis Martin," Praguefrank's Country Music Discographies, http://countrydiscography.blogspot. com/2013/01/janis-martin.html [posted January 21, 2013; last accessed June 29, 2018]).

120. Bill Pursell, interview with Terry Klefstad, February 22, 2013 (cited with the permission of the interviewer). Pursell told the same story in an interview with Klefstad, April 16, 2012.

121. Douglas B. Green, "Hargus 'Pig' Robbins: Top Nashville Studio Pianist," *Contemporary Keyboard* (July 1977): 20.

122. For more background (with a particular focus on the experiences of African American men), consult Terry Rowden, *The Songs of Blind Folk: African American Musicians and the Cultures of Blindness* (Ann Arbor: University of Michigan Press, 2009), esp. 1–14, 65–84.

123. Such practices continue today, although with significant differences between musical communities. See, for instance, Joseph Michael Abramo and Amy Elizabeth Pierce, "An Ethnographic Case Study of Music Learning at a School for the Blind," *Bulletin of the Council for Research in Music Education* no. 195 (Winter 2013): 18–19; Hyu-Yong Park and Mi-Jung Kim, "Affordance of Braille Music as a Mediational Means: Significance and Limitations," *British Journal of Music Education* 31, no. 2 (July 2014): 137–155.

124. For a detailed critique of this narrative, consult Sami Schalk, "Reevaluating the Supercrip," *Journal of Literary & Cultural Disability Studies* 10, no. 1 (2016): 71–86.

125. For more background on the "trainer" system, consult Lynn Abbot and Doug Seroff, *To Do This, You Must Know How* (Jackson: University Press of Mississippi, 2012).

126. Dewald van Deventer, "The Problems and Possibilities of Music Score Access for Blind Pianists: A Qualitative Account," *Musicus: A South African Journal for Music Teaching/'n Suid-Afrikaanse tydskrif vir musiekonderwys* 39, no. 1 (2011): 55–65.

127. Hargus "Pig" Robbins, qtd. in Douglas B. Green, "Hargus 'Pig' Robbins: Top Nashville Studio Pianist," *Contemporary Keyboard* (July 1977): 20.

128. Robbins, qtd. in Green, "Hargus 'Pig' Robbins," 20.

129. Green, "Hargus 'Pig' Robbins," 20.

130. Robbins, qtd. in Green, "Hargus 'Pig' Robbins," 20.

131. Robbins, qtd. in Green, "Hargus 'Pig' Robbins," 20. Robbins continues to record occasionally at the time of this writing (June 2018). See, for instance: Trigger, "An Ode to Robby Turner: Country Music's Man of Steel," *Saving Country Music* (posted January 4, 2016), https://www.savingcountrymusic.com/an-ode-to-robby-turner-country-musics-man-of-steel/ (last accessed June 29, 2018).

132. Green, "Hargus 'Pig' Robbins," 20.

133. The terms "hammer-on" and "pull-off" are widely attributed to Pete Seeger, who used the terms in his 1954 book *How to Play the 5-String Banjo*.

134. The recording was released in 1973, but the session was held on November 28, 1972 (Praguefrank, Michel Ruppli, Bill Daniels, Mario Manciotti, Richard Weize, Kurt

Rokitta, Phil Watson, Dik De Heer, Rene Pavlik, Ed Moench, Carl G. Cederblad, and Thieu Van DeVorst, "Charlie Rich," Praguefrank's Country Music Discographies, <http://countrydiscoghraphy2.blogspot.com/2015/04/charlie-rich.html> [posted April 12, 2015; last accessed June 29, 2018]). For more background on how the song came to Rich's attention, consult Lawrence Cohn, qtd. in Jarrett, *Producing Country*, 138–139.

135. Robbins, qtd. in Green, "Hargus 'Pig' Robbins," 20.

136. This extra bass sound may have been the product of the placement of the musicians in the studio. As engineer Lou Bradley indicated in an interview for *Mix* magazine, "The straight side of that piano, the bass side, was pushed up against a low divider between it and the drums—Jerry Carrigan was the drummer on that session. . . . Later, we made that wall higher, but at that time it was no higher than the piano. Henry Strzelecki's [electric] bass was also next to the piano—the bass and drums were under a shed that came out—and behind the piano and by that bass was a 6-string tic-tac bass guitar; Tommy Allsup played that" (Lou Bradley, qtd. in Barbara Schultz, "Classic Tracks: Charlie Rich 'Behind Closed Doors,'" *Mix* (September 1, 2011), https://www.mixonline.com/recording/classic-tracks-charlie-rich-behind-closed-doors-366297 (last accessed June 29, 2018).

An October 1973 *Time* magazine profile of Billy Sherrill noted that this sense of rhythm was essential to his success, observing that "Sherrill has no formula for that sound, but defines his stock in trade as feeling with a beat" ("The Sherrill Sound," *Time* [October 22, 1973], 85). A detailed description of the recording session and overdubs for "Stand by Your Man" can be found in Jimmy McDonough, *Tammy Wynette: Tragic Country* Queen (New York: Penguin Books, 2010), 160–163. For additional background, consult Jack Isenhour, *He Stopped Loving Her Today: George Jones, Billy Sherrill, and the Pretty-Much Totally True Story of the Making of the Greatest Country Record of All Time* (Jackson: University Press of Mississippi, 2011), 120–126; Charles Hughes, *Country Soul: Making Music and Making Race in the American South* (Chapel Hill: University of North Carolina Press, 2015), 171–174.

137. Young, interview with Morris Levy, December 18, 1997. For more background on this song, consult Bobby Braddock's recollections quoted in Jarrett, *Producing Country*, 155–156.

138. Green, "Hargus 'Pig' Robbins," 20.

139. J. Lester Feder, "'Song of the South': Country Music, Race, Region, and the Politics of Culture, 1920–1974," Ph.D. dissertation, University of California at Los Angeles, 2006, 148–191; Matthew D. Sutton, "Act Naturally: Charley Pride, Autobiography, and the 'Accidental Career,'" in *Country Boys and Redneck Women: New Essays in Gender and Country Music*, eds. Diane Pecknold and Kristine M. McCusker (Jackson: University Press of Mississippi, 2016), 44–63.

140. See, for instance, Brian F. Wright, "'A Bastard Instrument': The Fender Precision Bass, Monk Montgomery, and Jazz in the 1950s," *Jazz Perspectives* 8, no. 3 (December 2014): 281–303.

141. This phenomenon is particularly audible in many bluegrass recordings, particularly those recorded for local and regional labels.

142. For more background on the construction and wiring of RCA's facilities, consult Bill Porter, interview with John W. Rumble, February 23, 1994, Nashville, TN, *idem*, April 6, 1995, Nashville, TN, Country Music Foundation Oral History Collection, Country Music Foundation Library, OHC 190; *idem*, June 8, 1994, Nashville, TN, Country Music Foundation Oral History Collection, Country Music Foundation Library, OHC 228; *idem*, November 11, 1994, Fisherville, KY, Country Music Foundation Oral History Collection, Country Music Foundation Library, OHC 229; *idem*, November 13, 1994, Fisherville, KY, Country Music Foundation Oral History Collection, Country Music Foundation Library, OHC 230-LC; *idem*, April 6, 1995, Nashville, TN, Country Music Foundation Oral History Collection, Country Music Foundation Library, OHC 231; *idem*, September 13, 1995, Fisherville, KY, Country Music Foundation Oral History Collection, Country Music Foundation Library, OHC 232.

143. The term "sweet" jazz is a highly contentious one in jazz scholarship, but one that remains in usage today. See, for instance, Christopher Wilkinson, "Sweet Dance Music," *Grove Music Online*, June 29, 2018, http://www.oxford-musiconline.com/grovemusic/view/10.1093/gmo/9781561592630.001.0001/omo-9781561592630-e-1002276633.

144. Rich Kienzle, "First Bass: Bob Moore Has Witnessed and Made Music History Holding Down the Bottom End for Nashville's Studio A-Team," *No Depression* 77 (2009): 38–42.

145. Michael McCall, "Nashville Cats: Salute to Bob Moore," Country Music Hall of Fame and Museum, http://www.countrymusichalloffame.org/nashville-cats/bob-moore, posted February 17, 2007, last accessed October 18, 2017.

146. McCall, "Nashville Cats: Salute to Bob Moore"; Kienzle, "First Bass," 40–42.

147. Kienzle, "First Bass," 38.

148. Kienzle, "First Bass," 38.

149. Harold Bradley, interview with Morris Levy, February 22 or 23, 1996, ARC-0487, Rock and Roll Hall of Fame Archives and Library, Cleveland, OH.

150. Dave Roe, "Bob Moore, Music City Maven," *Bass Player* (August 2, 2011) http://www.bassplayer.com/artists/1171/bob-moore-music-city-maven/26503 (last accessed October 22, 2017).

151. In that same interview with Dave Roe, Moore notes that he was a particular fan of the RCA 44 ribbon microphone for recording the bass because "it just has such a nice, complete sound, without a lot of biting highs." He also noted a fondness for the "older Telefunken mics, as well, although I can't recall the model numbers" (Roe, "Bob Moore, Music City Maven").

152. Richard Weize, Michel Ruppli, Paul McPhail, Mario Manciotti, Praguefrank, Kittra Moore, Stephen Ford, and Phil Watson, "Conway Twitty—Part 1," *Praguefrank's Country Music Discographies* (posted March 27, 2011), http://countrydiscography.blogspot.com/2011/03/conway-twitty-part-1_27.html, last accessed August 27, 2018.

153. Harold Bradley, interview with John Rumble, May 14, 1991, Country Music Foundation Library, OHC-35. Bradley confirmed this in an interview with me in August 2014, noting that the tic-tac "gave you a click, and it also gave you a note,

and on a transistor radio, that note became important to my brother. He wanted that bass all the time" (Harold Bradley, interview with author, August 1, 2014, transcript, p. 9).

154. Bradley, interview with John Rumble, May 14, 1991, transcript, p. 17, interpolations in original. Bradley observed in an interview with me: "Well, we didn't really think about it, but to make it different from what the bass was playing. He's tonic and 5th, and then he'd play a run. He did bum-bum-bum-bum, and so while we were working it out, I'd made note of where he's doing the lead-ins, and then I made sure I was playing tonic and 5th. And then I'd play in-between notes, some notes that just kind of keep the record a little more lively. . . . [I]f you take it out, you'll miss it. But anyway, I had more leeway to play not exactly fills, but lead-ins than the bass. Because if you did that on the big bass, sounds like a cannon going off over there. But with that click . . . , if you put it in with the bass and mix it, it seems like it should be there. Some of the young musicians now, when I go in to play, are not sure of what it's supposed to sound like. Sometimes, they place it in the right place on the track, and sometimes they don't" (Bradley, interview with author, August 1, 2014).

155. Bradley told Morris Levy that he and Hank Garland purchased the first two Danelectro bass guitars in Nashville from Strobel's Music sometime between 1955 and 1958 (Bradley, interview with Levy, February 22 or 23, 1996). It is worth noting that this was not the Danelectro baritone guitar commonly used in its place, but a six-string bass guitar tuned an octave lower than a standard guitar. An example of the bass that Bradley and Garland used is in the collections of the Smithsonian Institution's Museum of American History ("Danelectro Electric Bass Guitar," http://americanhistory.si.edu/collections/search/object/nmah_1301424 [last accessed June 28, 2018]).

156. Bradley, interview with author, August 1, 2014, transcript, p. 9.

157. Bradley, interview with Levy, February 22 or 23, 1996.

158. Bradley, interview with author, August 1, 2014, transcript, p. 10.

159. The session was held on March 28, 1960 (Don Roy and Richard Weize, "Discography, 1956-1962," in liner notes for *Brenda Lee: Little Miss Dynamite* (Bear Family BCD 15772 DK, 1999), 57

160. For more background on music listening practices in automobiles, consult Karin Bijsterveld, Eefje Cleophas, Stephan Krebs, and Gijs Mom, *Sound and Safe: A History of Listening behind the Wheel* (New York: Oxford University Press, 2014), 72–106.

161. Sean MacLeod, *Phil Spector: Sound of the Sixties* (Lanham, MD: Rowman & Littlefield, 2018), 46–47.

162. Flory, *I Hear a Symphony*, 256n20; Per Elias Drabløs, *The Quest for the Melodic Bass: From Jamerson to Spenner* (Aldershot, UK: Ashgate, 2015; reprint ed., New York: Routledge, 2016).

163. Geoff Emerick, *Here, There, and Everywhere: My Life Recording the Music of the Beatles* (New York: Gotham Books, 2006), 114–116. See also: Russell Reising, *"Every Sound There Is": The Beatles' Revolver and the Transformation of Rock and Roll* (Aldershot, UK: Ashgate, 2002), 26–27, 35.

164. Bradley noted that "the bass drum eventually replaced the tic-tac pretty well, because they made it with a pop. Then it's too much competition with the tic-tac and the bass drum. It takes a lot of good precision playing to be together" (Bradley, interview with author, August 1, 2014).

165. Henry Strzelecki, interview with John Rumble, March 14, 1990, Country Music Foundation Oral History Project, Country Music Foundation Library, OHC 292-LC.

166. Strzelecki, interview with John Rumble, March 14, 1990.

167. In this interview, Strzelecki was often a bit loose with dates. He notes that his arrival was in November and then later suggests that it was in December (Strzelecki, interview with Rumble, March 14, 1990).

168. Strzelecki, interview with John Rumble, March 14, 1990. Bill Pursell recalled playing at the Carousel Club with African American bassist W. O. Smith, interviews with Terry Klefstad, Nashville, TN, June 19, 2012 and September 21, 2012 (cited with permission of the interviewer).

169. Strzelecki's first session with Eddy Arnold was on February 1, 1961 (Michael D. Freda, *Eddy Arnold Discography, 1944–1996* [Westport, CT: Greenwood Press, 199], 100). See also: Michael Streissguth, *Eddy Arnold: Pioneer of the Nashville Sound* (New York: Schirmer Books, 1997),155, 186–187.

170. Strzelecki, interview with John Rumble, March 14, 1990.

171. Henry Strzelecki, interview with John Rumble, March 22, 1990, Country Music Foundation Oral History Project, Country Music Foundation Library, OHC-293, transcript, p. 7.

172. Strzelecki, interview with John Rumble, March 14, 1990, transcript, p. 31.

173. Strzelecki, interview with John Rumble, March 22, 1990, transcript, pp. 3–4.

174. He recalled that he "had a '63 [Fender] Precision [Bass], or '64, and it got stolen. Chet and I went to Canada, and on the way up to Canada we went to Chicago. We were doing a TV show up there or a performance of some type. So on the way up they stole one of his instruments. They stole his Gretsch guitar—oh, and I tried a Gretsch bass, too, by the way; I didn't like it too well—and coming back they stole my bass and his Ramirez guitar, which was a gorgeous guitar and sounded so good. It was a classical guitar. It was worth a lot of money, and somebody stole it and probably hocked it for fifty bucks. . . . Those instruments meant a lot to us. Anyway, I ended up with a Fender Jazz [bass]. The next bass I got was a Fender Jazz bass. And that's the one that I used on practically everything from there on, from about 1965 or '66 on" (Strzelecki, interview with John Rumble, June 25, 1990, transcript, p. 13).

175. For a detailed history of Fender's basses, consult J. W. Black and Albert Molinaro, *The Fender Bass: An Illustrated History* (Milwaukee: Hal Leonard, 2001).

176. Strzelecki, interview with John Rumble, June 25, 1990, transcript, p. 12.

177. Strzelecki, interview with John Rumble, June 25, 1990.

178. Strzelecki, interview with John Rumble, June 25, 1990.

179. Praguefrank, Jeremy Roberts, Michel Ruppli, Chris Huskey, Richard Weize, Mario Manciotti, and Hans Sandberg, "Jerry Reed, Part 1," *Praguefrank's Country Music*

Discographies,   http://countrydiscoghraphy2.blogspot.com/2016/06/jerry-reed-part-1.html (posted June 28, 2016; last accessed June 29, 2018).

180. As Strzelecki opined, the bass often sounded fatter in the studio and even in the final mix than it did on the actual recordings because the grooves of the LP could not handle loud bass frequencies (Strzelecki, interview with John Rumble, June 25, 1990, transcript, p. 11).

181. Strzelecki, interview with John Rumble, June 25, 1990, transcript, pp. 11–12. Strzelecki also noted that the acoustic bass only really sounded good in certain keys: "Like E and F; E being a major country key, is not a great key. It wasn't for my instrument. E-flat was great, and D was great, but E and F were not really good. G was great. A, C, and so forth. But E and F were not really good keys. F was a little better than E. E was an awful key for my instrument, and of course we did so much in E, you know. . . . A lot of times it had to do with the weather. It was just a lot more dependable, the electric bass was" (Strzelecki, interview with John Rumble, June 25, 1990, transcript, p. 10).

182. Norbert Putnam, *Music Lessons: A Musical Memoir,* Vol. 1 (Nashville: Thimbleton House Media, 2017), 8–15.

183. Putnam, *Music Lessons,* 10.

184. Putnam, *Music Lessons,* 12–13.

185. Putnam, *Music Lessons,* 16.

186. Putnam, *Music Lessons,* 17–19.

187. Putnam, *Music Lessons,* 20–24; Carla Jean Whitley, *Muscle Shoals Sound Studio: How the Swampers Changed American Music* (Charleston, SC: The History Press, 2014); Rick Hall, *The Man from Muscle Shoals: My Journey from Shame to Fame* (Monterey: Heritage Builders, 2015), 173–181.

188. Hughes, *Country Soul,* esp. chs. 1, 5, and 6.

189. Travis D. Stimeling, "'To Be Polished More than Extended': Musicianship, Masculinity, and the Critical Reception of Southern Rock," *Journal of Popular Music Studies* 26, no. 1 (March 2014): 121–136.

190. Putnam, *Music Lessons,* 36–54.

191. Putnam, *Music Lessons,* 54.

192. Putnam, *Music Lessons,* 55.

193. Putnam, *Music Lessons,* 56–58.

194. Putnam, *Music Lessons,* 61.

195. Harold Bradley, interview with Morris Levy, February 22 or 23, 1996.

196. Putnam, *Music Lessons,* 62.

197. Putnam, *Music Lessons,* 62–64.

198. Putnam, *Music Lessons,* 64. Charlie McCoy came to session work in the same manner (McCoy with Stimeling, *Fifty Cents and a Box Top,* 50–51.

199. Putnam, *Music Lessons,* 65.

200. Hughes, *Country Soul,* 167–188.

201. Orr, ed., *Dylan, Cash, and the Nashville Cats*; Rose Drake, interview with author, Murfreesboro, TN, May 29, 2017. Pat McCoy, in conversation with me, noted that the influx of musicians from Memphis and Muscle Shoals led to significant growth

in her workload as the payroll processor for the Nashville Musicians Association (Pat McCoy, interview with author, Nashville, TN, May 28, 2017).

202. Putnam, *Music Lessons*, 66–93.

203. The session was held in June 1968; the specific date is unknown (Praguefrank, Michal Gololobov, Mario Manciotti, and Brent Emanuel, "Tony Joe White," *Praguefrank's Country Music Discographies*, http://countrydiscoghraphy2.blogspot.com/2013/11/tony-joe-white.html (posted November 30, 2013; last accessed June 29, 2018).

204. The single actually took several months before it reached the charts (Martin Doppelbauer, "Tony Joe White—His Life," <http://www.martin-doppelbauer.de/TJW/life2.htm> (posted November 2000, last accessed June 29, 2018).

205. Don Cusic, *Elvis and Nashville* (Nashville: Brackish, 2012).

206. Robert Walser, *Running with the Devil: Power, Gender, and Madness in Heavy Metal Music* (Middletown, CT: Wesleyan University Press, 1993), 42–43.

207. Here, I am influenced by Mark Katz's observations in *Capturing Sound: How Technology Has Changed Music* (Berkeley: University of California Press, 2004), 36, 78.

208. Roe, "Bob Moore, Music City Maven."

209. Boyd, *The Jazz of the Southwest; idem, Dance All Night: Those Other Southwestern Swing Bands*.

210. Western swing historian Cary Ginell notes that western swing bands did not use drums "on a widespread level . . . [until] World War II" (Cary Ginell, *Milton Brown and the Founding of Western Swing*, [Urbana: University of Illinois Press, 1994], *xxii*).

211. Kienzle, *Southwest Shuffle*, 254–257.

212. Edenton, interview with author, August 3, 2014.

213. Kent Blanton, telephone interview with author, September 8, 2014.

214. Drummer Farris Coursey, for instance, used body percussion on Red Foley's 1949 recording of "Chattanoogie Show Shine Boy" (Harold Bradley, interview with author, August 1, 2014; Cary Ginell, liner notes for *Red Foley: Old Shep—The Red Foley Recordings, 1933–1950* [Bear Family BCD 16759 FL, 2006], 66; Cary Ginell, Dave Sax, and Richard Weize, "The Discography, 1933–1950," in liner notes for *Red Foley: Old Shep—The Red Foley Recordings, 1933–1950* [Bear Family BCD 16759 FL, 2006], 84). Edenton, too, noted that he had "played brushes on a pasteboard box many times" (Edenton, interview with author, August 3, 2014).

215. Coursey's contributions to Foley's recordings are documented in Ginell, Sax, and Weize, "The Discography, 1933–1950," 83–86.

216. Of course, session musicians often make competing claims to being "the most recorded," but these claims are remarkably hard to verify. But there is no doubt that Harman's output—along with the output of most of the original Nashville A Team—puts him in a rather elite group of highly recorded musicians.

217. Harman, interview with Morris Levy, January 19, 1996.

218. Harman, interview with Morris Levy, January 19, 1996.

219. Harman, interview with Morris Levy, January 19, 1996.

220. Harman notes that Presley began using two drummers by around 1958 (Harman, interview with Morris Levy, January 19, 1996).

221. Harman, interview with Morris Levy, January 19, 1996.

222. Harman was the regular drummer for Hank Garland's jazz group at the Carousel Club. He recalled having the chance to play with members of the Four Freshmen, the Stan Kenton Orchestra, and Woody Herman's Thundering Herd during jam sessions at the Carousel Club, as well (Harman, interview with Morris Levy, January 19, 1996).

223. Harman, interview with Morris Levy, January 19, 1996.

224. Harman, interview with Morris Levy, January 19, 1996.

225. Jerry Carrigan, interview with Morris Levy, January 12, 1996, Morris Levy Interviews, Rock and Roll Hall of Fame Library and Archives, ARC-0487, Box 1, Folder 4.

226. Allen Smith, "Jerry Carrigan: Bama-Lam! Alabama's Drumming Legend," *Gritz* (July 2000), http://swampland.com/articles/view/title:jerry_carrigan (last accessed November 3, 2017). Carrigan also discussed this in more detail in a February 2009 interview with Bill Lloyd at the Country Music Hall of Fame and Museum ("Nashville Cats: Salute to Jerry Carrigan," http://countrymusichalloffame.org/ nashville-cats/jerry-carrigan [last accessed November 3, 2017] [NB: the website says that this happened on February 29, 2009, but there was no such date. Jim Ridley, writing for *Nashville Scene*, indicates that the interview took place on February 21, 2009 (Jim Ridley, "A Celebration of Jerry Carrigan at Country Music Hall of Fame," *Nashville Scene* [February 19, 2009], http://www.nashvillescene. com/arts-culture/article/13017590/a-celebration-of-jerry-carrigan-at-country-music-hall-of-fame (last accessed November 3, 2017)]).

227. "Nashville Cats: Salute to Jerry Carrigan."

228. Smith, "Jerry Carrigan."

229. Smith, "Jerry Carrigan."

230. Smith, "Jerry Carrigan." The session was held on March 16, 1965 (Michel Ruppli, Richard Weize, Martin Hawkins, Praguefrank, Chris Huskey, and David Mankelow, "Warner Mack," *Praguefrank's Country Music Discographies*, http://countrydis-coghraphy2.blogspot.com/2016/03/warner-mack.html [posted March 3, 2016; last accessed June 29, 2018]).

231. Smith, "Jerry Carrigan." Carrigan responded affirmatively to Smith's suggestion that he was "doing about 90 percent of RCA's Nashville sessions."

232. Carrigan, interview with Morris Levy, January 12, 1996.

233. "Sammi Smith—Something Old, Something New, Something Blue," *Discogs*, https://www.discogs.com/Sammi-Smith-Something-Old-Something-New-Something-Blue/master/852889 (last accessed June 29, 2018).

234. "Nashville Cats: Salute to Jerry Carrigan."

235. In 1969, Shelby Singleton opened a new studio that boasted "two four-track, two two-track and two monaural ampex [*sic*] units with all supporting equipment" ("Singleton Breaks New Ground," *Record World* [March 22, 1969], 22). By 1985, journalist John Lomax III noted that "most Nashville recording is accomplished

on twenty-four track machines" (John Lomax III, *Nashville: Music City USA* [New York: Abrams, 1985], 184).

236. Richard Osborne, *Vinyl: A History of the Analogue Record* (New York: Routledge, 2014), 84.

237. It is worth noting that negativity is virtually absent from reporting on and testimony about the Nashville recording scene during this time. As any workplace has a degree of friction from time to time, it is likely that negative opinions and frustrating situations were part of the environment, but they seem to be omitted from the archives and individual memories.

AFTERWORD

1. For more background on the progressive country music scene, consult, among others, Barry Shank, *Dissonant Identities: The Rock 'n' Roll Scene in Austin, Texas* (Hanover, NH: Wesleyan University Press, 1994); Travis D. Stimeling, *Cosmic Cowboys and New Hicks: The Countercultural Sounds of Austin's Progressive Country Music Scene* (New York: Oxford University Press, 2011).

2. For context, consult Michael Bane, *The Outlaws: Revolution in Country Music* (Nashville: The Country Music Press, 1978); Travis D. Stimeling, "'Phases and Stages, Circles and Cycles': Willie Nelson and the Concept Album," *Popular Music* 30, no. 3 (2011): 389–408; *idem*, "Narrative, Vocal Staging and Masculinity in the 'Outlaw' Country Music of Waylon Jennings," *Popular Music* 32, no. 3 (2013): 343–358; Michael Streissguth, *Outlaw: Waylon, Willie, Kris, and the Renegades of Nashville* (New York: itbooks, 2013); Kevin L. Glaser, *The Great Tompall: Forgotten Country Music Outlaw—The Authorized Biography of Tompall Glaser* (Oconomowoc, WI: Right Side Creations, 2014), 119–211.

3. Jason Mellard, *Progressive Country: How the 1970s Transformed the Texan in Popular Culture* (Austin: University of Texas Press, 2013), 171–198.

4. For some background, consult John Lomax III, *Nashville: Music City USA* (New York: Harry N. Abrams, 1985), 115–126, 198–210; David Gates, "Don't Get above Your Raisin': Ricky Skaggs, Alabama, and Their Contemporaries," in *Country: The Music and the Musicians from the Beginnings to the '90s*, rev. and updated ed., eds. Paul Kingsbury, Alan Axelrod, and Susan Costello Michael Kosser (Nashville: Abbeville Press, 1994), 360–385; Michael Kosser, *How Nashville Became Music City: 50 Years of Music Row* (Milwaukee: Hal Leonard Books, 2006), 211–223; Country Music Hall of Fame and Museum, "Nashville Cats: Salute to Session Player John Hobbs," https://countrymusichalloffame.org/nashville-cats/john-hobbs (posted March 10, 2012; last accessed July 20, 2018).

5. Buddy Harman, for instance, told interviewer Morris Levy: "I did go home and say, 'Where's the kids?' The wife said, 'They grew up and moved out'" (Buddy Harman, interview with Morris Levy, January 19, 1996, Morris Levy Interviews, Box 1, Folder 7, Rock and Roll Hall of Fame Archives and Library, Cleveland, Ohio). At the same time, Harold Bradley told Levy that "the demise of the players of that A Team [the Harman-Moore era] was some of them having disabilities because of poor health" (Harold Bradley, interview with Morris Levy, February 22 or 23, 1996,

Morris Levy Interviews, Box 1, Folder 2, Rock and Roll Hall of Fame Archives and Library, Cleveland, Ohio).

6. Such was the case with Ray Edenton, for instance.

7. Michael Streissguth, *Voices of the Country: Interviews with Classic Country Performers* (New York: Routledge, 2004), 47; Ben Ratliff, "Chet Atkins, 77, Is Dead: Guitarist and Producer Was Architect of the Nashville Sound," *New York Times* (July 2, 2011), < https://www.nytimes.com/2001/07/02/us/chet-atkins-77-dead-guitarist-producer-was-architect-nashville-sound.html> (last accessed July 23, 2018);

8. Charlie McCoy with Travis D. Stimeling, *Fifty Cents and a Box Top: The Creative Life of Nashville Session Musician Charlie McCoy* (Morgantown: West Virginia University Press, 2017), 109–143.

9. As recently as 2017, "Pig" Robbins contributed to Rhonda Vincent and Daryle Singletary's album *American Grandstand* (Upper Management 11, 2017) ("Daryle Singletary/Rhonda Vincent: American Grandstand," https://www.allmusic.com/album/american-grandstand-mw0003054342/releases [last accessed July 23, 2018]). Charlie McCoy still plays on sessions several times a year and continues to produce his own solo recordings; at the time of this writing, he is finishing production on his forty-first studio album.

10. The terms "local," "translocal," and "virtual" were applied to music scenes most notably by sociologists Andy Bennett and Richard A. Peterson in *Music Scenes: Local, Translocal, and Virtual* (Nashville: Vanderbilt University Press, 2004). See also Will Straw, "Systems of Articulation, Logics of Change: Communities and Scenes in Popular Music," *Cultural Studies* 5, no. 3 (1991): 368–388; Shank, *Dissonant Identities*; Holly Kruse, *Site and Sound: Understanding Independent Music Scenes* (New York: Peter Lang, 2003); idem, "Local Identity and Independent Music Scenes: Online and Off," *Popular Music and Society* 33, no. 5 (2010): 625–639.

11. See, among others: Louise Meintjes, "Reaching 'Overseas': South African Engineers, Technology, and Tradition," in *Wired for Sound: Engineering and Technologies in Sonic Cultures*, eds. Paul D. Greene and Thomas Porcello (Middletown, CT: Wesleyan University Press, 2004), 23–46; idem, "The Politics of the Recording Studio: A Case Study from South Africa," in *The Cambridge Companion to Recorded Music*, eds. Nicholas Cook, Eric Clarke, Daniel Leech-Wilkinson, and John Rink (Cambridge: Cambridge University Press, 2009), 84–97; Beverly Diamond, "Media as Social Action: Native American Musicians in the Recording Studio," in *Wired for Sound: Engineers and Technologies in Sonic Cultures*, eds. Paul D. Greene and Thomas Porcello (Middletown, CT: Wesleyan University Press, 2004), 129; Eliot Bates, *Digital Tradition: Arrangement and Labor in Istanbul's Recording Studio Culture* (New York: Oxford University Press, 2016).

12. Leonard Morton, Sr., interview with author, Nashville, TN, May 18, 2015; E. Mark Windle, *House of Broken Hearts: The Soul of 1960s Nashville* (n.p.: Blurb, 2017).

13. See, among many others: Jerome L. Rodnitzky, "The Decline of Contemporary Protest Music," *Popular Music and Society* 1, no. 1 (Fall 1971): 44–50; Jens Lund, "Fundamentalism, Racism, and Political Reaction in Country Music," in *The Sounds of Social Change: Studies in Popular Culture*, eds. R. Serge Denisoff and Richard

A. Peterson (Chicago: Rand McNally, 1972), 79–91;William S. Fox and James D. Williams, "Political Orientation and Music Preferences among College Students," *Public Opinion Quarterly* 38, no. 3 (January 1974): 352–371; Patricia Averill, "Esoteric-Exoteric Expectations of Redneck Behavior and Country Music," *Journal of Country Music* 4, no. 2 (Summer 1973): 34–38; Bill C. Malone, *Don't Get above Your Raisin': Country Music and the Southern Working Class* (Urbana: University of Illinois Press, 2001), 210–252; James E. Perone, *Songs of the Vietnam Conflict* (Westport, CT: Greenwood Press, 2001), 71–108; Peter LaChapelle, *Proud to Be an Okie: Cultural Politics, Country Music, and Migration to Southern California* (Berkeley: University of California Press, 2007), 180–207; Nadine Hubbs, *Rednecks, Queers, and Country Music* (Berkeley: University of California Press, 2014), 63–68; Doug Bradley and Craig Werner, *We Gotta Get Out of This Place: The Soundtrack of the Vietnam War* (Amherst: University of Massachusetts Press, 2015), 31–33.

14. Diane Pecknold, *The Selling Sound: The Rise of the Country Music Industry* (Durham, NC: Duke University Press, 2007), 209–226; Paula Jean Bishop, "The Roots and Influences of the Everly Brothers," Ph.D. dissertation, Boston University, 2011, esp. 110–112.

15. I would like to thank Paula Bishop for driving this point home to me in several conversations.

16. Albin J. Zak, III, *I Don't Sound like Nobody: Remaking Music in 1950s America* (Ann Arbor: University of Michigan Press, 2010).

17. See, for instance: "When Motown Went Country: The Supremes Sing Country, Western & Pop," *Highway Queens* (posted September 22, 2017), https://highwayqueens.com/2017/09/22/when-motown-went-country-the-supremes-sing-country-western-pop/ (last accessed July 23, 2018).

BIBLIOGRAPHY

ORIGINAL INTERVIEWS CONDUCTED

Bach, Byron T. "Ted." Telephone interview. August 29, 2014.
Bach, Carole Ann. Telephone interview. August 29, 2014.
Bradley, Harold. Nashville, TN. August 1, 2014.
Croft, Justin. Nashville, TN. May 26, 2017.
Dean, Ronnie. Telephone interview. August 21, 2014.
Drake, Rose. Murfreesboro, TN. May 29, 2017.
Edenton, Ray and Polly. Gallatin, TN. August 3, 2014.
Fott, Solie. Telephone interview. February 10, 2016.
Guenther, Cathy (Bach). Telephone interview. August 26, 2014.
McCoy, Charlie. Nashville, TN. July 30, 2014.
McCoy, Pat. Nashville, TN. May 28, 2017.
McElhiney, Bill, Jr. Telephone interview. August 7, 2014.
Morton, Leonard, Sr. Nashville, TN. May 18, 2015.
Moss, Wayne. Madison, TN. June 2, 2017.
Payne, Suzi Burgher. Telephone interview. February 3, 2015.
Robble, Gary. Nashville, TN. May 23, 2017.
Spicher, Buddy. Nashville, TN. July 29, 2014.
Stevens, Ray. Telephone interview. December 17, 2014.
White, Bergen. Telephone interview. September 5, 2014.

ARCHIVAL COLLECTIONS

Blonde on Blonde session tapes. Bob Dylan Archives. New York.
Byron Bach personal ledgers, 1972–1975. Personal collection of Cathy Bach Guenther. Nashville, TN.
Byron Bach personal papers. Personal collection of Carole Ann Bach. Nashville, TN.
Charles K. Wolfe Audio Collection. Center for Popular Music, Middle Tennessee State University. Murfreesboro, TN.

Country Music Foundation Library, Country Music Hall of Fame and Museum. Nashville, TN.
   Country Music Foundation Oral History Project Collection.
   Moving Images Collection.
   Neil Matthews, Jr., Lead Sheets.

PHOTOGRAPH COLLECTIONS

Louis T. Nicholas Papers, MSS 314, Special Collections Library. Vanderbilt University. Nashville, TN.
Morris Levy Interviews, ARC-0487. Rock and Roll Hall of Fame Library and Archives. Cuyohoga Community College. Cleveland, OH.
Nashville Banner Collection. Nashville Public Library. Nashville, TN.
Nashville Symphony Orchestra papers. Nashville Symphony Orchestra. Nashville, TN.
Southern Folklife Collection. University of North Carolina at Chapel Hill. Chapel Hill, NC.
Tennessee State University Special Collections. Nashville, TN.
William Pursell interviews. Personal collection of Terry Klefstad. Nashville, TN.

LINER NOTES

Dickerson, Deke, and Richard Weize. *George Hamilton IV: My North Country Home.* Bear Family BCD 17146 CH, 2011.
Escott, Colin, Arie den Dulk, Kurt Rokitta, and Richard Weize. *Jim Reeves: Welcome to My World.* Bear Family BCD 15656 PI, 1994.
Escott, Colin, Andrew Sandoval, Russ Wapensky, and Richard Weize. *The Everly Brothers: The Price of Fame.* Bear Family BCD 16511 GL, 2005.
Escott, Colin, and Richard Weize. *Classic Everly Brothers.* Bear Family BCD 15618 CI, 1992.
Escott, Colin, and Richard Weize. *Connie Smith: Born to Sing.* Bear Family BCD 16368 DI, 2001.
Escott, Colin, and Richard Weize. *Marvin Rainwater: Classic Recordings.* Bear Family BCD 15600 DI, 2007.
Escott, Colin, and Richard Weize. *Orbison.* Bear Family BC 16423 GL, 2001.
Ginell, Cary, Dave Sax, and Richard Weize. *Red Foley: Old Shep—The Red Foley Recordings, 1933–1950.* Bear Family BCD 16759 FL, 2006.
Guralnick, Peter, Ernst Mikael Jørgensen, and Erik Rasmussen. *Elvis: The King of Rock 'n' Roll—The Complete 50's Masters.* RCA 07863 66050-2, 1992.
Kienzle, Rich, and Richard Weize. *Ray Price and the Cherokee Cowboys.* Bear Family BCD 15843 JK, 1995.
Kienzle, Rich, and Richard Weize. *Willie Nelson: Nashville Was the Roughest.* Bear Family BCD 15831 HK, 2003.
Kingsbury, Paul, Don Roy, and Richard Weize. *Brenda Lee: Little Miss Dynamite.* Bear Family BCD 15772 DK, 1999.
Logsdon, Guy, Don Roy, and Richard Weize. *Marty Robbins: Under Western Skies.* Bear Family BCD 15646 DI, 1995.

Mazor, Barry, and Richard Weize. *Connie Smith: Just for What I Am.* Bear Family BCD 16814 EK, 2012.

Samuelson, Dave, Russ Wapensky, and Richard Weize. *Sonny James: Young Love.* Bear Family BCD 16373, 2007.

Skinker, Chris, Richard Weize, and Laurence J. Zwisohn. *Jean Shepard: The Melody Ranch Girl.* Bear Family BCD 15905-EI, 1996.

Vinicur, Dale, and Richard Weize. *Don Gibson: The Singer, The Songwriter: 1961–1966.* Bear Family BCD 15664 DI, 1991.

Wolfe, Charles K., and Richard Weize. *Hank Snow: The Singing Ranger—I'm Movin' On.* Bear Family BCD 15426, 1988.

PRINT AND ONLINE PUBLICATIONS

Abbott, Lynn, and Doug Seroff. *The Original Blues: The Emergence of the Blues in African American Vaudeville.* Jackson: University Press of Mississippi, 2017.

Abbott, Lynn, and Doug Seroff. *Ragged but Right: Black Traveling Shows, "Coon Songs," and the Dark Pathway to Blues and Jazz.* Jackson: University Press of Mississippi, 2007.

Abbott, Lynn, and Doug Seroff. *To Do This, You Must Know How.* Jackson: University Press of Mississippi, 2012.

Abramo, Joseph Michael, and Amy Elizabeth Pierce. "An Ethnographic Case Study of Music Learning at a School for the Blind." *Bulletin of the Council for Research in Music Education,* no. 195 (Winter 2013): 9–24.

Ackerman, Paul. "C. & W. Field Lauds BMI for Promotion of Rural Music." *Billboard* (November 17, 1956): 16, 20.

Altschuler, Glenn C. *All Shook Up: How Rock 'n' Roll Changed America.* New York: Oxford University Press, 2003.

Amendola, Billy. "An Interview with Hal Blaine." *Modern Drummer* (July 2005). https://www.moderndrummer.com/2005/07/hal-blaine-2/. Last accessed September 21, 2017.

Anderson, Tim. "'Buried under the Fecundity of His Own Creations': Reconsidering the Recording Bands of the American Federation of Musicians, 1942–1944 and 1948." *American Music* 22, no. 2 (Summer 2004): 231–269.

Anderson, Tim. *Making Easy Listening: Material Culture and Postwar American Recording.* Minneapolis: University of Minnesota Press, 2006.

Auslander, Philip. "Seeing Is Believing: Live Performance and the Discourse of Authenticity in Rock Music." *Literature and Psychology* 44, no. 4 (1998): 1–26.

Austin-Peay State University. *Farewell & Hail.* n.p., 1973.

Austin-Peay State University Office of Public Relations and Marketing. "Jazz Event to Honor Local Music Legend Solie Fott." https://www.apsu.edu/archived-news/2014/06/jazz-event-honor-local-music-legend-solie-fott.php. Posted June 4, 2014. Last accessed August 20, 2018.

Averill, Patricia. "Esoteric-Exoteric Expectations of Redneck Behavior and Country Music." *Journal of Country Music* 4, no. 2 (Summer 1973): 34–38.

Baade, Christina. "Airing Authenticity: The BBC Jam Sessions from New York, 1938/39." *Journal of the Society for American Music* 6, no. 3 (August 2012): 271–314.

Baade, Christina, Susan Fast, and Line Grenier. "Musicians as Workers: Sites of Struggle and Resistance." *MUSICultures* 41, no. 1 (2014): 1–9.

Bakker, Gerben. "Adopting the Rights-Based Model: Music Multinationals and Local Music Industries since 1945." *Popular Music History* 6, no. 3 (2011): 307–343.

Ball, Robert J. "Joseph Machlis and the Enjoyment of Music: A Biographical Appreciation of a Great Teacher." *Musical Quarterly* 95 (2013): 613–643.

Bane, Michael. *The Outlaws: Revolution in Country Music*. Nashville: Country Music Press, 1978.

Barker, Hugh, and Yuval Taylor. *Faking It: The Quest for Authenticity in Popular Music*. New York: W. W. Norton, 2007.

Barry, Ron. *The Elvis Presley American Discography*. Phillipsburg, NJ: Spectator Service, Maxigraphics, 1976.

Bashford, Christina. *The Pursuit of High Culture: John Ella and Chamber Music in Victorian England*. Woodbridge: Boydell Press, 2007.

Bates, Eliot. *Digital Tradition: Arrangement and Labor in Istanbul's Recording Studio Culture*. New York: Oxford University Press, 2016.

Bealle, John. *Public Worship, Private Faith: Sacred Harp and American Folksong*. Athens: University of Georgia Press, 1997.

Bennett, Andy, and Richard A. Peterson, eds. *Music Scenes: Local, Translocal, and Virtual*. Nashville: Vanderbilt University Press, 2004.

Bennett, Rebecca. "Debating Music 'Appreciation' outside the American Classroom, 1930–1950." *Journal of Historical Research in Music Education* 33, no. 2 (April 2012): 128–151.

Berry, Chad. *Southern Migrants, Northern Exiles*. Urbana: University of Illinois Press, 2000.

Bertrand, Michael T. *Race, Rock, and Elvis*. Urbana: University of Illinois Press, 2000.

Biggar, George C. "The WLS National Barn Dance Story: The Early Years." In *Exploring Roots Music: Twenty Years of the JEMF Quarterly*. Ed. Nolan Porterfield. Lanham, MD: Scarecrow Press, 2004, 34–44.

Bijsterveld, Karin, Eefje Cleophas, Stephan Krebs, and Gijs Mom. *Sound and Safe: A History of Listening behind the Wheel*. New York: Oxford University Press, 2014.

Bird, Rick. "Herzog Is Hallowed Ground." *CityBeat* (Cincinnati, OH). November 16, 2009. https://www.citybeat.com/music/music-feature/article/13015806/herzog-is-hallowed-ground. Last accessed March 25, 2018.

Bishop, Paula Jean. "The Roots and Influences of the Everly Brothers." Ph.D. dissertation, Boston University, 2011.

Biszick-Lockwood, Bar. *Restless Giant: The Life and Times of Jean Aberbach and Hill and Range Songs*. Urbana: University of Illinois Press, 2010.

Black, J. W., and Albert Molinaro. *The Fender Bass: An Illustrated History*. Milwaukee: Hal Leonard, 2001.

Blaine, Hal, with Mr. Bonzai. *Hal Blaine and the Wrecking Crew*. Ed. David M. Schwartz. Alma, MI: Rebeats Publications, 2010.

Booth, Greg. *Behind the Curtain: Making Music in Mumbai's Film Studios*. New York: Oxford University Press, 2008.

Boehm, Lisa Krissoff. "Chicago as Forgotten Country Music Mecca." In *The Hayloft Gang: The Story of the* National Barn Dance. Ed. Chad Berry. Urbana: University of Illinois Press, 2008, 101–118.

Boyd, Jean A. *Dance All Night: Those Other Southwestern Swing Bands, Past and Present.* Lubbock: Texas Tech University Press, 2012.

Boyd, Jean A. *The Jazz of the Southwest: An Oral History of Western Swing.* Austin: University of Texas Press, 1998.

Boyd, Jean A. *"We're the Light Crust Doughboys from Burrus Mill": An Oral History.* Austin: University of Texas Press, 2003.

"The Boys in the Band." *Billboard* 81, no. 42 (October 18, 1969): A42.

Brackett, David. *Interpreting Popular Music.* Cambridge: Cambridge University Press, 1995; reprint ed., Berkeley: University of California Press, 2000.

Brackett, David. *Categorizing Sound: Genre and Twentieth-Century Popular Music.* Berkeley: University of California Press, 2016.

Bradley, Andy, and Roger Wood. *House of Hits: The Story of Houston's Gold Star/Sugarhill Recording Studios.* Austin: University of Texas Press, 2010.

Bradley, Doug, and Craig Werner. *We Gotta Get Out of This Place: The Soundtrack of the Vietnam War.* Amherst: University of Massachusetts Press, 2015.

Brady, Erika. "Contested Origins: Arnold Schultz and the Music of Western Kentucky." In *Hidden in the Mix: The African American Presence in Country Music.* Ed. Diane Pecknold. Durham, NC: Duke University Press, 2013, 100–118.

Brady, Erika. *A Spiral Way: How the Phonograph Changed Ethnography.* Jackson: University Press of Mississippi, 1999.

Bragg, Rick. *Jerry Lee Lewis: His Own Story.* New York: HarperCollins, 2014.

Brasseaux, Ryan. *Cajun Breakdown: The Emergence of an American Made Music.* New York: Oxford University Press, 2009.

Breen, T. H. "The Great Wagon Road." *Southern Cultures* 3, no. 1 (1997): 22–57.

Brislin, Tom. "The Floyd Cramer Style." *Keyboard* (September 2008): 36–37.

Broughton, Chad. *Boom, Bust, Exodus: The Rust Belt, the Maquilas, and a Tale of Two Cities.* New York: Oxford University Press, 2015.

Broume, P. J., and Clay Tucker. *The Other Music City: The Dance Bands and Jazz Musicians[,] 1920 to 1970.* Nashville: American Press Printing, 1990.

Broven, John. *Record Makers and Breakers: Voices of the Independent Rock 'n' Roll Pioneers.* Urbana: University of Illinois Press, 2009.

Broyles, Michael. "Lowell Mason on European Church Music and Transatlantic Cultural Identification: A Reconsideration." *Journal of the American Musicological Society* 38, no. 2 (Summer 1985): 316–348.

Buck, Mick, and John W. Rumble, eds. *Patsy Cline: Crazy for Loving You.* Nashville: Country Music Foundation, 2012.

"Buddy Harman: The Original Country Drummer." *Modern Drummer* (January 2011). https://www.moderndrummer.com/2011/01/buddy-harman/. Last accessed September 21, 2017.

Bufwack, Mary A., and Robert K. Oermann. *Finding Her Voice: Women in Country Music, 1800–2000.* Nashville: Country Music Foundation Press and Vanderbilt University Press, 2003.

Burns, Debra Brubaker, Anita Jackson, and Connie Arrau Sturm. "Unsung Heroines: Contributions of Selected Early Twentieth-Century Women to American Piano Pedagogy." *American Music Teacher* 52, no. 3 (December 2002–January 2003): 24–28.

Burns, Gary. "A Typology of 'Hooks' in Popular Records." *Popular Music* 6, no. 1 (January 1987): 1–20.

Burns, Martha Dennis. "A Gallery of Teachers and Students: The Female Piano Teacher in Antebellum America." In *Piano Roles: A New History of the Piano*. Ed. James Parakilas. New Haven, CT: Yale University Press, 2002, 134–140.

Burns, Martha Dennis. "The Power of Music Enhanced by the Word: Lowell Mason and the Transformation of Sacred Singing in Lyman Beecher's New England." *Annual Proceedings of the Dublin Seminar for New England Folklife* 21 (1998): 139–150.

Butt, John. *Playing with History: The Historical Approach to Musical Performance*. Cambridge: Cambridge University Press, 2002.

Cage, John. "Lecture on Nothing." In Cage, *Silence: Lectures and Writing*. Middletown, CT: Wesleyan University Press, 1961, 109–127.

Campbell, Gavin James. *Music and the Making of a New South*. Chapel Hill: University of North Carolina Press, 2004.

Campelo, Isabel. "'That Extra Thing': The Role of Session Musicians in the Recording Industry." *Journal on the Art of Record Production* no. 10 (July 2015). http://arp-journal.com/that-extra-thing-the-role-of-session-musicians-in-the-recording-industry/. Accessed January 25, 2018.

Cantor, Louis. *Dewey and Elvis: The Life and Times of a Rock 'n' Roll Deejay*. Urbana: University of Illinois Press, 2005.

Cantwell, Robert. *When We Were Good: The Folk Revival*. Cambridge, MA: Harvard University Press, 1996.

Carter, Walter. *The Mandolin in America: The Full Story from Orchestras to Bluegrass to the Modern Revival*. Milwaukee: Backbeat Books, 2017.

Chew, Geoffrey, and Richard Rastall. "Notation III.4.ii. Notes: Shapes, Colours, Abbreviations." In *Grove Music Online*. https://doi.org/10.1093/gmo/9781561592630.article.20114. Last accessed April 10, 2018.

Ching, Barbara. *Wrong's What I Do Best: Hard Country Music and Contemporary Culture*. New York: Oxford University Press, 2001.

Christgau, Robert. "Rockism Faces the World." *The Village Voice* 35 (January 2, 1990). Archived at https://www.robertchristgau.com/xg/rock/decade-89.php. Last accessed August 22, 2018.

Christian, Jim. "Buddy Spicher: Master of Double Stops." *Fiddler Magazine* 5, no. 3 (Fall 1998): 19–23.

Church Music in Baptist History. Nashville: Historical Commission of the Southern Baptist Convention; Southern Baptist Historical Society, 1984.

Clausius, Katharina. "Historical Mirroring, Mirroring History: An Aesthetics of Collaboration in *Pulcinella*." *Journal of Musicology* 30, no. 2 (Spring 2013): 215–251.

"Clement in Tennessee Waltz with Country Music Support." *Billboard* (August 11, 1962): 20.

Coates, Norma. "(R)evolution Now? Rock Music and the Political Potential of Gender." In *Sexing the Groove: Popular Music and Gender*. Ed. Sheila Whiteley. London and New York: Routledge, 1997, 50–64.

Cobb, Buell E., Jr. *The Sacred Harp: A Tradition and Its Music*. Athens: University of Georgia Press, 2004.

Cockrell, Dale. *Demons of Disorder: Early Blackface Minstrels and Their World*. Cambridge: Cambridge University Press, 1997.

Cohen, Sara. "Men Making a Scene: Rock Music and the Production of Gender." In *Sexing the Groove: Popular Music and Gender*. Ed. Sheila Whiteley. London and New York: Routledge, 1997, 12–36.

Cohodas, Nadine. *Spinning Blues into Gold: The Chess Brothers and the Legendary Chess Records*. New York: St. Martin's Press, 2000.

Comentale, Edward P. *Sweet Air: Modernism, Regionalism, and American Popular Song*. Urbana: University of Illinois Press, 2013.

"Como Cuts Record Despite Cold." *Nashville Tennesseean* (February 10, 1965).

Cook, Nicholas. "Methods for Analysing Recordings." In *The Cambridge Companion to Recorded Music*. Eds. Nicholas Cook, Eric Clarke, Daniel Leech-Wilkinson, and John Rink. Cambridge: Cambridge University Press, 2009, 221–245.

Cooper, B. Lee. "Charting Cultural Change, 1953–57: Song Assimilation through Cover Recording." In *Play It Again: Cover Songs in Popular Music*. Ed. George Plasketes. Aldershot, UK: Ashgate, 2010; reprint ed., New York: Routledge, 2016, 43–76.

Cooper, B. Lee. "Promoting Social Change through Audio Repetition: Black Musicians as Creators and Revivalists, 1953–1978." *Tracking: Popular Music Studies* 2, no. 1 (Winter 1989): 2–46.

Cooper, Peter. "Sheldon Kurland—Violinist, String Arranger—Dies at 81." *Nashville [Tenn.] Tennessean* (February 6, 2010). http://blogs.tennessean.com/tunein/2010/01/06/sheldon-kurland-violinist-string-arranger-dies-at-81/. Last accessed September 18, 2015.

"Country Music: The Nashville Sound." *Time* (November 27, 1964): 80.

Country Music Hall of Fame and Museum. "Nashville Cats: Salute to Jerry Carrigan." http://countrymusichalloffame.org/nashville-cats/jerry-carrigan. Posted February 2009. Last accessed November 3, 2017.

Country Music Hall of Fame and Museum. "Nashville Cats: Salute to Session Player John Hobbs." https://countrymusichalloffame.org/nashville-cats/john-hobbs. Posted March 10, 2012. Last accessed July 20, 2018.

Country Music Hall of Fame and Museum. "Night Train to Nashville: Music City Rhythm & Blues." https://countrymusichalloffame.org/exhibits/exhibitdetail/night-train-to-nashville-music-city-rhythm-blues#.WrpGqNMbPOQ. Last accessed March 27, 2018.

Country Music Hall of Fame and Museum. "Sonny James." https://countrymusichalloffame.org/Inductees/InducteeDetail/sonny-james. Last accessed May 7, 2018.

Cowie, Jefferson. *Capital Moves: RCA's Seventy-Year Quest for Cheap Labor*. Ithaca, NY: Cornell University Press, 1999; paperback ed., New York: New Press, 2001.

Coyle, Michael. "Hijacked Hits and Antic Authenticity: Cover Songs, Race, and Postwar Marketing." In *Rock over the Edge: Transformations in Popular Music Culture*. Eds.

Roger Beebe, Denise Fulbrook, and Ben Saunders (Durham, NC: Duke University Press, 2002, 133–158.

Crane, Larry, and Kyle Lehning with Bergen White. "Fred Foster: Monuments of Sound." *Tape Op* 118 (March–April 2017): 38–48.

Cummings, Alex. "Collectors, Bootleggers, and the Value of Jazz, 1930–1952." In *Sound in the Age of Mechanical Reproduction*. Eds. David Suisman and Susan Strasser. Philadelphia: University of Pennsylvania Press, 2010, 95–114.

Cusic, Don. *Elvis and Nashville*. Nashville: Brackish Publishing, 2012.

Cusic, Don. "In Defense of Cover Songs: Commerce and Credibility." In *Play It Again: Cover Songs in Popular Music*. Ed. George Plasketes. Aldershot, UK: Ashgate, 2010; reprint ed., New York: Routledge, 2016, 223–229.

Dandaneau, Steven P. *A Town Abandoned: Flint, Michigan, Confronts Deindustrialization*. Albany: State University of New York Press, 1996.

"Danelectro Electric Bass Guitar." http://americanhistory.si.edu/collections/search/object/nmah_1301424. Last accessed June 28, 2018.

Daniel, Wayne W. *Pickin' on Peachtree: A History of Country Music in Atlanta*. Urbana: University of Illinois Press, 1990.

"Daryle Singletary/Rhonda Vincent: American Grandstand." https://www.allmusic.com/album/american-grandstand-mw0003054342/releases. Last accessed July 23, 2018.

Dettmar, Kevin J. H. *Is Rock Dead?* New York: Routledge, 2006.

DeVeaux, Scott. *The Birth of Bebop: A Social and Musical History*. Berkeley: University of California Press, 1997.

Diamond, Beverly. "Media as Social Action: Native American Musicians in the Recording Studio." In *Wired for Sound: Engineers and Technologies in Sonic Cultures*. Eds. Paul D. Greene and Thomas Porcello. Middletown, CT: Wesleyan University Press, 2004, 118–137.

DiBlasi, Alex. "In Defense of the Monkees." *American Music Review* 41, no. 2 (Spring 2012). http://www.hisam.org/. Last accessed January 29, 2018.

Diekman, Diane. *Twentieth Century Drifter: The Life of Marty Robbins*. Urbana: University of Illinois Press, 2012.

Discogs.com. https://www.discogs.com/. Last accessed August 24, 2018.

Dockwray, Ruth, and Allan F. Moore. "Configuring the Sound-Box, 1965–1972." *Popular Music* 29, no. 2 (May 2010): 181–197.

Doerschuk, Robert L. "Beyond Floyd: The Harmonic Convergence." *Keyboard* (March 1993): 118, 123.

Doppelbauer, Martin. "Tony Joe White—His Life." http://www.martin-doppelbauer.de/TJW/life2.htm. Posted November 2000. Last accessed June 29, 2018.

Dorgan, Howard. *The Old Regular Baptists of Central Appalachia: Brothers and Sisters in Hope*. Knoxville: University of Tennessee Press, 2001.

Dougan, John. "Objects of Desire: Canon Formation and Blues Record Collecting." *Journal of Popular Music Studies* 18, no. 1 (2006): 40–65.

Drabløs, Per Elias. *The Quest for the Melodic Bass: From Jamerson to Spenner*. Aldershot, UK: Ashgate, 2015; reprint ed., New York: Routledge, 2016.

Elsdon, Peter. *Keith Jarrett's The Koln Concert*. New York: Oxford University Press, 2012.

Emerick, Geoff. *Here, There, and Everywhere: My Life Recording the Music of the Beatles.* New York: Gotham Books, 2006.

Emery, Ralph, with Tom Carter. *Memories: The Autobiography of Ralph Emery.* New York: Macmillan, 1991.

Escott, Colin. *Hank Williams: The Biography.* New York: Back Bay Books, 2004.

Escott, Colin, with Martin Hawkins. *Good Rockin' Tonight: Sun Records and the Birth of Rock 'n' Roll.* Paperback ed. New York: St. Martin's Griffin, 1992.

Eskew, Harry L. "Southern Baptist Contributions to Hymnody." *Baptist History and Heritage* 19, no. 1 (January 1984): 27–35.

Eskew, Harry L. "Southern Harmony and Its Era." *The Hymn: A Journal of Congregational Song* 41, no. 4 (October 1990): 28–34.

Eskew, Harry L. "William Walker's 'Southern Harmony': Its Basic Editions." *Latin American Music Review/Revista de Música Latinoamericana* 7, no. 2 (Autumn–Winter 1986): 137–148.

Fairchild, Frederick D. "Roy C. Knapp." Percussive Arts Society Hall of Fame. http://www.pas.org/about/hall-of-fame/roy-knapp. Last accessed November 2, 2017.

Faragher, Scott. *Nashville in Vintage Postcards.* Charleston, SC: Arcadia, 1999.

Farrugia, Rebekah, and Nancy Gobatto. "Shopping for Legs and Boots: Tori Amos's *Original Bootlegs*, Fandom, and Subcultural Capital." *Popular Music and Society* 33, no. 3 (July 2010): 357–375.

Fatherley, Richard W., and David T. MacFarland. *The Birth of Top 40 Radio: The Storz Stations' Revolution of the 1950s and 1960s.* Jefferson, NC: McFarland, 2014.

Feder, J. Lester. "'Song of the South': Country Music, Race, Region, and the Politics of Culture, 1920–1974." Ph.D. dissertation, University of California at Los Angeles, 2006.

Feder, Stuart. *Charles Ives, "My Father's Song": A Psychoanalytic Biography.* New Haven, CT: Yale University Press, 1992.

Firestone, Ross. *Swing, Swing, Swing: The Life and Times of Benny Goodman.* New York: W. W. Norton, 1993.

Flory, Andrew. *I Hear a Symphony: Motown and Crossover R&B.* Ann Arbor: University of Michigan Press, 2017.

Fong-Torres, Ben. *The Hits Just Keep on Coming: The History of Top 40 Radio.* San Francisco: Backbeat Books, 2001.

Fontenot, Kevin S. "Country Music's Confederate Grandfather: Henry C. Gilliland." In *Country Music Annual 2001.* Eds. Charles K. Wolfe and James E. Akenson. Lexington: University Press of Kentucky, 2001, 189–204.

Fontenot, Kevin S. "Uncle Henry and Captain Mose: New Insights into Two Country Music Pioneers." Paper presented to the International Country Music Conference, Belmont University, Nashville, TN, June 2, 2017.

Forbis, Wesley L. "The Sunday School Board and Baptist Church Music." *Baptist History and Heritage* 19, no. 1 (January 1984): 17–26.

Fox, Aaron A. *Real Country: Music and Language in Working-Class Culture.* Durham, NC: Duke University Press, 2004.

Fox, Aaron. "White Trash Alchemies of the Abject Sublime: Country as 'Bad' Music." In *Bad Music: The Music We Love to Hate.* Eds. Christopher J. Washburne and Maiken Derno. New York: Routledge, 2004, 39–61.

Fox, Jon Hartley. *King of the Queen City: The Story of King Records*. Urbana: University of Illinois Press, 2009.

Fox, Pamela. *Natural Acts: Gender, Race, and Rusticity in Country Music*. Ann Arbor: University of Michigan Press, 2009.

Fox, Pamela, and Barbara Ching, eds. *Old Roots, New Routes: The Cultural Politics of Alt. Country*. Ann Arbor: University of Michigan Press, 2008.

Fox, William S., and James D. Williams. "Political Orientation and Music Preferences among College Students." *Public Opinion Quarterly* 38, no. 3 (January 1974): 352–371.

Freda, Michael D. *Eddy Arnold Discography, 1944–1996*. Westport, CT: Greenwood Press, 1997.

Fresne, Jeannette. "History of the Stamps Baxter Singing Schools." *Journal of Historical Research in Music Education* 30, no. 1 (October 2008): 21–38.

Frith, Simon. "Pop Music." In *The Cambridge Companion to Pop and Rock*. Eds. Simon Frith, Will Straw, and John Street. Cambridge: Cambridge University Press, 2001, 91–108.

Frith, Simon. *Sound Effects: Youth, Leisure, and the Politics of Rock 'n' Roll*. New York: Pantheon Books, 1981.

Frizzell, Scott. "Not Just a Matter of Black and White: The Nashville Riot of 1967." *Tennessee Historical Quarterly* 70, no. 1 (Spring 2011): 26–51.

Gant, Alice M. "The Musicians in Nashville." *Journal of Country Music* 3, no. 2 (Summer 1972): 24–44.

Garrett, Charles Hiroshi. *Struggling to Define a Nation: American Music and the Twentieth Century*. Berkeley: University of California Press, 2008.

Gates, David. "Don't Get above Your Raisin': Ricky Skaggs, Alabama, and Their Contemporaries." In *Country: The Music and the Musicians from the Beginnings to the '90s*. Rev. and updated ed. Eds. Paul Kingsbury, Alan Axelrod, and Susan Costello. Nashville: Abbeville Press, 1994, 360–385.

Gebhardt, Nicholas. *Vaudeville Melodies: Popular Musicians and Mass Entertainment in American Culture, 1870–1929*. Chicago: University of Chicago Press, 2017.

Gibson, Nathan D. "What's International about International Country Music?: Country Music and National Identity around the World." In *The Oxford Handbook of Country Music*. Ed. Travis D. Stimeling. New York: Oxford University Press, 2017, 495–518.

Gibson, Nathan D., with Don Pierce. *The Starday Story: The House That Country Music Built*. Jackson: University Press of Mississippi, 2011.

Gilbert, Calvin. "Unsung Heroes Honored at Musicians Hall of Fame Induction." *CMT News* (November 27, 2007). http://www.cmt.com/news/1575159/unsung-heroes-honored-at-musicians-hall-of-fame-induction/. Last accessed January 28, 2018.

Ginell, Cary. *Milton Brown and the Founding of Western Swing*. Urbana: University of Illinois Press, 1994.

Glaser, Kevin L. *The Great Tompall: Forgotten Country Music Outlaw—The Authorized Biography of Tompall Glaser*. Oconomowoc, WI: Right Side Creations, 2014.

Goff, James R., Jr. *Close Harmony: A History of Southern Gospel*. Chapel Hill: University of North Carolina Press, 2002.

Gomery, Douglas. *Patsy Cline: The Making of an Icon*. Bloomington: Trafford Publishing, 2011.

Gomery, Douglas. *Sam Phillips: The Man Who Invented Rock 'n' Roll*. New York: Little, Brown, 2015.

Gooley, Dana. "The Outside of 'Sitting In': Jazz Jam Sessions and the Politics of Participation." *Performance Research* 16, no. 3 (September 2011): 43–48.

Graham, Hugh Davis. "Desegregation in Nashville: The Dynamics of Compliance." *Tennessee Historical Quarterly* 25, no. 2 (Summer 1966): 135–154.

Green, Archie. "Hillbilly Music: Source and Symbol." *Journal of American Folklore* 78, no. 309 (July–September 1965): 204–228.

Green, Archie. "Laborlore." In *Torching the Fink Books and Other Essays on Vernacular Culture*. Chapel Hill: University of North Carolina Press, 2001, 47–50.

Green, Douglas B. "Hargus 'Pig' Robbins: Top Nashville Studio Pianist." *Contemporary Keyboard* (July 1977): 20, 50–51.

Green, Douglas B. *Singing in the Saddle: The History of the Singing Cowboy*. Nashville: Country Music Foundation Press and Vanderbilt University Press, 2002.

Green, Lucy. *How Popular Musicians Learn: A Way Ahead for Music Education*. Aldershot, UK: Ashgate, 2001.

Greenfield, Robert. *The Last Sultan: The Life and Times of Ahmet Ertegun*. New York: Simon & Schuster, 2011.

Gregory, James N. *The Southern Diaspora: How the Great Migrations of Black and White Southerners Transformed America*. Chapel Hill: University of North Carolina Press, 2005.

Grier, Miles Parks. "Said the Hooker to the Thief: 'Some Way Out' of Rockism." *Journal of Popular Music Studies* 25, no. 1 (March 2013): 31–55.

Grissim, John. *Country Music: White Man's Blues*. New York: Coronet, 1970.

Grundy, Pamela. "'We Always Tried to Be Good People': Respectability, Crazy Water Crystals, and Hillbilly Music on the Air, 1933–1935." *Journal of American History* 81, no. 4 (March 1995): 1591–1620.

Guralnick, Peter. *Last Train to Memphis: The Rise of Elvis Presley*. New York: Back Bay Books, 1995.

Haas, Michael. "Studio Conducting." In *The Cambridge Companion to Conducting*. Ed. José Antonio Bowen. Cambridge: Cambridge University Press, 2003, 28–39.

Hall, Rick. *The Man from Muscle Shoals: My Journey from Shame to Fame*. Monterey: Heritage Builders, 2015.

Hall, Tom T. *The Storyteller's Nashville: A Gritty and Glorious Life in Country Music*. Rev. and expanded ed. Nashville: Spring House Press, 2016.

Hall, Wade. *Hell-Bent for Music: The Life of Pee Wee King*. Lexington: University Press of Kentucky, 1996.

Hamm, Charles. *Yesterdays: Popular Song in America*. New York: W. W. Norton, 1979.

Hammond, Angela Denise. "Color Me Country: Commercial Country Music and Whiteness." Ph.D. dissertation, University of Kentucky, 2011.

Harker, Brian. *Louis Armstrong's Hot Five and Hot Seven Recordings*. New York: Oxford University Press, 2011.

Harkins, Anthony. *Hillbilly: A Cultural History of an American Icon*. New York: Oxford University Press, 2004.

Harrington, Beth. *The Winding Stream: An Oral History of the Carter and Cash Family.* Georgetown, MA: PFP, 2014.

Hartman, Kent. *The Wrecking Crew: The Inside Story of Rock and Roll's Best-Kept Secret.* New York: Thomas Dunn Books, 2012.

Havighurst, Craig. *Air Castle of the South: WSM and the Making of Music City.* Urbana: University of Illinois Press, 2007.

Hawkins, Martin. *A Shot in the Dark: Making Records in Nashville, 1945–1955.* Nashville: Vanderbilt University Press and Country Music Foundation Press, 2006.

Healy, Scott. "Hammond B-3 Basics for Pianists." *Keyboard* (April 27, 2010). https://www.keyboardmag.com/lessons/hammond-b-3-basics-for-pianists. Last accessed June 28, 2018.

Heinonen, Yrjö. "The Creative Process of the Beatles Revisited: A Multi-level Analysis of the Interaction between Individual and Collaborative Creativity." *Popular Music History* 9, no. 1 (2014): 32–47.

Hemphill, Paul. *The Nashville Sound: Bright Lights and Country Music.* New York: Simon & Schuster, 1970; paperback ed., New York: Ballantine Books, 1975.

Hennion, Antoine. "The Production of Success: An Anti-Musicology of the Pop Song." *Popular Music* 3 (1983): 159–193.

Henry, Murphy Hicks. *Pretty Good for a Girl: Women in Bluegrass.* Urbana: University of Illinois Press, 2013.

Hill, Jeremy. *Country Comes to Town: The Music Industry and the Transformation of Nashville.* Amherst: University of Massachusetts Press, 2016.

Hill, Jeremy. "'Country Music Is Wherever the Soul of a Country Music Fan Is': Opryland U.S.A. and the Importance of Home in Country Music." *Southern Cultures* 17, no. 4 (2001): 92–111.

Hill, Trent. "The Enemy Within: Censorship in Rock Music in the 1950s." *South Atlantic Quarterly* 90, no. 4 (Fall 1991): 675–707.

Hirsch, Lily E. "Weaponizing Classical Music: Crime Prevention and Symbolic Power in the Age of Repetition." *Journal of Popular Music Studies* 19, no. 4 (2007): 342–358.

"Historic RCA Studio B." https://www.reddstewart.com/historic-rca-studio-b. Last accessed July 23, 2018.

Hodgson, Jay. *Understanding Records: A Field Guide to Recording Practice.* New York: Continuum, 2010.

Holmes, Tim. "US and Them: American Rock's Reconquista." *Popular Music and Society* 30, no. 3 (July 2007): 343–353.

Holt, Fabian. *Genre in Popular Music.* Chicago: University of Chicago Press, 2007.

Horowitz, Joseph. *Classical Music in America: A History of Its Rise and Fall.* New York: W. W. Norton, 2005.

Howe, Sandra Wieland. *Women Music Educators in the United States: A History.* Lanham, MD: Scarecrow Press, 2014.

Hubbs, Nadine. *Rednecks, Queers, and Country Music.* Berkeley: University of California Press, 2014.

Huber, Patrick. "Black Hillbillies: African American Musicians on Old-Time Records, 1924–1932." In *Hidden in the Mix: The African American Presence in Country Music.* Ed. Diane Pecknold. Durham, NC: Duke University Press, 2013. 19–81.

Huber, Patrick. *Linthead Stomp: The Creation of Country Music in the Piedmont South.* Chapel Hill: University of North Carolina Press, 2008.

Huber, Patrick. "The New York Sound: Citybilly Recording Artists and the Creation of Hillbilly Music, 1924–1932." *Journal of American Folklore* 127, no. 504 (Spring 2014): 140–158.

Huber, Patrick. "The 'Southernness' of Country Music." In *The Oxford Handbook of Country Music.* Ed. Travis D. Stimeling. New York: Oxford University Press, 2017, 31–53.

Hughes, Charles L. "Country Music and the Recording Industry." In *The Oxford Handbook of Country Music.* Ed. Travis D. Stimeling. New York: Oxford University Press, 2017, 205–228.

Hughes, Charles L. *Country Soul: Making Music and Making Race in the American South.* Chapel Hill: University of North Carolina Press, 2015.

Indraganti, Kiranmayi. *Her Majestic Voice: South Indian Female Playback Singers and Stardom, 1945–1955.* New Delhi: Oxford University Press, 2016.

Inglis, Ian. "Embassy Records: Covering the Market, Marketing the Cover." *Popular Music and Society* 28, no. 2 (May 2005): 163–170.

Isenhour, Jack. *He Stopped Loving Her Today: George Jones, Billy Sherrill, and the Pretty-Much Totally True Story of the Making of the Greatest Country Record of All Time.* Jackson: University Press of Mississippi, 2011.

Ivey, Bill. "The Bottom Line: Business Practices That Shaped Country Music." In *Country: The Music and the Musicians from the Beginnings to the '90s.* Rev. and updated ed. Eds. Paul Kingsbury, Alan Axelrod, and Susan Costello. New York: Abbeville, 1994, 280–311.

Ivey, Bill. "Chet Atkins." In *Stars of Country Music.* Eds. Bill C. Malone and Judith McCulloh. Urbana: University of Illinois Press, 1975; paperback ed., New York: Da Capo Press, 1991, 274–288.

Ivey, Bill. "Commercialization and Tradition in the Nashville Sound." In *Folk Music and Modern Sound.* Eds. William Ferris and Mary L. Hart. Jackson: University Press of Mississippi, 1982, 129–138.

"James Holds Trio." *Billboard* 76, no. 36 (5 September 1964): 16.

Jarrett, Michael. *Producing Country: The Inside Story of the Great Recordings.* Middletown, CT: Wesleyan University Press, 2014.

Jasen, David A. *Tin Pan Alley: The Composers, the Songs, the Performers, and Their Times—The Golden Age of American Popular Music from 1886 to 1956.* New York: D. I. Fine, 1988.

Jensen, Joli. *The Nashville Sound: Authenticity, Commercialization, and Country Music.* Vanderbilt University Press, 1998.

Johnson, Timothy A. *Baseball and the Music of Charles Ives: A Proving Ground.* Lanham, MD: Scarecrow Press, 2004.

Johnston, Richard, and Dick Boak. *Martin Guitars: A Technical Reference.* Milwaukee: Hal Leonard, 2009.

Jones, Loyal. *Country Music Humorists and Comedians.* Urbana: University of Illinois Press, 2008.

Jones, Roben. *Memphis Boys: The Story of American Studios.* Jackson: University Press of Mississippi, 2011.

Jones, Todd R. "The Relationship Between Lowell Mason and the Boston Handel and Haydn Society, 1815–1827." Ph.D. dissertation, University of Kentucky, 2017.

Jordan, Larry. *Jim Reeves: His Untold Story.* n.p.: Page Turner Books, 2011.

Kahunde, Samuel. "Repatriating Archival Sound Recordings to Revive Traditions: The Role of the Klaus Wachsmann Recordings in the Revival of the Royal Music of Bunyoro-Kitara, Uganda." *Ethnomusicology Forum* 21, no. 2 (August 2012): 197–219.

Katz, Mark. *Capturing Sound: How Technology Has Changed Music.* Rev. ed. Berkeley: University of California Press, 2010.

Katz, Mark. *Groove Music: The Art and Culture of the Hip-Hop DJ.* New York: Oxford University Press, 2012.

Keefe, Simon P. "'Die Ochsen am Berge': Fran Xaver Süssmayr and the Orchestration of Mozart's Requiem, K. 626." *Journal of the American Musicological Society* 61, no. 1 (Spring 2008): 1–65.

Kehrberg, Kevin Donald. "'I'll Fly Away': The Music and Career of Albert E. Brumley." Ph.D. dissertation, University of Kentucky, 2010.

Kenney, William Howland. *Recorded Music in American Life: The Phonograph and Popular Memory, 1890–1945.* New York: Oxford University Press, 1999.

Kienzle, Rich. "First Bass: Bob Moore Has Witnessed and Made Music History Holding Down the Bottom End for Nashville's Studio A-Team." *No Depression* 77 (2009): 36–47.

Kienzle, Rich. "Floyd Cramer, 1933–1997." *Country Music* (March–April 1998): 54.

Kienzle, Rich _. "For Gary Burton, It Started in Nashville. Really." *Community Voices* (October 3, 2013). http://communityvoices.post-gazette.com/arts-entertainment-living/get-rhythm/item/37465-for-gary-burton-it-started-in-nashville-really. Last accessed June 28, 2018.

Kienzle, Rich. "Hank Garland: Legendary Country-Jazz Artist." *Guitar Player* (January 1981): 76–86.

Kienzle, Rich. "Ray Edenton: Nashville Studio Rhythm Specialist." *Guitar Player* (May 1981): 76–80.

Kienzle, Rich. *Southwest Shuffle: Pioneers of Honky-Tonk, Western Swing, and Country Jazz.* New York: Routledge, 2003.

King, Rob. *Hokum!: The Early Sound Slapstick Short and Depression-Era Mass Culture.* Berkeley: University of California Press, 2017.

Kingsbury, Henry. *Music, Talent, and Performance: A Conservatory Cultural System.* Philadelphia: Temple University Press, 2001.

Kingsbury, Paul, Michael McCall, and John Rumble, eds. *The Encyclopedia of Country Music.* 2nd ed New York: Oxford University Press, 2012.

Klefstad, Terry. *Crooked River City: The Musical Life of Nashville's William Pursell.* Jackson: University Press of Mississippi, 2018.

Kosser, Michael. *How Nashville Became Music City: 50 Years of Music Row.* Milwaukee: Hal Leonard Books, 2006.

Kraft, James P. *Stage to Studio: Musicians and the Sound Revolution, 1890–1950.* Baltimore, MD: Johns Hopkins University Press, 1996.

Kramer, Michael J. "Rocktimism?: Pop Music Writing in the Age of Rock Criticism." *Journal of Popular Music Studies* 24, no. 4 (December 2012): 590–600.

Kreyling, Christine, Wesley Paine, Charles W. Waterfield, Jr., and Susan Ford Wiltshire. *Nashville: Athens of the South.* Nashville: Vanderbilt University Press, 1996.

Kronengold, Charles. "Accidents, Hooks, and Theory." *Popular Music* 24, no. 3 (October 2005): 381–397.

Krueger, Alan B., and Alexandre Mas. "Strikes, Scabs, and Tread Separations: Labor Strife and the Production of Defective Bridgestone/Firestone Tires." National Bureau of Economic Research, NBER Working Paper Series, Working Paper 9524. http://www.nber.org/papers/w9524. Posted February 2003. Last accessed July 2, 2018.

Kruse, Holly. "Local Identity and Independent Music Scenes: Online and Off." *Popular Music and Society* 33, no. 5 (2010): 625–639.

Kruse, Holly. *Site and Sound: Understanding Independent Music Scenes.* New York: Peter Lang, 2003.

Kurland, Sheldon. *An Adult Guide to the Orchestra.* Nashville: Darkhorse Books, 2002.

LaChapelle, Peter. *Proud to Be an Okie: Cultural Politics, Country Music, and Migration to Southern California.* Berkeley: University of California Press, 2007.

Lagos, Taso G. "Poor Greek to 'Scandalous' Hollywood Mogul: Alexander Pantages and the Anti-Immigrant Narratives of William Randolph Hearst's *Los Angeles Examiner.*" *Journal of Modern Greek Studies* 30, no. 1 (May 2012): 45–74.

Laird, Tracey E. W. *The Louisiana Hayride: Radio and Roots Music along the Red River.* New York: Oxford University Press, 2014.

Lange, Jeffrey J. *Smile When You Call Me a Hillbilly: Country Music's Struggle for Respectability.* Athens: University of Georgia Press, 2004.

Lawrence, Robb. *The Early Years of the Les Paul Legacy, 1915–1963.* Milwaukee: Hal Leonard, 2008.

Lawson, Colin. "Recreating History: A Clarinettist's Retrospective." In *The Cambridge Companion to Recorded Music*, eds. Nicholas Cook, Eric Clarke, Daniel Leech-Wilkinson, and John Rink. Cambridge: Cambridge University Press, 2009, 263–266.

Ledbetter, April, and Lance Ledbetter, comp. *Never a Pal like Mother: Vintage Songs and Photographs of the One Who's Always True.* Atlanta: Dust-to-Digital, 2011.

Leech-Wilkinson, Daniel. *The Changing Sound of Music: Approaches to Studying Recorded Musical Performance.* London: CHARM, 2009.

Leech-Wilkinson, Daniel. "Recordings and Histories of Performance Style." In *The Cambridge Companion to Recorded Music.* Eds. Nicholas Cook, Eric Clarke, Daniel Leech-Wilkinson, and John Rink. Cambridge: Cambridge University Press, 2009, 246–262.

Leitzel, Galen E. "The History and Development of the American Public School Concert Band (1920–1941) and Its Influence on Concert Band Repertoire." DMA dissertation, Shenandoah Conservatory, 2006.

Leppert, Richard, and George Lipsitz. "'Everybody's Lonesome for Somebody': Age, the Body, and Experience in the Music of Hank Williams." *Popular Music* 9, no. 3 (October 1990): 259–274.

Levin, Robert D., Richard Maunder, Duncan Druce, David Black, Christoph Wolff, and Simon P. Keefe. "Finishing Mozart's Requiem: On 'Die Ochsen am Berge': Franz

Xaver Süssmayr and the Orchestration of Mozart's Requiem, K. 626." *Journal of the American Musicological Society* 61, no. 3 (Fall 2008): 583–608.

Levine, Lawrence W. *Highbrow/Lowbrow: The Emergence of Cultural Hierarchy in America*. Cambridge, MA: Harvard University Press, 1988.

Levy, Morris. "Nashville Sound-Era Studio Musicians." In *Country Music Annual 2000*. Eds. Charles K. Wolfe and James E. Akenson. Lexington: University Press of Kentucky, 2000.=, 22–29.

"Lillian Vann Hunt." *Nashville Tennessean* (May 10, 2009).

Lindvall, Terry, and Andrew Quicke. *Celluloid Sermons: The Emergence of the Christian Film Industry, 1930–1986*. New York: New York University Press, 2011.

Linn, Karen. *That Half-Barbaric Twang: The Banjo in American Popular Culture*. Urbana: University of Illinois Press, 1991.

Locke, Ralph P. "Music Lovers, Patrons, and the 'Sacralization' of Culture in America." *19th-Century Music* 17, no. 2 (Autumn 1993): 149–173.

Lockheart, Paula. "A History of Early Microphone Singing, 1925–1939: American Mainstream Popular Singing at the Advent of Electronic Microphone Amplification." *Popular Music and Society* 26, no. 3 (2003): 367–386.

Lomax, John, III. *Nashville: Music City USA*. New York: Harry N. Abrams, 1985.

Lund, Jens. "Fundamentalism, Racism, and Political Reaction in Country Music." In *The Sounds of Social Change: Studies in Popular Culture*. Eds. R. Serge Denisoff and Richard A. Peterson. Chicago: Rand McNally, 1972, 79–91.

Macfarland, Malcolm, and Ken Crossland. *Perry Como: A Biography and Complete Career Record*. Jefferson, NC: McFarland Press, 2009.

MacLeod, Sean. *Phil Spector: Sound of the Sixties*. Lanham, MD: Rowman & Littlefield, 2018.

Malone, Bill C. *Don't Get above Your Raisin': Country Music and the Southern Working Class*. Urbana: University of Illinois Press, 2001.

Malone, Bill C. "Patsy Cline and the Transformation of the Working-Class South." In *Sweet Dreams: The World of Patsy Cline*. Ed. Warren R. Hofstra. Urbana: University of Illinois Press, 2013, 17–21.

Malone, Bill C., and Jocelyn R. Neal. *Country Music, U.S.A*. 3nd rev. ed. Austin: University of Texas Press, 2010.

Malone, Bill C., and David Stricklin. *Southern Music/American Music*. Rev. and expanded ed. Lexington: University Press of Kentucky, 2003.

Manning's Ithaca Directory 1957. Schenectady: H. A. Manning, 1957.

Mansfield, Brian. "Pioneering Nashville Guitarist Velma Smith Dies." *USA Today* (August 1, 2014). https://www.usatoday.com/story/life/music/2014/08/01/velma-smith-nashville-guitarist-dies/13454861/. Last accessed September 14, 2017).

Marovich, Robert M. *A City Called Heaven: Chicago and the Birth of Gospel Music*. Urbana: University of Illinois Press, 2015.

Marshall, Lee. "For and against the Record Industry: An Introduction to Bootleg Collectors and Tape Traders." *Popular Music* 22, no. 1 (January 2003): 57–72.

Matthews, Neil, Jr. *The Nashville Numbering System: An Aid to Playing by Ear*. 2nd ed. Milwaukee: Hal Leonard, 1984.

May, Lissa Fleming. "Early Musical Development of Selected African American Jazz Musicians in Indianapolis in the 1930s and 1940s." *Journal of Historical Research in Music Education* 27, no. 1 (October 2005): 21–32.

Mazor, Barry. *Ralph Peer and the Making of Popular Roots Music.* Chicago: Chicago Review Press, 2015.

McCall, Michael. "Nashville Cats: Salute to Bob Moore." Country Music Hall of Fame and Museum. http://www.countrymusichalloffame.org/nashville-cats/bob-moore. Posted February 17, 2007. Last accessed October 18, 2017.

McClary, Susan. *Feminine Endings: Music, Gender, and Sexuality.* Minneapolis: University of Minnesota Press, 1991.

McCommon, Paul. "Trends in Southern Baptist Church Music since 1915." *Baptist History and Heritage* 21, no. 3 (July 1986): 50–56.

McCoy, Charlie, with Travis D. Stimeling. *Fifty Cents and a Box Top: The Creative Life of Nashville Session Musician Charlie McCoy.* Morgantown: West Virginia University Press, 2017.

McCracken, Allison. *Real Men Don't Sing: Crooning in American Culture.* Durham, NC: Duke University Press, 2015.

McCusker, Kristine M. *Lonesome Cowgirls and Honky-Tonk Angels: The Women of Barn Dance Radio.* Urbana: University of Illinois Press, 2008.

McCusker, Kristine. "Rose Lee Maphis and Working on Barn Dance Radio, 1930–1960." In *The Women of Country Music: A Reader.* Eds. Charles K. Wolfe and James E. Akenson. Lexington: University Press of Kentucky, 2003, 61–74.

McDonough, Jimmy. *Tammy Wynette: Tragic Country Queen.* New York: Penguin Books, 2010.

McElrath, Hugh T. "Turning Points in the Story of Baptist Church Music." *Baptist History and Heritage* 19, no. 1 (January 1984): 4–16.

McRaven, William H. *Nashville: Athens of the South.* Nashville: Tennessee Book Company, 1949.

Meintjes, Louise. "The Politics of the Recording Studio: A Case Study from South Africa." In *The Cambridge Companion to Recorded Music.* Eds. Nicholas Cook, Eric Clarke, Daniel Leech-Wilkinson, and John Rink. Cambridge: Cambridge University Press, 2009, 84–97.

Meintjes, Louise. "Reaching 'Overseas': South African Engineers, Technology, and Tradition." In *Wired for Sound: Engineering and Technologies in Sonic Cultures.* Eds. Paul D. Greene and Thomas Porcello. Middletown, CT: Wesleyan University Press, 2004, 23–46.

Meintjes, Louise. *Sound of Africa!: Making Music Zulu in a South African Studio.* Durham, NC: Duke University Press, 2003.

Mellard, Jason. *Progressive Country: How the 1970s Transformed the Texan in Popular Culture.* Austin: University of Texas Press, 2013.

Melton, Gary Warren. "An Examination of the Bootleg Record Industry and Its Impact upon Popular Music Consumption." *Journal of Popular Music Studies* 26, nos. 2–3 (June 2014): 399–408.

Mercer-Taylor, Peter. "Two-and-a-Half Centuries in the Life of a Hook." *Popular Music and Society* 23, no. 2 (Summer 1999): 1–15.

Messer, Susan Kitts. "The Southern Baptist Children's Choir Curricula from 1941 through 1985 and Influences of Major Music Education Trends upon the Curricula." Ph.D. dissertation, Louisiana State University, 1988.

Middleton, Richard. *Voicing the Popular: On the Subjects of Popular Music.* New York: Routledge, 2006.

Millard, Andre. *America on Record: A History of Recorded Sound,* 2nd ed. Cambridge: Cambridge University Press, 2005.

Miller, Bonny H. "A Mirror of Ages Past: The Publication of Music in Domestic Periodicals." *Notes* (Second Series) 50, no. 3 (March 1994): 883–901.

Miller, Karl Hagstrom. *Segregating Sound: Inventing Folk and Pop Music in the Age of Jim Crow.* Durham, NC: Duke University Press, 2010.

Miller, Kiri. *Traveling Home: Sacred Harp Singing and American Pluralism.* Urbana: University of Illinois Press, 2008.

Moore, Allan F. "Authenticity as Authentication." *Popular Music* 21, no. 2 (May 2002): 209–223.

Moore, Allan F. *Song Means: Analysing and Interpreting Recorded Popular Song.* Farnham, UK: Ashgate, 2012.

Moore, Allan F., and Ruth Dockwray. "The Establishment of the Virtual Performance Space in Rock." *Twentieth-Century Music* 5, no. 2 (September 2008): 219–241.

Moore, Allan F., Patricia Smith, and Ruth Dockwray, "A Hermeneutics of Spatialization for Recorded Song." *Twentieth-Century Music* 6, no. 1 (March 2009): 83–114.

Moorefield, Virgil. *The Producer as Composer: Shaping the Sounds of Popular Music.* Cambridge, MA: MIT Press, 2005.

Morton, David. *Off the Record: The Technology and Culture of Sound Recording in America.* New Brunswick, NJ: Rutgers University Press, 2000.

Morton, David L., Jr. *Sound Recording: The Life Story of a Technology.* Baltimore, MD: Johns Hopkins University Press, 2004.

Murphy, Clifford. *Yankee Twang: Country and Western Music in New England.* Urbana: University of Illinois Press, 2014.

Music, David W. "Tunes by Lowell Mason and Thomas Hastings in Southern United States Shape-Note Tune Books of the Early Nineteenth Century." *Journal of Musicological Research* 26 (2007): 325–352.

Musicians Hall of Fame. "Shelly Kurland." http://www.musicianshalloffame.com/virtual-tours/shelly-kurland/. Last accessed September 25, 2015.

Myers, Marc. *Anatomy of a Song: The Oral History of 45 Iconic Hits that Changed Rock, R&B and Pop.* New York: Grove Press, 2016.

Myers, Marc. "Interview: Gary Burton (Part 1)." http://www.jazzwax.com/2010/07/interview-gary-burton-part-1.html. Posted July 26, 2010. Last accessed August 20, 2018.

Nashville Symphony Orchestra. "About: Mission & History." https://www.nashvillesymphony.org/about/history. Last accessed September 25, 2015.

Neal, Jocelyn R. "Analysis and Performance across the Canon: 'When Recollection Is All We've Got': Analytical Exploration of 'Catchy' Songs." *College Music Symposium* 47 (2007): 12–22.

Neal, Jocelyn R. "The Metric Makings of a Country Hit." In *Reading Country Music*. Ed. Cecilia Tichi. Durham, NC: Duke University Press, 1998. 322–337.

Neal, Jocelyn R. "Narrative Paradigms, Musical Signifiers, and Form as Function in Country Music." *Music Theory Spectrum* 29 (2007): 41–72.

Neal, Jocelyn R. "'Nothing but a Little Old Pop Song': Patsy Cline's Music Style and the Evolution of Genre in the 1950s." In *Sweet Dreams: The World of Patsy Cline*, ed. Warren R. Hofstra. Urbana: University of Illinois Press, 2013, 128–153.

Neal, Jocelyn R. "The Twang Factor in Country Music." In *The Relentless Pursuit of Tone: Timbre in Popular Music*. Eds. Robert Fink, Melinda Latour, and Zachary Wallmark. New York: Oxford University Press, 2018, 43–64.

Negus, Keith. *Music Genres and Corporate Cultures*. New York: Routledge, 1999.

Nelson, Ken. *My First 90 Years Plus 3*. Pittsburgh: Dorrance, 2007.

Nettl, Bruno. *Heartland Excursions: Ethnomusicological Reflections on Schools of Music*. Urbana: University of Illinois Press, 1995.

Neumann, Mark, and Timothy A. Simpson. "Smuggled Sound: Bootleg Recording and the Pursuit of Popular Memory." *Symbolic Interaction* 20, no. 4 (February 1997): 319–341.

Noles, Randy. *Orange Blossom Boys: The Untold Story of Ervin T. Rouse, Chubby Wise, and the World's Most Famous Fiddle Tune*. Anaheim Hills, CA: CENTERSTREAM, 2002.

Noonan, Jeffrey J. *The Guitar in America: Victorian Era to Jazz Age*. Jackson: University Press of Mississippi, 2008.

Noonan, Jeffrey. *The Guitar in American Banjo, Mandolin, and Guitar Periodicals, 1882–1933*. Middleton, WI: Music Library Association, 2009.

Noonan, Jeffrey. "Highbrow, Lowbrow and Middlebrow: An Introduction to America's Progressive Era Mandolin Orchestra." *Musique, Images, Instruments: Revue française d'organologie et d'iconographie musicale* 12 (2010): 170–189.

Norton, Kay. *Baptist Offspring, Southern Midwife: Jesse Mercer's Cluster of Spiritual Songs (1810)—A Study in American Hymnody*. Warren, MI: Harmonie Park, 2002.

Nunn, Erich. *Sounding the Color Line: Music and Race in the Southern Imagination*. Athens: University of Georgia Press, 2015.

Olmsted, Tony. *Folkways Records: Moses Asch and His Encyclopedia of Sound*. New York: Routledge, 2003.

"On the Passing of Shelly Kurland, Peter's Father." *Film Nashville*. Posted January 9, 2010. https://filmnashville.org/on-the-passing-of-shelly-kurland-peters-fathe/. Last accessed September 18, 2015.

Orr, Jay, ed. *Dylan, Cash, and the Nashville Cats: A New Music City*. Nashville: Country Music Foundation, 2015.

Orr, Jay, ed. *Home of 1,000 Hits: Historic RCA Studio B, Nashville*. Nashville: Country Music Foundation, 2016.

Osborne, Richard. *Vinyl: A History of the Analogue Record*. New York: Routledge, 2014.

Park, Hyu-Yong, and Mi-Jung Kim. "Affordance of Braille Music as a Mediational Means: Significance and Limitations." *British Journal of Music Education* 31, no. 2 (July 2014): 137–155.

Patoski, Joe Nick. *Willie Nelson: An Epic Life*. New York: Little, Brown, 2008.

"The Peabody Semicentennial." *Peabody Journal of Education* 2, no. 5 (March 1925): 278–281.

Pearson, Valerie. "Authorship and Improvisation: Musical Lost Property." *Contemporary Music Review* 29, no. 4 (August 2010): 367–378.

Pecknold, Diane. "The Country Music Association, the Country Music Foundation, and Country Music's History." In *The Oxford Handbook of Country Music.* Ed. Travis D. Stimeling. New York: Oxford University Press, 2017, 55–84.

Pecknold, Diane. "Making Country Modern: The Legacy of *Modern Sounds in Country and Western Music.*" In *Hidden in the Mix: The African American Presence in Country Music.* Durham, NC: Duke University Press, 2013. 82–99.

Pecknold, Diane. "Negotiating Gender, Race, and Class in Post-Civil Rights Country Music: How Linda Martell and Jeannie C. Riley Stormed the Plantation." In *Country Boys and Redneck Women: New Essays in Gender and Country Music.* Eds. Diane Pecknold and Kristine M. McCusker. Jackson: University Press of Mississippi, 2016, 146–165.

Pecknold, Diane. *The Selling Sound: The Rise of the Country Music Industry.* Durham, NC: Duke University Press, 2007.

Pemberton, Carol Ann. "Lowell Mason: His Life and Work." Ph.D. dissertation, University of Minnesota, 1971.

Perone, James E. *Songs of the Vietnam Conflict.* Westport, CT: Greenwood Press, 2001.

Peterson, Richard A. *Creating Country Music: Fabricating Authenticity.* Chicago: University of Chicago Press, 1997.

Peterson, Richard A. "The Dialectic of Hard-Core and Soft-Shell Country Music." In *Reading Country Music: Steel Guitars, Opry Stars, and Honky-Tonk Bars.* Ed. Cecelia Tichi. Durham, NC: Duke University Press, 1998, 234–255.

Pethel, Mary Ellen. *Athens of the New South: College Life and the Making of Modern Nashville.* Knoxville: University of Tennessee Press, 2017.

Philip, Robert. *Performing Music in the Age of Recording.* New Haven, CT: Yale University Press, 2004.

Pierce, Charles L. "A History of Music and Music Education of the Seventh-Day Adventist Church." DMA dissertation, Catholic University of America, 1976.

Pierce, Jennifer Ember. *Playin' Around: The Lives and Careers of Famous Session Musicians.* Lanham, MD: Scarecrow Press, 1998.

Pinch, Trevor, and Karin Bijsterveld. "New Keys to the World of Sound." In *The Oxford Handbook of Sound Studies.* Eds. Trevor Pinch and Karin Bijsterveld. New York: Oxford University Press, 2011, 3–35.

Platte, Nathan. "Music for *Spellbound* (1945): A Contested Collaboration." *Journal of Musicology* 28, no. 4 (Fall 2011): 418–463.

Poe, William Allen. "Nashville, Tennessee." In *The Encyclopedia of Religion in the South.* 2nd ed. Eds. Samuel S. Hill and Charles H. Lippy. Macon: Mercer University Press, 2005, 538–539.

Polk's Nashville Suburban Director. n.p.: R. L. Polk, 1958.

Porcello, Thomas. "Music Mediated as Live in Austin: Sound, Technology, and Recording Practice." In *Wired for Sound: Engineering and Technologies in Sonic Cultures.* Eds.

Paul D. Greene and Thomas Porcello. Middletown, CT: Wesleyan University Press, 2005, 103–117.

Porcello, Thomas. "'Tails Out': Social Phenomenology and the Ethnographic Representation of Technology in Music-Making." *Ethnomusicology* 42, no. 3 (Autumn 1998): 485–510.

Porterfield, Nolan. *Jimmie Rodgers: The Life and Times of America's Blue Yodeler.* Urbana: University of Illinois Press, 1979.

Portis, Charles. "That New Sound from Nashville." *Saturday Evening Post* (February 12, 1966): 30–38.

Praguefrank's Country Music Discographies. http://countrydiscography.blogspot.com and http://countrydiscoghraphy2.blogspot.com. Last accessed August 24, 2018.

Pruett, David B. "Music City, U.S.A.: Charlotte, North Carolina." Paper presented to the Society for American Music, Tempe, AZ, March 2003.

Pruett, David B. "Commercial Country as Process: WBT, Charlotte, and the Creation of a Country Music Center." Paper presented to the International Country Music Conference, Belmont University, May 2003.

Pugh, Ronnie. *Ernest Tubb: The Texas Troubadour.* Durham, NC: Duke University Press, 1996.

Pyall, Nicholas. "Guitar Stringing in Late Nineteenth-Century North America: The Emergence of Steel." *Journal of the American Musical Instrument Society* 40 (2014): 29–74.

Ramsey, Sonya. "'We Will Be Ready Whenever They Are': African American Teachers' Responses to the *Brown* Decision and Public School Integration in Nashville, Tennessee, 1954–1956." *Journal of African American History* 90, no.1–2 (Winter 2005): 29–51.

Randel, Don Michael. "The Canons in the Musicological Toolbox." In *Disciplining Music: Musicology and Its Canons.* Eds. Katherine Bergeron and Philip V. Bohlman. Chicago: University of Chicago Press, 1992, 10–22.

Ratliff, Ben. "Chet Atkins, 77, Is Dead: Guitarist and Producer Was Architect of the Nashville Sound." *New York Times* (July 2, 2011). https://www.nytimes.com/2001/07/02/us/chet-atkins-77-dead-guitarist-producer-was-architect-nashville-sound.html. Last accessed 23 July 2018.

Rebelo, Pedro. "Dramaturgy in the Network." *Contemporary Music Review* 28, nos. 4–5 (August–October 2009): 387–393.

Reising, Russell. *"Every Sound There Is": The Beatles' Revolver and the Transformation of Rock and Roll.* Aldershot, UK: Ashgate, 2002.

Reynolds, Simon. "Lost in Music: Obsessive Record Collecting." In *This Is Pop: In Search of the Elusive at Experience Music Project.* Ed. Eric Weisbard. Cambridge, MA: Harvard University Press, 2004, 289–307.

Reynolds, William J. "The Graded Choir Movement among Southern Baptists." *Baptist History and Heritage* 19, no. 1 (January 1984): 55–62.

Rhodes College. *The Lynx.* Memphis, 1952.

Ridley, Jim. "A Celebration of Jerry Carrigan at Country Music Hall of Fame." *Nashville Scene* (February 19, 2009). http://www.nashvillescene.com/arts-culture/article/

13017590/a-celebration-of-jerry-carrigan-at-country-music-hall-of-fame.   Last accessed November 3, 2017.

Ritchie, Fiona, and Doug Orr. *Wayfaring Strangers: The Musical Voyage from Scotland and Ulster to Appalachia*. Chapel Hill: University of North Carolina Press, 2014.

Roberts, John Storm. *The Latin Tinge: The Impact of Latin American Music on the United States*. 2nd ed. New York: Oxford University Press, 1999.

Rodger, Gillian M. *Champagne Charlie and Pretty Jemima: Variety Theater in the Nineteenth Century*. Urbana: University of Illinois Press, 2010.

Rodman, Ron. "Radio Formats in the United States: A (Hyper)Fragmentation of the Imagination." In *Music and the Broadcast Experience: Performance, Production, and Audiences*. Eds. Christina L. Baade and James Deaville. New York: Oxford University Press, 2016, 235–258.

Rodnitzky, Jerome L. "The Decline of Contemporary Protest Music." *Popular Music and Society* 1, no. 1 (Fall 1971): 44–50.

Roe, Dave. "Bob Moore, Music City Maven." *Bass Player* (August 2, 2011). http://www. bassplayer.com/artists/1171/bob-moore-music-city-maven/26503.   Last accessed October 22, 2017.

Rosenberg, Neil V., and Charles K. Wolfe. *The Music of Bill Monroe*. Urbana: University of Illinois Press, 2007.

Rowden, Terry. *The Songs of Blind Folk: African American Musicians and the Cultures of Blindness*. Ann Arbor: University of Michigan Press, 2009.

Ruppli, Michel, comp. *The King Labels: A Discography*. Vol. 1. Westport, CT: Greenwood Press, 1985.

Rumble, John W. "Behind the Board with Bill Porter, Part One." *Journal of Country Music* 18, no. 1 (1996): 27–40.

Rumble, John W. "Behind the Board with Bill Porter, Part Two." *Journal of Country Music* 18, no. 2 (1996): 20–30.

Rumble, John W. "Behind the Board with Bill Porter, Part Three." *Journal of Country Music* 19, no. 1 (1997): 24–31.

Rumble, John W. "The Emergence of Nashville as a Recording Center: Logbooks from the Castle Studio, 1952–1953." *Journal of Country Music* 7, no. 3 (December 1978): 22–41.

Rumble, John W. "Fred Rose and the Development of the Nashville Music Industry, 1942–1954." Ph.D. dissertation, Vanderbilt University, 1980.

Rumble, John W. *Home of 1,000 Hits: Historic RCA Studio B, Nashville*. Nashville: Country Music Foundation Press, 2016.

Rumble, John W., ed. *Chet Atkins: Certified Guitar Player*. Nashville: Country Music Foundation, 2011.

Russell, Tony. "Country Music on Location: 'Field Recording' Before Bristol." *Popular Music* 26, no. 1 (January 2007): 23–31.

Russell, Tony. *Country Music Records: A Discography, 1921–1942*. New York: Oxford University Press, 2004.

Russo, Alexander. "Passing Pappy's Biscuits: Dynamics of Uneven Modernization in Regional Radio Voices." In *Music and the Broadcast Experience: Performance,*

Production, and Audiences. Eds. Christina Baade and James A. Deaville. New York: Oxford University Press, 2016, 173–190.

Safford, Sean. *Why the Garden Club Couldn't Save Youngstown: The Transformation of the Rust Belt*. Cambridge, MA: Harvard University Press, 2009.

Samples, Mark Christopher. "A Package Deal: Branding, Technology, and Advertising in Music of the 20th and 21st Centuries." Ph.D. dissertation, University of Oregon, 2012.

Sanjek, David. "What's Syd Got to Do with It?: King Records, Henry Glover, and the Complex Achievement of Crossover." In *Hidden in the Mix: The African American Presence in Country Music*. Ed. Diane Pecknold. Durham, NC: Duke University Press, 2013, 306–338.

Sanjek, Russell, and David Sanjek. *American Popular Music Business in the 20th Century*. New York: Oxford University Press, 1991.

"Savoy Records Discography: 1945." *JazzDisco.org*. https://www.jazzdisco.org/savoy-records/discography-1945/. Accessed April 4, 2018.

Sawyer, Kathy. "Perry Como Sings Praise of Good Old Nashville." *Nashville Tennesseean* (August 22, 1967).

Schalk, Sami. "Reevaluating the Supercrip." *Journal of Literary & Cultural Disability Studies* 10, no. 1 (2016): 71–86.

Schlappi, Elizabeth Roe. *Roy Acuff, the Smoky Mountain Boy*. 2nd ed. Gretna, LA: Pelican Publishing, 1997.

Schloss, Joseph G. *Making Beats: The Art of Sample-Based Hip-Hop*. Middletown, CT: Wesleyan University Press, 2004.

Schmidt Horning, Susan. *Chasing Sound: Technology, Culture, and the Art of Studio Recording from Edison to the LP*. Baltimore, MD: Johns Hopkins University Press, 2013.

Schorer, Dylan, Jim Ohlschmidt, and Thom Bresh. "Travis Style: The Life and Legacy of Thumbpicking King Merle Travis." *Acoustic Guitar* 9 (December 1998): 52–63.

Schultz, Barbara. "Classic Tracks: Charlie Rich 'Behind Closed Doors.'" *Mix* (September 1, 2011). https://www.mixonline.com/recording/classic-tracks-charlie-rich-behind-closed-doors-366297. Last accessed 29 June 2018.

Seabrook, John. *The Song Machine: Inside the Hit Factory*. New York: W. W. Norton, 2015.

Segrave, Kerry. *Payola in the Music Industry: A History, 1880–1991*. Jefferson, NC: McFarland, 1994.

Senneh, Kalefa. "The Rap against Rockism." *New York Times* (October 31, 2004). http://www.nytimes.com/2004/10/31/arts/music/31sann.html. Last accessed November 9, 2012.

Shank, Barry. *Dissonant Identities: The Rock 'n' Roll Scene in Austin, Texas*. Hanover, NH: Wesleyan University Press, 1994.

Shearon, Stephen. "Kieffer, Aldine." In *Encyclopedia of American Gospel Music*. Ed. W. K. McNeil. New York: Routledge, 2005, 215–217.

Shearon, Stephen, Harry Eskew, James C. Downey, and Robert Darden. "Gospel Music 2. Southern Gospel Music." In *Grove Music Online* https://doi-org.www.libproxy.wvu.edu/10.1093/gmo/9781561592630.article.A2224388. Last accessed April 11, 2018.

"Shelly Kurland." *New York Times* (January 9, 2010). https://archive.nytimes.com/query. nytimes.com/gst/fullpage-9E07EEDC123AF93AA35752C0A9669D8B63.html. Last accessed December 16, 2019.

Shelton, Alan. "Chet Atkins and the Nashville Sound." *Country Music World* no. 10 (August 5–18, 1981): 27.

"The Sherrill Sound." *Time* (October 22, 1973): 85.

Shuker, Roy. "Beyond the 'High Fidelity' Stereotype: Defining the (Contemporary) Record Collector." *Popular Music* 23, no. 3 (October 2004): 311–330.

Shuker, Roy. *Wax Trash and Vinyl Treasures: Record Collecting as a Social Practice.* Farnham, UK: Ashgate, 2016.

Shuker, Roy. *Popular Music: The Key Concepts*, 4th ed. New York: Routledge, 2017.

Simons, David. "Ray Edenton's 'A-Team' Memories." *The Country Music Journal* 55 (June–July 2000): 11–12.

Simons, David. *Studio Stories: How the Great New York Records Were Made.* San Francisco: Backbeat Books, 2004.

Simpson, Kim. "Country Radio's Growing Pains in the Music Trades, 1967–1977." *American Music* 27, no. 4 (Winter 2009): 500–514.

"Singleton Breaks New Ground." *Record World* (March 22, 1969): 22.

Skates, Sarah. "New Procedures for Election to the Country Music Hall of Fame." *Music Row* (February 25, 2009). https://musicrow.com/2009/02/new-procedures-for-election-to-the-country-music-hall-of-fame/. Last accessed January 27, 2018.

Smith, Allen. "Jerry Carrigan: Bama-Lam! Alabama's Drumming Legend." *Gritz* (July 2000). http://swampland.com/articles/view/title:jerry_carrigan. Last accessed November 3, 2017.

Smith, Richard D. *Can't You Hear Me Calling: The Life of Bill Monroe, Father of Bluegrass.* Boston: Little, Brown, 2000.

Smith, W. O. *Sideman: The Long Gig of W. O. Smith: A Memoir.* Nashville: Rutledge Hill Press, 1991.

Smith, Wes. *The Pied Pipers of Rock 'n' Roll: Radio Deejays of the '50s and '60s.* Marietta, GA: Longstreet, 1989.

Spottswood, Dick. *Banjo on the Mountain: Wade Mainer's First Hundred Years.* Jackson: University Press of Mississippi, 2010.

Spottswood, Richard K. *Ethnic Music on Records: A Discography of Ethnic Recordings Produced in the United States, 1893–1942.* 7 vols. Urbana: University of Illinois Press, 1990.

Snyder, Robert W. *The Voice of the City: Vaudeville and Popular Culture in New York.* New York: Oxford University Press, 1989.

"The Southern Gentlemen." https://www.sonnyjames.com/hof/photo-galleries/the-southern-gentlemen/. Last accessed May 7, 2018.

Sprigge, Martha. "Tape Work and Memory Work in Post-War Germany." *Twentieth-Century Music* 14, no. 1 (February 2017): 49–63.

Stahl, Matt. "Public, Private, Popular: Pop Performers, Liberalism and the Limits of Rights." *MUSICultures* 41, no. 1 (2014): 94–114.

Stamper, Pete. *It All Happened in Renfro Valley.* Lexington: University Press of Kentucky, 1999.

Steel, David Warren, with Richard H. Hulan. *The Makers of the Sacred Harp.* Urbana: University of Illinois Press, 2010.

Sterne, Jonathan. *mp3: The Meaning of a Format.* Durham, NC: Duke University Press, 2012.

Sterne, Jonathan. "Sounds like the Mall of America: Programmed Music and the Architectonics of Commercial Space." *Ethnomusicology* 41, no. 1 (January 1997): 22–50.

Sterner Miller, Tim. "This Machine Plays Country Music: Invention, Innovation, and the Pedal Steel Guitar." In *The Oxford Handbook of Country Music.* Ed. Travis D. Stimeling. New York: Oxford University Press, 2017, 177–204.

Stevens, Ray, with C. W. "Buddy" Kalb. *Ray Stevens' Nashville.* Tallahassee: Father & Son, 2014.

Stilwell, Robynn J. "Vocal Decorum: Voice, Body, and Knowledge in the Prodigious Singer, Brenda Lee." In *She's So Fine: Reflections of Whiteness, Femininity, Adolescence, and Class in 1960s Music.* Ed. Laurie Stras. Burlington, VT: Ashgate, 2010, 57–88.

Stimeling, Travis D. *Cosmic Cowboys and New Hicks: The Countercultural Sounds of Austin's Progressive Country Music Scene.* New York: Oxford University Press, 2011.

Stimeling, Travis D. "Narrative, Vocal Staging and Masculinity in the 'Outlaw' Country Music of Waylon Jennings." *Popular Music* 32, no. 3 (2013): 343–358.

Stimeling, Travis D. "'Phases and Stages, Circles and Cycles': Willie Nelson and the Concept Album." *Popular Music* 30, no. 3 (2011): 389–408.

Stimeling, Travis D. "Situating Country Music Studies." In *The Oxford Handbook of Country Music.* Ed. Travis D. Stimeling. New York: Oxford University Press, 2017, 1–12.

Stimeling, Travis D. "Taylor Swift's 'Pitch Problem' and the Place of Adolescent Girls in Country Music." In *Country Boys and Redneck Women: New Essays in Gender and Country Music.* Eds. Diane Pecknold and Kristine McCusker. Jackson: University Press of Mississippi, 2016, 84–101.

Stimeling, Travis D. "'To Be Polished More than Extended': Musicianship, Masculinity, and the Critical Reception of Southern Rock." *Journal of Popular Music Studies* 26, no. 1 (March 2014): 121–136.

Stone, Robert L. *Sacred Steel: Inside an African American Steel Guitar Tradition.* Urbana: University of Illinois Press, 2010.

Straw, Will. "Sizing Up Record Collections: Gender and Connoisseurship in Rock Music Culture." In *Sexing the Groove: Popular Music and Gender.* Ed. Sheila Whiteley. New York: Routledge, 1997, 3–16.

Straw, Will. "Systems of Articulation, Logics of Change: Communities and Scenes in Popular Music." *Cultural Studies* 5, no. 3 (1991): 368–388.

Streissguth, Michael. *Eddy Arnold: Pioneer of the Nashville Sound.* New York: Schirmer Books 1997.

Streissguth, Michael. *Outlaw: Waylon, Willie, Kris, and the Renegades of Nashville.* New York: itbooks, 2013.

Streissguth, Michael. *Voices of the Country: Interviews with Classic Country Performers.* New York: Routledge, 2004.

Sullivan, Jill M. "Women Music Teachers as Military Band Directors during World War II." *Journal of Historical Research in Music Education* 39, no. 1 (October 2017): 78–105.

Sullivan, Jill M., and Amy E. Spears. "All-Female School Bands: Separate Spheres and Gender Equality." In *Women's Bands in America: Performing Music and Gender*. Ed. Jill M. Sullivan. Lanham, MD: Rowman & Littlefield, 2017, 95–125.

Sutton, Matthew D. "Act Naturally: Charley Pride, Autobiography, and the 'Accidental Career.'" In *Country Boys and Redneck Women: New Essays in Gender and Country Music*. Eds. Diane Pecknold and Kristine M. McCusker. Jackson: University Press of Mississippi, 2016, 44–63.

Tackley, Catherine. *Benny Goodman's Famous 1938 Carnegie Hall Jazz Concert*. New York: Oxford University Press, 2012.

Taylor, Mike. "Hank Williams Sessions." *Hank Williams—A Comprehensive Discography*. http://www.hankwilliamsdiscography.com/HankWilliams/HWSession.php. Last accessed July 24, 2018.

Taylor, Timothy D., Mark Katz, and Tony Grajeda, eds. *Music, Sound, and Technology in America: A Documentary History of Early Phonograph, Cinema, and Radio*. Durham, NC: Duke University Press, 2012.

Temperley, Nicholas. "The Old Way of Singing: Its Origins and Development." *Journal of the American Musicological Society* 34, no. 3 (Autumn 1981): 511–544.

Théberge, Paul. *Any Sound You Can Imagine: Making Music/Consuming Technology*. Hanover, NH: Wesleyan University Press, 1997.

"A Thumb Pickers Family Tree: Seminal Sources for Muhlenberg County, Kentucky Guitar Style from Shultz and Jones to Atkins." *Journal of Country Music* 22, no. 1 (2001): 25.

"Top Billing Signs Floyd Cramer." *Country Music Telegram* (July 1978): 3.

Toynbee, Jason. *Making Popular Music: Musicians, Creativity, and Institutions*. London: Arnold, 2000.

Traut, Don. "'Simply Irresistible': Recurring Accent Patterns as Hooks in Mainstream 1980s Music." *Popular Music* 24, no. 1 (January 2005): 57–77.

Tribe, Ivan M. "The Economics of Hillbilly Radio: A Preliminary Investigation of the 'P.I.' System in the Depression Decade and Afterward." *JEMF Quarterly* 20 (Fall–Winter 1984): 76–83.

Tribe, Ivan M. *Mountaineer Jamboree: Country Music in West Virginia*. Lexington: University Press of Kentucky, 1984.

Tribe, Ivan M. *The Stonemans: An Appalachian Family and the Music that Shaped Their Lives*. Urbana: University of Illinois Press, 1993.

Trigger. "An Ode to Robby Turner: Country Music's Man of Steel." *Saving Country Music* (January 4, 2016). https://www.savingcountrymusic.com/an-ode-to-robby-turner-country-musics-man-of-steel/. Last accessed June 29, 2018.

Troutman, John. *Kika Kila: How the Hawaiian Steel Guitar Changed the Sound of Modern Music*. Chapel Hill: University of North Carolina Press, 2016.

Truax, Barry, ed. *Handbook for Acoustic Ecology*. 2nd ed. Burnaby, BC: Cambridge Street, 1999. https://www.sfu.ca/sonic-studio/handbook/Soundmark.html. Last accessed June 27, 2018.

Turner, Dale. "Hole Notes with Dale Turner: The Signature Open-G-Tuned Rhythm Style of Don Everly." *Guitar World* (April 21, 2014). https://www.guitarworld.com/uncategorized/hole-notes-dale-turner-signature-open-g-tuned-rhythm-style-don-everly. Last accessed November 28, 2017.

Tyler, Paul L. "The Rise of Rural Rhythm." In *The Hayloft Gang: The Story of the National Barn Dance*. Ed. Chad Berry. Urbana: University of Illinois Press, 2008, 19–71.

van Deventer, Dewald. "The Problems and Possibilities of Music Score Access for Blind Pianists: A Qualitative Account." *Musicus: A South African Journal for Music Teaching/'n Suid-Afrikaanse tydskrif vir musiekonderwys* 39, no. 1 (2011): 55–65.

VanCour, Shawn. *Making Radio: Early Radio Production and the Rise of Modern Sound Culture*. New York: Oxford University Press, 2018.

Vander Wel, Stephanie. "'I Am a Honky-Tonk Girl': Country Music, Gender, and Migration." Ph.D. dissertation, University of California at Los Angeles, 2008.

Vander Wel, Stephanie. "The Singing Voice in Country Music." In *The Oxford Handbook of Country Music*. Ed. Travis D. Stimeling. New York: Oxford University Press, 2017, 157–175.

Vanderbilt University Peabody College of Education and Human Development. "History." http://peabody.vanderbilt.edu/about/explore/history.php. Last accessed September 18, 2015.

Waksman, Steve. *Instruments of Desire: The Electric Guitar and the Shaping of Musical Experience*. Cambridge, MA: Harvard University Press, 1999.

Wald, Gayle F. *Shout, Sister, Shout!: The Untold Story of Rock-and-Roll Trailblazer Sister Rosetta Tharpe*. Boston: Beacon Press, 2007.

Walker, Katherine. "Cut, Carved, and Served: Competitive Jamming in the 1930s and 1940s." *Jazz Perspectives* 4, no. 2 (August 2010): 183–208.

Walser, Robert. *Running with the Devil: Power, Gender, and Madness in Heavy Metal Music*. Middletown, CT: Wesleyan University Press, 1993.

Ward, Brian, and Patrick Huber. *A&R Pioneers: Architects of American Roots Music on Record*. Nashville: Vanderbilt University Press, 2018.

Ward, Ed. "Willie Nelson: Breakthrough of a Lone-Star Legend." *Rolling Stone* 204 (January 15, 1976): 18.

Waring, Virginia. *Fred Waring and the Pennsylvanians*. Urbana: University of Illinois Press, 1997.

Warren, Wilson J. *Tied to the Great Packing Machine: The Midwest and Meatpacking*. Iowa City: University of Iowa Press, 2007.

Watson, Jada. "Changing *Billboard* Methodologies and Ecological Diversity in Hot Country Songs." Paper presented at International Country Music Conference, Belmont University, June 2018.

Watson, Jada. "'Girl on the Billboard': Changing *Billboard* Methodologies and Ecological Diversity in Hot Country Songs." Paper presented at International Association for the Study of Popular Music—US Branch, Nashville, TN, March 2018.

Watson, Jada. "Toward a Data-Driven Analysis of Gender Representation in *Billboard* Country Songs Chart, 1985–Present." Paper presented at the International Country Music Conference, Nashville, TN, June 2017.

Weisbard, Eric. "Country Radio: The Dialectic of Format and Genre." In *The Oxford Handbook of Country Music*. Ed. Travis D. Stimeling. New York: Oxford University Press, 2017, 229–248.

Weisbard, Eric. *Top 40 Democracy: The Rival Mainstreams of American Music*. Chicago: University of Chicago Press, 2014.

Weisethaunet, Hans, and Ulf Lindberg. "Authenticity Revisited: The Rock Critic and the Changing Real." *Popular Music and Society* 33, no. 4 (October 2010): 465–485.

Wennerstrom, Mary H. "The Undergraduate Core Music Curriculum at Indiana University." *Journal of Music Theory Pedagogy* 3, no. 1 (Spring 1989): 153–176.

"When Motown Went Country: The Supremes Sing Country, Western & Pop." *Highway Queens* (posted September 22, 2017). https://highwayqueens.com/2017/09/22/when-motown-went-country-the-supremes-sing-country-western-pop/. Last accessed July 23, 2018.

Whitburn, Joel. *Top Country Singles, 1944 to 2001*. Menomonee Falls, WI: Record Research, 2002.

White, Robert George, Jr. "Martin Block and WNEW: The Rise of the Recorded Music Radio Format, 1934–1954." Ph.D. dissertation, Bowling Green State University, 1981.

Whitley, Carla Jean. *Muscle Shoals Sound Studio: How the Swampers Changed American Music*. Charleston, SC: The History Press, 2016.

Who's Who in American Music: Classical. 1st ed. New York: R. R. Bowker, 1983.

Wilcox, Glenn, ed. *The Southern Harmony and Musical Companion* by William Walker. Facsimile edition. Lexington: University Press of Kentucky, 1993.

Wilkinson, Christopher. "Sweet Dance Music." *Grove Music Online*. http://www.oxford-musiconline.com/grovemusic/view/10.1093/gmo/9781561592630.001.0001/omo-9781561592630-e-1002276633. Last accessed June 29, 2018.

Williams, Chas. *The Nashville Number System*. 7th ed. n.p.: Chas Williams, 2005.

Williams, Gilbert A. "The Black Disc Jockey as a Cultural Hero." *Popular Music and Society* 10, no. 3 (1986): 79–90.

Williams, James Alan. "Phantom Power: Recording Studio History, Practice, and Mythology." Ph.D. dissertation, Brown University, 2006.

Wilson, Joe. *Lucky Joe's Namesake: The Extraordinary Life and Observations of Joe Wilson*. Ed. Fred Bartenstein. Knoxville: University of Tennessee Press, 2017.

Williams, John Alexander. *Appalachia: A History*. Chapel Hill: University of North Carolina Press, 2002.

Williams, Michael Ann. *Staging Tradition: John Lair and Sarah Gertrude Knott*. Urbana: University of Illinois Press, 2006.

Williamson, John. "Cooperation and Conflict: The British Musicians' Union, Musical Labour and Copyright in the UK." *MUSICultures* 41, no. 1 (2014): 73–92.

Windle, E. Mark. *House of Broken Hearts: The Soul of 1960s Nashville*. n.p.: Blurb, 2017.

Wolfe, Charles K. "The Bristol Syndrome: Field Recordings of Early Country Music." In *Country Music Annual 2002*. Eds. Charles K. Wolfe and James E. Akenson. Lexington: University Press of Kentucky, 2002, 202–221.

Wolfe, Charles K. *Classic Country: Legends of Country Music*. New York: Routledge, 2001.

Wolfe, Charles K. *A Good-Natured Riot: The Birth of the Grand Ole Opry*. Nashville: Country Music Foundation Press and Vanderbilt University Press, 1999.

Wolfe, Charles K. *In Close Harmony: The Story of the Louvin Brothers*. Jackson: University Press of Mississippi, 1996.

Wolfe, Charles K. *Kentucky Country: Folk and Country Music of Kentucky*. Lexington: University Press of Kentucky, 1982.

Wolfe, Charles K. *Tennessee Strings: The Story of Country Music in Tennessee*. Knoxville: University of Tennessee Press, 1977.

Wolk, Douglas. "Thinking about Rockism." *Seattle Weekly* (May 4, 2005). http://www. seattleweekly.com/2005-05-04/music/thinking-about-rockism.php/. Last accessed November 9, 2012.

Wright, Brian F. "'A Bastard Instrument': The Fender Precision Bass, Monk Montgomery, and Jazz in the 1950s." *Jazz Perspectives* 8, no. 3 (December 2014): 281–303.

Wynn, Linda T. "The Dawning of a New Day: The Nashville Sit-Ins, February 13–May 10, 1960." *Tennessee Historical Quarterly* 50, no. 1 (Spring 1991): 42–54.

Zagorski-Thomas, Simon. *The Musicology of Record Production*. Cambridge: Cambridge University Press, 2014.

Zak, Albin J., III. *I Don't Sound like Nobody: Remaking Music in 1950s America*. Ann Arbor: University of Michigan Press, 2010.

Zak, Albin J., III. "No-Fi: Crafting a Language of Recorded Music in 1950s Pop." In *The Art of Record Production: An Introductory Reader for a New Academic Field*. Eds. Simon Frith and Simon Zagorski-Thomas. Farnham, UK: Ashgate, 2012. 43–56.

Zwonitzer, Mark, with Charles Hirshberg. *Will You Miss Me When I'm Gone?: The Carter Family and Their Legacy in American Music*. New York: Simon & Schuster, 2004.

FILMOGRAPHY

Altman, Robert, dir. *Nashville*. Paramount, 1975.

Barrett, David. "Charlie McCoy Interview Snippet for BluesHarmonica.com with David Barrett." https://www.youtube.com/watch?v=UPaZenhUhGE. Posted August 30, 2013. Last accessed June 28, 2018.

Blank, Les, dir. *A Poem Is a Naked Person*. Les Blank Films, 1974; released 2015.

Blanton, Kent. https://www.youtube.com/channel/UC6-8f7r19PwVVm1UjdaGWZQ. Last accessed April 2, 2018.

BluegrassLibrary. "Jordanaires—Workin' on a Building." https://www.youtube.com/watch?v=tADJ7vLv4hk. Posted June 19, 2009. Last accessed September 21, 2017.

Camalier, Greg, dir. *Muscle Shoals*. Magnolia Pictures, 2014.

Collins, Preston, and Jim Dennett, dirs. *Music City, U.S.A.* Gemini Pictures, 1966.

Elfstrom, Robert, and David Hoffman, dirs. *The Nashville Sound*. The Nashville Co., 1970.

Justman, Paul, dir. *Standing in the Shadows of Motown*. Artisan Entertainment, 2002.

MisterStereo. "The Jordanaires—Dig a Little Deeper." https://www.youtube.com/watch?v=YKKM9aIFLt4. Posted July 28, 2010. Last accessed April 11, 2018.

Neville, Morgan, dir. *20 Feet from Stardom*. Tremolo Productions/Gil Friesen Productions, 2013.

Rise, Leif, dir. *Road to Nashville*. Crown International Pictures, 1967.

Shearon, Stephen, and Mary Nichols, *I'll Keep on Singing: The Southern Gospel Convention Tradition*. DVD. Murfreesboro: Middle Tennessee State University, 2010.

Sheridan, Jay J., dir. *Nashville Rebel*. American International, 1966.

Tedesco, Danny, dir. *The Wrecking Crew!* Magnolia Pictures, 2008/2015.

Va HOSS. "Jim Reeves . . . Recording 'Blue Canadian Rockies' in Studio (Live Video from 1963-HQ)." https://www.youtube.com/watch?v=1ejFPPXQoGc. Posted November 7, 2013. Last accessed May 1, 2018.

For the benefit of digital users, indexed terms that span two pages (e.g., 52–53) may, on occasion, appear on only one of those pages.

Tables and figures are indicated by *t* and *f* following the page number